NEW PERSPECTIVES ON THE FINANCIAL SYSTEM

Edited by Laurence Harris, Jerry Coakley, Martin Croasdale and Trevor Evans, all Department of Social Studies, The Open University

The British financial system, and the City in particular, is currently undergoing substantial changes. These changes have resulted from a considerable amount of research into the operation of the financial system over several years. This book presents and explains the results of research conducted since 1980 within or related to the Open University's Financial Studies Research Group. It consists of distinctly separate studies linked around a common theme and represents a new departure in studying the financial system. Informed by a Marxist theoretical perspective, the studies span theoretical, institutional and econometric research so that the book is the first to combine a radical theoretical approach with careful empirical research.

New Perspectives on the Financial System

Edited by Laurence Harris
Jerry Coakley
Martin Croasdale
Trevor Evans

With an Introductory Essay by Michael Meacher MP

CROOM HELM
London • New York • Sydney

Croom Helm Ltd, Provident House, Burrell Row,
Beckenham, Kent, BR3 1AT
Croom Helm Australia, 44-50 Waterloo Road,
North Ryde, 2113, New South Wales

Published in the USA by
Croom Helm
in association with Methuen, Inc.
29 West 35th Street
New York, NY 10001

British Library Cataloguing in Publication Data
New perspectives on the financial system.
1. Finance
I. Harris, Laurence
332 HG173
ISBN 0-7099-3741-5

Library of Congress Cataloging-in-Publication Data
New perspectives on the financial system.
"Published in the USA by Croom Helm in association
with Methuen, Inc." — T.p. verso.
Includes index.
1. Finance — Great Britain. I. Harris, Laurence.
HG186.G7N44 1988 332'.0941 87-15723
ISBN 0-7099-3741-5

Printed and bound in Great Britain by
Biddles Ltd, Guildford and King's Lynn

CONTENTS

PREFACE

In 1979 a programme of research on the financial system was initiated at the Open University and soon took a more structured, research group form as the Financial Studies Group. This book brings together a number of the main writings of the group from that date to the end of 1986. The majority of them have not been published before. Each author was a member of the Financial Studies Group at the time his or her chapter was written, except for Michael Meacher, Robin Murray and Alan Lipietz whose chapters are based on their contribution to a conference, 'The Future of Finance', organised by the Group in January 1983.

The chapters were written by a variety of authors, engaged on different research projects, and at different times; and their style and method varies from discursive, theoretical and historical pieces to econometric studies and detailed empirical surveys. But they comprise a cohesive and complementary body of writing reflecting the fact that the various projects are elements in a coherent overall research programme. Broadly speaking, the main questions to which that programme is directed are: what are the principal developments in the financial system in recent decades? How can their implications for the economy as a whole be evaluated? and what are their implications for policy? The motivation for this programme and its coherence was greatly enhanced by the renewed prominence of the City and controversies over it, for the programme questions bear directly upon them. Each writer approaches these questions from a theoretical position which differs from orthodox, neo-classical writings to a greater or lesser degree (while sometimes using neo-classical principles where appropriate) and, in total, the whole offers significantly new perspectives on the financial system.

Naturally, since they reflect the work of the Financial Studies Group over a period, the individual chapters were written at different times. We have decided to publish them here without updating the earlier ones for two reasons: first their different dates of birth convey a sense of the work of a research group as a living entity more accurately than a homogenised set of papers could; and, second, we believe that the arguments and conclusions of the earlier papers have stood the test of time well. This is not to deny that the rapid pace of change in the City will soon warrant another book discussing the young, upwardly mobile world of finance after the Big Bang. Nor is it to deny that, even apart from these great changes, there are significant areas of finance not covered in the present book (such as the Third World debt crisis).

The Financial Studies Group brings together academic researchers, but, in fact, its strengths are founded upon the organizational, secretarial and joke-appreciating skills of Iris Manzi who is the exception to the academic rule that no-one is indispensable. The high quality of the finished book is due to Iris Manzi's care and diligence over the enormous amount of typing, with a valuable contribution by Ann Boomer, and our gratitude goes to both of them.

Too many people have made valuable comments on individual chapters to register our thanks here. We do gratefully acknowledge financial support from the Open University, Leverhulme Trust, and the University of California.

Milton Keynes
January 1987

ACKNOWLEDGEMENTS AND SOURCES

Permission is gratefully acknowledged to reprint the following chapters, which were first published elsewhere: Chapter 3, Money Makes the World Go Round, in *Capital & Class*, No 24, 1985, Chapter 4, The Internationalisation of Bank Capital, in *Capital & Class*, No 23, 1984 Chapter 5, Industry, the City and the Foreign Exchanges: Theory and Evidence, in *British Review of Economic Issues*, Vol 4, No 10, 1983; Chapter 6, Evaluating the Role of the Financial System, in *Socialist Economic Review*, Merlin Press, 1982; Chapter 14, Pension Funds and Local Authority Investment, and Chapter 14, Pension Funds: An Alternative View, in *Capital & Class*, No 20, 1983.

AUTHORS

Jerry Coakley* Lecturer in Economics, City of London Polytechnic

Martin Croasdale* Economist, CEGB

Trevor Evans* Research Fellow, Open University

Laurence Harris* Professor of Economics, Open University

Alan Lipietz Economist, CEPREMAP, Paris

Michael Meacher Shadow Employment Spokesperson, The Labour Party

Richard Minns* Chief Executive, Greater London Enterprise Board

Robin Murray Fellow, Institute of Development Studies; formerly Chief Economic Adviser to the Greater London Council

Sonja Ruehl* Lecturer in Economics, The Hatfield Polytechnic

Stephen Smith* Lecturer in Sociology, Kingston Polytechnic; former member of the Open University Technology Policy Group

Dave Wield* Lecturer in Technology, Open University; member of the Open University Technology Policy Group

* Member or former member of the Open University Financial Studies Research Group

Part I

QUESTIONS OF POLICY AND THEORY

Chapter One

THE FUTURE OF FINANCE

Michael Meacher

Those who are interested in radical reform in this country and in other European countries, and I'm thinking particularly of France, have in my view over-emphasised the importance of controlling the commanding heights of the economy in industry but given far too little attention to control over the commanding heights of other very significant areas of national policy. One of those I would certainly say is control of communications and the whole question of the reform of the media and how you get your message across but we're not discussing that today. The other of even more immediate importance is control over the commanding heights of finance.

I don't think one has to be a Marxist in order to accept that the dominant mode of capitalism today and for a long time past is the financial mode and the confidence of the financial markets is all too often treated today as the touchstone of the practicability of policies. Whether that is so or not is a matter of controversy but the importance of the claim is undoubtedly crucial. In fact in a recent debate only last week in the House the Chancellor of the Exchequer attacked the opposition's policies, not because he was actually able to find anything wrong (or at least he didn't say so) about the industrial or economic policies but on two grounds - one on the question of inflation and how it should be handled and secondly, on the grounds of confidence. Let me just read you this one sentence. 'He (that is, Peter Shore) sought in that respect to enlist the Treasury Model in support of his fantasy. (But this requires) the model to assume the two things that simply could not be assumed: that he would have success in restraining the growth of incomes on a scale that his party has totally failed to secure so far, and that the implementation of his programme would have no adverse effects on confidence' and it was the second that he went on to emphasise very strongly. That is an absolute critical issue.

Let us speak plainly. I think everyone knows that the immediate check or barrier to the success of alternative policies, whatever particular form it takes in terms of a return towards full employment, to high public spending and high investment is the virtual certainty of a full scale financial crisis. We will be faced with the City and with international financiers refusing to underwrite the party's programme which will certainly lead to a collapse of the markets for government securities and to the likelihood that that pushes up interest rates sky high. That's one problem - if you are trying to finance a programme which even modestly under Labour policies are put at spending programmes of many billion pounds of extra government spending to regenerate the economy. Secondly, the demand which will certainly exist and indeed probably exists in the first few weeks, let alone months or years to transfer funds out of sterling and into other currencies will of course have drastic effects on the exchange rate, particularly at a time when now we are seeing money being moved abroad at the rate of £12 billion a year. If one tries to stymie that flow one can imagine the consequences. We saw those consequences - they were immediately apparent in 1964 with a Bank Rate which was then at a crisis level of 7 per cent; it makes us laugh today but it was crisis level then. The figures will be slightly different today but it will be the same crisis within a matter of two months. It happened again in 1966 which many people see I think as the watershed in the switch from what might have been regarded as socialist policies to a very conventional social democratic programme. That rightward shift was produced by the financial crisis more than any other single factor. And again in 1976 a financial crisis led to the agreement with the IMF and a Letter of Intent which caused the Labour government to cut public expenditure dramatically.

I think no-one has any doubts about this; if we do not control the financial markets, they will certainly control us. The question is how is that control to be achieved?

Now I think the grounds for concern are all too clear. The financial institutions, I'm sure we are all aware, are now the new capitalists. They certainly control more than half of the shares on the Stock Exchange, totally replacing rich individuals of perhaps three or four decades ago. Funds under the control of institutions have grown to an enormous size. I think they control funds today of something of the order of £600 billion with an income of the Pension and Insurance Funds of something up to £10 billion a year. The banks are lending overseas £40 billion or more. These are absolutely enormous sums and relatively unregulated. I sometimes think that the nationalisation of the Bank of England gave the Bank of England a chance to do a reverse takeover of the Treasury (perhaps we need to renationalise the Bank of England); but certainly beyond that our powers have never been exerted and are probably non existent. There is an over-concentration of power. There are probably less than 30 institutions who control three-quarters of this enormous turnover of fund monies and what we're really talking about is something like two or three hundred men (and there are no women in that particular group at this level!) two or three hundred men who control, almost totally unregulated by the state, the quite colossal sums of money which are perfectly capable of ditching any economic or industrial strategy.

I think the financial system has not served industry well and I think that fact is well understood. We have a financial system that has not provided long term funds for industry at viable rates of interest. The interest rate differential for our industrialists compared to Germany's and Japan's is something like five of ten per centage points, a very large difference indeed, and as I've already said there has been massive over-investment overseas. This year and for the last few years we have been in a situation where more money is being invested overseas than the total of domestic investment in the whole of the UK which I think is a remarkable fact. Money is going abroad today at the rate of £1 billion a month since the Tories abolished exchange controls in 1979, with pension funds committing something like a quarter of all of their monies now to foreign lending. Now I think that that is a familiar analysis but what I think is not at all familiar and indeed far too little discussed is what we actually do about it and I just want to posit four questions at this stage.

First of all, how do we prevent the institutions disposing of government securities or refusing to buy them (exactly the problem which we had in 1976/7) and how do we prevent them funnelling money out of the country? How exactly do we do that and what would be the full implications of whatever measures we might adopt.

Secondly, how do you fix the exchange rate, what is the impact on monetary policy? The question is how sterilised the intervention is, how do you regulate interest rates and how do you ensure above all that there is an adequate supply of funds being fed to government in order to underpin this very large refinancing programme through the public sector. How actually do you do that and ensure that those funds will be available and that there won't be a bottleneck in the financial system?

Thirdly, how do you actually achieve democratic accountability? We're all agreed that there is far too great a concentration of power, but how do you achieve decentralisation of power. Does the planning agreement model which has been talked about for industry have any relevance here, or does one do it through the public ownership route? And how do you ensure that there is adequate backup at the local enterprise board level?

And lastly, if people argue for nationalisation, exactly what are the alternative criteria by which the financial system should then operate. It's easy to talk about the instrument, but what I think needs to be much more talked about is the change in the pattern of operations which would then result.

Those are, I think, the questions of the day.

NOTE

This is an edited version of the introductory speech Michael Meacher gave from the Chair at 'The Future of Finance' Conference, of the Open University Financial Studies Group, 21 January 1983.

Chapter Two

ALTERNATIVE PERSPECTIVES ON THE FINANCIAL SYSTEM

Laurence Harris

In the first half of the 1980s the City of London took centre stage in British affairs in a manner not quite seen before, and certainly different from its public position in the last half-century. In the two previous periods when the City had been seen to dominate political life in modern Britain, the image of finance and financiers as a dark force was to the fore. In 1931 and the 1960s Labour politicians (echoing the sentiments of a broader based industry lobby) saw themselves struggling against City interests which wielded terrific power. At times politics appeared to hinge on the City's manipulation of money, exchange rates and interest rates, supposedly to the detriment of everyone except the 'Gnomes of Zurich' or the 'bankers' ramp'. In the 1980s, by contrast, the City's highly public face was as the dynamic partner of government and people, the section of our society striding most assuredly toward a hi-tech post-industrial and wealthy age. At least, until the Guinness scandal.

This new dynamic world of finance has touched everyone's lives in Britain, and especially in the South East. Most people have seen its tangible side in the easy use of credit cards and in the effect on housing and consumer spending of greatly liberalised mortgage credit. Equally, the sales to the public of shares in British Telecom, British Gas, British Airways and other national industries, have, through the media, had an impact on the national consciousness that could never have been imagined in the old days before the Post Office, the Gas Board and BEA/BOAC gave way to such sterling modern names. These technically accomplished privatisation sales were remarkable both for the size of the capital sums raised (unparalleled since the state's borrowing to finance World War II and the post-war nationalisations) and the fact that share applications and market premiums, which in the 'popular capitalism' ethic of the 1950s had remained the preserve of professional 'stags', now become the small talk of ordinary people.

Accompanying these ubiquitous signs of change in the financial system have been changes with more fundamental long run effects but which are directly felt mainly by the market operators, banks and large corporations themselves. They are all, in one form or another, aspects of a radical increase in the internationalisation of finance. Under it finance in Britain has become one element of a world-wide financial system. Although London is one of that system's main centres, it is its international circuits rather than its links with British business that dominate it. That orientation has characterised the City since its beginning. (1) What is new is that the international system of which it is part is now almost wholly supra-national instead of being the international extension of particular countries' capitalisms as it was in the financial expansion of the late nineteenth century.

The radical internationalisation of the City has occurred in creating this supra-national world system over the past two decades. The first step in the 1960s and 1970s was the internationalisation of bank deposits and bank credit or in other words the creation of Eurodollar markets at the centre of which were British and foreign banks located in London. By the end of 1986 potentially the most far-reaching change was the internationalisation of London's equity market in the 'Big Bang' reforms of that year. Between those two changes, London's trading in international bonds had been transformed by the development of Eurobonds, and new international commodity markets had been created with new forms of futures trading in commodity and financial futures.

These changes in the financial system prompt theoretical questioning. Are new perspectives in economic theory required to comprehend the issues raised by the new developments in finance? In this chapter I outline the elements of a new theoretical perspective. They are organised around two broad concepts: the specific forms of economic power wielded by financial institutions; and the financial system's role in regard to state policy and regulation of the economy. The approach is loosely derived from Marxian economic theory, but I argue that neither the classic Marxian work by Hilferding nor orthodox neo-classical theory is adequate for understanding the modern financial system. The resulting lacuna makes the development of a new perspective a valid enterprise. The essays in this book, although diverse, are linked by their contribution to that task and the notes to this chapter indicate their links to specific aspects of a new perspective.

FINANCIAL INSTITUTIONS AND ECONOMIC POWER

At one level it is trite to recognise that financial institutions are powerful; it is commonplace to refer to powerful banks and financiers. But in most economic theory they are not treated as wielding power; the concepts for theorising their economic power are not there and its existence and character is not posed as a theoretical question. Yet without such a concept, theory cannot address some of the questions that have figured in the non-theoretical discussion of politicians, journalists and everyday conversation. For example, the financial institutions' economic power is implicit in every discussion of whether Britain's industrial problems have resulted from the City's failure to supply appropriate finance; of whether monetary policy can 'work'; and of the causes of the City's internationalisation.

In neo-classical economics, agents, whether individuals, firms, or specifically financial firms are assumed to be powerless unless they have a degree of monopoly in the markets on which they sell their output or buy inputs; a degree of market power. If they do have some monopoly its effect is only to give them some power over the prices at which they buy and sell. For example, if financial institutions have some monopoly power they can set interest rate margins on their loans and deposits, as the cartel of UK commercial banks did explicitly before the 1971 policy 'Competition and Credit Control'. But restricting the concept of economic power to such market power, as does neoclassical economics, prevents analysis of financial institutions' economic power for two reasons: first, financial markets are highly developed and exhibit many of the defining characteristics of perfectly competitive rather than monopolistic markets; and, second, financial institutions' economic power is broader and more complex than their ability to influence market prices. Let us examine those aspects briefly.

The high degree of competition on financial markets is not pre-given; it is increased at particular times by particular developments and has been marked by several phenomena in recent years. Dealers on markets for short-term credit, foreign exchange markets, bond markets and, to a lesser extent, equity markets, have a high degree of access to information - a fundamental condition of competitive markets - and this has increased in a qualitative leap with the adoption of new information technology. (2) Barriers to entry in the markets for particular types of financial instruments are low as has been seen in the entry of different institutions into others' traditionally protected markets; for example, the entry of commercial banks into the building societies' traditional mortgage market, and the building societies' entry into the business of cheque (demand) deposits. And the effect of these market conditions is seen in the squeeze on profit margins which often occurs when an initially profitable new form of financial trading is established. For example, the growth of Eurobond markets with rising issues of various types of floating rate notes in the 1980s led, by 1986, to a sharp competitive squeeze on the margins of the banks managing the issues. These characteristics of the markets in which they operate mean that financial institutions do not, in principle, systematically wield market power (in setting interest rates, for example), so in neo-classical economics that means they have no economic power. (3)

But economic power is broader and more complex than that. Market power is defined in terms of the ability to influence the terms of the institution's own contracts, but the power under discussion in debates over 'finance versus industry' or 'finance versus the state' is the power of financial institutions to constrain, regulate, or undermine the plans of industrial enterprises or the state. One means of achieving this could be the monopolistic market power of, say, particular banks in special circumstances, but that is only one and, in its absence, other, more fundamental characteristics of the economic power of the financial system can be identified.

This power has three characteristics: it relates to the financial system as a whole rather than individual institutions; it is based in part on the system's control of specialised forms of capital; and in part it is based on its control of money as the means of circulation. None of these is absolute (the financial system does not have a monopoly of money, for example) but simplifying by assuming they are enables us to get to the heart of the problem.

The power of the City stems from the fact that, as a system, it occupies a specialised and distinct position in the circuits of capital so that whatever the differences are between the different institutions (between pension funds and building societies, for example) they are secondary compared to the difference between financial institutions on one hand and enterprises in industry or agriculture on the other.

This special position means that the financial institutions control blocs of capital which are distinct from the productive capital employed in industry and agriculture and the commodity capital employed in trade and in productive enterprises. Although distinct from the capital controlled by other enterprises this capital in the hands of financial institutions is part of the interlocking circuits of capital of the economy as a whole and profitable accumulation requires its deployment in industrial and other enterprises. In this, the financial institutions controlling it have a potential power over other enterprises. In principle the other sectors of the economy potentially also have power over finance, for either can influence the terms of the connection between financial and other capital, but the characteristics of each are such that the potential power of finance is, in fact, an actual domination. The difference between them is that financial capital is universal and hence mobile to a degree that other forms of capital are not. Productive capital in industry is tied to specific lines of production and operates as if its profit is determined by the production carried out in the enterprise. The profits of the financial system, however, have their origins in the world economy as a whole, and the logic of financial institutions is to operate so as to draw on these sources wherever they are. (4)

Financial capital's universality explains the economic power the financial system has over industrial capital for it gives rise to a great asymmetry. Look at it from the point of view of industry first. Industry needs credit and financial capital in the form of equity finance in order to accumulate. Without it, a firm can only expand on the basis of its own retained profits but with external finance it can draw upon the accumulated profits of the system as a whole. (5) Thus, although industry may rely for long periods on retained profits as a source of finance for investment, as British manufacturing firms have done, it is a restrictive basis for accumulation. (6) If outside funds of the appropriate types are denied to a firm or industry by the financial system or if banks withdraw from lending in one direction to place funds in other lines accumulation in the first will be forced to decline relatively. Thus, the financial system has the power to determine the amount and terms of industry's access to the specialised forms of capital, financial capital, which link individual capitals into the world system. Looked at from the other direction, financial capital ultimately depends on the profits generated in 'the real economy' of production but that does not give industry reciprocal power over finance. The universality of financial capital means that its revenue does not only come from its direct relations with sections of industrial capital, its interest and dividends on credit and shares in firms, so the financial system as a whole is not directly threatened by industrial weakness. One reason is that because of its universality, financial capital's revenue is drawn from the world system of industrial capital as a whole, so that a reduction in the profit flow from one sector does not weaken the financial system as a whole (indeed it is part of its mode of operating) and in a financial system as well developed as London's, is not generally a threat even to individual banks. The second is that the financial institutions lend to states, and place funds in land and property and with each other. The result, as I argue below, is that the financial system is dominatd by 'fictitious capital' which enables it to appropriate industrial profits indirectly and with relative security even when the profitability of production is weak. The revenue from credit to the state in advanced capitalist countries is secure even if the state's own revenue is viewed as deriving from the profits of private production; because the state has powers of taxation and compulsion to obtain its revenue the financial system receives its share of industrial profits indirectly, via its profits from the state, even in industrial slumps. Thus, the interdependence between the financial system's specialised forms of capital and other sectors of the economy is an asymmetrical one in which the financial system has an economic power which, although not unconditional, is dominant over industry.

The third factor in the economic power of the financial system is that its institutions, particularly the banks, operate the economy's money. They transfer, exchange and account for all agents' money balances which are the means through which exchange, trade and circulation are carried out. In addition, the financial system changes the volume of money and determines what is and is not money. These functions give the financial system economic power in relation to the state and policy, which I examine in the next section. Before doing so, however, I would like to consider further the emphasis placed on the financial system as a whole in this discussion of its economic power. The notion that the power of finance resides in the financial system as a whole and the distinct nature of its capital does not deny that individual financial institutions have great power over firms and other bodies; instead, it is the framework within which that power of individual banks and finance houses is located. Several studies in the US (7) and Britain (8) have discussed the power that banks in particular have over corporations either through the terms of the credit they give or through their control of shareholdings. Moreover, the efforts of individual institutions to strengthen their relative position against other institutions within the financial system is a major force in the system's dynamic. A side of this which is neglected in financial studies is the financial institutions' concern with their own labour costs and their efforts to increase labour productivity through new technology under the pressure of competition. (9) But an aspect of competition which is well recognised is the struggle between whole blocs of finance for leading positions in the world financial system, a competitive process in which, as the City competes with New York and other centres, the state has played a central role. (10)

FINANCIAL SYSTEM AND STATE REGULATION

The special economic power of financial institutions gives them a key role in the regulation of the economy and, hence a central position with regard to state policy. The impact speculation against sterling has had on the policies and politics of successive Labour (and Tory) governments is a well-established phenomenon of British politics testifying to this. (11) But here I am concerned with the more abstract and general dimensions of the problem. I think they give grounds for arguing that in a modern capitalist economy the financial system generally weakens the state's economic sovereignty.

I focus on one aspect of the state, its responsibility for

money. It is easy to imagine that this responsibility varies with political persuasions since right wing governments promulgate 'monetarism' as an ideology and political programme and right wing parties have appropriated the idea of 'sound money' or 'honest money' as their own. But in fact responsibility for money is fundamental to all states. It has two dimensions: first, the state has to have a monopoly of money to some degree; second, it must effectively regulate money to support the monetary standard (ensure 'sound money'). Consider each of these in turn.

The existence of a unified national currency and the state's monopoly of it is generally a condition of national sovereignty. Nations dominated by foreign states are marked by the absence of their own independent currency. The colonies of the British Empire had monetary authorities such as currency boards which maintained the domination of the pound as their monetary standard. Today, Swaziland's and Lesotho's absence of effective national sovereignty under South Africa's regional domination is marked by their membership of the Rand Monetary Area and use of South Africa's currency within their countries. A minimum condition of effective sovereignty is the existence of a national currency. In advanced capitalist economies the state's control of it takes legal forms through laws prescribing legal tender, banking law and regulations concerning the convertibility of national money into foreign currency but it does not have a direct monopoly in the creation of money within the economy. The stock of money in circulation consists of both cash (which is formally a state monopoly) and, principally, bank deposits which are created by the banking system. Therefore the state has to attempt to control money creation by the banks in order to maintain its national monopoly. (12)

Maintaining (or, rather, attempting to create) the state's monopoly of national money differs from the state's responsibility for regulating money to maintain its standard, although the two are closely related. For money to operate effectively in the circulation of commodities, the rate at which it exchanges with them has to be stable. In the traditional right-wing cry for 'sound money' that means zero inflation, but in growing capitalist economies it requires a stable and moderate rate of inflation. (13) However it is regarded, the state has responsibility for ensuring that stability. It is part of its responsibility for the conditions which support the circulation of commodities and accumulation of capital. In Marx's analysis, the exchange value of money in circulation was stabilised by the value of the monetary commodity, gold (even in the case where convertibility into gold was temporarily suspended), and the values of the commodities in circulation. But dealing with present day money which has no gold base the nation state has sole responsibility for maintaining stable money.

That monetary stability refers to internal circulation, but it is inseparable from the state's responsibility for regulating and maintaining the integration of domestic monetary circuits with international ones. (14) Examples abound where hyperinflation, extreme instability of the national money in domestic circulation, leads to the replacement of national money by foreign money in domestic trade and to a loss of international use of national money, a 'soft currency'. A recent example is the high inflation in Israel in the years preceding 1985, which led to widespread use of the US dollar in Israel and almost to the official adoption of a policy to dollarise the economy. (The idea was quashed because of its implication for national sovereignty.) More generally, the monetary circulation of any single economy is bound up with the world's monetary flows (15) so that if the state is to succeed in maintaining the stability of money in domestic circulation it is also responsible for those links. (16)

These two sides of the state's monetary role - its monopoly of money and its responsibility for stable money - are highly problematic. They involve relations with the financial system which are in principle antagonistic and they illuminate a further aspect of the power of financial institutions. In the last section we considered their power largely in relation to finance and the accumulation of capital; in the present context their power relates to the role of money in the circulation of commodities.

The state's responsibility for money is problematic because it cannot operate directly either on the stock of money or on its circulation. It is not as if the state controls a printing press which is the sole source of money (as it appears to do in simple macro-economic models); or enforces strict ratios between gold reserves and the stock of money in circulation (as simple theories of the gold standard would have it); or can control the total money stock by strictly controlling the monetary base of high-powered money created by the state and allowing banks to reach an equilibrium position (as modern advocates of monetary base control would have it). The money stock consists principally of financial instruments which appear on the balance sheets of financial institutions, traditionally defined as bank deposits of various types. Their quantity, character and role depend on the financial institutions' own behaviour in relation to other agents. Thus, to exercise its responsibility for money the state has to act upon the financial institutions rather than upon money itself; much of the disarray of macroeconomic theory in recent decades can be attributed to its failure to recognise the need to replace its assumption of an exogenously controlled money supply with an analysis of financial institutions. In fact, monetary policy in Britain since the beginning of the nineteenth century has turned on how the state relates to and attempts to control the financial institutions even when the theory has been concerned with the simpler conceptual framework of 'control of the money stock'.

The main point to note is that, although the state has to attempt to carry out its monetary responsibilities through control over financial institutions their nature makes it impossible for the state to achieve a monopoly of money or to achieve control of the supply of money in the pursuit of 'sound money'. At least, these goals are not attainable unless the nature of the financial system itself is changed by incorporating the financial institutions within the state in some way.

The difficulties created for the state's monetary control by the financial system's role arise from the two features of financial institutions I have touched on earlier; the universal, non-specific character of financial capital; and the unification of two functions, money-dealing and credit in banks' operations.. Their effect can be illustrated by four difficulties that have dogged British governments' attempts to control the stock of money. Each attempt, of necessity, has required the authorities to define the money supply by identifying which financial instruments do operate as money, but financial institutions are such that any such definition has run into one or other of these difficulties.

First, 'financial innovation' by the institutions means that financial instruments change so that the operational definition of money is unstable. (17) Two decades ago, for example, there was controversy over whether time deposits in banks as well as demand deposits (cheque accounts) should count as money. Changes in the conditions banks attach to each have made them more comparable so that common treatment is the norm. But at the same time building societies have changed the character of deposits held with them toward greater similarity with bank deposits, and there is uncertainty over whether they should be included as money.

Second, a response to state controls over the institutions is to 'disintermediate' or carry out financial transactions which are formally outside the institution. For example, instead of a bank seeking deposits from big corporations and using them as the basis of its loans to other corporations, it may effectively act as a broker by bringing the first and second corporations directly into contact and guaranteeing the credit. As a result, financial capital which would otherwise have come under the control of banks and appeared in their accounts as deposits, a form of money, is kept out of the institutions and, hence, does not become an element of money that the state can control. This occurs both when the state attempts to control the institutions to exercise its control over money (as when the UK authorities' 'corset' controls attempted to restrict bank deposits in three periods between 1973 and 1980), and when the state's regulations on matters such as the ratio of an institution's shareholders' stake to its deposits are designed to maintain the institutions' stability.

The third difficulty the state faces through having to carry out its monetary responsibilities through the financial institutions is that the financial system is highly internationalised. Of all the advanced capitalist countries, this is particularly true for Britain. British banks have a high proportion of deposits and loans denominated in dollars and other foreign currencies, the City has a large number of foreign banks and finance companies, and British corporations use both foreign and British currency accounts in their trading and investment. (18) State control of financial institutions in carrying out its monetary responsibility is, therefore, undermined by the character of the institutions. There can be no effective meaning to a monopoly of national money if the institutions themselves operate with a mix of domestic and foreign financial instruments which is ever changing, and if this internationalisation directly relates to the operations of firms in production and trade.

These arguments indicate the dimensions of the financial system's power in relation to the state's monetary responsibilities. They are not accidental, nor do they result from capriciousness or political bias of the financial institutions. Instead, they are characteristics of the types of capital that operate within the financial system. By its nature it is universal, highly mobile and has an underlying tendency toward developing new forms of financial instruments and operations to maintain and heighten those qualities, for without them financial capital would ultimately cease to be distinct from industrial capital, commercial capital, or state finance.

States in capitalist societies have tried to confront these problems in various ways ranging from nationalisation of banks and other financial institutions to direct controls and regulations over them. In recent years 'liberalisation' and 'privatisation' have dominated policy in many countries, apparently increasing the dominant role of the financial system and decreasing the power of national states in the sphere of money. (19) Britain and the US have followed that path; Japan, the oustanding example of an advanced capitalist country with (in appearance, at least) strong state regulation of the financial system, has taken significant liberalisation measures; (20) and France, despite extending the nationalised banking sector when President Mitterand first gained power, (21) has also given increased freedom to finance. And in the 1980s many Third World countries have been forced to reduce state controls over finance, although Korea, whose 1965 policies are often quoted as an example they should follow, is really an example of state regulation of finance. (22) These are only the most prominent examples of the many countries where the overriding issue in economic policy has become the deregulation of finance. It is the agenda for the 1980s and has much wider implications than its financial effects, for it affects the state's own position in fundamental ways.

MARXIST THEORY: FICTITIOUS CAPITAL AND FINANCE CAPITAL

This chapter's perspective on the financial system differs from that of orthodox theory in that it emphasises the system's character as a distinct bloc of capital, the economic power that relates to this, and the problems this poses for the relationship between the state and finance. Instead, neo-classical theory omits the financial system from its standard models of macro-policy (in favour of a concept of a simple and exogenous money supply) and the neo-classical theory of banks and financial institutions does not recognise their specificity. They are treated as financial intermediaries, simply mediating between ultimate lenders and ultimate borrowers and, in the process, producing and selling financial services (such as risk reduction and maturity transformation). As such they comprise a service industry on a par with manufacturing industries such as steel with the only difference being in the tangibility of their products. In the 1980s this concept has come to play a powerful role in economic policy with trade negotiations in GATT focussing on free trade in services in return for free trade in commodities, and with relations between the US and Japan centring on the freedom for American banks and finance houses to sell their financial services in Tokyo in return for Japanese freedom to sell other products in the US.

The argument of this chapter, which, by contrast, emphasises the specificity of the financial system is derived from Marxist concepts. In the remainder of the chapter I spell out the Marxian concepts of capital which relate to the financial system and underlie the perspective I have adopted here. The notion of 'fictitious capital' is most prominent in this framework. I conclude by arguing that Hilferding's classic Marxist text on financial institutions, Finance Capital, (23) is, despite its outstanding theoretical merits, wrong in its main line of argument. The concept of finance-capital which is much used by Marxists (and frequently misused) does not accord with the main line of Marx's theory.

Let me start with Marx's concepts pertaining to the financial system's capital, and examine the nature of fictitious capital. I shall take banks as the representative financial institution. In Marx's work two particular forms of capital are comprised in banks' operations; a form of merchant or commercial capital dedicated to money-dealing, and interest-bearing capital. The commercial capital banks command yields a profit by buying, selling and transferring money, or, in effect, dealing in money and financial instruments in ways which parallel merchants' dealings in commodities. Profit is appropriated by the spread on the buying and selling prices of foreign exchange, by commissions and by charges for the transfer of funds and the clearing of cheques. (24) The interest-bearing capital banks command consists, strictly speaking, of the loans they make to industry (using the term here to stand for productive capital in general) and its yield comes in the form of interest which is a deduction from the surplus value produced in industry. (25) Marx regarded bank capital as comprising both these elements, and their development is interconnected. Two points about them are particularly significant for appraising the modern role of banks: first, both types of capital connect with a basic characteristic of finance, a drive toward mobility, liquidity, or, at least, away from being tied to specific sectors and operations; second, as a result of this tendency other types of capital become prominent element in banks' operations, particularly fictitious capital in various forms.

Interest-bearing capital is different from the productive capital committed to industry precisely because, to its owner, the act of lending it enables a share of surplus value to be obtained in the form of interest without any direct involvement in the productive enterprise. If conflicts between labour and capital over the production process or over wages, weaken an industry's profits, or if this results from the periodic re-structuring of capital as a whole, the lender of interest-bearing capital withdraws it and invests in other sectors instead of having to intervene directly in the industry. That characteristic is at the heart of all interest-bearing capital, but in the hands of banks it is especially important because of the liquidity of their liabilities. Their deposits, which (for commercial banks at least) form the basis of their money-dealing operations are highly liquid since depositors are not tied to one particular bank; with well-developed banking systems personal knowledge and trust do not enter the relation so that deposits and other monetary instruments are non-specific and anonymous forms in which capital can be held. The money-dealing that banks carry out, and competition within banking facilitates this distancing of money and deposits from specific ties. Since both elements of bank capital are based on universality, mobility and liquidity, the dynamic of each is a tendency to increase this freedom as far as possible.

The freedom of interest-bearing capital, however, has its limits for, being loaned to industry, it is directly articulated with productive capital without any mediation. One institution which increases its liquidity despite this tie is the stock market, the secondary market in corporate bonds for those bonds then represent interest-bearing capital which can be bought and sold enabling the owner to move it freely; it reduces the directness of the connection. Marx saw the same institution as providing another route for overcoming the limitations of interest-bearing capital, the creation of another form of investment, fictitious capital. (26) Fictitious capital consists of financial assets created by the capitalisation of an income stream where the asset does not have a counterpart in an equivalent sum of productive capital. The representative example of fictitious capital examined by Marx was shares in joint-stock companies traded on the stock exchange where the price, being the capitalised value of the entitlement to future dividends that they represented, exceeded the value of the funds invested in the company through the initial share subscription.

Fictitious capital embodied in the market value of corporate equity is at one remove from productive capital itself, for, although its value depends upon industry's ability to generate profits it can also be increased by control and manipulation of stock markets. An expansion of banking can be achieved by banks investing in shares as well as credit to industry since the former, to the extent that they are fictitious capital, give more scope for banks to control the value of their assets than would direct ownership of productive capital. Hilferding, in his theory of finance-capital, argued that banks develop in this direction, and I examine this view later. For the present, I shall consider fictitious capital further in order to emphasise that it exists in many other forms apart from the stock market values of equities and these other types of fictitious capital have, in fact, underpinned the modern expansion of international banking.

Bonds issued by sovereign states and bank loans to states are both types of fictitious capital for their value represents the capitalised stream of future interest payments by the state while, in general, the credit obtained by the state through these instruments is not mobilised as capital. That is, states do not, on the whole, use them to finance the production of commodities for profit (although, of course, the state's spending can indirectly support the profits of some sectors of private industry); the corollary is that the interest banks can receive on such bonds is not paid directly from the uncertain profits of productive enterprises. Instead, the interest paid by the state to its creditors is ultimately financed by the state's powers of taxation. The strength of the state's tax base itself depends upon the economy's vigour, (27) and, depending partly on the relative ability of workers and capital to shift their tax burden, taxes may deplete corporate profits, but the fact that the state's interest payments are based on the power of taxation means that the state mediates between the banks who are its creditors and productive capital to a degree that makes the banks' ownership of this fictitious capital quite divorced from the vicissitudes of industry.

The fictitious capital comprised by state debt is, therefore, a form of capital in which banks invest while preserving a high degree of independence from production itself. It gives banks much greater freedom from being tied to specific firms and sectors than either interest-bearing capital (loans to firms) or equity ownership could. Its liquidity is enhanced when well-developed markets exist to trade state debt. It is, therefore, not surprising that such sovereign debt has underpinned today's international banking system.

Another feature of today's financial system is the high degree of 'layering' or, in other words, the extent to which banks and other financial houses lend their funds to other banks and financial corporations. The bonds and certificates which act as repositories for these funds comprise another form of fictitious capital which gives the banks that invest in it a greater distance from industry than could be achieved by bank credit to industrial enterprises. In this case the separation may appear valid to an individual bank although the layering makes the banking system as a whole more vulnerable to the shocks produced by industrial crises and, since central banking cannot give a complete guarantee against bank failures, this form of fictitious capital may be less firmly freed from production than a state debt (with its support in the power of taxation). Nevertheless, it provides banks with sources of revenue which are sufficiently removed from specific ties to industry to meet finance's needs for liquidity and independence.

In Marx's perspective this independence is ultimately illusory for the profits of the banking system as a whole are treated as dependent on the production of surplus value. However, the drive for independence shapes the banking system and individual banks can achieve a distance and high degree of independence from production.

Marx developed the concept of fictitious capital in the context of the rise of the joint-stock company, and the same phenomenon was seen by Hilferding as the key to the development of another form of capital, finance capital.

However, the dynamic implied in the two forms of capital is quite different; while fictitious capital is marked by the looseness of its connection to industrial capital and the production of surplus value, finance capital is marked by the extreme closeness of its involvement.

Finance capital is a combination of two simpler forms of capital, money capital in the hands of banks and industrial capital. These two forms of capital, specialised types in Marx's scheme, are seen by Hilferding as having been combined in the leading capitalist countries to produce by the end of the nineteenth century a system where large banks and industry were completely interlocked through banks investing in industry. In this combination banks are seen as, in a general sense, the dominant partner and the question of whether banks do in fact, control industry has dominated much of the modern American and British literature within this tradition. (28)

The idea that banks control industry in a one-way relationship is somewhat removed from Hilferding's own conception, for he saw banks' domination as occurring in a complex, mutually dependent relationship. For example, the creation of giant trusts and cartels among banks on one hand and firms on the other, go hand in hand and mutually reinforce each other, with the impetus to the formation of giant banks ultimately stemming from the tendency toward concentration and centralisation of productive capital. Another example of the mutual character of the relationship, is that the individuals and class fractions involved are seen as becoming merged; the dependence of industrial on banking capital and their linking in finance-capital 'does not mean that the magnates of industry also become dependent on banking magnates' but, instead, that a class of capitalists with unified interests in finance and industry emerges. (29)

Nevertheless, however complex the interrelationships between banks and industry, the concept of finance-capital does firmly emphasise the dominance banks have over industry in this combination. With the creation of finance-capital banks own industrial firms' equity, they control the allocation of bank credit upon which firms increasingly depend to finance the growth of productive capital, and a significant proportion of their profit comes as 'promoters' profit' from their control over the creation of industrial equity capital and its marketing on the stock exchange. Because banks control firms' access to finance in these ways they are seen to control industry's operations:

> The banks exercise a direct control over the employment of capital in corporations which they support with credit, and this control is applied ever more systematically as the tendency for industry to become increasingly dependent on the banks progresses.

Finance-capital's characteristic of banks dominating industry is related to another distinctive feature, the closeness of the ties between the two; the laws of development of capitalism 'bring bank and industrial capital into an ever more intimate relationship (through which) capital assumes the form of finance capital'. (31)

Hilferding and his contemporaries saw this closeness between banks and industry as a new dimension. In Marx's scheme, industrial capital and the financial capital in which banks operate (32) are specialised forms of capital; the circulation of each is related to the others, and ultimately industrial capital is seen as determining what happens to financial capital, but each is a distinct and separate form of capital. For example, interest-bearing capital is quite distinct from industrial capital, (33) and although banks obtain interest on it by lending to industry and thereby claiming a share of the surplus value produced in industry, the credit is at arm's length so that separateness is preserved. But as the links between banks and industry develop into finance capital, it was argued, the relationship ceases to be at arm's length.

Thus, compared with Marx's, Hilferding's conception implies a reversal in the roles of finance and industry in a double sense; finance comes to dominate industry instead of being surbordinate to it, and their arm's length relationship becomes one where they are closely merged. These reversals are theorised as the results of the laws of development analysed by Marx rather than as being in opposition to Marx's theory; indeed, Kautsky and Bauer viewed Hilferding's book Finance Capital as the completion of Marx's ideas on the stage of capitalism that was only just emerging before his death. Finance capital arose principally from two of the phenomena Marx had identified. Concentration and centralisation had created monopolistic firms in industry while the rise of a modern credit system had concentrated into the hands of banks the savings of all classes; the two merged as the monopolistic firms had nowhere else to go for the large blocs of finance needed to facilitate their accumulation while the banks had no profitable alternative to investing their large inflows of funds in industry. Those highly specific assumptions underlay Hilferding's theory.

But there is an apparent contradiction between finance-capital and Marx's category of fictitious capital which he had identified as a key development in the rise of the modern credit system. While the latter is as we have seen, characterised by its relative independence from productive capital, finance-capital appears completely tied. If banks control industrial firms' finance and are unified with industry through this they are also dependent on industrial enterprise. It would seem that if banks own equity in industry, lend heavily to it, profit from floating new companies and control firms' productive operations in order to regulate and protect their financial investment, their fortunes are directly tied to those of 'their' firms. If firms in an industry enter a profits crisis, banks that are tied to them cannot simply withdraw credit from that industry and place it elsewhere since their finance is tied and specific; any withdrawal would destroy a large part of the bank's assets and, instead, banks are compelled to supervise the reconstruction of 'their' firms' operations directly.

This contradiction gives grounds for thinking that Hilferding's concept fails to capture the effect of the laws Marx identified, for they pointed to a system where finance was increasingly independent of production, where financial operations were strongly separated from productive by layers of fictitious capital. For Marx, the tendency of finance was to become increasingly abstract and free rather than specific and tied, whereas finance capital appears to be quite the opposite.

Before exploring this contradiction further and reappraising the role of Hilferding's concept in the development of Marxist theory, a pause for reflection is necessary for it may be only an apparent contradiction. Hilferding seems not to have seen it as real, for he argues that finance capital, instead of being tied and specific, is a form of capital which is 'its supreme and most abstract expression'. (34) And he gives specific reasons for thinking that in economic crises (precisely when finance's independence is most forcefully tested by its ability to avoid being broken by industry's dislocation) banks are able to maintain their stability within a system of finance-capital better than they could previously. One reason is that the industrial enterprises with which they are linked are highly cartelised in a largely successful attempt to insulate them from the anarchy of the market, with the result that they are able to withstand economic crises with less harm than enterprises in sectors with lower degrees of concentration. Another is that the destabilising speculation that formerly characterised the commodity and stock exchanges and helped to transmit and generalise the effects of a capitalist crisis of production is reduced both by a reduction in the significance of merchant capital as financial and industrial trusts develop, and by banks' domination and regulation of stock markets. (35)

Hilferding's emphasis throughout his analysis of finance-capital is on the high degree of regulation and order that the unity of big banks and big firms seek to impose on the economy, controlling market forces and insulating themselves from the instability that unregulated markets bring. Bank capital is able to maintain its stability while being tied to industry because '(i)ndustrial earnings acquire a more secure and regular character' (36) in this stage of capitalism, or at least, the earnings of the cartels and trusts are more secure so that the small and medium enterprises bear an extra burden of economic crises. If the thrust of finance in Marx's conception is toward increased independence so that its profits can be obtained from surplus value without being tied to productive capital's vicissitudes, in Hilferding its ties are unproblematic since they are part of a system within which the fluctuations are regulated and smoothed.

That approach does not offer a satisfactory resolution of the contradictions for, however regulated and stabilized the world of monopoly capital is, if banks are joined with its productive enterprises their capital is tied to particular sectors and they are forced to intervene directly in the production of surplus value as capital is continually restructured and unevenly accumulated. The logic of finance capital in Hilferding is that 'the banks ... become ... industrial capitalists' and this contradicts the general Marxian conception that finance is universal and mobile; in Hilferding's own words finance capital implies the 'immobilization of bank resources in industry' (37) and, although he saw this as partial, it lies at the core of finance capital.

Historical Specificity

If, as I have argued, Marx's view of financial capital as liquid, mobile and relatively independent from production corresponds well to today's world of finance, and if Hilferding's concept of finance-capital is inconsistent with it, two questions arise. First, in terms of the development of the discourse itself, how was Hilferding's concept developed out of Marx's own; what assumptions and emphases took it in a contradictory direction? Second, what insight does the concept of finance capital give into the historical development of capitalism?

The crucial link in Hilferding's development of the concept of finance capital out of Marx's categories is the concept of fictitious capital; the fictitious capital represented by share values above the value of the capital subscribed to the firm. He considers this in the form of a new category, promoters' profit. Banks can obtain promoters' profit by founding industrial companies and issuing shares whose market value, when profits are discounted at the prevailing discount rate, is higher than the money advanced in the company. This was seen as a significant driving force behind banks' increased involvement in industry. But this leads Hilferding in the opposite direction from the general implications of fictitious capital because he concentrates on only one of its forms. The fictitious capital represented by share values and, particularly, the capital gains on new shares is the type of which is most closely linked to productive enterprises so Hilferding considers that to gain maximum benefit from it banks have to be closely involved with industry.

This line of reasoning reflects Hilferding's great emphasis on the sphere of production which makes it difficult for him to see the many mediations that may lie between any particular financial operation and the production of surplus value. Two examples illustrate the one-sidedness of this approach. First, as the vast takeover and greenmail operations of the last few years illustrate, banks obtain large profits from the expansion of fictitious capital in shares without themselves becoming involved directly in the operation or supervision of industrial capital. Second, fictitious capital in corporate equities is not the only or most significant form of fictitious capital in the expansion of banking and the modern credit system. The bonds, bills, certificates and credit instruments issued by states, state-backed institutions, and purely financial corporations themselves have been the most significant form of capitalised revenue streams in the development of the credit system. As I have outlined above, the expansion of international banking across the Euro-markets and other international markets has been to a large extent based on such fictitious capital, but Hilferding's concentration on a specific, different form of fictitious capital directed his analysis along quite different lines. Hilferding thought finance capital resulted from banks having no alternative use for their vast inflow of funds but to invest in industry, but they have created alternatives at every turn.

These problems mean that the concept of finance-capital remains valuable for understanding capitalism's historical development, but only when it is seen as a historically specific and limited form of capital. This contrasts directly with Hilferding's own assessment. Seeing finance capital as capital's 'supreme and most abstract expression' he argued that the phenomena observed in Germany where 'universal banks' invested directly in industry and controlled industrial trusts 'is a necessary and unavoidable tendency' while the division between deposit banking and merchant banking in Britain was backward and a (superficial) hindrance to banks' essential role of integrating with industry. He saw the English separation between banks and industry as a historically specific system, 'an outmoded one (which) is everywhere on the decline because it makes the control of the loaned-out bank capital more difficult and hence obstructs the expansion of bank credit itself.' (38)

The implication of the arguments presented here is that the tendency to dissociate banks' operations from industry's is the rule and their direct linking is the exception. Sweezy presents one way in which the historical limits of finance capital may be conceived. He saw the direct dominance of bankers in industry as a transitional phenomenon in the emergence of 'monopoly capital' so that 'Bank capital, having had its day of glory, falls back again to a position subsidiary to industrial capital'. (39) The issue of whether banks dominate industry or *vice versa* is different from the one emphasised in this essay; financial capital operated by banks may well have a generally dominating role but finance capital would only exist if the relation between banks and industry is a close one with banks' dominance being through direct intervention. The question of its historical specificity relates, therefore, to the circumstances under which direct control predominates.

At specific periods in specific economies forms of finance-capital have existed even if, as at present, international banking is characterised by an absence of direct involvement in industry; the classic example is German banking since the late nineteenth century, and another, typical of some third world countries today, is Chile in the second half of the 1970s. The original character of the German system is well known from Hilferding and Lenin. The system in modern Chile evolved after 1973 when (in 1974 and 1975) Pinochet's government, in an extreme reaction to socialist forms of intervention opened up the financial system to private ownership and competition. The subsequent rapid growth of banking led to the creation of large conglomerates in which banks and other enterprises were closely meshed. Foxley summarised their character as follows:

> By the end of 1978, five economic conglomerates controlled 53% of the total assets of Chile's 250 largest private enterprises. Nine conglomerates, including these five, controlled 82% of the assets of the Chilean banking system. These nine groups also controlled 60% of total bank credits and 64% of loans made by financial institutions. (40)

Diaz-Alejandro notes that by late 1982 'extreme indebtedness was found among those (private firms) that controlled banks - interpenetration of economic and financial power appears to have reached extraordinary levels. The two largest business groups in Chile by late 1982 controlled the principal insurance companies, mutual funds, brokerage houses, the largest private company pension funds and the two largest private commercial banks - by late 1982 many banks had lent one quarter or more of their resources to affiliates.' (41) These are examples of the numerous cases where the structures typical of finance capital have emerged in specific circumstances, but finance capital is the opposite of financial capital's basic tendency and role.

The conditions which can generate finance-capital's type of conglomerates in such specific cases relate to the configuration of the state and the degree of development of financial markets for these determine the expansion of forms of fictitious capital other than that comprised in industrial equities. London's operation as a financial centre where banks preserved the looseness of their links with industry (following the nineteenth-century banker's advice: 'reject ... anything that is not readily convertible into money ... mind your own business') (42) was possible because financing state deficits and having large, internationally oriented and well-developed secondary markets in financial instruments permitted the creation of a wide variety of forms of fictitious capital in which banks could operate. (43) In the late nineteenth century, Germany did not have those conditions but, instead, an interventionist state that directly encouraged the creation of bank-industry trusts in the pursuit of industrialisation. Chile in the late 1970s, also lacking indigenous forms of fictitious capital on financial markets, was directed by a state which directly encouraged the creation of such conglomerates. They were founded on the bourgeoisie's ability to buy banks and enterprises from the state at low prices when the military regime privatised them; Foxley calculates that they were able to buy them at approximately 30 per cent below the value of their assets. (44)

Because London's modern banking system developed on the basis of a wide range of fictitious capital instead of being based on the specific relations involved in finance-capital, it had the basis to become the world centre of the international (Euro-) banking system that developed in the 1970s for it is a system dominated by fictitious capital and, in that, it appears to be an advanced effect of the inherent tendency of bank capital to seek liquidity and universality, avoiding immobilisation. However, as bankers have found in the 1980s the problem is that even fictitious capital cannot avoid its ultimate dependence on the productivity of industry; when the accumulation of productive capital is dislocated even state debt is risky, and banks' capital can indeed become immobilized by the crisis at times.

NOTES

Parts of this chapter are based on a paper delivered at the American Social Science Associations meetings, New York, December 1985. I am grateful to the participants and to the members of the Open University Financial Studies Group for comments.

1. The international orientation of the City has long been known and the subject of critical comment. A major theme in historical writings is the thesis developed by Perry Anderson (1966). A different perspective on it, which emphasises the supranationality of the international finance system and the historical changes in the position of international finance in Britain has been developed by several contributors to this book, both here and elsewhere. Books by Coakley and Harris (1983) and Fine and Harris (1985) cover much of this ground, while in this volume Trevor Evans' 'Money Makes the World Go Round', Jerry Coakley's 'The Internationalisation of Bank Capital', and Coakley and Harris' 'The City, Industry and the Foreign Exchanges' contribute to this new perspective.

2. The neo-classical theory of markets treats access to information as axiomatic (the 'perfect knowledge' assumption). Properly specified in those terms it implies that information is instantaneously available to all market participants at low cost and, in the limit, zero cost. New information technology has radically decreased the marginal cost of such information. It should be noted that in most neo-classical models it is assumed that the relevant information has to be 'true', but this is not a necessary requirement in fact and the information now made available to markets is often relevant because it is believed to be relevant not because it is truly an indicator of an external economic reality. As Keynes noted, the herd instinct and self-generated beliefs are what count on financial markets.

3. See the chapter by Coakley and Harris, 'Evaluating the Role of the Financial System'.

4. Industrial enterprises have a strong tendency to develop activities similar to financial institutions' in order to overcome their relative lack of universality and mobility. Thus multinational corporations allocate financial capital internally in a manner which to varying degrees imitates financial markets. Morover, as Jerry Coakley's chapter 'Bank Lending and the Control of Industry: An Empirical Study' discusses, large UK corporations have increasingly developed treasury divisions which, in the extreme, are in-house banks.

5. In Marxian terms, even if a firm expands only on the basis of its retained profits it may be drawing on the surplus value of the whole capitalist system to some extent for, as a result of equalisation of profit rates, the selling price of its commodities will generally differ from their

value (profit per unit will differ from surplus value per unit). See Fine and Harris (1979). But the financial system provides greater, and different, access to overall profits.

6. In this book the role of internal finance for UK firms is discussed in Croasdale and Harris 'Internal Funds and Investment' and Croasdale 'Modelling the Finance of Investment'.

7. For example, Kotz (1978).

8. A seminal contribution was Minns (1980). In the present book, the two chapters by Jerry Coakley ('Bank Lending and British Industry: An Empirical Study' and 'American Banks' Credit to UK Industry') and Richard Minns' chapter ('The Management of Shareholdings in Large Manufacturing Corporations') directly relate to this issue. Both writers develop significant new approaches to the problem.

9. The two chapters by Smith and Wield, 'Banking on New Technology' and 'New Technology and Bank Work', mark a significant innovation in their investigation of the relation between new technology, competition and labour organisation.

10. The chapters by Trevor Evans, Jerry Coakley, and Coakley and Harris in Part II of this volume examine these questions. See also Coakley and Harris (1983) and Fine and Harris (1985).

11. See below, J. Coakley and L. Harris 'The City, Industry and the Foreign Exchanges'.

12. It is worth noting that the concept employed here of the state needing a national monopoly of money differs from the neoclassical treatment. Neoclassical writers argue that states' monopoly of the money supply confers a financial advantage on the state in the form of seignorage. This is the command over real resources, the acquisition of commodities, the state gains without cost by the creation of money. Thus, if the state seeks a monopoly over money it is in order to maximise its own 'profit' or 'utility' in the manner of a pre-capitalist war lord. Here, by contrast, the state's monopoly over money is conceived as a pre-condition for its exercise of its responsibility for national capitalist accumulation.

13. This proposition, deriving from the Latin American structuralist theories of inflation, sees inflation as a necessary mechanism providing flexibility within which the unevenness of capitalist growth can occur.

14. See de Brunhoff.

15. See the chapter by Trevor Evans 'Money Makes the World Go Round'.

16. The state's responsibility for the links between national and international money can also be interpreted as having an element of seignorage although with more plausibility than the neo-classical theory of seignorage relating to national money in a closed economy. Thus, the British state's promotion of the pound sterling as an international currency almost until the end of the Sterling Area enabled Britain to obtain net imports without a short-term real foreign exchange cost (as evidenced by the famous 'sterling balances' accumulated by India and other countries). Similarly, the international use of the US dollar has enabled the US to run cumulative trade deficits, particularly in periods such as the Vietnam war and Reagan's military expansion when the military budget generates large balance of payments deficits.

17. In recent years a version of this phenomenon has been known as Goodhart's Law, after Charles Goodhart (then at the Bank of England) who noted that when a given set of financial instruments is defined as money and attempts are made to control its supply, financial innovation leads to other instruments, which are uncontrolled, taking on some of money's functions, so thwarting the controls.

18. See the chapter by Jerry Coakley, 'The Internationalisation of Bank Capital'. A significant new twist to the upward spiral of increased internationalisation was the judgement in 1987 that a London bank, the Scandinavian Bank, could have its capital denominated in a basket of currencies because its deposits were in various denominations.

19. In this context the chapters by Robin Murray 'Pension Funds and Local Authority Investments' and Richard Minns 'Pension Funds: An Alternative View' are interesting since they discuss the scope for financial interventions by the local state rather than national states.

20. The character of the system that is being reformed or replaced in Japan is discussed in Sonja Ruehl's chapter 'Interest Rate Regulation and Credit Rationing in Japan: The Evidence'.

21. Alan Lipietz' chapter 'The Limits of Bank Nationalisation in France' discusses the character and limits of those nationalisation measures.

22. This thesis is argued below in my chapter 'Financial Reform and Economic Growth: A New

Interpretation of South Korea's Experience'.

23. R. Hilferding (1910).

24. Although Marx paid considerable attention to the importance of money-dealing capital in the financial system, it has not figured prominently in subsequent writings except for Hilferding, op. cit.; G.C. Ingham (1984); and J. Coakley and L. Harris (1983).

25. L. Harris (1976).

26. Marx, Capital, vol. III.

27. J. O'Connor, The Fiscal Crisis of the State.

28. Hilferding, op. cit., p.225, 'The dependence of industry on the banks is therefore a consequence of property relations. An ever-increasing part of the capital of industry does not belong to the industrialists who use it. They are able to dispose over capital only through the banks ...' The literature discussing the empirical validity of the hypothesis of bank control over industry in the US includes P. Sweezy, (1942); R. Fitch and M. Oppenheimer, D. Kotz, (1978). For the UK it includes R. Minns, (1980) and the chapters by Jerry Coakley in Part III of this book.

29. Hilferding, op. cit., p.225.

30. Hilferding, op. cit., p.293.

31. Hilferding, op. cit., p.22.

32. 'Financial capital' being used here to include both interest-bearing capital and money-dealing capital.

33. A difference marked by the differences between the former obtaining revenue as interest and the latter as profit-of-enterprise.

34. Hilferding, op. cit., p.22.

35. The effectiveness of regulation in limiting crises is discussed particularly in Hilferding, op. cit., Ch. 20. In addition, Hilferding reasons that banking crises became less prevalent because their system of cash reserves became more flexible and permitted greater elasticity in the money supply (ibid, p.290-1). He also treated the bank-industry relations of finance-capital as only one element in banks' operations, for although banks were tied to particular firms, the size of banks' capital and its internationalisation meant that they could spread their risks.

36. Ibid, p.225.

37. Ibid, p.291.

38. Ibid, p.293.

39. P. Sweezy, op. cit., p.268.

40. A. Foxley (1983), pp. 81-83.

41. C.F. Diaz-Alejandro (1984), p.20.

42. Advice given under the pen-name 'Bullion' to nineteenth-century bankers. Quoted in B. Fine and L. Harris (1985), p.129.

43. These conditions and their historical significance are discussed more fully in B. Fine and L. Harris (1985).

44. Foxley, op. cit.

REFERENCES

Anderson, P. (1966) 'The Origins of the Present Crisis' in P. Anderson and R. Blackburn (eds) Towards Socialism, Ithaca, Cornell University Press.

J. Coakley and L. Harris (1983) The City of Capital, Oxford, Basil Blackwell.

S. de Brunhoff (1978) State, Capital and Economic Policy, London, Pluto Press.

C.F. Diaz-Alejandro (1984) 'Goodbye Financial Repression, Hello Financial Crash', Kellogg Institute Working Paper, no.24.

B. Fine and L. Harris (1983) Rereading Capital, London, Macmillan.

------ (1985) The Peculiarities of the British Economy, London, Lawrence and Wishart.

A. Foxley (1983) Latin American Experiments in Neo-Conservative Economics, Berkeley, University of California Press.

L. Harris (1976) 'On Interest, Credit and Capital, Economy and Society, vol. 5, no. 2.

R. Hilferding (1910) Das Finanz Kapital, Vienna. English translation, edited by Tom Bottomore, Finance Capital, London (1981).

G.C. Ingham (1984) Capitalism Divided? London, Macmillan.

D. Kotz (1978) Bank Control of Large Corporations in the United States, Berkeley, University of California Press.

R. Minns (1980) Pension Funds and British Capitalism, London, Heinemann.

J. O'Connor (1973) Fiscal Crisis of the State, New York, St. Martins Press.

P. Sweezy (1942) The Theory of Capitalist Development, New York, Monthly Review Press.

Part II

FINANCE AND THE INTERNATIONAL SYSTEM

INTRODUCTION TO PART II

Laurence Harris

The role of money and finance in Britain and other economies is inseparable from its international dimension. In one sense finance is essentially international and an understanding of its world role is a prerequisite for analysing its operation within a country.

Trevor Evans' chapter, Money Makes the World Go Round, gives a thorough overview of the changing character of the international monetary system since World War II. It examines the links between finance and the 'real' economy of production, trade and capital accumulation, and the connections linking the US and UK economies with the developing international system.

In The Internationalisation of Bank Capital Jerry Coakley is also concerned with the modern development of the international system, but from a different angle. While Evans focusses on money, state policy and the 'real' economy, Coakley examines the growing internationalisation of the banks. These are the (mainly private) institutions that actually operate the international and domestic financial system, or, at least, dominate the operations of all other financial institutions, and the chapter is a valuable application of the view that the financial system has to be seen in terms of its specific institutions as well as the more universal or abstract concepts of 'money', 'finance' and 'the financial system'. Coakley shows how the specific position of banks in different countries has affected their role in internationalisation and provides an explanation for the predominance of the City of London as a centre of international finance.

In Industry, the City and the Foreign Exchanges: Theory

and Evidence Jerry Coakley and I examine an argument that has dominated British politics and economic policy for decades. In general it is the idea that the international character of the City of London has had a harmful effect on British industry so that the integration between national and international finance that Evans writes of has been damaging in Britain. This chapter reports an empirical study of one aspect of the general thesis; the proposition that the exchange rate policies pursued by British governments (especially in the period of the Bretton Woods international monetary system) depressed the profits of industrial and commercial enterprises. Its concerns relate directly to those of Part III where we concentrate on the relations between finance and industry in the UK.

Chapter Three

MONEY MAKES THE WORLD GO ROUND

Trevor Evans

The world economy has been going through a crisis for just over ten years. It began with the 1974-5 recession, which was the deepest and most widespread to have occurred since before World War II. This was followed by a period of recovery that was strong in the US and the newly industrialising countries of Latin America and South-East Asia, but weak in Europe, Japan and the Third World. Then in 1980 the world was plunged into a recession that was even more severe than the previous one. Unemployment increased to record post-war levels in all the advanced capitalist economies, and the fall in primary commodity prices had a devastating effect on the economies of the Third World. Although a strong recovery has been underway in the US since 1983, the upturn has been uneven and weak elsewhere.

This article is about the relation between the crisis in the world economy and international finance. At the end of the second world war what became known as the Bretton Woods international monetary system was established with the intention of giving governments greater control over international economic relations. This system collapsed in the early 1970s and gave way to one that was dominated by the operation of private markets. I will attempt to show that these private markets have been one of the principal mechanisms by which the crisis has been imposed on national economies. While it is true that in Britain the Thatcher government chose to pursue monetarist policies, it would have been very difficult for it to have chosen not to. This is not meant to imply that there are no other policies that could be pursued, but rather that any viable alternative would have to mount a more radical challenge to the system of private financial markets than is often envisaged.

The article will mainly be concerned with trying to outline how the international financial system has developed in response to accumulation in the advanced capitalist economies. The main focus will be on the US and Britain although, because of its global implications, the international debt crisis will also be touched on. First, however, it might help to say a little about the importance of money.

The Power in your Purse

Capitalism is a monetary economy. This is in some respects so obvious that it is easy to take it for granted. There are so few activities that do not involve money in some way that it can appear to be a rather ordinary feature of everyday life. Yet it is in reality one of the more remarkable products of human society. A process has been created by which virtually every type of qualitative distinction can be reduced to a difference between one quantity of money and another. Goods and services, artefacts and land, even people's abilities and attributes - all can be expressed as a sum of money. It is the universality of money that makes the task of understanding its social function so difficult.

In a capitalist economy, production is organised in a large number of separate enterprises. There is however no institution which consciously decides how much of society's labour should be employed in producing any particular commodity. Instead this is decided after a commodity has been produced by whether it can be sold for money. Money provides the link between producers and consumers, and is the means by which society validates a particular expenditure of labour. Money is therefore a social bond which both unites and regulates people in this decentralised system of production.

But money is not just a bond: its possession confers control over social production. Most people have to spend their lives working, often at meaningless tasks, in order to get the money that is necessary to live. As a result, those who have money can command the labour of those that don't. It is this that makes it possible to throw money into circulation and make more money, a profit. Money that circulates in this way is capital and, as capital, it constitutes an enormous concentration of social power.

Although capital employs this social power to promote production, in general it will only do so if it is profitable, and it does not do so smoothly. On the contrary, periods of profitable investment have always run into social obstacles that impose a limit on the process. The limit manifests itself initially as a widespread inability to sell commodities for money and results in a cutback in investment and a downturn in the economy. This is the basis of the business cycle that has been a permanent feature of capitalist development since the early nineteenth century. It is downturns in the business cycle that underly the financial crises that still periodically rock even the strongest capitalist economies and force them to transform themselves and adapt to a changing world.

Because money exercises such a pervasive influence, reaching into every pore of social life, it provides an extremely powerful weapon for curbing any social demands which are incompatible with the pursuit of profit. The fact that money is the bond which links people together in a capitalist society makes it very difficult to resist attacks which are launched through that bond, as the trade union movement has found when confronted by the strategy of monetarism. At a time of crisis, therefore, it is through money that the imperatives of a capitalist economy are reasserted over those of social life.

National Money

Money used to be made out of valuable commodities such as silver or gold. This type of money is known as commodity money, and its face value was related to the value of the metal it contained. However, in order to avoid having to continuously weigh out quantities of metal in order to use it as money, it needed to be minted into coins of a standard weight. This task required a public authority and it fell to the state, which either minted the coins itself or supervised their production by someone else. From the outset then, money has involved the state and has had a distinctively national character.

Commodity money however was expensive to produce and its supply was quite inadequate for the phenomenal growth of a monetary economy which occurred with the development of capitalist commerce and industry. The rise of capitalism was consequently associated with the development of other forms of money. This resulted in a system of national money based on a combination of money issued by the state (state money) and money issued by the banking system (credit money).

There are two ways in which banks can create money: one is to issue bank notes; the other is to credit an account with a deposit which can then be drawn on by cheque. When a cheque is used to make a payment, the deposit is transferred to another account, the deposit can be transferred again and again, but it will still exist even after the original advance of credit has been repaid. Most money is of this type and it exists only as an entry in a bank's books or, with modern technology, as just a pulse on a computer tape.

Banks can provide an extremely flexible supply of money, but because this money can be created so easily, there is a problem about ensuring its quality. (In the United States during the nineteenth century the notes issued by many banks were often only accepted elsewhere at a substantial discount on their face value.) The state has therefore become deeply involved in the regulation of the monetary system and the institution through which this is exercised is the Central Bank. The Central Bank sits at the apex of a banking system. The money it creates is backed by the state and it provides the means by which other banks settle the balance on their transactions with each other. The quality of the credit money created by commercial banks rests on its exchangeability with the state money issued by the Central Bank.

The Bank of England has been the Central Bank through which the state has regulated the monetary system in Britain - even though it was privately owned until as late as 1946. The Bank's practice evolved in the course of the nineteenth century as the government attempted to ameliorate the consequences of recurrent financial crises. The issue of bank notes, which had been practised by all banks, was restricted to the Bank of England, and it was only permitted to issue notes up to a ceiling related to the size of its gold reserves. The notes were convertible into gold on request, and the standard of value was a £1 gold coin. The state therefore tried to ensure the quality of the credit money created by commercial banks by linking it, through the Bank of England's money, to the value of gold.

The direct link between the value of Bank of England money and gold was finally broken after the international financial crisis in 1931. Since then the state has tried to ensure the quality of money by a system of reserve requirements. This means that the amount of money that banks can create is supposed to be limited to a fixed multiple of their reserves of state money, which includes Bank of England money and some forms of government debt. Since the state controls the supply of this high quality money, it should be able to control the total amount of money that is created. However, because commercial banks make their profits by extending credit, they tend to be very innovative in finding ways round any restrictions on the ability to meet the demand for loans. Recent evidence from Britain and the US suggests that if reserves are not supplied to the commercial banks, the competition between them for the reserves that are available will send interest rates sharply up, but that this will have little direct effect on the amount of money that the banks create.

Regulating the Economy

The development of a system of national money that is not convertible domestically for gold has meant an important shift in the way that money serves to regulate a capitalist economy. In the nineteenth century, the expenditure of labour on producing a commodity was socially validated when that commodity was sold for money. When there was a downturn in the business cycle and companies could not sell their products, they would be unable to repay their bank loans and a rash of bank failures would follow. Any outstanding money that had been issued by these banks would become worthless, and the destruction of one part of the total money in circulation added a further deflationary twist to the situation. As recession purged the economy of its least productive enterprise those that remained would be the ones that had adopted new techniques. They could produce commodities more cheaply and so sell them at prices commensurate with the reduced level of monetary demand.

In order to prevent cyclical downturns escalating into a complete financial collapse, the Bank of England developed the practice of acting as lender of last resort. This ensured that if one bank collapsed, it would not endanger the whole financial system. It should be noted that by lending money to a bank that was threatened with a shortage of liquidity, the Central Bank was effectively guaranteeing the exchangeability of all the money created by the banking system. This was an important change.

The role of the Central Bank as lender of last resort and the domestic inconvertibility of money are the two main characteristics of the monetary systems that have operated in the advanced capitalist countries since the second world war. When there is a downturn in the business cycle, this still appears as an inability to sell commodities at their old prices. There is not enough money to buy all the commodities and, as unsold stocks build up, firms will be faced with a shortage of money and so want to borrow more. Freed from the constraint of convertibility the Central Bank can provide the banking system with the reserves necessary to meet the additional demand for credit. This is the strategy of Keynesianism. The commodities will be sold but at a higher price. A deep recession is avoided but the underlying problem has merely been displaced. The problem of validating the labour expended in producing commodities no longer occurs at the point where the commodities are exchanged for money, it has been shifted to the point where the quality of credit money used to buy the commodities is guaranteed through its relation to state money. Because the Central Bank now guarantees the exchangeability of all money, it is no longer possible to devalue the total supply of money by destroying the money created by just a few banks; what happens instead is that the value of all money is partially devalued through inflation.

If the Central Bank underwrites the creation of money in this way it facilitates the function of money as a means of circulation. It promotes the exchange of commodities and, at least in the short term, continued economic reproduction. However, there is a contradiction between the function of money as a medium of circulation and that of money as a store of value. A capitalist economy is dependent on the existence of a credit system which collects idle money and concentrates it as capital at that point in the economy where it can most profitably be employed. If money's function as a store of value is seriously undermined, idle capital will be withdrawn from the credit system and stored in some other form, such as oil paintings or real estate. If the idle capital can be retained it is only at a rate of interest that is so high that it cuts into profits and undermines the ability of firms to invest.

The appeal of the monetarist strategy, whose rationale

was based on little more than the dogma of sound money, was that it attempted to reassert the value of money by refusing to provide the reserve assets that would underwrite the creation of money by the banking system. Where governments have chosen to follow this strategy it has resulted in acute recessions. However, where governments have not themselves chosen to follow monetarist policies, they have found their management of the economy constrained by the relation between their national money and the international monetary system.

Geofinance. BW.

International money

The type of monetary system which exists in each capitalist economy depends on state regulation and exists on a national basis. Capitalism however has always been an international system. In practice, a stable international monetary system has depended on one state being sufficiently financially dominant to impose its money on the rest of the world economy. Before 1914 this role was played by Britain; since 1945 it has been fulfilled by the United States.

The international monetary system that came into operation after the second world war was set up at a conference attended by 44 nations in 1944 at the North American holiday resort of Bretton Woods. The mighty US economy had finally lifted itself out of depression with the onset of the war, and between 1940 and 1944 its industrial output doubled. As the war drew to a close a debate developed within the US state over how to ensure that this rate of accumulation could be maintained. A younger generation of more radical economists at the Treasury argued for a Keynesian-oriented system of national planning. It was however the State Department's view which prevailed. This favoured a free-market system, but argued that its success would depend on the US running a substantial export surplus. To achieve such a surplus, US capital would have to gain access to those large parts of the world economy that were closed by protective barriers, most notably the markets of the British empire. The US therefore set about trying to create a multi-lateral system of international trade, and it was with this aim in mind that it participated in the Bretton Woods conference.

At the end of the war the US controlled 70 per cent of

the world's reserves of gold, and it used this financial power to achieve an international monetary system in which the dollar played a central role. The British government felt obliged to accept the US proposals because of its dependence on huge US loans to finance day-to-day imports of food and raw materials. (The secret treaties by which the US maintains military bases in Britain were agreed under the same circumstances.)

There were three main features of the system that was established at Bretton Woods. Firstly, gold was to act as the international store of value, but the dollar was to act alongside it, 'as good as gold', on the basis that the US government would convert dollars into gold at the rate of $35 an ounce. Secondly, the value of other currencies was fixed in terms of the dollar at a rate that was pegged, but could under certain conditions be adjusted. Thirdly, the International Monetary Fund was founded to regulate the exchange-rate system and to provide short-term loans to countries while they overcame balance of payments deficits.

The Bretton Woods system provided a framework within which international economic relations could be conducted using a national money, namely the dollar. In countries other than the US, the national money was to be exchangeable with the dollar through the Central Bank. Governments were allowed to impose controls on the exchange of capital for overseas investment, but otherwise different currencies were supposed to be freely convertible, although it was not in fact until the late 1950s that this was fully achieved. The system can be described as politically managed because it required constant intervention in foreign-exchange markets by national monetary authorities in order to maintain the pegged level of exchange rates. This international arrangement made possible an unprecedented expansion of the world economy in the two decades after the second world war, but as the dollar came to play an increasingly large international role, this put US capital in a privileged international position.

The Privileges of the Dollar

Since World War II governments have been responsible for managing their national economies, but they have had to do so within limits imposed through the international monetary system. Until the early 1970s this constraint operated through the balance of payments. It was this process that gave rise to the stop-go-cycle that dominated British economic policy in the 1950s and 1960s. Governments would facilitate accumulation by providing the banking system with the reserves necessary to expand the supply of money. But if this was pursued beyond a certain point, it would result in a balance of payments deficit. Then the government would be forced to introduce a more contractionary policy. Because it was possible to borrow from the IMF, the downturn could be cushioned but it could not be avoided.

The one country where this did not apply was the US. Because its national money also served as international money, the US economy was not constrained in the same way from running a balance of payments deficit. If a company in Britain wants to buy something in the world market it needs dollars, and it gets these by purchasing them from the Bank of England. The Bank of England will only be able to supply these if there are companies earning dollars abroad and exchanging them for sterling. Companies in the US, by contrast, could simply buy items in the rest of the world and pay for them with their own national money. Paul Sweezy has likened the situation to having a free gold mine at the bottom of the garden. Since the dollar was as good as gold, and dollars were created in the US, it was possible for the private and government enterprises that make up the US economy to acquire resources from the rest of the world without having to part with items of comparable value themselves. US enterprises were able, on balance, to spend more abroad than they earned, resulting in the payments deficit.

In fact, the US ran a substantial trade surplus through the 1950s and most of the 1960s due to the large international demand for its consumer goods and, above all, its sophisticated means of production. However, this trade surplus was more than offset by two other items. One was the aid and military expenditure which the US state incurred as a result of assuming the role of dominant world power. The other was the extensive programme of direct investment which US corporations embarked on first in Canada and then in Europe. The overall balance of payments was consequently in deficit.

As a result of the US deficit there was a steady flow of dollars out of the US, although this was initially welcomed by other states who were anxious to build up their reserves of international money. Nevertheless, by the early 1960s the size of the outflow was beginning to create a problem. Under the terms of the Bretton Woods agreement the United States was obliged to convert foreign dollar holdings into gold on request, and by the early 1960s the scale of these foreign holdings was larger than the US reserve of gold. The first serious sign of trouble occurred in 1960 when there was a speculative run on the London gold market. (Speculation occurred because it was believed that if the US government could not convert all the outstanding dollars at the rate of $35 per ounce of gold, the dollar value of gold might have to be increased. In that event anyone holding gold would be able to sell it at a much higher dollar price than they had paid.)

The issue came to a head because, in addition to the underlying structural deficit, the US balance of payments was also affected by flows of money capital that were closely related to the business cycle. In 1958 full convertibility had finally been established between the national currencies of the main capitalist countries, and this removed an important barrier to the international mobility of capital. Then in 1960 the US economy entered a recession and, once the demand for credit had declined, interest rates began to fall. This affected international capital flows in two ways. Firstly, there was a spate of bond issues in New York by foreign companies and governments who took advantage of the low interest rate and then exported the capital they had raised. Secondly, an even greater amount of short-term capital left the US in search of higher interest rates elsewhere. The combined effect of these capital flows was to sharply exacerbate the size of the US deficit.

The Kennedy government was eager to use Keynesian techniques to boost the economy out of recession, but it was worried by the danger that a further fall in interest rates might, by pumping yet more dollars into the rest of the world, lead to another run on gold. It can therefore be seen that, although the US was not constrained in the same way as other countries from running a balance of payments deficit, it too was subject to limits imposed by the international monetary system.

The next move of the US government was to try and increase its room for manoeuvre by controlling the flow of capital out of the country. While this was successful in its immediate objective, it led to a major transformation of the international financial system that resulted in government policy becoming even more tightly constrained by the operation of private capital markets.

The Rise of the Eurodollar

US Capital Controls

Between 1963 and 1965 the US government introduced a series of measures to control the flow of capital out of the country. US corporations, however, were already engaged on a strategy of investing overseas, and had a programme of future investments lined up when the capital controls were introduced. Instead of raising the finance for overseas investment in the US and then sending it abroad, these corporations therefore began to use their overseas subsidiaries to borrow from banks in other countries.

A novel feature of this borrowing was that although it was contracted outside the US it was denominated in dollars. If a bank in Europe lent in dollars, because it was located in Europe it could escape the regulation of the US government, and loans to non-residents in dollars were not subject to regulation by a European government. A money market that is based in one country and denominated in the currency of another is known technically as an off-shore, or transnational, money market. But because this market developed initially in Europe it has become known more generally as the Eurocurrency market, or, in view of the predominance of dollar-denominated issues, the Eurodollar market. A small market in Eurodollars had existed since 1949 - it originated because the Soviet and Chinese government wanted to keep their reserves of dollars where they could not be impounded by the US government! It was however the imposition of US capital controls that was a major impetus to the growth of a large-scale Eurodollar market, and in the mid-1960s it began to grow very rapidly.

A further impetus to the growth of the Euromarkets came as a result of another, more long-standing US government measure, Regulation Q. This imposed a ceiling on the interest rate that banks could pay for deposits, and had been introduced in the 1930s at the time of the New Deal to keep the price of bank loans down. In 1966, accumulation in the US slackened, and as the demand for credit increased, interest rates hit the maximum permitted level. Banks in the US were unable to raise the interest rate on deposits any further, and this encouraged US corporations to deposit any idle earnings in the Euromarkets, where the interest rate was not controlled.

The main centre of this rapidly growing international financial market was the City of London. London had a long history as an international financial centre, although until the 1960s it was still oriented towards the remnants of the British empire. The City quickly recognised the importance of the Eurodollar and, with a zeal that was in marked contrast to that of British industry, it set about restructuring its operations so as to capture the new market for itself. In this, it was aided by the fact that of all the financial centres that then existed, London was one of the least regulated in the world.

US banks rushed to open overseas branches, especially in London, and in 1966 they replaced British and European banks as the dominant force in the Euromarkets. By 1967 the importance of the new market had become so established that the US government felt compelled to lift those of its capital controls that affected the overseas branches of US banks so that they would not be handicapped in competing with other banks.

The rise of the Euromarkets meant the beginning of an important shift from international financial relations being conducted through the official channels of the Bretton Woods system towards the private markets of the Eurodollar system. An international financial market had already begun to develop in the late 1950s and early 1960s. US banks appear to have first opened overseas branches as a result of following their corporate customers abroad. It was therefore the increasing international organisation of production that led to the growth of international movements of money capital. But the growth of large-scale units of capital within banking was itself an impetus to major banks developing their international activities. The imposition of controls on capital flows by the US government determined the form that this international development took. When the government tried to limit the growth of international financial dealings based in the US, the private-market system transformed itself and, with remarkable agility, established itself on a new basis outside the control of any national state. Although the controls succeeded in limiting the size of capital flows out of the US, it failed to stem a growing private-market system that was increasingly undermining the tenability of the politically-managed international monetary system based on the dollar.

The Crisis of the Dollar

The position of the dollar as international money had rested on the massive industrial supremacy of the US economy at the end of the war. The US had acquired a large proportion of the world's international reserves and, through a combination of financial muscle and political dominance, created a new world-market order in its image. The dollar-based system facilitated a rapid expansion of the world economy, but there were several features of this process that tended to undermine its success. Firstly, the boom in other capitalist economies was based on adopting the highly productive techniques that had been pioneered by US industry before the war. This involved new branches of industry and, above all, the introduction of the moving assembly line, or Fordist organisation of production, that enabled employers to impose a far higher intensity of labour on workers than had been possible hitherto.

Secondly, while there was a rapid deepening of the economic interconnections between the advanced capitalist economies, firms based in different countries participated in this in different ways. During the 1950s and 1960s, many US companies supplied foreign markets by investing abroad (as did British companies); in most other countries companies concentrated on investing in domestic production that could be used to supply exports to other economies. Although productivity in the US remained at a high level by international standards, it grew more slowly than in virtually any other advanced capitalist country, and while the US share of world trade began to fall, that of other economies began to rise. This was particularly marked in the case of Japan and West Germany.

The US actually ran a trade deficit in 1968 for the first time since the war, and even with controls on capital flows the size of the overall deficit was growing. Opposition to the massive US deficit began to mount. The French government in particular objected vehemently to the ability of US capital to buy up European companies by just flooding other countries with dollars, and in 1965 it had begun to convert its dollar reserves into gold. Gold was the weak link for the US so long as it was committed to converting dollars held abroad, and in 1967 the US government obtained a promise from the West German government not to convert their dollar reserves into gold.

The publication of the 1967 US balance of payments

accounts in February 1968 revealed the overall deficit to be larger than ever, and by March there was an enormous rush on gold as market operators tried to beat the revaluation of gold that they felt was inevitable. The US President, Lyndon Johnson, had the British government close the London gold market, and when it opened again two weeks later it was on the basis of a two-tier system. The US government would continue converting dollars into gold at the official rate of $35 an ounce for Central Banks; private holders of dollars on the other hand would be subject to a free market rate that would certainly be higher. This heralded an important shift in relations between the US and other capitalist states.

In the 1950s other capitalist states had welcomed the dollar-based international monetary system. (Britain even played a subordinate part in running it through the minor role that sterling continued to occupy as a reserve currency until the late 1960s.) In the 1960s, as the US deficit grew, the system was still accepted although it was now widely believed that it would have to be reformed so as to end the privileged position of the US economy that enabled it to spend more dollars abroad than it earned. This acceptance in turn gave way in the late 1960s to a situation where more serious differences emerged as the US began to impose its will on the other capitalist countries.

The basis for the shift in US policy was laid out in several articles published by academic economists in the late 1960s. These advocated what was known as the 'Passive Strategy for the Balance of Payments'. This argued that instead of accepting responsibility for the size of the US balance of payments deficit, the government should pursue the policies that would run the US economy at the optimal level irrespective of the size of the payments deficit; countries that didn't want to absorb more dollars should revalue their currencies. (If a country revalued, it would make the dollar price of any purchases in that country less attractive. By discouraging purchases by US-based concerns, this was supposed to reduce the size of the dollar inflow into that country's reserves.) The attraction to the US government of this Passive Strategy was that it shifted the responsibility for the US deficit onto the governments of other countries.

The immediate crisis of the dollar was relieved by the operation of the business cycle. The upturn that began in the early 1960s finally came to an end in 1969. This was the first recession to take hold since the Euromarkets had become important. High interest rates in the US now attracted short-term capital from the Euromarkets on a scale that was sufficient to offset the underlying payments deficit. But recession afforded only a precarious relief.

The Collapse of Bretton Woods

In 1970 the recession led to what was then the largest bankruptcy in US history, that of the Penn Central Railroad Company. Because it was linked by short-term loans to many other large corporations, the Federal Reserve was fearful of a widespread financial collapse, and it encouraged a vigorous expansion of credit by commercial banks. As interest rates fell, short-term capital left the US on a scale that was quite unprecedented at the time. From a previous peak balance-of-payments deficit of $3.4 billion in 1967, and a modest surplus of $2.7 billion in 1969, the deficit jumped to $9.8 billion in 1970 and a staggering $29.7 billion in 1971. This was the Passive Strategy with a vengeance.

The scale of these capital flows put irresistible pressure on other countries to revalue their currencies. This achieved what was in effect the first major devaluation of the dollar, but although the US did agree to a small devaluation of the dollar against gold, most of the adjustment between the dollar and other currencies was forced onto the other countries. Because most of the adjustment was not made by devaluing the dollar against gold, the US avoided what would have been a relative increase in the importance of gold at the expense of the dollar. The effective devaluation of the dollar cheapened US exports and, by temporarily overcoming the consequence of the slow growth of productivity in the US, it helped check the decline in the US share of world trade.

The US however still faced one vulnerability: the huge sums of dollars that had been pumped into the rest of the world and were now held by Central Banks could, under the two-tier system established in 1968, be presented for conversion into gold. On 15 August 1971 Richard Nixon resolved this problem quite simply by announcing that the US would no longer honour its post-war commitment to convert dollars into gold. The final fixed link between money and gold was broken. Although gold has continued to serve as part of some countries' reserves, its price had fluctuated widely. In the absence of any alternative, the world was forced to accept an international monetary system based on a dollar standard.

In 1973 the dollar was effectively devalued for a second time. The publication of figures showing the size of the 1972 balance of payments deficit led to another run on the dollar. As short-term capital flooded out of the US again in an attempt to beat the anticipated devaluation, adjustment was once more forced predominantly onto other countries. The turbulence that was engendered by these huge flows resulted in the closure of foreign exchange markets for two weeks. When they reopened it was not on the basis of the system of fixed exchange rates adopted at Bretton Woods, but a system of floating exchange rates which fluctuated in response to market forces.

Floating exchange rates had been advocated for some time by Milton Friedman and other monetarist economists. They argued that if a country ran either a surplus or a deficit on its balance of payments, this would be smoothly and automatically eliminated by allowing the exchange rate to adjust in response to supply and demand in the market for foreign exchange. This is wrong because the main force in foreign exchange markets since the late 1960s has not arisen from trade or investment imbalances, as monetarist theory tended to assume, but from short-term flows of money capital. Multinational banks keep their reserves and idle money capital in the country where it will earn the highest rate of interest. Small changes in interest rates can result in large flows of capital and this has a marked effect on the demand for foreign exchange. Once exchange rates were also free to adjust, this made yet larger flows of short-term capital likely. If the value of a currency was falling, or merely expected to fall, capital would move out in order to avoid a loss of value; conversely, in the case of a currency's value rising, capital would move in. Far from adjusting smoothly, a system of floating exchange rates is likely to exacerbate any imbalance, and can lead to highly unstable gyrations in the value of exchange rates.

Ending gold convertibility and the introduction of floating exchange rates marked the collapse of the Bretton Woods system. It had been undermined by large flows of money capital associated with the internationalisation of financial markets. The US government had tried to control these flows so that they didn't inhibit its attempts to boost the US economy, but this only succeeded in driving the emerging international financial market to organise itself outside the control of the US or any other national government. When the 1960s boom finally came to an end and threatened widespread bankruptcies, the US state provided the reserves for an enormous expansion of credit. Because of the international role of the dollar, the expansion of credit resulted in huge sums of dollars being pumped into the rest of the world, from where they could be presented to the US for conversion into gold. The link between the dollar and gold was the point at which all the contradictions of private accumulation and the international state system had become focused. When that link could no longer be maintained it signalled, perhaps more clearly than any other single event, that the underlying conditions that had made possible the post-war boom had come to an end.

The 1974 Slump

At the same time that the US government was trying to reflate its economy, similar policies were being pursued in the other advanced capitalist economies, which had also been affected by the recession in 1970. In Britain it was the time of the Heath government's U-turn and the so-called Barber boom. Throughout the advanced capitalist world there was a massive expansion of credit as Central Banks provided the reserves to finance growing government and private debt. For the first time since the war, an upturn in the business cycle occurred simultaneously in all the advanced capitalist economies.

The synchronised upturn resulted in an unusually large increase in the demand for primary commodities and their price began to rise sharply. On top of this, many of the dollars that had flooded out of the US were deposited in the Eurodollar market by Central Banks eager to earn some interest on their large holdings, and these dollars were then used to finance extensive speculation in primary commodities, so sending prices still higher. Between 1971 and 1974 primary commodity prices tripled and this was a key factor in the world-wide acceleration in inflation that occurred at the time.

The upturn itself, however, was largely dependent on government and consumer expenditure, and with very little real investment, it would have been difficult to sustain. According to the US National Bureau of Economic Research, which has a sophisticated procedure for monitoring the business cycle, the upturn had already begun to slow down in Spring 1973. This was a short time before the US monetary authorities, anxious at the rising rate of inflation, moved to restrict the supply of reserves to the banking system. By Summer 1973, interest rates had risen to record levels, and in November the US economy entered its most serious recession since the 1930s. Expansionary policies in some countries managed to postpone the downturn, but by 1974 the recession had hit all the advanced capitalist economies and in the twelve months between April 1974 and April 1975, industrial production in the OECD economies slumped by 10 per cent.

The underlying cause of the slump was that in the course of the post-war boom there had been a massive accumulation of capital. At the same time, it became increasingly difficult to generate a surplus that was large enough to maintain the rate of return on capital, and by the 1960s a decline in the rate of profit was becoming marked in all the advanced capitalist economies. A recession had tried to break in the US in 1966 but had been suppressed following a large increase in government expenditure on the New Society Program and the Vietnam war. In West Germany, a serious recession in 1966-7 had promoted sufficient restructuring to result in a strong cyclical upturn. In Britain, following the Labour government's deflationary response to the balance of payments crisis in 1966, unemployment increased significantly for the first time since the war. Economic growth in the US and other countries became increasingly dependent on a growing expansion of credit to finance expenditure, partly by governments, but above all by private consumers and corporations.

The expansion of credit postponed a major slump, but when it finally occurred in 1974 the banking system was very over-extended and this led to a serious domestic and international banking crisis. Important banks went bankrupt in several countries, of which the largest were the Franklyn National in the US and the Herstadt in West Germany. In Britain, where a secondary bank called the London and Counties went bankrupt, the Bank of England mounted a major rescue operation - 'the lifeboat' - to prevent a collapse of secondary banks which had become hopelessly overstretched in the property market.

The most serious international aspect of the crisis was in the unregulated Euromarkets, where many banks made substantial losses. In the absence of an international lender of last resort, a serious collapse of confidence between banks was only averted as a result of concerted action by several Central Banks, most notably the US Federal Reserve and the Bank of England. Together with the Bank for International Settlements, the Basle-based bank to Central Banks, a rudimentary system of responsibility for international banking transactions was fashioned.

The onset of the recession was marked by mounting stocks of unsold commodities, and financially pressed corporations were anxious for credit. But once production had been cut back and it was clear that capital could not be invested profitably, there was both an abrupt decline in the corporate demand for loans and an increase in deposits as corporations placed their over-accumulated capital in the Euromarkets. This coincided with the influx of petro-dollars from the newly rich oil-exporting countries. The hard-pressed Eurobanks were desperate to find customers to lend this capital to, and their attention shifted from corporate to sovereign borrowers. This initially involved financing the balance of payments deficits incurred, partly because of the oil-price rise, by several of the advanced capitalist countries, of which Britain, Italy and France were the most important. But from 1975 bank lending was directed increasingly towards Third World countries who wanted to finance ambitious development programmes. The capital that could not be invested at a sufficiently attractive rate of profit in the advanced capitalist economies was being deposited in the Euromarkets and from there lent to the Third World.

Third World countries until then had to rely for external finance almost entirely on official development aid, either from multilateral institutions such as the World Bank, or from the bilateral aid programmes run by individual countries. The rapid growth of private bank lending therefore meant a shift from official to private, market-based channels of finance. While the official finance had been spread over a large number of countries, often after an extensive appraisal of investment projects, the new private finance was heavily concentrated on a relatively small number of newly industrialising countries.

The pressure on the international banking system was relieved by an upturn in the world economy in Spring 1975. This was exceptionally strong in the US, where a large number of new jobs were created, and it was also strong in the newly industrialising countries. In Europe, Japan and the non-oil developing countries, however, the recovery was, by post-war standards, weak. Bankers began to congratulate each other on what they perceived as their success in recycling petro-dollars. But this was based on a very short-term view of the problem.

A Weak Upturn and an even Bigger Slump

The recovery in Europe and Japan after 1975 was constrained by the balance of payments, which now had to bear the added burden of higher oil prices. In Britain the Labour government attempted to loosen this constraint by devaluing the pound. This was intended to cheapen exports and so compensate for the slow growth of productivity. With the system of floating exchange rates that had existed since 1973, governments did still intervene in foreign exchange markets, in theory just to smooth out disruptive fluctuations. In practice many governments could not resist the temptation to try and influence the underlying level of the exchange rate too. (That is why the system is sometimes referred to as 'dirty floating'.) When it became clear in 1976 that the pound was being nudged down, there was a large outflow of short-term capital from Britain. The Labour government had to introduce a deflationary package in order to stem a collapse of the exchange rate and this was the mechanism that ensured that the recovery in Britain was weak even by European standards. This episode also marked the beginning of explicitly monetarist policies by a British government.

The strong recovery in the US from 1975 was made possible because the international role of the dollar enabled the US to run a balance of payments deficit and, now that convertibility had been ended, there was no longer the danger of a run on its gold reserves. The US ran a trade surplus in 1975 as a result of the large fall in imports that accompanied the recession. But once the recovery was underway, the trade balance moved into deficit in 1976 and the size of the deficit increased through 1977 and 1978. Much of the competitive advantage that US exports had gained after the devaluations of 1971 and 1973 had been eroded as other countries in turn devalued their currencies. The Carter government therefore tried to achieve a third devaluation of the dollar. From late 1977 the dollar was allowed to float down on the foreign exchange market, but this turned to a rout in Autumn 1978 as short-term capital cut and fled, and deflationary measures had to be introduced in order to push up interest rates and stem the flow. This succeeded temporarily by attracting short-term capital back to the US. But it did not touch the problem that as a result of the underlying US deficit, the rest of the world was being forced to accept huge sums of dollars.

The situation culminated in a major crisis of the dollar in Autumn 1979; as the exchange rate fell there was a massive move out of the dollar in foreign exchange markets, one result of which was the explosion in the price of gold which occurred at the time. This coincided with a crisis in domestic US credit markets where, as a result of inflation, there was a move out of the dollar and into other stores of value such as real estate. In order to protect the dollar, the Federal Reserve introduced a series of measures that sent the US prime rate of interest shooting up to a then unprecedented level of 15 per cent. This attracted sufficient short-term capital back to the US to stem the fall in the exchange rate, but at the beginning of 1980 the economy entered another recession. The importance of this episode is that it illustrates the bounds within which the US government is able to influence the regulation of its national economy. The ending of convertibility had removed the danger of a run on US gold reserves, but the limits to accumulation were reasserted through the dollar's exchange rate. Once again it showed that the US is also subject to the constraints of the international financial system. The limits of the strategy introduced under Nixon and continued under Carter had been reached even before Ronald Reagan assumed office.

The Reagan government inaugurated a new strategy by supporting policies that sent the prime rate of interest soaring to over 20 per cent. The huge sums of capital this attracted pushed the value of the dollar up in a complete reversal of the policies that had been pursued over the previous decade to cheapen exports. As high interest and exchange rates cut into corporate receipts the recession that had followed the policies introduced under Carter was seriously deepened.

Monetarist policies had been introduced in Britain in 1976, but after the election of the Thatcher government in 1979 they were pursued with far greater vigour. A tight restriction on the supply of reserves to the banking system led to a sharp rise in interest rates. As in the US, this attracted short-term capital into Britain and pushed up the exchange rate of the pound, thereby reducing the sterling value of foreign earnings. The financial pressure on industrial and commercial companies led to a large fall in output and resulted in an even deeper slump than 1974. The Thatcher government was completely committed to this course, but unless it had cut the financial links between Britain and the rest of the international capitalist economy, it would have found its options seriously limited.

The high interest rates that the US had to maintain to protect the dollar meant that short-term capital would be attracted from any country where interest rates were significantly lower. Given the volatility of the floating exchange rate system, this could rapidly lead to a collapse of the exchange rate. This is what happened in France at the beginning of 1983 when the government was forced to abandon its reflationary policies in order to protect the franc.

The 1980-2 recession in the US was consequently transmitted to all the other advanced capitalist economies as a result of the international mobility of money capital.

The International Debt Crisis

The most acute impact of the recession was not however on the advanced capitalist economies but on the highly indebted countries of the Third World. By the summer of 1982, the total international debt of the non-OPEC developing countries was $550 billion of which $270 billion was owed to private banks. Furthermore, over half the total bank lending was to just three countries: Argentina, Brazil and Mexico.

The onset of recession affected the ability of Third World countries to service their debts in two ways. Firstly, there was a sharp decline in the demand for primary commodities and, as a result, their price fell. Since primary commodity exports are a major source of income for most Third World countries this combination of lower sales and lower prices meant a marked reduction in their foreign earnings. Secondly, most of the bank loans had been contracted at variable rates of interest, and these were adjusted at regular intervals to keep them in line with current market rates. Consequently when interest rates shot up, so did the cost of servicing the outstanding debt. Third

World sovereign debtors were therefore squeezed between falling incomes and rising interest changes.

The debt crisis came to a head in August 1982 when Mexico in effect defaulted on its international payments. The banks, however, were anxious not to declare a formal default as this would have required them to write off their loans to Mexico as a loss. As Keynes said: 'If you owe the bank a thousand pounds you have a problem; if you owe your bank a million pounds your bank has a problem.' Although the loans were arranged through consortia involving in total as many as 200 banks, much of the debt was owed to a small number of very big international banks. In 1982 the nine largest US banks had outstanding loans to the Third World that were equal to twice the value of their capital, and their loans to Mexico alone amounted to half the value of their capital.

Rather than write these loans off, the banks embarked on what is known as rescheduling. This involves postponing scheduled repayments of capital and, most importantly, lending a country yet more money so that it can meet at least some of its interest payments and thereby avoid having to be declared legally in default. Instead of having to record a substantial loss, by pursuing this course banks could acquire a further interest-earning asset for their books! It is of course a relatively short-term solution since, unless a country can increase its foreign earnings sufficiently, this might just result in an even larger non-performing loan that will have to be written off in the future.

Since the Mexican default, the focus of the crisis has shifted from one country to another as Brazil, Venezuela, Argentina and other smaller debtors were unable to meet their debt-service payments. Although banks and debtor countries wanted to avoid a formal default, both sides employed knife-edge tactics while bargaining over the terms of rescheduling agreements, and this inevitably carries a risk. Since every loan is subject to a cross-default clause, declaring any one loan in default would trigger the default clause in every other loan to the same country. Because of the over-exposure of the big banks, there was a widespread fear that if a country defaulted, it might bankrupt at least one major bank, and because of banks' interdependence, this might in turn precipitate an international banking collapse.

The growth of sovereign lending after 1975 appeared to offer the possibility of appropriating surplus from the Third World at a much higher rate than was possible from the working class in the advanced capitalist countries. But when the credit-financed boom in the US threatened a collapse of the dollar in 1979, the consequences of the recession that followed made it impossible for the Third World countries to service their debts. The crisis that had broken in the advanced capitalist countries in 1974 had been displaced through the international financial system onto the Third World.

The immediate crisis in Mexico - and subsequently in Brazil and Argentina - was stalled by the emergence of an international lender of last resort. Coordinated through the Bank for International Settlements, the US Federal Reserve, the Bank of England and the International Monetary Fund assembled short-term loans and pressured reluctant private banks to participate in new medium-term loans.

The position that the IMF had come to occupy was now a far cry from that envisaged at Bretton Woods. The reserves of this official institution had become dwarfed by the huge growth of those associated with private international financial markets. No longer the major source of financing for balance of payments deficits, the IMF became responsible for negotiating the terms of a small pilot loan, and the successful completion of the negotiations would be the signal for private banks to provide the bulk of the new finance required. The IMF's terms are strongly influenced by modern free-market principles, which economists employed by the Fund have played a leading part in elaborating. Instead of making loans that would ensure the political control of a market system, the IMF has therefore become the instrument by which the terms of market-based private finance are agreed.

The conditions attached to an IMF loan focus on achieving short-term monetary targets. They require a big cut in state intervention and result in a severe deflation. The reduction in the government's need for finance and in the general level of imports is supposed to ensure that the balance of payments will provide enough foreign exchange to meet future debt-service payments. The consequences for living standards, especially for the urban poor, have been horrific, and the introduction of IMF policies has on several occasions led to breakdowns in public order. But the result of the IMF's policies, which occurred at the same time as a large decline in new loans, has been to achieve a substantial net transfer of capital from Latin America to the US.

Conclusion: Paying for MX

The possibility of an international banking crisis has receded as a result of the remarkably vigorous recovery that began in the US in 1983. Interest rates came down slightly and primary commodity prices stopped falling. Quite inadvertently, the Reagan administration appears to have stumbled onto one of the few combinations of policy that could have succeeded in the US. The upturn has been boosted by huge government spending, above all on armaments. This has resulted in a budget deficit that is on a larger scale than that advocated by any European social democratic administration.

Reagan's novelty is to run this deficit at the same time as a relatively tight monetary policy. Because government borrowing comes on top of a huge amount of lending to the private sector, interest rates have remained at an unusually high level for a period of recovery. High interest rates have attracted short-term capital to the US and pushed the dollar exchange rate to higher and higher levels.

The dilemma that US governments have faced for the last quarter century has been how to boost the national economy while avoiding the international consequences of a balance of payments deficit that could lead to a run on gold or, more recently, a collapse of the exchange rate. The upturn that began in 1983 sucked in imports on a huge scale while the high exchange rate meant that exports remained depressed. The result has been that the US has run a trade deficit of unparalleled proportions. Because of the dollar's role as international money, other countries have had to accept the dollars that have been forced on them. In effect the rest of the world is granting credit to the US equal to the size of its deficit.

If foreign holders of dollars began to sell, it could lead to an even more dramatic collapse of the dollar than in 1979. What has prevented this so far has been the high level of US interest rates. This has ensured that sufficient capital has flowed into the US to temporarily offset the underlying balance of payments deficit. Foreign Central Banks are keeping the dollars that have flowed into their reserves in the US and investing them in short-term Treasury Bills. (These commonly have a maturity of three months but can easily be sold at short notice.) Foreign dollar holdings are therefore simultaneously financing both the US balance of payments deficit and the US government deficit. (Compare the following US estimates for 1984: balance of payments current account deficit, $178 billion; Federal government deficit, $182 billion; military expenditure, $234 billion.) The rest of the world is not only constrained by high US interest rates, it is also financing the US recovery.

As the former basis of US dominance in the world economy was eroded, the US government hit on a strategy of financial manipulation that has helped to re-establish its dominance on a new basis. But it is a precarious strategy. The real strength of the recovery depends on the extent to which both the recession and the upturn have promoted a transformation in the structure of the productive economy. The credit system in the US remains under great stress and the high level of interest and exchange rates squeezes all but the most profitable corporations. The biggest ever bail out amounting to $4.5 billion had to be mounted by the Federal Reserve in June 1984 in order to prevent a major bank, Continental Illinois, from collapsing. Some estimates have claimed that the dollar is over-valued by as much as 30 per cent, and if US interest rates should fall at all, this would risk a serious run on the dollar. If that happened the monetary authorities would have to act quickly to push up interest rates to whatever level was necessary to attract capital back to the US. At that point the Third World debt crisis would again become an immediate issue.

US capital has been able to benefit from the current system of international financial relations based on private markets and the dollar. However the shift away from the politically regulated system set up at Bretton Woods has in general meant that the limited space within which national governments could pursue independent economic policies has been yet further constrained. An urgent objective for any government wishing to pursue an independent policy will be to close the channels by which international financial flows impose the logic of the market on elected governments. A democratic economic policy will involve acting at an international level with other countries to construct an alternative to the dollar-based system and to wrest control over international economic relations away from private markets and into the hands of institutions that can be subjected to some type of popular accountability.

Table 3.1: Non-Oil Developing Countries Debt

	External Debt $bn	Of which Private Mkt, %	Debt Service $bn	Debt Service ratio to exports %
1973	96.8	50.0	15.3	14.0
1974	120.1	51.4	17.1	11.5
1975	146.8	53.7	21.1	14.0
1976	181.4	54.7	24.6	13.9
1977	221.8	55.7	30.7	14.0
1978	276.4	57.5	44.7	17.3
1979	324.4	58.9	60.2	18.1
1980	375.4	58.6	68.1	16.3
1981	436.9	59.8	92.3	21.0
1982	505.2	60.5	107.8	22.3

Source: International Monetary Fund, World Economic Outlook

Table 3.2: Total External Debt, end 1982, $ billions

21 major LDC borrowers	514.5
Latin America	288.1
Argentina	38.8
Brazil	86.3
Chile	17.2
Colombia	10.2
Ecuador	6.6
Mexico	84.6
Peru	11.2
Venezuela	33.2
Asia	108.8
Indonesia	21.9
Korea	37.2
Malaysia	8.6
Phillippines	20.7
Taiwan	9.3
Thailand	11.1
Middle East and Africa	117.6
Algeria	14.8
Egypt	21.8
Israel	28.0
Ivory Coast	8.4
Morocco	10.8
Nigeria	11.2
Turkey	22.6

Source: Morgan Guarantee, World Finance Markets

SELECT BIBLIOGRAPHY

Bank for International Settlements, Annual Reports

Block, Fred (1977) The Origins of the International Economic Disorder, University of California Press

Brett, E. et. al., Planned Trade, Labour Part of Policy and US Intervention, History Workshop Journal, No 13, Spring 1982

Calleo, David P., (1982) The Imperious Economy, Harvard University Press

Coakley, Jerry & Harris, Laurence (1983), City of Capital, Basil Blackwell

Lipietz, Alain, (1982) Credit Money: A Condition Permitting Inflationary Crisis, Review of Radical Political Economy, Volume 14, Number 2

Mendelsohn, M. Stegan (1979) Money on the Move, The Modern International Capital Market, McGraw Hill

Parbonni, Ricardo (1981) The Dollar and its Rivals, New Left Books

Wojnilower, A. (1980) The Central Role of Credit Crunches in Recent Financial History, Brookings Papers on Economic Activity, Number 2, 277-337

Chapter Four

THE INTERNATIONALISATION OF BANK CAPITAL

Jerry Coakley

The ability of Japanese industrial capital successfully to compete via exports and the internationalisation of production against US and European industrial capital is well known. By contrast Japanese bank capital still remains somewhat of an enigma: few people in Britain will be aware that Dai-Ichi Kangyo Bank and Fuji Bank are the largest two Japanese commercial banks in terms of total assets whilst one would expect rather more people to know that Citicorp and Bankamerica are the two leading American commercial banks. At the end of 1982 the two American banks ranked first and second and the two Japanese banks eighth and tenth respectively, in a listing of the Top 500 commercial banks in the world. (1) It is paradoxical that Japanese banks should remain relatively unknown in Britain for since January 1982 their share of international bank lending from their United Kingdom offices has surpassed (with the exception of a short break in mid-1982) that of both British banks and American banks in London, the other leading international lenders.

The fact that British bank capital has been relegated to second place in international lending (prior to 1982 American bank capital held the lion's share) from its own base in the City of London does suggest that the nature of both international banking and of the City itself has been changing. The purpose of this article is to explain these transformations. The task will be approached through a detailed examination of the internationalisation of bank capital seen from the perspective of the City of London, the preeminent world banking centre since the 1960s. In turn the novel features of international banking in the City today will be related back to domestic banking systems in which various forms of state regulation play a leading role. In the concluding section an attempt will be made to draw out some implications of the internationalisation of bank capital.

The theoretical framework which informs this article is that of the internationalisation of circuits of capital. Within this tradition the internationalisation of the productive and commodity circuits of capital each has received a good deal of attention as Jenkins (1984) shows in his careful survey. However, as Jenkins' survey reveals the literature on the internationalisation of the circuit of money capital is rather thin. This article should be seen as the beginning of an attempt to fill this lacuna by focusing on the dominant vehicle in the internationalisation of the circuit money capital, namely bank capital and on the leading international financial centre, the City of London. Before examining internationalisation proper the nature of bank capital is briefly discussed since this also is a relatively neglected area within the Marxist tradition. (2)

THE NATURE OF BANK CAPITAL

Bank capital must be one of the world's most heavily state regulated sections of capital. It is this state regulation which gives rise to the confusing variety of domestic banking structures globally and which in recent years has come under increasing pressure from the movement towards deregulation. Generally a minimum of two state bodies (and even more in some countries) are centrally involved in the regulation of all domestic banking systems: these are the Central Bank (whose constitutional position varies widely across countries) and the Treasury or Ministry of Finance. This is not the place to describe the specifics of bank regulation; suffice it to say that the central position of bank capital in the credit system of advanced capitalist countries is underlined by the fact that Central Banks through their lender-of-last-resort facility effectively underwrite the profitability of commercial banking. But one aspect of regulation which is relevant here is the degree of segmentation of banking activities. At the risk of gross over-simplification, a breakdown of the three major types of activity undertaken by bank capital is presented below. For illustrative purposes it may prove helpful to bear in mind that the domestic activities of Japanese bank capital are segmented along these lines.

Commercial Banking

Commercial banking is familiar to most people as High Street banking. One of its central domestic functions is the operation of the domestic clearing and money transmission system which involves the processing of cheques and money transfers such as standing orders and direct debits. The banks which operate this system in Britain are known as the clearing banks. The operation of the clearing system used to be the jealously guarded monopoly of domestic bank capital but recently pressures have built up to open it to selected overseas banks. (3) Despite the latter it is likely that domestic banks will still retain a virtual monopoly of their respective clearing systems and this is one of the reasons why it is valid to employ the concept of domestically-based blocs of bank capital such as Japanese or British bank capital.

Thus far commercial banking has been treated as a homogeneous activity but following Coakley and Harris (1983) it will prove helpful in describing its other functions to differentiate between retail and wholesale banking. Retail banking is concerned chiefly with the mobilisation of the savings of working people and with the advancement of consumer credit (and some housing finance) to the middle strata. In this context we could view savings banks including Post Office savings banks as the epitome of retail commercial banking where the emphasis is on (savings) deposits rather than on credit. Although savings banks are not generally large by commercial banking standards, it should be remembered that Japan's Post Office Savings Bank with assets of $350 billion could arguably claim to be the world's largest bank since Citicorp's total assets by contrast were only $128 billion at the end of 1982.

Wholesale commercial banking on the other hand involves a focus on the credit relations between bank and other capital and involves a qualitatively different scale of transaction. The development of the Euromarkets (see below) and the post-war internationalisation of commercial banking have almost exclusively been concerned with the global expansion of wholesale banking. At this stage it should be emphasised that leading commercial banks engage in both retail and wholesale banking though a small minority of mainly consortium banks have opted for specialisation in wholesale banking.

Trust Banking

Trust banking is segmented from commercial banking activities in Japan and Canada on the grounds of conflict of interest (4) but commercial banks in other countries are generally free to engage in it. Trust banking involves banks advising on or managing for a fee, the investment portfolios of wealthy individuals and more significantly, of pension funds; it involves operating unit trust and other portfolios. Minns (1982) has shown in his pioneering study of British pension funds that as much as 40 per cent of their assets were managed and effectively controlled by bank capital. The recent trend in the United Kingdom has been for both commercial and investment (merchant) banks to compete for a share of this lucrative business given the growing international portfolio diversification of pension fund assets.

Investment Banking

Investment and commercial banking were separated under the 1933 Glass-Steagall Act in the US following the 1929-33 Great Crash and banking crisis. Japan followed suit in the post-war reorganisation of its domestic banking system. The essence of investment banking is that is involves dealing in securities (buying, selling, underwriting) both on banks' own behalf and on behalf of others for a fee. Different types of financial institutions specialise in investment banking although the recent trend has been to follow the model of US investment banks like Merrill Lynch and, to a lesser extent, of Japanese securities firms like Nomura Securities. Since the late 1970s a number of legislative changes have contributed to the development of international markets in equities and in securities more generally. These changes include the abolition of exchange controls in the UK in 1979 and in Japan in 1980 and the US pensions legislation advocating the diversification of pension fund portfolio.

The international diversification of pension fund assets has provided an impetus for the internationalisation of investment banking activities. It is in this light that we should view the recent flurry of ownership changes in the London Stock Exchange firms where British and overseas banks and others have been purchasing stakes in firms with dealing and other securities-related expertise. Significantly leading US (and other) commercial banks have for some years been providing investment banking services from London subsidiaries which do not fall within the remit of the Glass-Steagall Act since the latter applies only to banking in the United States.

These then are the three major types of activity in which bank capital engages. At the level of banking institutions there is unfortunately no neat one-to-one correspondence between banking activities and types of bank. As a general rule, however, commercial banks tend to engage in more of these activities than other types of banks and this may be considered as the basis of their hegemonic role within the various nationally-based blocs of bank capital. At one extreme, in West Germany all of these activities are combined within what are aptly called universal banks: thus universal banks like Deutsche Bank advance loans, manage investment portfolios and underwrite security issues so their hegemony is virtually unchallenged. At the other extreme, in Japan the major banking activities have been legally segmented and are undertaken by distinct types of bank though there is now some evidence of deregulation.

The present climate of change seems to be moving inexorably towards the German or Hanseatic model of universal banks even if the pace of change varies between countries. First indications are that commercial banks are likely to consolidate their hegemony within the various blocs of bank capital. The larger commercial banks have moved to purchase stakes in stock exchange firms in London, to form partnership deals with securities firms in Japan and to take over other financial services firms in countries like the USA. However, this is speculation about the future. In the following sections the focus is on the internationalisation of commercial banking since this is by far the most internationalised aspect of bank capital. This is done through examining the development of the City of London, the leading international commercial banking centre.

THE CITY OF LONDON - BANKER TO THE WORLD

To understand the City's current leading role in international commercial banking it is necessary to refer briefly to the City's previous golden age, at the turn of the century and to its subsequent demise. During the apogee of the British Empire and the international gold standard from 1870-1914 the City of London could readily lay claim to the title of banker to the world. (5) London's pre-eminence in that epoch was closely intertwined with the global hegemony of European bank capital up to the First World War. (6) However the war was to change all this for the ensuing devastation of or disruption to the economies of the major European protagonists undermined their banking systems and allowed the United States with New York as its leading centre to emerge as the predominant bank capital bloc of the day.

In the interwar period and during the 1950s London attempted to recoup its former glory at the hub of the group of Commonwealth and other countries which comprised the Sterling Area. (7) The impact of this on London's status as an international banking centre pales into insignificance when compared with the impetus furbished by the development in the 1960s and 1970s of a new set of banking and bond (debt) markets called the Euromarkets. (8)

The Euromarkets have re-established London as a world banking centre. The basis of its new found pre-eminence is not an exact replay of history but has itself been reconstituted in some significant aspects. London's pre-World War I position is aptly summarised by Feis (1930):

> Half a hundred types of financial institutions played a part in the process of investment of British capital (overseas - JC). The huge commercial banks, where most checking accounts were kept, which financed commodity movements throughout the world, were the greatest source of credit, yet they played but an indirect part in the security issue business. Alongside of them stood the banks public and private, of the British Dominions. These, growing to power, kept establishments in London to employ their funds, to share in the profit of trade financing, to handle governmental financial affairs (1930, p.7).

In other words, the principal role of big British commercial banks (recall that by the turn of the century the five precursors of today's 'Big Four' clearing banks had already emerged) was the short-term financing of international trade since sterling then operated as the international currency par excellence. The possibilities of financing trade encouraged the internationalisation of British and European bank capital through the establishment of overseas offices and subsidiaries. By means of loans and purchases the commercial banks also supported the equally important business of foreign securities (bonds and preferred shares) transactions of the capital markets even though this field still remained the speciality of the merchant banks. We shall see that London's more recent re-emergence as a banking centre contrasts in many respects with its erstwhile imperial role. One way of understanding this is to outline a typology of categories of bank lending which is presented in Table 4.1.

Table 4.1: Typology of bank lending from London

	Residents	Overseas
Sterling Lending	A	B
Foreign Currency Lending	C	D

Sterling lending to the overseas sector (category B) and, by implication, sterling deposits from overseas formed the basis of London's pre-First World War role but from 1939 until 1979 had been curtailed by exchange controls. In any case, since the 1960s foreign or Eurocurrency lending overseas (category D) has eclipsed all other international lending. This partly reflects the demise of sterling as a trading currency and the rise of the dollar as international money but, perhaps more significantly, it represents a shift in the role of international bank lending. Within the latter, medium-term lending for accumulation purposes clearly outweighs that of short-term trade financing.

The banking business associated with foreign currency loans to overseas states and corporations we shall describe as Eurobanking since this type of lending is the hallmark of the Euromarkets and represents a new departure for London and other Eurobanking centres. In Table 4.2 the relative importance of different categories of bank lending and the share of total international lending in aggregate bank lending are presented. Here international lending is taken to comprise not only foreign currency loans to overseas residents - its principal component - but also foreign currency lending to residents and sterling lending to overseas residents. It will be apparent that the contemporary significance of the latter category of lending has been rather unimpressive by comparison with Euromarket lending until the late 1970s, but it has staged a recovery since the abolition of exchange controls in 1979 and at the end of 1983 it accounted for some 5 per cent of international bank lending. This still lags behind international trends where domestic currency loans in 1983 comprised almost 10 per cent of gross international bank lending. (9)

Table 4.2: Lending by banks in the United Kingdom 1970-82

	Sterling Lending		Foreign Currency Lending		Total International Bank Lending	%
	Resid-ents	Over-seas	Resid-ents	Over-seas		
1970	17087	1054	1169	14417	16646	(49.3)
1971	20382	1372	1418	16451	19241	(48.6)
1972	25275	2775	2345	28839	27959	(52.5)
1973	32294	1967	4345	36167	42479	(56.9)
1974	35578	2256	6353	43966	52575	(59.6)
1975	37291	3185	8252	58954	70391	(65.4)
1976	40223	3831	10522	81698	96051	(70.5)
1977	45550	4236	11173	83890	99299	(68.6)
1978	50234	5096	11239	100838	117173	(70.0)
1979	60258	5074	10659	123607	139332	(69.8)
1980	72195	7879	17043	142981	167903	(71.9)
1981	100888	11743	16590	213237	241570	(72.8)

Source: Bank of England Quarterly Bulletin.

From the table it is seen that the 1970s represented a turning point as far as the nature of banking in the UK is concerned: since 1972 total international bank lending for the first time exceeded purely domestic bank lending and since 1976 it has accounted for more than 70 per cent on average of total lending from the UK. By 1982 it had reached the staggering total of 75 per cent.

On the basis of this mushrooming of international

lending one can understand the growth and consolidation of London as an international banking centre. Table 4.3 indicates the growth since 1967 of the UK share of international banking business which for our purposes may be taken as coterminous with the share of the City of London. (10)

Table 4.3: UK Share of International Banking Business 1976-84

	1967	1972	1977	1982	1983	1984
UK share as per cent of total	26.7	31.4	26.1	26.9	26.6	24.9

Sources: Bank of England Quarterly Bulletin. The Wilson Report, Cmnd 7937.

We see that the City of London's share of international banking has fluctuated between approximately one quarter and one third of the total but that in 1984 it dipped under the one quarter mark for the first time since the mid-1960s. But this is only part of the picture and begs the question of competition from other centres and especially New York.

Table 4.4 shows the relative market shares of the UK and its main competitors over the last five years. At first sight the puzzling feature to emerge from the table is the apparently low level of the US (and by implication New York's) share of international bank lending which in 1980 only just exceeded that of France (Paris). The weakness of New York's share is explained by various state restrictions on Eurocurrencies in the United States until the establishment of international banking facilities (IBFs) substantially free from these restrictions in December 1981. The jump in the US share since 1982 can then be largely attributed to the operation of IBFs and the influx of foreign banks into the United States which they have encouraged. Indeed according to International Monetary Fund calculations New York is poised to overtake London in terms of market shares on a narrower definition of international lending. (11)

At this stage, it may be tempting to conclude that, due to London's pre-eminence, British bank capital rules the waves as it did to a large extent in the imperial epoch. Such a conclusion would be to ignore the impact on London of Eurobanking. Prior to that the City's banking community

Table 4.4: International Banking Centres

	Total International Bank Lending ($ billion)	UK		US		Of Which Japan		France		Bahamas	
Sept 1980	1778	459	(25.8)	165	(9.3)	107	(8.0)	110	(9.0)	126	(7.1)
Sept 1981	2094	559	(26.7)	214	(10.2)	149	(7.1)	165	(7.9)	155	(7.4)
Sept 1982	2387	642	(26.9)	346	(14.5)	180	(7.5)	172	(7.2)	134	(5.6)
Sept 1983	1492	662	(26.6)	384	(15.6)	215	(8.6)	175	(7.0)	131	(5.3)
Sept 1984	2682	669	(14.9)	403	(15.0)	245	(9.1)	178	(6.6)	na	

Source: Bank of England Quarterly Bulletin.

Table 4.5: International Bank Lending from UK

		Total Outstanding ($ billion)	UK Banks	US Banks	Japanese Banks	Other Overseas Banks	Consortium Banks
Sept	1980	459	24.1	25.7	19.4	25.7	9.1
Sept	1981	559	23.6	22.3	22.8	27.4	3.9
Sept	1982	642	22.3	21.5	25.5	27.0	3.8
Sept	1983	na	21.8	20.9	25.2	30.0	3.8
Sept	1984	674	20.1	18.7	28.3	30.0	3.0

Source: Bank of England Quarterly Bulletin.

was comprised of British and Commonwealth banks. Even at the time of the Radcliffe Report, London's foreign bank community numbered a mere 40 but by the end of 1983 no less than 399 foreign banks were directly represented in London as against a corresponding total of 294 for New York, its nearest rival (Blanden, 1984). Another way of attempting to measure the impact of Eurobanking is to examine the relative market shares of the international bank lending from the UK by UK and other overseas banks with offices in the City (Table 4.5).

Even allowing for some participation in consortium banks it emerges that British bank capital is responsible for rather more than one fifth of all international bank lending from the UK. Indeed their market share is exceeded by Japanese bank capital which in 1982 took over from US bank capital as the dominant international banking bloc. More recently Arab banks have also appeared as yet another emergent banking bloc within the City. In other words the domination of the City of London in the world of international banking is no longer synonymous with the domination of British bank capital. Instead of Lombard Street decisions deciding the flows of international credit those of Tokyo and Wall Street play an equally if not more significant role. We qualify the latter since many routine decisions by Japanese and American banks relating to international credit are still made in London but generally decisions on very large syndicated and jumbo credits are a matter for head office in their respective countries.

The fact that London has to some extent become the centre through which Eurocurrency loans are booked and packaged rather than where all the crucial financial decisions are made is one of the novel features of its current role. The international nature of Eurobanking has led Coakley and Harris (1983) to describe London's new banking role as an enclave role to highlight its lack of connection with the UK real economy. Japanese banks in London provide a vivid illustration of this. Of their total sterling and foreign currency assets of £105.5 billion in February 1983 only a mere 3.6 per cent represented loans to the UK non-monetary real sector. US banks had rather more links with the UK economy: one eighth of their asset portfolio of £97.8 billion could be identified as loans to the UK real sector. In aggregate only one twelfth of all overseas banks' assets consisted of loans to the non-bank sector. This evidence is consistent with overseas banks concentrating their lending on the multinational corporations in the UK.

In other words Eurobanking being a truly internationalised form of banking serves to highlight the disjuncture between London's role as an international banking centre and the development of both the UK productive economy and the UK bank capital. It helps to explain why the City in its role as banker to the world and British bank capital to a lesser extent can flourish whilst the economy languishes in a crisis reminiscent of that of the 1930s and the process of deindustrialisation proceeds apace. However this raises the issue of why Eurobanking has been the major form of the internationalisation of commercial banking since the 1960s and that issue is now examined.

THE INTERNATIONALISATION OF COMMERCIAL BANKING

It has been suggested in the previous section that London's new international banking role involves a novel development in bank lending. The bulk of London's international business is now denominated in dollars and other foreign currencies rather than in sterling and the greater part of international lending is conducted by foreign and not British bank capital. One question which arises is whether Eurobanking can be viewed as a novel phenomenon and to answer this we need to examine its characteristics and predecessors a little more closely. In doing this we distinguish two major systems of commercial banking, branch banking and unit banking, which while not totally mutually exclusive have each tended to predominate in different epochs both at the national and international levels. These two systems of commercial banking correspond approximately to the distinction between retail and wholesale commercial banking made in the first section. Eurobanking is the international extension of unit banking.

Unit Banking

The overriding characteristic of unit banking is the centralised nature of its domestic operations, its paucity of branches within countries and its consequent wholesale banking orientation. Historically and logically it precedes branch banking, the other major type of banking system.

England had a unit banking system until the middle of the nineteenth century as does the United States today where its survival rests on legal restrictions on interstate banking. Becuase of its paucity of domestic branches unit banking has lead to a distinct pattern of domestic interbank (between banks) relationships known as correspondent banking and a specialised market known as the interbank market. So the much vaunted international interbank market of the Euromarkets today enjoys a long heritage even if the scale of domestic interbank markets has remained comparatively small: Sayers (1967) estimates that domestic interbank deposits accounted for just 7 per cent of the total US bank deposits in the mid-1960s.

Unit banking systems did not require a quantum leap to extend correspondent banking on an international scale; indeed correspondent banking has long been regarded as synonymous with international correspondent banking; the following description from a <u>Financial Times</u> survey of <u>World Banking</u> is typical:

> Historically, correspondent banking has been an interbank relationship where banks effected each others settlements, undertook local exchange transactions, trade financing, collection services, international money transfers and all the other services involved in making payments across state boundaries ... Today banks are each other's biggest customers ... some 90% of all foreign exchange dealings are interbank (16 May, 1983, <u>Financial Times</u>).

So long as the function of international banking was confined to financing trade and overseas payments, correspondent banking proved to be a perfectly adequate vehicle of internationalisation. Moreover, correspondent banking neither required nor encouraged banks to have a widespread overseas branch presence. The spread of multinational corporations within and between the advanced capitalist economies and the newly industrialising countries (NICs) after World War II was to change this picture. By 1959 no less than 700 US multinationals had a UK subsidiary or affiliate while only seven US Banks were directly represented here. Given that, the subsequent influx of American bank branches into London is hardly surprising.

Because American banks' existing expertise lay in wholesale banking, their internationalisation strategy generally involved the establishment of foreign wholesale branches or units, a phenomenon I shall refer to as Eurobanking. This is the international counterpart of domestic unit banking. It differs from international branch banking and offshore (tax-haven) centres of a strictly limited number of de novo wholesale units rather than subsidiaries incorporating networks of retail branches. The advantage for Eurobanks of overseas branches rather than subsidiaries is that the expansion of branch assets are limited only by the parent banks' equity base rather than by the equity base of the subsidiaries and that branches are more amenable than subsidiaries to head office control. Since the 1970s other groups of banks most notably the Japanese, have similarly pursued a strategy of Eurobanking and have established wholesale units in London and other financial centres. Eurobanking has now become the predominant form of international banking across the globe. However it has not completely displaced international branch banking.

Branch Banking

Extensive branch networks and their associated retail deposit bases are the epitome of branch or retail banking. Branch banking has long characterised the banking systems in Britain, Europe and the former Commonwealth countries and it currently seems likely to make larger inroads into the US domestic unit banking system. Historically unit banking has been superseded by branch banking in the UK as the generally smaller country banks have been swallowed up by their town or city counterparts to form part of the latters' branch structure. As such, branch banking appears more consonant with the centralisation or amalgamation tendencies identified by Hilferding as inherent in capitalist banking.

Branch banking has enjoyed a long tradition of internationalisation. Before the First World War the British, French and German banks had relatively extensive overseas branch networks. However these networks were generally confined to the imperial blocs and economic satellites associated with their parent countries. Thus, for example, British banks could boast of branches in the former Commonwealth countries and those other 'friendly' states which, in aggregate, were later to comprise the members of the Sterling Area. But banking business between these imperial blocs had to be conducted largely via correspondent banking relationships.

In the post-World War II period, the internationalisation of branch banking has developed albeit slowly in a new direction. The banks of the advanced countries have embarked on a strategy of absorbing banks in those other advanced countries and NICs where state regulation did not prevent foreign takeovers. For example, some British and Japanese banks have acquired relatively large branch networks in the US but foreign takeover bids for British banks were temporarily halted by the Monopolies Commission 1981 decision not to allow overseas bids for the Royal Bank of Scotland to proceed. Similarly, other states like Japan and West Germany have in recent decades adopted a rather restrictive attitude towards takeovers of the domestic banks. This, contrasted with the positive encouragement given to Eurobanking in most if not all countries until now, has meant that international branch banking has been forced to play second fiddle in bank capital's overall internationalisation strategies. However the recent trend towards deregulation may encourage more foreign takeovers of banks and redress the balance back towards international branch banking.

Conclusion

Since the 1960s bank capital has expanded on an enormous scale through the development of what we have described as Eurobanking. The latter has involved the internationalisation of one system of commercial banking (unit banking) based on leading financial centres and specialising in lending largely to multinational corporations and sovereign states. Eurobanking enabled the City of London to recapture its role as banker to the world which it was forced to cede to New York in the interwar period. Moreover it has permitted American and Japanese bank capital to emerge as the leading nationally based blocs of bank capital in terms of international lending, even from the home base of British bank capital.

What are the implications of these developments in bank capital? They lend support to many of the conclusions contained in Andreff's (1984) important article on the international centralisation of capital which is one of the few successful attempts to link the internationalisation of productive and bank capital. By a selective and differential focus on leading financial centres (including tax havens) Eurobanking has contributed towards the integration of newly industrialising countries (NICs) and oil-exporting countries with the advanced capitalist countries and to the relative isolation of the rest of the Third World. By the same token the geographic pattern of Eurobanking has tended to follow that of multinational corporations (MNCs) and has thereby enhanced the latter's focus on advanced economies and NICs.

In this sense I fully agree with Andreff's major conclusion that the development of NICs and the international credit economy (Eurobanking) are complementary and interdependent. It should be added that Eurobanking also supports what Andreff calls the international centralisation of capital since Eurocredits are increasingly employed to finance giant takeovers and mergers.

One question which remains is whether the development of Eurobanking can be fully explained by its relationship with MNCs. The answer has to be no for as the recent international debt crisis illustrates one of the major outlets for Eurobanking has been sovereign state lending. Moreover the focus of Eurobanking on leading financial centres like London and New York has to be explained by banking factors as well as by relationships with MNCs. Primary among the former is the role of state regulation as witnessed by the rise of New York since the relaxation of banking legislation of the United States in December 1981 to allow the operation of Eurobanking through the establishment of international banking facilities. The future internationalisation of bank capital seems set to hinge on the extent and pace of deregulation in the future.

NOTES

This is a revised version of a paper originally presented at the CSE Annual Conference at Sheffield in July 1983. I am grateful to participants especially Wladimir Andreff, Peter Burgess, Jane Humphries and Hank Overbeck for a stimulating discussion and to Laurence Harris for helpful comments on several drafts of this paper.

1. The Banker, June 1983.

2. Exceptions are Andreff (1984), Coakley and Harris (1983), Harvey (1982), Minns (1980) and Overbeck (1980).

3. Overseas banks can join the United States clearing system while in Britain Citicorp and Standard Chartered Bank have indirectly joined the clearing system.

4. For a discussion of conflicts of interest in the US context see Herman (1975).

5. See De Cecco (1974).

6. See Feis (1930).

7. See Coakley & Harris (1983) Ch 2.

8. Ibid, Ch 3.

9. World Financial Markets, January 1984.

10. Here as in Coakley and Harris (1983) the City of London is defined to comprise the UK financial system.

11. The Banker, March 1984, pp.9-10. The Bank of England's interpretation of the data receives support from Morgan Guaranty's World Financial Markets, January 1984.

REFERENCES

Andreff, W. (1984) The International Centralisation of Capital and the Reordering of World Capitalism, Capital and Class, no.22.

Blanden, M. (1984) Foreign Bank: the Impetus Slackens, The Banker, February.

Coakley, J. and Harris, L. (1983) The City of Capital, Oxford, Basil Blackwell.

de Cecco, M. (1974) Money and Empire, Oxford, Basil Blackwell.

Feis, H. (1930) Europe the World's Banker 1870-1914, New Haven, Yale University Press.

Harvey, D. (1982) The Limits to Capital, Oxford, Basil Blackwell.

Herman, E.S. (1979) Conflict of Interest: Commercial Banks' Trust Department, New York, Twentieth Century Fund.

Jenkins, R. (1984) Divisions over the International Division of Labour, Capital and Class, no. 22.

Kotz, D. (1984) Bank Control of Large Corporations, Berkley, University of California Press.

Minns, R. (1980) Pension Funds and British Capitalism, London, Heinemann.

Overbeck, H. (1980) Finance Capital and the Crisis in Britain, Capital and Class, no. 11.

Sayers, R.S. (1967) Modern Banking, Oxford, Clarendon.

Chapter Five

INDUSTRY, THE CITY AND THE FOREIGN EXCHANGES: THEORY AND EVIDENCE

Jerry Coakley and Laurence Harris

In diverse areas of economics there is an idea that the financial system and the industrial system are distinct and may have conflicting interests. At the level of pure theory Marx distinguished financial capital from productive capital with the former being unable to produce surplus value. At the level of the concrete analysis of the British economy, writers within different paradigms have often argued that the City of London has pursued policies which are not in the interests of industry. The exact nature of the supposed conflict varies from writer to writer. Some have concentrated on the assertion that the City has failed to provide the finance necessary for high rates of fixed capital formation and has thereby held back productivity growth. Such arguments gave a stimulus to the establishment of the Wilson Committee. Others have argued the City has adopted policies with respect to exchange rates which have not coincided with industry's interests and that its representatives have succeeded in establishing them as government policies. Such arguments were particularly frequent before the 1967 devaluation of sterling when writers posed a clear dichotomy between the City and industry. The former supposedly was anxious to maintain the exchange rate at $2.80 = £1 while industry's profits suffered from having such a high exchange rate.

In this chapter we do two things. First, we examine the nature of the different arguments which have been put forward regarding a general conflict between the City and industry and attempt to relate this to conflict over the foreign exchanges and state economic policy. Second, we report on an empirical study of one aspect of the theory of a

City/industry conflict. This study concerns the relation between foreign exchange variables and the profits of industry and the City in the UK. Its results support the hypothesis that industrial profits did suffer from the City's defence of the pound and the overvaluation of the exchange rate and the study distinguishes different elements in this effect. It shows that writers who concentrate solely upon the harm done to profits by deflation fail to capture the full effect of the foreign exchanges. Conversely the defence of sterling and related state policies have, by maintaining the City's international role, boosted the City's profits. (1)

THE BASIS OF CONFLICT BETWEEN INDUSTRY AND THE CITY

Whilst numerous writers postulate a conflict of interest between industry and the City, relatively few have elaborated a theoretical basis for such a conflict. Below, two types of approaches are examined. The first refers to studies of policy interventions where the writers have referred to a variety of specific formulations of the City/industry conflict but where the theoretical basis is only implicit. The second consists of theoretical formulations of the City/industry conflict, using a range of Marxist approaches.

Policy interventions

Versions of this approach span Sraffian and Keynesian writers and have been instrumental in public policy debates in Britain at least since the 1930s. Within this tradition different writers have concentrated upon different aspects of policy as the crucial indicator of the divergence between the City and industry. G.D.H. Cole (1933) in a volume of socialist economists' essays on money, expresses one view; that bankers were deflationists while industrialists required and pressed for expansion. Glyn and Sutcliffe (1972), like the Cambridge Political Economy Group (1974), are examples of writers who take as a crucial indicator of the conflict of interest, a predilection on the part of the City for investing abroad rather than in British industry. (2) Another approach postulating that the City has had an interest in maintaining a faulty international financial system irrespective of the effects on industry, overlaps with the idea that it has several times maintained too high an exchange rate, been deflationist, and been the cause of a degree of foreign investment which is deleterious for industry. If the City supported the return to the Gold Standard in 1925 as the financial mechanism that was appropriate to the foreign investment of Britain's imperialist tradition they did so, Keynes argued in The Economic Consequences of Mr Churchill, at the wrong exchange rate thereby forcing deflation (and the social injustice of wage cuts). If it struggled to maintain the exchange rate in the 1960s the City, argued writers such as Brittan (1964, 1971), saw devaluation as spelling the end of sterling's role as a reserve currency with consequent damage to the City's position as an international capital market.

These theses of a conflict of interest between the City and industry have several weaknesses. A problem which is fundamental to all of them is their neglect of a theoretical framework for analysing the inter-connections between the City and industry; for without one it is difficult to make precise the notion of the 'interests' of each element and it is impossible to provide any hypothesis as to why they should conflict. If they have an underlying implicit assumption that the City and industry have an 'objective' common interest, either in maintaining industrial efficiency or in full employment and the welfare of the nation, it is necessary for writers who postulate a conflict to give some reason as to why that common interest is consistent with a conflict. Two unsatisfactory types of explanation have been given.

One is that the City is, at times, obsessed with irrational goals which blind it to the common interest. Stewart (1978) writes of the importance the City attached to its own self-esteem in 1967. There is undoubtedly some truth in this as a description of the psychology of the City's members. The Governor of the Bank of England, in his first public speech after the 1967 devaluation, exemplified the City attitude that it had been shamed by its failure to win the confidence of the world and maintain the pound. (3) But concentrating on irrational psychology is a poor foundation for economic analysis and it may be postulated that it is a reflection in individual thought of material circumstances. As Keynes argued, if conservative bankers raise such irrational issues as trust it is likely to be a reflection of vested material interests. (4) A second type of explanation is that it was impossible for the City to operate on the basis of its common interest with industry because of a breakdown in the information system; partly because British industry has historically relied to a relatively large extent upon internal financing rather than the credit system and partly for other reasons, it has been argued that the City has been chronically out of touch with industry's needs in respect of finance, demand management or the foreign exchanges. Thus Harrod (1951, p.345) describes Keynes's view of the Treasury and the Bank (if we can take them as representative of the City's views):

> Keynes believed that the old boys were fundamentally trustworthy and well-meaning; but they were blind and complacent, and greatly needed prodding

and writing of the period 1951-64 Brittan (1964, p.64) argues that, as 'the spokesman of the City' the Bank of England's

> judgements of the business situation at home depend on the mood its executive directors pick up from individual businessmen, rather than on any elaborate calculation of national income trends.

The idea of informational breakdown or 'blindness', too, may correspond to a real phenomenon at times, but it is hard to sustain as a basic cause of divergence. For one thing the City's representatives have not always been ignorant of the needs of industry; under Montague Norman the Bank played an active interventionist role in particular areas of industrial restructuring. For another, the hypothesis of informational breakdown only removes the question one step back; why did the Bank and City institutions not take steps to improve their information and gathering system until the middle of the decade following the Radcliffe Committee's condemnation of its paucity?

Theoretical Formulations

To answer the question of how the City and industry can diverge if they have common interests it is necessary to begin by considering the nature of those common interests. Marxist economics provides one theoretical framework for doing so. Its postulate that the interest on money capital and the part of bank profits obtained through operating the monetary payments mechanism are forms of surplus value, together with the contention that the latter arises only in the production of commodities by 'industrial' capital imply that financial capital is ultimately completely dependent on industry. (5) Inefficient industry is a weak source for the profits of financial capital and if we identify the interests of the City with its revenue from interest and profits it appears within this framework that policies which are in the interests of industrial capital in the sense of stimulating its profitability are in its own interests. Only one exception is possible at the present level of analysis; if all other things are held constant the City may raise its own profit at the expense of industry's if it engineers a rise in interest rates, but we are not concerned with that issue here. To analyse a divergence in the policies of the two fractions despite the common basis of their profits it is possible to move forward in two ways. Both require us to postulate the existence of differentiation within industrial capital itself. One concerns the effects of generalised competition between firms and industries, the type considered by Marx at the level of abstraction which was concerned with many-capitals (as against capital-in-general). The other concerns the effect of distinct blocs or fractions of industrial capital. Let us begin with the latter.

Marxist writings in the twentieth century have moved beyond the categories that Marx used to distinguish different fractions of capital according to their position in the circuit of capital (merchant capital, financial or interest-bearing capital and so on). They have identified different fractions of industrial or productive capital itself, postulating distinctions between international and national capital, and between monopoly capital and small-medium capitals. These distinctions are not without theoretical difficulties, but to the extent that they are sustainable they provide a basis for the idea that there is a conflict between the City and industry. For it may be postulated that there is a connection between the interests of financial capital and those of one fraction of industrial capital such that they are opposed to the remaining sections of industry; the City/industry polarisation is thereby conceived as a polarisation of the city and one part of industry. Aaronovitch (1955) (1961) typifies the view that there has been a merging of interests between financial capital and large industrial capital which act in combination against the interests of small and medium capital.

He argues that initially financial capital was entirely distinct but in modern times has merged with 'the monopolies' to bring to Britain the financial-industrial relations typified by the 'finance capital' that Lenin, Hilferding and others saw in Germany and America at the beginning of the century. If one seeks in Marx's theory for a reason why large industrial capital which becomes allied to financial capital should have interests different from those of small and medium capital it has to be found in the logic of his 'law of increasing concentration and centralisation.' According to this the growth of large capitals is part of the competitive process of innovation: the production of relative surplus value and the concomitant adoption of mechanised and then automated processes is a necessary development under capitalism, and, since it requires the centralisation of existing capitals, large firms must, to be successful, represent a permanent threat to their smaller competitors. (6) Longstreth (1979) and Blank (1977) employ the possibility of a different division within industrial capital. Instead of a division between large and small capital, they postulate one which distinguishes international from national capital and argue that the City has become allied to the former. Longstreth describes this as 'a coincidence of interests between imperialists and the City' while Blank describes its political aspect as an overseas or sterling lobby. Aaronovitch (1981) in a similar vein refers to the overseas orientation of the City. By this he means the alliance between the City, manufacturing and trading multinationals and segments of colonial capital once based in London. The possibility of a division between a financial-international-industrial fraction and a national fraction of capital cannot be founded on simple deductions from Marx's theoretical framework, it requires historical analysis of Britain's development in relation to other capitalist nations and in relation to non-capitalist societies. However, if the division exists it is simple to see how it could influence the policies adopted by 'the overseas lobby' in directions different from national capital's policies. The diversion of finance to foreign investment at the expense of domestic investment in response to differential profit rates might, for example, lead financial and international capital to favour policies such as free trade whereas national capital might have an interest in selective import controls, for example. Within such a perspective, the City and international capital have no concern to stem the 'de-industrialisation' of Britain since the geographical location of the source of their revenue is irrelevant, whereas national capital, by definition, is interested in the profitability of capital operated at home.

These frameworks, concentrating on the division of industrial capital itself into distinct blocs which are in alliance with or opposition to financial capital, provide one possible material basis for an opposition between financial capital and at least one section of industrial capital. Although they are often open to misuse by those who emphasise the conspiratorial nature of one or other bloc of capital, such a faulty approach is not inherent in the frameworks themselves. An entirely different approach, however, is one which instead of focusing on the relation between financial capital and distinct sections of industrial capital, concerns its relation to industrial capital as a whole. Despite the postulate that financial capital is ultimately dependent on the surplus generated by industrial capital as a whole, the Marxian system does give a role to a conflict between them.

The key to this theory is the distinction between capital-in-general and many-capitals in competition. At the level of analysis where competition is considered, the theory has to study the mechanisms by which the individual capitals are coordinated and through which the laws of competition are effected. In Capital the most salient mechanism is the market for commodities, it is in that context that Marx analyses the ways in which competition establishes market values, (7) influences technical progress and establishes prices of production and the tendency toward the formation of the average rate of profit. Thus, the commodity market is a mechanism which constrains the activities of individual capital; in Marx's framework it controls their operation in accordance with the nature of capital in general. A less obvious mechanism with a similar function in Marx's theory is the credit market. Its activity complements that of the commodity market since credit facilitates the movement of capital from one branch to another to finance innovation, influence market values, equalise rates of profit and form prices of production. According to Marx the credit market, unlike the commodity market, takes on the explicit character of something over and above individual capitals. Money capital assumes the nature of a concentrated organised mass which is subject to the control of the bankers, the representatives of social capital. He argues, for example, that the rate of interest on financial capital is a single, clear and unified representation of the general rate of profit, and as such it fulfils a role which the rates of profit on individual industrial capitals cannot, for in their tendency toward the average rate they are always at different distances from it. (8) This representation is also conceived by Marx to exist at the international level. On one hand he refers to the historical pre-existence in international centres of interest-bearing capital from the era before the advent of industrial capital and the fact that a traditional general rate of interest existed even then. On the other, Marx maintains that the function of the interest rate as a representation in the capitalist mode of production is achieved through the greater direct influence of the world market in establishing the interest rate as compared with the rate of profit. In other words, financial capital can be viewed as operating as a mechanism of competition vis-a-vis individual capitals at the level of the world credit market. The significance of the Eurocurrency markets that have developed since the 1960s lies in the face that they have greatly strengthened this role of world credit markets in enforcing conformity of rates across national boundaries.

An extension of this perspective of Marx's to the problem of whether industrial and financial capital can have distinct interests leads to the view that they may at a conjunctural level whilst fundamentally sharing a common interest. At a fundamental level financial capital represents the interests of capital as a whole in increasing the production of surplus value and its accumulation. However, when one moves to the level of a concrete example such as the UK the possibilities for conjunctural conflict become apparent. On one hand industrial capitals competing on the markets (many capitals) pursue narrower and less unified interests than capital in general. In this context the historical absence of a unified position by UK industry has often been remarked. On the other hand the immediate interests of the City entail international competition with other financial blocs or centres. Characteristically this can imply advocating foreign exchange policies which accentuate credit market competition and, hence, conflict with the immediate interests of industry.

The implications of the proposition that the conflicts between financial capital (representing capital as a whole) and industrial capital (as many capitals) are conjunctural is that the City's interests coincide with those of different sectors of industrial capital at different times. In contrast with the idea that financial capital is permanently bound to one fraction such as international capital or big capital, here it is conceived that the interests of financial capital sometimes accord with those of one and sometimes with those of another sector of industrial capital according to circumstances. The only constant is, in general terms, that the policies pursued are those which promote the production of surplus value in Britain and the other areas of the world from where financial capital draws its profits.

Representing the City's interests in quite such general terms is not adequate, however, for interpreting history. It is necessary to examine the ways in which those interests are pursued. We concentrate on one of the many; the City's policies with respect to the foreign exchanges. These policies are significantly related to the City's interests in two ways. First, policy regarding the exchange rate helps to discipline industrial capital operating in the UK (a strong exchange rate, for example, stimulating competition and the restructuring of capital) and affects the terms on which the internationalisation of capital proceeds. Second, the City's members do not necessarily formulate policy consciously as the protectors of capital in general (although we give instances of Bank of England views which are in such terms). They have a more immediate interest which is sustainable and consistent with those general interests: the protection of the international competitive position of the City itself. In the following paragraphs we examine the City's role in that context.

THE CITY AND THE FOREIGN EXCHANGES

In this section the links between the City and foreign exchange policies are examined. First, we discuss how the immediate interests of the City are related to the theoretical framework outlined in the previous section. We go on to identify the major role commercial banks play in the foreign exchange market. Through this role it is argued that the City is integrated in the operation of foreign exchange policies relating to UK official reserves. This leads to a discussion of the links between the post-war sterling crises and foreign exchange policies. The section ends with a brief discussion of the 1967 illustration of the conjunctural conflict between industry and the City.

How does the City's conception of its interests relate to the theoretical framework outlined in the previous section? At the outset it should be stressed that the concept of the interests of a fraction of capital is a difficult one. In the previous section it has been argued that the fundamental interests of financial capital involve representing capital in general in increasing the production of surplus value and its accumulation. The question which now arises is how this is manifest at a conjunctural level particularly since the different parts of the City have different roles within the whole. Here we make the assumption that international considerations are paramount for financial centres like London associated with relatively small open economies. In other words the immediate interests of the City are determined by international competition with other blocs of financial capital and financial centres and these are taken to predominate over considerations of competition within the City itself. That is, the immediate interests of the City are taken to be coterminous with the maintenance of the City's leading position amongst world foreign exchange markets. The Bank of England (1980, p.437) explains the City's leading position, thus:

> Because of the United Kingdom's geographical position, banks in London can deal with the Far East, Middle East and North America, as well as with the rest of Europe, in the course of the working day. This consideration, together with the experience gained when sterling was the main international currency and the presence in London of many other international markets which bring foreign exchange business with them, helps the London foreign exchange market to maintain a leading position.

And it is not only in foreign exchange markets that London has had a lead over other centres. It has been an international leader in reinsurance, certain commodity markets, and, in the last decade, in international bank credits (Eurocurrency credits). However, for the City to be the leading financial centre in the world it has to compete; it has had to take steps to maintain its position and strengthen it in order to ensure that London does not lose international financial business to New York.

The devaluation of 1967 marks a divide between two areas in the way that City thinking conceived the steps that had to be taken to maintain its competitive position vis-a-vis New York. Until 1967 it was believed that the strength of sterling, a strong and stable value for the pound, was an essential foundation for the City's international business, but in the 1970s it was seen that despite the decline and fluctuations of sterling's exchange rate the City could maintain and strengthen its hold on international financial business as long as it succeeded in limiting government controls over it. The change between the two periods explains why although before 1967 City spokesmen described devaluation as a potential catastrophe, in the 1970s London's bankers and financial institutions made exceptional profits, expanded fast and were unruffled by sterling's vicissitudes: devaluation had proved not to be a catastrophe. The change in attitudes reflected the changed nature of the City's business. In the earlier years, its international business had been based on its position at the centre of a sterling-using world, the sterling system; it was a system where sterling was both a reserve currency and trading currency and it was founded upon the City's credit being good enough to enable it to build up debts repayable in sterling balances. Opposition to devaluation was based on the view that the governments which held these sterling balances would have their confidence shaken by the reduction in their value that devaluation would cause and the keystone of the City's international borrowing would be taken away. In the 1970s, however, the City's reliance on the sterling balances as a source of funds was replaced by the growth of Eurodollar business; sterling almost ceased to be a reserve currency and instead of primarily borrowing and lending pounds the City borrowed and lent Eurodollars and other currencies. Becoming the world centre for Eurodollar credits, the City's profitable foreign business ceased to rest mainly on confidence in sterling and the City lived with, even welcomed, fluctuating exchange rates.

Nevertheless, the exchange rate remains important for the British economy as a whole and the City's attitudes to exchange rate policy are central to the study of the relation between the City and industry. It is worth noting that City institutions are no outsiders in the execution of those policies; the banks have been integrated with the state in consequence of their participation in the wholesale foreign exchange markets. The major direct participants in the markets comprise the commercial banks and broking firms and these act as agents for the other participants in the market - state central banks, suprastate bodies and multinational corporations. Moreover banks are the market-makers in the various currencies. The central role of banks in the foreign exchange markets forms the basis for their integration with the state in the operation of UK foreign exchange policies related to official reserves.

The first example of this integration concerns the Exchange Equalisation Account (EEA) which was established in 1932 and is formally under the control of the Treasury. During the post-war period the purpose of the EEA has been the management of the UK's official foreign exchange reserves. The Bank of England has responsibility delegated to it for the day-to-day management of the EEA. The Bank, in turn, has developed a system of co-operating with banking capital in its operation. This is described by the Bank of England (1980, p.442).

> The Bank usually intervenes covertly through the agency of commercial banks (and may continue to deal in other markets outside normal trading hours in London). These banks will handle the Bank's business with the discretion and confidentiality which they would give any other customer.

Intervention in respect of the EEA was heavy under the Bretton Woods system when it was directed at defending sterling's parity. Intervention has declined somewhat since the floating of sterling in June 1972 but still constitutes the basis of the managed or so-called 'dirty' floating.

The other example of a foreign exchange policy involving the integration of the City with the state is the system of exchange control operated in the UK from the outbreak of World War II until October 1979. Its purpose was to conserve and increase the UK's gold and foreign exchange reserves and to improve the balance of payments. The powers of control were vested in the Treasury but their administration was delegated to the Bank of England, and via the latter, to commercial banks, stockbrokers and others.

Given the integration of the City with the state in the operation of UK official reserves policies and given the explicit purpose of these policies of conserving and increasing official reserves the punctuation of the 1950-76 period by sterling crises may appear puzzling at first sight. Two aspects of such 'crises' are striking. Firstly, they were invariably associated with the weakness (that is, the relative overvaluation) of the sterling exchange rate. This suggests that the existing parity was being unduly defended through sales of official reserves and other policies. Secondly, and with the exception of the 1967 devaluation, the 'crises' were ultimately resolved largely through deflationary policies leaving foreign exchange policies unchanged. Such policies restored confidence in sterling temporarily but adversely affected production and, indirectly, the profits of industry. The question which remains is why sterling remained relatively overvalued particularly in the 1950s and 1960s. The implicit constraint on the operation of exchange control offers one explanation:

> Throughout the past thirty years the control has been administered, so far as was compatible with the need to conserve foreign exchange, to cause as little damage as possible to the international use of sterling and to the country's overseas earning power. (Bank of England, 1967, p.245)

That is, in the 1960s international competition dictated a strong exchange rate to be in the immediate interests of the City, a rate which, moreover, could be defended by exchange control on <u>outward</u> capital movements. In this context the imperative of maintaining the international competitiveness of the City as a whole was thought to demand a strong exchange rate policy. It was also a policy which, as we shall show, harmed the short-term profitability of UK industry but was seen as a discipline to stimulate restructuring and the more profitable long-term operation of industry.

The 1967 Devaluation

The question of whether the exchange rate of sterling could or should be maintained at $2.80 was at the centre of policy debates in the three years after the election of Labour in 1964. It was widely believed that the City of London was firmly against devaluation and that it had succeeded in persuading the government to 'defend the pound.' The view of Longstreth is typical of this belief. Commenting on the Prime Minister's 1965 justification for not devaluing Longstreth (1979, p.183) writes:

> Maintaining the exchange rate was in other words still the top priority in deference to the City and its international support in the IMF and the United States.

and he illustrates his argument with a quotation from The Banker of October 1967:

> ... the main reason for the City's acquiescent mood is that, contrary to expectations, the government has endorsed the City's order for priorities. It has put sterling first (Longstreth, 1979, p.185)

Michael Stewart (1978, p.83) describes a similar view of the City's and the government's policies by noting their reaction to devaluation when it occurred:

> The Government had talked and acted for so long as if devaluation was a fate worse than death that it is hardly surprising that when it came many people should have regarded it as a major national defeat and humiliation ... Predictably, it was the City of London which reacted worse of all. Obsessed with its traditional role as a world financial centre, and with the traditional role of sterling as a world reserve and trading currency, it had failed to notice that Britain had become a second rank industrial power with a sluggish growth rate and an uncompetitive exchange rate. Devaluation was seen not as a belated and essentially technical adjustment to changed economic conditions, but as a crushing blow to the City's self-esteem.

There is no doubt that views in the City did insist upon the maintenance of the exchange rate. The retort to critics that the Governor of the Bank of England offered in his Mansion House speech of 20 October 1966 was typical of many pronouncements made by Governors in those years:

> Another favourite taunt in some circles is that we are sacrificing the people to save the pound. On the contrary, the pound is being protected for the sake of the people ... The Government's firm stand on this subject is most heartening. (9)

At the same time that the City was pursuing its anti-devaluation views, many economists took the view that the maintenance of the exchange rate was harming the British economy in general, or industry in particular. This view is summarised in the proposition that changes in the world economy and Britain's trading and capital position in it rendered the old exchange rate inappropriate, that attempts to maintain it led to alternating periods of reflation and deflation ('stop-go'), and that these cycles had a deleterious effect on investment and production. Writing in 1968 the authors in the Brookings Institution report, Britain's Economic Prospects, summarised this view:

> For nearly two decades prior to the sterling devaluation of November 1967, (Britain) coped with periodic crises in her international payments largely by using a mixture of fiscal and monetary policies to hold down domestic aggregate demand ... Restraint of demand as a remedy for a payments deficit is usually effective, since a lower level of employment both reduces domestic spending on imports and slows the upward creep of the price level improving the international price competitiveness of the nation's traded goods: but it is expensive. We have not been able to measure the costs imposed by periodic demand restraint but believe them to have been substantial. Although the level of unemployment was low on the average, output was foregone when aggregate demand had to be cut back; workers and equipment were idled to protect the trade balance; and the efficiency of business investment was reduced in a setting where businessmen were uncertain about the future size of their markets because of the Government's recurrent disturbance of the level of employment and growth rate of aggregate demand ... (some) evidence suggests that stop-go-policies, induced by periodic difficulties with international payments, have forced British businesses into hand-to-mouth investment policies which perpetuate old and inefficient plant layouts (Caves et al., 1968, pp.487-8)

This provides one link between the interests of industry and the foreign exchanges which will be tested below.

INDUSTRY AND THE FOREIGN EXCHANGES: EMPIRICAL EVALUATION

One phenomenon of recent British experience that has focussed attention on relations between the City and industry is the problem of foreign exchange policy. In particular, attention has focused on the question of whether the exchange rate was maintained at an artificially high rate by City interests before the 1967 devaluation (and the question was posed again by the high exchange rate that accompanied the 1980-81 industrial crisis) and whether it was opposed by industry because it damaged profitability. Each of the theoretical frameworks we have elaborated can provide an answer to these questions. The ideas that the City was irrational or lacked information about industry could explain such an apparent illogicality and the idea that the City is essentially interested in supporting a particular fraction of industrial and merchant capital - international capital - could explain its desire to avoid a disruption to the international financial system and its own role as the banker to international capital. Moreover, the last idea (that the City is interested in maintaining the credit market's forces of discipline over individual capitals on behalf of capital-in-general) can explain the City's opposition to lowering the exchange rate on the grounds that maintenance of the exchange rate was thought to damage profitability only in the short term while this was necessary to stimulate future profitability; it was conceived by the City interests as a necessary discipline to force increases in productivity. On this view, the lowering of the exchange rate was conceived as 'a soft option' to be avoided, and although maintenance of the exchange rate may induce deflation the consequent reduction in profitability has the long-run effect of stimulating the adoption of technical innovations and more profitable working methods (as well as disciplining the workforce). Thus, on this view the City's opposition to such a course of action is conceived as stimulating the long-run profitability of industry based in Britain. It is a view which is consonant with City pronouncements in the mid-1960s and in recent years. One example, was the Mansion House speech of the Governor of the Bank of England where, after renouncing the idea that investment and new methods should be stimulated by increases in aggregate demand he presented the defence of the pound as an essential discipline; the pound 'cannot be treated as a sort of fascinating toy for bright boys to play with. I do not believe in the future of any economy where nothing ever gives way except the exchange rate'. (10) The exchange rate should be maintained to ensure that in industry old working methods, old 'attitudes' and inefficient firms gave way instead, while in the world of finance, the City could maintain its international position.

The competing versions of the hypothesis that the City and industry have conflicting interests are not easily susceptible to empirical tests to discriminate between them. However, their common proposition that industry's interests were opposed to the City's policies can be related to data, if we simplify by assuming that industry's and the City's interests can be reduced to their own profitability. (11) Then the theories share the proposition that the profitability of industry and the City is affected by the foreign exchanges. The proposition is that a strong exchange rate and other related policies designed to protect the City's international role affected industry's profitability adversely. Conversely, these same policies boosted the profits of the City. If these propositions were to be false, the relevance of the City versus industry hypothesis to the interpretation of modern economic experience would be seriously questioned. In the following pages we report on an empirical study of the proposition; it suggests that, as postulated by the various theories, the City's 'defence of the pound' did indeed adversely affect the profits of industry whilst benefiting the City's own profits. But it also suggests that the mechanisms through which profits were affected cannot be reduced to the dampening effect of deflation and 'stop-go' policies as had been assumed in the writings surveyed.

Under the regime of semi-fixed exchange rates as existed under the Bretton-Woods system the profits of industry and commerce in an open economy like Britain's are affected by movements on the foreign exchanges in two ways. The first is direct: to the extent that they occur, changes in the exchange rate themselves have an impact on profitability by affecting the costs of imported raw materials, the selling price of industry's produce on the home and export markets and the sterling value of profits on foreign operations. To the extent that British industry is highly internationalised, one might expect the latter effect to outweigh the former and raise profits. As part of this direct influence they also affect the balance between real wages and profits. Neo-classical balance of payments theory postulates that the direct effect of a fall in the exchange rate is to increase profits in a range of cases. The second influence of the foreign exchanges is indirect: foreign exchange movements lead to government action such as deflation of domestic demand which affects profits. Foreign exchange movement or 'crises' which trigger this indirect effect are not always observable as falls in the exchange rate; under semi-fixed rates governments respond to sales of the domestic currency by intervening to buy the currency and stabilise the exchange rate, and in consequence the deterioration on the foreign exchanges is observed as a fall in the country's reserves rather than (or in combination with) the fall in exchange rate.

Likewise it is possible to identify two effects of the foreign exchanges on the City's profitability but these effects operate through different channels. On one hand foreign exchange policies are used to protect the City's international role. In the 1960s these policies assumed the form of averting devaluation and even in the 1970s when the basis of the City's international business became less dependent on sterling it remained the case that the sterling exchange rate was at times defended. We would expect these policy effects to be captured by the level of reserves and the dollar-sterling exchange rate. On the other hand other financial instruments are used to reinforce foreign exchange policies the most significant of which is interest rate policy. In both the 1960s and 1970s high interest rates have been deployed at various times in efforts to defend the foreign exchanges. In the 1960s the objective was to defend sterling's par value but as international markets have become more integrated in the 1970s the focus has shifted to more open competition between the leading financial centres. However, a perverse if unintended effect of high interest rates is to boost the City's profits, particularly those of bank capital. Since high interest rates are a usual component of deflationary packages, this once again highlights the conflict between the City and industry.

In accordance with the various hypotheses of the City's foreign exchange policies having adversely affected industry's profits we therefore postulate that the latter is a function of the exchange rate, foreign exchange reserves and lagged profits and we test the resulting equation which contains the following variables:

$$YI_t = C_0 + \sum_{j=0}^{j} \left[\alpha_{1j} D_{t-j} + \alpha_{2j} R_{t-j} + \alpha_{3j} YI_{t-1-j} \right] + e_t \qquad (1)$$

We chose a maximum lag of four periods (J=4) for the regressors. D denotes the US dollar sterling exchange rate, R the level of UK reserves, YI the profits of industry and commerce, and e_t an error term. In the estimated equation the regression coefficient on (D) reflects the direct effect of exchange rates and also the indirect effect that arises from government demand management in response to the exchange rate's level in relation to the par or target value. The coefficient on R reflects only the indirect effect. Finally the coefficient on lagged YI captures the lag in the effects upon profits.

Fitting a form of equation (1) to quarterly unadjusted data (1961 (I) - 1981 (II)) by ordinary least squares yielded

$$\begin{aligned} YI = {} & \underset{(677.17)}{3703.45} - \underset{(286.73)}{610.51D} + \underset{(0.02)}{0.04\,R} - \underset{(309.51)}{620.77D_{t-4}} \\ & + \underset{(0.02)}{0.06R_{t-3}} + \underset{(0.11)}{0.50\,YI} \end{aligned} \qquad (2)$$

$$SER = 344.81; \quad \bar{R}^2 = 0.97$$

Since equation (2) employs a lagged dependent variable the use of the DW statistic is not valid. We applied an LM test which indicated that we could not reject the null hypothesis of no first order serial correlation at the 95 per cent confidence level.

The results of equation (2) provide support for the hypotheses we discussed above. The negative coefficients D and D_{t-4} suggest an inverse relationship between industry's profits and the dollar-sterling exchange rate. Equation (2) however does not allow us fully to judge the separate effects of the elements yielding these negative coefficients. In the absence of further work we can only surmise that the combined direct effects (of a change in the exchange rate) relating to the selling price of industry's produce, to the sterling value of its overseas profits and to the balance between real wages and profits outweigh the direct effect of the costs of imported raw materials and any indirect effect expressed through the exchange rate. The positive coefficients on R and R_{t-3} provide evidence of the indirect effects of the foreign exchanges on industry's profits by triggering deflationary policies once reserves reach a critical level. Finally the positive coefficient on YI_{t-1} suggests that current profits are positively associated with past profits.

Equation (2) thus has provided some evidence that the pursuit of foreign exchange policies has at times adversely affected industrial profitability. But this supports only one side of the general City versus industry conflict. Might it not be the case that foreign exchange policies have also depressed the City's profits? To test this side of the hypothesis we test the following equation for financial profits (YF):

$$YF_t = C_o + \sum_{j=o}^{j} \left[\beta_{1t} D_{t-j} + \beta_{2t} R_{t-j} + \beta_{3t} TB_{t-j} \right] + U_t \qquad (3)$$

D and R are defined as in equation (1) and TB denotes the Treasury bill rate. Using a maximum lag of four periods (J=4) and fitting equation (3) to quarterly unadjusted data for the period 1961(I) - 1981 (II) we obtained:

$$\begin{aligned} YF = -\ &1554.54 + 0.10R + 15289.9TB + 3796.09TB_{t-4} \\ &(280.52) \quad (0.005) \quad (986.30) \quad (1090.63) \\ +\ &194.23D_{t-4} \\ &(93.44) \end{aligned} \qquad (4)$$

$$SER = 191.04;\ \bar{R}^2 = 0.97;\ DW = 0.64$$

The low value for the DW statistic probably indicates that the dynamics of equation (4) are not yet adequately specified so that the results must be treated as preliminary rather than final. Nevertheless the results do appear to be consistent with our hypothesis on the City's profits. The positive coefficients on R and D_{t-4} suggest that large reserves and a strong exchange rate are associated with the City's role as a leading international financial centre and, thus, its profitability. The positive sign on the lagged exchange rate coefficient is particularly significant since it contrasts with the negative sign on the corresponding coefficient for the industrial profits equation. This provides tentative evidence of a conflict of interest between the City and industry over the foreign exchanges. Further evidence of this conflict is furbished by the positive coefficients on the current and lagged values of the Treasury bill rates. In other words, policies such as high interest rates adopted to defend the exchange rate are positively associated with the City's profitability.

Effects of Devaluation and Floating on Profitability

The tests reported support the idea that the profits of industry and the City have been affected by the foreign exchanges. The data used span a period in which major changes took place in British policy toward the foreign exchanges. One change was the devaluation of 1967, another was the move toward managed floating of the exchange rate after 1972. We first wish to examine the extent to which these changes have caused shifts in the relationship between foreign exchange variables and industry's profitability. Did the 1967 devaluation, for example, change the relationship between the foreign exchanges and industry's profitability? The City versus industry hypothesis suggests that it would have had an effect on industry's profitability (that, according to the theory, is what the conflict over policy was about) but this required careful interpretation: the hypothesis does not suggest that devaluation would have changed the relationship between foreign exchange variables and profitability. It would still be the case after devaluation that the level of the exchange rate has a direct effect on profitability and that, as long as the par-value system operates, the indirect effect of the foreign exchanges would operate through demand management policies. We employed a Chow test to examine whether there had been any shift in the relationship that underlies equation (2). Dividing our data into the sub-periods (1961 (I) - 1967 (II)) and (1967 (IV) - 1972 (I)) we obtained the F statistic:

$$F = 2.71 > F^*_{0.95}(6,34) \approx 2.38$$

The statistic is significant at the 5 per cent level and we cannot accept the null hypothesis that the 1967 devaluation had no effect on the relationship between the foreign exchanges and the profits of industry and commerce. However we stress the tentative nature of this result since the null hypothesis cannot be rejected at the 1 per cent significance level. How is this explained? The argument must be that although the relationship is unchanged, the level of profits is raised in the short run by devaluation. One way in which this occurs is through the favourable direct effects of lower exchange rates on profits. The second channel is that after devaluation the government still operates the indirect effect, deflating when the foreign exchanges worsen, but this may occur less often because the devaluation is designed to cause deviations from par value to be less frequent and less intense. (12) Studies by Artus (1975), Horne (1979) and the National Institute of Economic and Social Research (1972) suggest that the 1967 devaluation did succeed in improving the current balance and thereby lessen the downward pressures on the exchange rate. In consequence, devaluation did succeed to some extent in reducing foreign-exchange induced deflationary policies with their associated pressure on profits.

On balance, therefore, the predictions of the City versus industry hypothesis regarding the effect of the 1967 devaluation on industrial and commercial profits are borne out. But since the devaluation could not be expected to change completely the relationship between profits and the foreign exchanges had therefore left profits subject to future restrictions as the new par value became inappropriate, would it not have been more in the interests of industry to press for a change in the relationship itself? Instead of pressing for devaluation on the grounds that it would assist industry, should industry not have pressed for an end to the Bretton Woods system? The end did, in fact, come through a combination of circumstances in 1971 and a system of floating rates was adopted in 1972. We have investigated the extent to which this change did alter the relationship between profits and the foreign exchanges. The results are not clear cut because the move did not lead to a complete abandonment of management of the foreign exchanges. As Dornbusch and Fischer (1979) have found by fitting an equation for the period 1969 (IV) - 1978 (II) the authorities continued to intervene in the market to reduce exchange rate fluctuations and therefore had, at various times, targets for the exchange rate even though there were no par values. Therefore it is probable that the foreign exchanges' indirect effect through government-induced deflation continued to operate to some extent (as it clearly did in precipitating a deflationary policy in 1976).

Employing the Chow test for the stability of Equation (2) between the sub-periods (1961 (I) - 1972 (II)) and (1972 (III) - 1981 (II)) yielded:

$$F = 1.25 < F^*_{0.95} \quad (6,65) \approx 2.24$$

At the 5 per cent level of significance we cannot reject the null hypothesis that the relations between profits and the foreign exchange variables were not shifted by the breakdown of the Bretton Woods system. Further work would be required to test for the relative strength of the separate effects on industry's profits during the 1970s.

So far we have focused on the effects of foreign exchange changes on industry's profits. We now consider the shift in the City's approach from the defence of sterling's parity in the 1960s to its support for floating exchange in the 1970s. We have argued that the 1967 devaluation marked a turning point in the sense that it heralded a shift within the City from sterling business to Eurocurrency business. Since this change was gradual rather than abrupt we have taken the floating of sterling as an approximate cut-off point to test whether the nature of the City's business affected the relationship between its profitability and the foreign exchanges.

The Chow test for the stability of equation (4) between the sub-periods (1961 (I) - 1972 (II)) and (1972 (III) - 1982 (II)) yielded:

$$F = 4.89 > F^*_{0.95} \quad (6.65) \approx 2.24$$

So at the 5 per cent significance level we cannot accept the null hypothesis that the more international nature of the City's business in the 1970s had no effect on the relationship between its profitability and the foreign exchanges. This goes some way towards explaining why the City, having vigorously defended the sterling parity during the 1960s, could have adopted a stance of non-opposition towards and even support for floating exchange rates in the 1970s.

CONCLUSION

The idea that there is a conflict between financial and industrial capital in Britain can be given a theoretical foundation in several ways. It can be argued that it has a basis in irrationality, poor information, a structural alliance between financial capital and one section of industrial capital against the rest, or in the financial system's function as a force which controls and disciplines the activities of all industrial capital. Each approach has limitations. Underlying each is an assumption that it is in principle possible to separate industrial from financial capital and underlying the 'overseas lobby' version of a structural alliance is the assumption that international and national sectors of industrial capital can be considered separate. Each of these assumptions can be questioned. Moreover, the concept of interests that can be represented involves assumptions that warrant further discussion. Nevertheless, our discussion makes clear that as a working hypothesis the idea of a conflict between financial and industrial capital can be maintained.

Our empirical work focuses on one aspect of the conflict which others have claimed to be important in the context of the United Kingdom. It is the hypothesis that the profits of industry and the City are sensitive to foreign exchange policies so that aims pursued by the City with respect to them have at times conflicted with the interests of industry and commerce. Our results indicate that profits are sensitive in that way, but they are not conclusive. Declines in foreign exchange reserves do appear to have caused deflationary policies which, through their effect on capacity utilisation, harm industrial and commercial profits. Stop-go policies in 'defence of the pound' did have a harmful effect on profits in the short run, and were not completely eliminated by the adoption of partially floating rates since 1972. Moreover, a high exchange rate itself has had a direct harmful effect on industrial profits whilst benefiting those of the City. The City's profits have in the past also been boosted by the use of high interest rates to defend the exchange rate.

Further study of the relationship between the foreign exchanges, the City and industry will necessitate specification of the government reaction function and a more complete specification of the determinants of each sector's profits in order to distinguish better between direct and indirect effects. In particular, it will be desirable to examine the extent to which the direct effect of exchange rate changes make itself felt through its impact on the conversion of overseas profits into sterling (rather than on the costs and prices of home operations) and whether this has changed through time. The work on which we report here, however, indicates that the relationships are significant and are not inconsistent with contemporary views of economic policy since the war.

NOTES

1. This chapter is based on research funded by the Faculty of Social Sciences, the Open University, for which we register our thanks. We are grateful to colleagues and the Open University Financial Studies Research Group for comments on earlier papers, and in particular to Martin Croasdale for helpful econometric advice. We have also benefited from helpful referee's comments.

2. Although we categorise Glyn and Sutcliffe as writers who concentrate on the City's foreign investment as being in opposition to industry's interests on their p.43, in later pages they argue that industry itself has invested abroad and they postulate that City and industry have merged. They also write of the City's deflationary and anti-devaluation policies.

3. Calling the devaluation 'that unhappy occurrence' he declared 'the responsibility is ours in the UK ... for many years past it has been our inadequate performance that has undermined confidence in us and in ourselves. We all too thoroughly provided the raw material for a bearish view of sterling and have no right to complain.' Bank of England Quarterly Bulletin, 8, 2, June 1968, p.171.

4. Harrod (1951) p.341.

5. The statement that in Marxist theory commodities and surplus value are produced only by 'industry' is a short-hand. In this context the term includes all production under the direct control of capital (including such non-industrial activities as agriculture and the

production of some services). The term is being used here to delineate the sphere of productive labour (on which see Fine and Harris (1979) Ch.3) and note that in Marxist theory it does not include the activities of the financial system. Similar assumptions are implicit in several non-Marxist frameworks too. For example, the model of Gurley and Shaw (1960) distinguishes financial intermediaries from ultimate borrowers with the latter alone owning physical capital and paying interest out of the profits received from its operation.

6. See Fine and Harris (1979).

7. Marx (1971), Ch. X.

8. 'As concerns the perpetually fluctuating market rate of interest, however, it exists at any moment as a fixed magnitude, just as the market price of commodities, because in the money-market all loanable capital continually faces functioning capital as an aggregate mass, so that the relation between the supply of loanable capital on one side and the demand for it on the other, decides the market level of interest at any given time ... On the other hand, the general rate of profit is never anything more than a tendency, a movement to equalise specific rates of profit' (Marx, 1971 p.366). Although Marx thought the interest rate 'represented' the rate of profit, it was not quantitatively equal. The image painted by Marx is one where industrial capital in competition inevitably speaks with many tongues whereas financial capital speaks with one voice for them all. It does so because it is located within a mechanism that co-ordinates and controls them all.

9. Bank of England Quarterly Bulletin, 6 (4), December 1966, p.353.

10. Bank of England Quarterly Bulletin 6 (4), December, 1966, pp.353-5. A further advantage of the theory that the City acts for capital-in-general in a shifting relation with individual capitals is that it can explain the sharp shifts that have occurred in City policies. In the 1950s the City and sections of the Treasury were anxious to restore convertibility of sterling even though it would mean devaluation and perhaps floating rates. In the 1970s the City has welcomed floating rates in a way that seemed inconceivable in 1967.

11. Due to the well-known difficulties in defining rates of profit, profitability is taken to imply the levels of pre-tax income. This is deemed to be the measure of profitability which best accords with our underlying

theoretical framework. See Data Definitions and Sources for exact definition (below).

12. It is the case that devaluations including the 1967 one, frequently are accompanied by deflationary policies.

DATA DEFINITIONS AND SOURCES

D US dollar-sterling exchange rate from Economic Trends.

R total official UK reserves from Economic Trends.

TB Treasury bill tender rate from International Financial Statistics.

YI pre-tax profits of industrial and commercial companies: defined as income after stock appreciation arising in the UK. From Economic Trends.

YF pre-tax profits of financial companies and institutions: defined as income arising in the UK. From Economic Trends.

REFERENCES

Aaronovitch, S. (1955) Monopoly, London, Lawrence and Wishart.

------ (1961) The Ruling Class, London, Lawrence and Wishart.

------ (1981) The Relative Decline of the UK, Ch. 6, in S. Aaronovitch, R. Smith et al. (1981), The Political Economy of British Capitalism: A Marxist Analysis, London, McGraw Hill.

Artus, J.R. (1975) 'The 1967 Devaluation of the Pound Sterling', IMF Staff Papers, vol. 22, pp.595-640.

Bank of England (1967) 'The UK Exchange Control: a Short History', Bank of England Quarterly Bulletin, vol. 7 (3), pp.245-60.

------ (1980) 'The Foreign Exchange Market', Bank of England Quarterly Bulletin, vol. 20 (4), pp.437-44.

Blank, S. (1977) 'Brittan - the Politics of Foreign Economic Policy, the Domestic Economy and the Problem of Pluralist Stagnation', International Organization, vol. 31 (4).

Brittan, S. (1964) The Treasury under the Tories 1951-1964, Harmondsworth, Penguin.

------ (1971) Steering the Economy, Harmondsworth,

Penguin.
Cambridge Political Economy Group (1974) Britain's Economic Crisis, Spokesman Pamphlet, no. 44.
Caves, R.E. and Associates (1968) Britain's Economic Prospects, Washington DC, Brookings Institution.
Cole, G.D.H. (1933) 'The Socialisation of Banking' in G.D.H. Cole (ed), What Everyone wants to know about Money, London, Gollancz.
Dornbusch, R. and Fischer, S. (1979) 'Sterling and the External Balance', National Bureau of Economic Research Working Paper, no. 327.
Fine, B. and Harris, L. (1979) Rereading Capital, London, Macmillan.
Glyn, A. and Sutcliffe, B. (1972) British Capitalism, Workers and the Profits Squeeze, Harmondsworth, Penguin.
Gurley, J.G. and Shaw, E.S. (1960) Money in a Theory of Finance, Washington DC, Brookings Institution.
Harrod, R.F. (1951) The Life of John Maynard Keynes, London, Macmillan.
Horne, J. (1979) 'The Effect of Devaluation on the Balance of Payments and the Labour Market: United Kingdom 1967', Economica, vol. 46, no. 181, pp.11-25.
Keynes, J.M. (1972) 'The Economic Consequences of Mr. Churchill' as reprinted in, Essays in Persuasion, Collected Writing, vol. IX, London, Macmillan.
Longstreth, F. (1979) 'The City, Industry and the State' in C. Crouch (ed) State and Economy in Contemporary Capitalism, London, Croom Helm.
Marx, K. (1971) Capital, vol. III, Moscow, Progress Publishers.
National Institute of Economic and Social Research (1972) The effects of the devaluation of 1967 on the Current Balance of Payments, Economic Journal, vol. 82 (Supplement), pp.442-64.
Stewart, M. (1977) The Jekyll and Hyde Years: Politics and Economic Policy since 1964, Oxford, Pergamon.

Part III

THE CITY AND INDUSTRY

INTRODUCTION TO PART III

Laurence Harris

In the first chapter of this book Michael Meacher identifies the City's inadequate financing of British industry as one of the principal shortcomings which a socialist financial strategy would have to address. His argument that the City has failed industry is shared by many, and its acceptance has probably increased since the mid-1960s when a small number of commentators like Andrew Shonfield and Fred Hirsch argued that the City's defence of sterling's high exchange rate imposed a great penalty on industry. The feelings of industrialists 20 years later are well indicated by this excerpt from a Financial Times editorial in 1986:

> The new Confederation of British Industry committee on relations between industry and the City will have its work cut out. The CBI's membership has been broadened to include financial institutions, but evidently fellow-membership has not yet turned to fellow-feeling. After a sometimes passionate debate on a motion attacking the City for taking excessively short-term views, the president tactfully declined to count the vote. (Financial Times, 12 November 1986)

When a particular view on Britain's malaise becomes common place there is a particularly strong need for empirical investigation, for it is often the case that repetition alone gives currency to the view and it is assumed to be true without careful enquiry. The breadth and generality of the 'City has failed Industry' argument makes it difficult to pin down for empirical study, but the thesis can be interpreted as a group of distinct specific propositions. The research and arguments presented in the following chapters engage with several of them.

The Wilson Committee was established by James Callaghan's Labour government precisely in order to inquire into the role of the City and it was especially concerned with the adequacy of the supply of finance for industry. Its Report gave the City an almost completely clean bill of health in this regard, although there were suggestions of some shortages of venture capital. The first chapter in this Part, Evaluating the Role of the Financial System, is a critical evaluation of the Wilson Committee's Report. It is worth emphasising that the article does not contest Wilson's view that there has not been a quantitative shortfall of finance for industry. The radical, but now widespread, argument that industry has been starved of funds or that the supply of funds of the right type (long-term capital) has generally and chronically fallen short of industry's sustainable demand for them does not have strong empirical support and there are sound theoretical reasons for doubting it. However, that is not to deny that the City has had a significant and deleterious effect upon industry in Britain. Even if financial markets work in a sufficiently textbook manner to prevent quantity constraints in the funding of industry, their prices - rates of interest and exchange rates - have undoubtedly often been too high for industrial growth (as the previous chapter suggests). And even if the overall quantity of funds has not been deficient, financial institutions have used their funding arrangements to influence corporate management while not giving priority to the long-term growth of profitable production in this respect. In Evaluating the Role of the Financial System Jerry Coakley and I argue that the Wilson Committee was unable to investigate these phenomena properly because of its neo-classical theoretical basis which prevented it from analysing the institutional structure of the power the financial system wields.

That chapter distinguishes the money and credit markets on one hand from the securities markets on the other and argues that each has distinct channels and connections to industry through which financial institutions operate. The next chapter, by Richard Minns, focuses on securities; the following two by Jerry Coakley are concerned with credit; while the concluding chapters in this Part (Martin Croasdale, and Croasdale and Harris) take an approach which bears on the impact of both credit and equity finance.

In The Management of Shareholdings in Large Manufacturing Companies Richard Minns reports on research which involved a structured survey of the share registers of the 50 largest UK manufacturing companies. The research was partly a development of the pathbreaking work Minns published in Pension Funds and British Capitalism (London, Heinemann, 1980) in which he showed that banks' potential influence over non-financial companies is much greater than would appear from their low ownership of shares, for they manage and control a high proportion of the shares owned by pension funds. In the present chapter Minns examines other aspects of the divergence between the ownership and control of shares, greatly contributing to our knowledge in this area by using information provided under Section 27 of the 1976 Companies Act to penetrate behind nominee shareholdings. Minns' work is exceptional in the UK for, unlike the USA and West Germany, the conventional wisdom had assumed that banks have no influence on firms through control of shares and the question had hardly been considered a worthwhile research topic. Minns' work has shown the error of that assumption. Although it was completed before the dramatic changes in the securities markets in the mid-1980s, its revelation of banks' (and other institutions') powerful position with regard to corporate managements through their share register pre-figured the even greater use (and mis-use) of such power in the insider-trading scandals with which the names of Guinness, Morgan-Grenfell and others have been connected on the City pages.

In addition to shareholdings, banks' credit to companies, which is their main financial connection, acts as a potential channel of influence. If it were true that the quality of management in industry and commerce were a source of the British economy's weakness, the conditions attached to bank loans could have offered a route for banks to intervene and strengthen company operations (as banks seem to do, through different channels, in West Germany), but it has been argued that bank credit has been made available too unconditionally and it is dominated by short-term credit. Both these claims are investigated in surveys conducted by Jerry Coakley and reported in his two chapters in Part III.

In Bank Lending and the Control of Industry: An Empirical Study Coakley reports on a survey of large UK corporations in non-electrical engineering. He finds that at the time the Wilson Committee was considering the claim that UK commercial banks were not giving medium-term loans, they had already changed their practice to some extent and were doing so rapidly, so that the industrial companies surveyed borrowed medium-term credit from them as well as from other banks. The changes taking place were, Coakley found, related to developments within firms themselves, particularly the development of treasury functions within large firms. This implies that instead of seeing changes in the type of finance as emanating only from innovation by financial institutions they have to be related to changes in the borrowers' own financial decision-making. This chapter carefully examines the types of conditions banks attach to their credit and concludes that although changes in them and in other aspects of their operations have given banks closer involvement with companies they still do not have the great influence over strategic planning and real investment decisions that banks in some other countries have.

In American Banks' Credit to UK Industry Jerry Coakley is concerned with a similar issue: the conditions attached to banks' loans to firms, but this chapter is based on a survey of US banks in London. American banks' lending to large UK companies has been notable for two features: its rapid growth in recent years and the difference between their type of lending operation and the traditional British commercial banks'. This survey shows that their rapid expansion in this area began after the 'competition and credit control' policy was initiated by the UK authorities in 1971. It is argued that the survey's findings concerning their concentration on large corporate business, the high proportion of medium-term lending, credit appraisal and the types of conditions they attach to their loans all reflect the banks' roots in the wholesale banking that is a well-developed feature of US banking. As the Wilson Committee noted, the conditions US banks attach to their loans are different from the traditional British banks' for, instead of securing their loans by collateral (which insures against the collapse of the firm and frees the lender from involvement with its ongoing operations), US banks' medium-term loans prescribe conditions to be observed while the firm is a going concern. Jerry Coakley's survey provides the first systematic information on the precise types of conditions US banks do attach to their corporate lending. Although they are concerned with firms' current behaviour, it is interesting to note that neither they nor the banks' methods of credit appraisal run significantly counter to the 'hands-off' tradition in banking. Like the conditions found in the survey of engineering companies these are concerned with balance sheet ratios and financial structure and the bankers appear to be not involved with production and real investment decisions.

The potential for banks' involvement in industry is relatively restricted by UK firms' extraordinarily high degree of reliance on their own internal funds, including retained profits, as a source of investment finance. Although aggregate UK data on gearing ratios (of debt to equity) are historically weak it is clear that the proportion of external finance in UK companies' sources of funds is very low in comparison to other countries. For advocates of the thesis that the City has starved industry of funds, this fact is sometimes taken as supporting evidence, but it cannot really serve that role since the relative proportions of different types of finance reflect both firms' own decisions and the external constraints. The existence of a high degree of internal finance, however, does suggest an alternative approach to the relation between finance and investment from the neo-classical approach. While neo-classical theory emphasises the influence of the cost of capital (a measure of the price of finance) on investment decisions, it can be argued that the quantity of internal finance acts as a quantity constraint on investment (either in combination with the cost of capital or other variables). This does not automatically follow from the existence of a high degree of reliance on internal funds, but it can do so if the latter is evidence that firms are not indifferent between sources of finance.

Martin Croasdale's article Modelling the Finance of Investment discusses the theoretical basis of arguments that firms' investment is positively related to their stock of internal finance. Croasdale reviews the existing theoretical and empirical literature, the leading examples of which relate to US experience. His critical evaluation is based on a significant theoretical advance which emphasises that internal finance can still influence investment while not being an absolute constraint since firms can respond to changes in internal finance not only by adjusting their investment but also by changing other sources and uses of funds. Previous writers have generally failed to take into account such a general adjustment process and Croasdale shows that this leads to the inclusion of cash flow variables in their econometric models whereas a more valid method of capturing the effect of changes in sources and uses would be the inclusion of a borrowing variable.

In Internal Funds and Investment Martin Croasdale and I fit a model based on these principles to quarterly data for the UK industrial and commercial sector. Our purpose in this chapter is not purely theoretical, but, instead, to evaluate a question of policy. When interest rates are high, as they have been in Britain whenever there has been a sterling crisis or when, as under Margaret Thatcher's governments, they are used to restrain the money supply, industrialists bemoan their effect on real investment. Their argument is not (or not only) that the cost of capital is too high compared to the real return on investment (an issue that concerned the Wilson Committee) but is frequently expressed in terms of a quantity constraint; high interest rates cause a drain on profits to pay the financial system and thereby reduce firms' internal funds and restrict their investment. Fitting our econometric model to UK data produced results which conformed to this view. The estimated effect of interest rates on investment was small but statistically significant through this route.

It is interesting to note the connection between this chapter and the chapter by Coakley and Harris in Part II. There it was found that under a fixed exchange rate regime a City policy of defending high exchange rates harms industry partly through indirect channels. One such channel would, from the Croasdale and Harris chapter, appear to be that defending the exchange rate leads to high interest rates which, by acting as a drain on internal funds, restrict firms' investment. The power of the financial system with respect to industry is many sided and interconnected.

Chapter Six

EVALUATING THE ROLE OF THE FINANCIAL SYSTEM

Jerry Coakley and Laurence Harris

It is widely recognised that the financial system has a pivotal role in the British economy. Conflicts over economic policies have involved exchange rates, interest rates and the direction and conditions of credit as often as wages and the labour process. Such financial variables are important because of their effects on the 'real' economy. The financial system's significance lies in its impact on these variables but its influence also works through other channels. We argue that to understand the effect of financial processes on the 'real' economy one needs to consider the workings of the financial system itself, and in particular, the differences that exist within it.

Financial 'processes' is a rather abstract term; it is easier to think in terms of the institutions in which the processes are at work. Thus, what we are really looking at is how the banks, insurance companies, pension funds and other financial institutions ('the City' for convenience), have operated with respect to industrial and commercial capital in the UK.

The significance of the City lies in the specific nature of the power exercised by its institutions; it is a power which has several dimensions and political discussion sometimes concentrates on one dimension rather than another. In the present monetarist episode, as in earlier periods, the power of the City to force the government to adopt deflation and unemployment as a strategy has been at the fore. This, itself, can arise either from the direct political activities of the City or from its power to influence exchange rates and interest rates-key variables which act as constraints on governments' ability to plan and expand state expenditure. The power to influence exchange and interest rates illustrates the specificity of financial institutions as compared with other firms and bodies: for whereas any firm importing or exporting, or even any worker holidaying in Benidorm, may have an indirect influence on the demand/supply balance for foreign exchange, the financial institutions' position and role in the economic structure is to concentrate financial balances in their hands and thereby dominate the exchange market and credit markets. It is they, rather than industrial firms or other agents that act in the wholesale money and foreign exchange markets where interest and exchange rates are set. Some discussions of the City's power are concerned with another of its dimensions - its pivotal role in determining the adequacy, price and direction of finance for industry; questions about this power often ask whether the City has been instrumental in channelling capital abroad and thereby starving productive capital operating in the UK of funds. (1) Finally, the potential for influencing the supply of finance to industry gives rise to the possibility of another dimension of financial institutions' power, the ability to influence industry or control it in some circumstances. This is the aspect of the City's power on which this chapter focuses.

The workings of the financial system have recently been examined by the Wilson Committee, the latest in a line of official reports on the City. Its report (2) carried the general message that all is well with the City and no significant changes are necessary or desirable. Although some members signed a note of dissent supporting the TUC proposal for a new investment facility, such a fund would hardly affect the City's operation; since the need for it was thought to arise from a gap in the funds supplied by the City, it would not even compete with the existing financial institutions. In the present paper, we reach a different conclusion on the need for government intervention in the City. We also employ a different theoretical approach from Wilson's. The Wilson Committee assumes that financial institutions are decision-making individual economic agents much like any other firm and that their decisions have the same status as those of any firm or household. We start from the assumption that the financial system as a whole is a distinct bloc (rather than a summation of its individual institutions), its operations and effects are quite specific and its position in the economy embodies specific forms of power over the other agents.

The Wilson Committee's view that all economic agents are equally significant and financial institutions have no special power implies that those institutions are essentially passive conduits (3): their principle function is seen as merely channelling funds from one sector of the economy to another and making only technical decisions on the disposition of funds. By contrast we think it is significant that City institutions have specific objectives - the specific aim of strengthening their own competitive position.

This drive has an important implication for Wilson's central problem of financing industry. It has been at the root of particular conflicts between the interests of the City and of industry in Britain in spite of their common long-term interest in profitable accumulation. Strengthening the City's own competitive position has meant improving it as an <u>international</u> finance centre vis-a-vis those of New York, Frankfurt and others. At crucial conjunctures this has required policies to maintain a relatively high exchange rate (although that is not a permanent policy) and to ensure high interest rates irrespective of their effects upon industrial profits and accumulation. (4) This strategy, which has been predicated on a policy of allowing London's international financial business to develop relatively unhampered by controls, has succeeded in making London the strongest international centre of money and credit markets.

The City's international competition for financial business is one aspect of its specific power and dynamic that distinguishes it from other sectors of the economy. But it would be wrong to see the City as a monolith, whether as a unified conduit for funds to industry or as an entity in international competition. Distinct elements within the City have distinct roles and in the following paragraphs we examine the specific power exercised by different elements in financing industry.

Below we examine the UK's two main types of financial markets and then return to their common characteristic - their short-term perspective.

1. The Role and Nature of Financial Markets

The Wilson Committee's individualist perspective, with its assumption that all decision makers are equally significant, obscures the specificity of the power of the City as a whole. It also clouds the distinctions between the different parts of the financial system itself. We shall consider these distinctions by concentrating on the division of labour which has emerged between two types of 'financial markets', the money and credit markets on one hand and the securities or capital markets on the other. The differences between them are such that there is an ever present potential for conflict between the institutions engaged in each type of market. The markets for money and credit are dominated by banks engaged in obtaining and making short and medium-term loans; broadly speaking the loans do not give any legal rights of ownership (although they confer some real power on the lender to affect the borrower's actions). The capital market, whose institutional framework is centred on the stock market and the bodies which operate within and around it (insurance companies, pension funds, brokers, jobbers and trusts) trades in securities which are created as a means of raising long-term capital for enterprises and which in the case of shares (but not, generally speaking, bonds) confer some legal ownership rights. A third important type of market is the wholesale foreign exchange market. Although it does overlap and interweave with the money and credit markets because of the dominant role played by London banks in Eurocurrency transactions, we do not explicitly discuss it in this paper.

The possibility of conflicts between the institutions engaged in each type of market becomes especially important at times of economic crisis. In the past year financial institutions, under the informal leadership of the Bank of England, have negotiated rescue packages for several major enterprises. In these deals the differences between banks with existing loans at risk and institutions holding equity capital have been at the fore. Moreover, at times of high interest rates the benefits accruing to banks because a high proportion of their deposits are obtained at low or zero interest (the endowment effect) bring no direct benefits to pension funds; insurance companies and others in the capital market. Thus, the degree of support for high interest rate policies differs, and this difference is fostered by the fact that high interest rates (and the expectation that they will eventually fall) causes industry to favour raising loans by borrowing from banks instead of the capital (bond) market.

(a) **The securities markets.** The securities markets refer to the series of markets in which share capital and various bonds are floated and traded. The securities market can be further subdivided into the corporate stock market which is concerned with share capital, company loan stock and debentures, and the gilt-edged market for the issue and trading of government bonds. In this section we are concerned mainly with the stock market and particularly share capital although much of what we have to say about institutional domination may also apply to the gilt-edged market. At the outset it should be pointed out that the Wilson Report did point to some of the salient features of the stock market (5) but in that context it failed to analyse them or relate them to the ongoing debate on the ownership and control issue (a debate which is central to any evaluation of how changes in the financial system can affect industry).

The stock market really comprises two interrelated markets corresponding to its two basic functions. The first is the new issues market which raises money capital for the joint stock companies issuing new or additional shares. In the UK context the first thing to be noted about new issues is the dramatic decline in their relative contribution to industrial and commercial companies' external finance (6) from an average of over 30 per cent in the 1963-70 period to an average of only 12 per cent in the 1971-9 period. This is all the more striking because the decline occurred during a period of unprecedented growth in institutional cash flow. The second feature of the new issues market is that rights issues by larger companies (often for takeover purposes) have raised most of the money capital. A rights issue involves a company offering its existing shareholders the right to subscribe at a discount for further shares in proportion to their shareholdings. To sum up: the stock market's contribution to companies' external finance has been relatively minor during the 1970s but one cannot conclude that it has exercised no influence over industry.

Of far greater quantitative importance than the new issues market is the secondary market where existing shares and bonds can be bought and sold. This corresponds to the second basic function of the stock market which is to facilitate the conversion of investors' existing shares into money and which forms the basis for investors' short-term outlook. The secondary market is where the increasing institutional domination of the stock market is proceeding. Basically this is a transfer or distributional shift in the ownership of shares, typically from the personal sector to financial institutions, for example pension funds and insurance companies. It does not itself involve raising any additional money capital for the companies whose shares are changing hands. But their role on the secondary market gives institutions a strong role in the new issues market too, since the principle type of new issue is the 'rights issue' where existing shareholders are the main suppliers of new funds. Now, ordinary share capital represents the risk-bearing capital of a company and confers certain ownership rights on the shareholders. In normal circumstances these rights include dividend payments and a note per share on the appointment or removal of directors, and in the event of insolvency, a residual claim on the company's assets after all creditors have been fully repaid. It is important to bear in mind these ownership rights for they have frequently been misunderstood or exaggerated in the context of the ownership and control debate - a topic which the Wilson Report does not even mention although it implicitly discusses some related issues.

The ownership and control debate arose as a criticism of the neo-classical theory of the owner/entrepreneur profit-maximising firm. The most popular alternative (the managerial theory of the firm) to the neo-classical theory saw the modern firm as characterised by a separation between its ownership and its control or management. The joint stock form of enterprise has seen the replacement of the owner/entrepreneur by a range of shareholders all holding relatively small stakes in the enterprise. In the absence of any large shareholders, claims the theory, management stepped into the power vacuum and began running companies on a different basis. Instead of maximising profits, management was seen as pursuing growth as an objective usually subject to some financial constraint such as a minimum level of dividends or a stock market value constraint. (7) Failure to comply with the financial constraint implied a threat of takeover and the possible replacement of management.

If the managerial theory of the firm were valid it would have important implications for the Alternative Economic Strategy for it would decrease the significance of taking enterprises into public ownership. Has the increased institutional domination of the stock market, the concentration of shareholdings in the hands of big financial blocs, weakened the basis of the theory? Prais (1976) thinks not on the grounds that institutions spread their holdings across a range of companies (in order to reduce risk) so that no individual institution holds controlling interests in individual companies. Managers remain autonomous. Wilson similarly emphasises the dispersion of shareholdings. However, the power that institutional shareholders can exert as owners over managers is not obliterated by superficial dispersal, because shareholdings can be aggregated into financial groups to exert pressure. A common device used by the institutions to this end is the 'Investment Protection Committee' (IPC).

In the insurance companies' IPC for example, an average of ten to 20 cases per year in the 1970s have dealt with a management problem whilst a somewhat larger number have involved questions of shareholders' voting rights and the rights of consultation on major changes in company structure. (8) Moreover, since some two-thirds of pension fund assets are externally managed by merchant banks as Minns has shown, (9) the concentration of such assets in the hands of a small number of merchant banks confers the possibility of effective control on them. At the end of 1976 the merchant banks had some £7½ billion funds under management on behalf of other institutions and individuals. However, the Wilson Report failed to see this concentration of funds as a source of control. The managerial theories also underestimate the constraints on companies from outside the stock market, particularly from the bank credit market. This raises the possibility of conflict between shareholders and banks not only in the more obvious cases of bank-imposed dividend restrictions and residual claims on liquidated companies' assets but also over the range of a company's major decisions. We explore this more fully in the context of the money/credit markets.

(b) **The money/credit markets.** The money/credit markets refer to those markets where banks provide short and medium-term credit facilities and other specialist services such as trade financing. Until the late 1970s the City's sophisticated money/credit markets have been unique in their failure to supply medium-term bank credit on a more general level. This is not to deny the significance of bank credit in the financing of industry and trade at the aggregate level. As the Bank of England indicates:

> The banks increased their share of industrial and commercial companies' external finance in the 1970s. In the 1960s ... they had provided rather less than half of the total, while in the 1970s they contributed about 60% of it, often more. (10)

At least part of the increased importance of bank credit can be explained by the decline of the industrial bond market and the increased willingness of American banks in particular to supply term facilities. Now whilst it is difficult to quibble with the report's conclusion that no general shortage of funds for industry exists in the UK at present, it is arguable whether this has been the case for different types of bank credit until the late 1970s. There is a distinction between bank credit to finance circulating capital and that to finance fixed capital. Broadly, until the latter half of the 1970s, this led to a distinction between the lending practices of British clearing banks and American commercial banks in London and different implications for the relationship between the financial and productive sectors.

Historically, the UK clearing banks have developed a tradition of overdraft financing which still survives today. For example, overdraft facilities in 1980 accounted for some 70 per cent of the portfolio of the leading clearing bank (11) and are estimated to be at least 80 per cent of two other clearers' portfolios. Although the Radcliffe Report in 1959 recommended the development of term facilities by the clearers the latter have responded rather reluctantly. (12) This contrasts with the view expressed by the Wilson Committee that the British banks have moved substantially toward medium-term lending in their credit to British industry. And the fact that overseas banks have captured more than 30 per cent of the UK corporate lending market seems to suggest that the clearers' adherence to overdraft financing cannot be explained by the lack of demand for term facilities.

The nature of clearing bank finance, the fact that it has not been well designed as a means of funding long-term planning for the development of productive capital, is indicated not only by its short-term nature. Equally significant is the type of security that is required against the credit; until the late 1970s the preponderant situation was one where banks required a security which could protect the bank if the firm became unprofitable instead of one which considered the firm as a going concern. But even the latter type of approach has caused problems. Let us explore this further.

For all but the largest companies overdraft and medium-term credit facilities are secured against a company's assets to protect the clearers' interests in cases of insolvency. Security normally limits a company's power to dispose of any of its fixed assets and, in the case of a floating charge (simply a legal claim on a company's floating assets such as stocks and debtors), confers on the bank the power to appoint a receiver. The latter power becomes quite crucial at times of crisis and indeed the number of receiverships has increased sharply in recent years. (13) Since security requirements are normally calculated on the assumption of the liquidation of the company concerned and the forced sale of its assets, the clearing banks' approach to credit analysis has been characterised as the 'liquidation' or 'gone concern' approach. Clearly this approach, involving short-term facilities and a focus on a company's balance sheet, is not the most appropriate for financing industry's fixed capital formation. Also since all secured borrowing ranks ahead of unsecured borrowing, and as shown in insolvencies, the banks' power to appoint a receiver is critical and constitutes a potential source of conflict between banks and shareholders.

Since the early 1970s American commercial banks have promoted medium-term bank credit normally on an unsecured basis to finance fixed capital. The approach of the American banks to credit analysis has been described as the 'going concern' approach in that it focuses on company cash flow and profitability as a viable and not a liquidated concern. In this form of credit, security requirements are replaced by detailed loan agreements. Fixed capital finance has several important features. It is available over a fixed term subject to compliance with the conditions specified in the loan agreement. For our purposes it is possible to distinguish four broad types of loan agreement conditions which circumscribe a company's operations during the term of its facility. (14)

The first is financial covenants such as dividends or gearing restrictions. Banks can stipulate both capital gearing and income gearing (interest cover) ratios/limits for all but prime quality borrowers. In a regime of sustained high interest rates the income gearing ratio assumes critical importance. Note, however, that this ratio is expressed in terms of the amount of interest payments (reflecting capital gearing and interest rates); by contrast the Wilson Report emphasises interest rates as (the major component of) the cost of capital. The Bank of England's (1980A) estimate that the income gearing of UK industrial and commercial companies rose from 17 per cent in 1978 to 14 per cent in

1979 at a time when capital gearing fell from 19 per cent to 18 per cent, illustrates the restrictive effects of this covenant. The second type of condition is standard for all unsecured borrowing and is designed to protect the bank against the possibility of future creditors taking security and so ranking ahead of it in the event of insolvency. The most common form of this type of condition is the negative pledge which prohibits further secured borrowing by enterprises. The third and perhaps most sensitive condition is that which specifies events of default. As well as failure to pay interest and principal where due, or breach of financial covenants, events of default can include catch-all clauses such as the 'no material adverse change' clause which is normally determined at the discretion of the Bank. Finally, a cross default clause is now standard in all loan agreements. In the case of a multi-banked company, cross default clauses imply that an event of default under <u>any</u> agreement automatically triggers default in <u>all</u> agreements. The engineering firm, Stone-Platt, is a good example of a UK company which recently fell victim to a cross default clause. The importance of cross default clauses lies in the fact that in the event of financial problems a company is not confronted by individual banks acting separately but by a group of banks representing the interests of bank capital against any other possible interests in the company. They are a symptom of the competition and conflicts of interest that can exist between different financial institutions.

The significance of the loan agreements used by American banks is that they define a new basis for relations between the banks and industry. These agreements require the creditor banks regularly to review or monitor not only their outstanding facilities but more significantly the financial performance of enterprises in respect of the loan agreement conditions. In normal circumstances this monitoring implies access to enterprises' published accounts and regular contact between bank and enterprise management. Should an enterprise be in default of any condition with any bank the cross default clause places the enterprise's banks in a powerful position to accelerate their debt which forces the enterprise into drastic short-term measures such as disposal of assets or rationalisation.

The bias of bank finance in the UK toward short-term lending is thought to have been instrumental in causing industry to take a short-term view of its investment plans, emphasising quick returns rather than long-term development. It may be asked, however, whether the existence of the capital market counteracts this influence: noting particularly the rise of the institutional shareholder may it not be the case that the stock market provides a source of funds which permit firms to take a long-term perspective? Apart from the fact that industry relied to only a small extent upon finance from the capital market, it is doubtful whether institutional investors can be characterised as taking the long view. There is some evidence that the institutions which manage pension fund assets aim for short-term profits (15) and, indeed, such a policy would be consistent with the high turnover of shares and high price volatility during the 1970s that Wilson noted. Certainly, fund managers have readily disposed of shares for short-term gains during the recent spate of 'dawn-raid' takeovers. The importance of the short-term bias of bank lending could also be qualified by noting the dependence of industry upon internal finance (retained profits and reserves) as a source of funds of accumulation. Surely managers can take a long-term view of investment and use the internal funds under their own control to finance it? Here is a specific test of the managerialist theory of the firm. The British experience suggests that the low profitability and associated low dividends that would in the short run result from that policy leaves firms vulnerable to a takeover because the price of their shares on the stock market, the secondary capital market, is driven down. Thus, even though the capital market is not often used to raise new finance, it constrains the use that is made of other finance, and it reinforces the short-term bias of bank lending.

In a general sense then UK financial markets with their short-term outlook have not been favourably disposed towards fixed capital accumulation by British industry and so may have contributed to deindustrialisation - but this theme cannot be pursued here. Instead we turn to one of the conditions which underly London's role as an international finance and trading centre - namely the relative absence of state controls - and discuss the case for, and some of the problems associated with, such controls in respect of the financing of industry.

2. Control and Nationalisation of the City

The issue of whether the major financial institutions should be controlled or nationalised has to be seen in the light of the way they have operated. But, first, the issue itself has to be stated clearly since the words 'control' and 'nationalisation' are too general and, in consequence, the programmes of left-wing parties and right-wing populists (or even fascist parties) can appear to coincide on the need to control the financiers. Socialists have no prerogative over a distrust of money.

It is important to be clear about why one should argue for the control or nationalisation of the City. The choice of argument is itself a political judgement. On the one hand, you can argue for control of the City on the basis of the view that relatively unfettered institutions are not working well enough for capitalism, while on the other hand, you can argue for control because you think they work too well for capitalism. The Wilson Committee employed only the first criterion: are the financial institutions meeting the needs of small business? Is the growth of the institutional shareholder weakening the efficiency of the stock market? Socialists should be concerned with the second criterion and base their argument on the institutions' ability to strengthen monopoly capital and inhibit socialist policies.

We employ the second criterion here but the choice is not so stark and we will qualify it in due course. A related problem is the meaning of those terms themselves, for the financial institutions of all capitalist countries are already controlled and, in some cases, nationalised to a greater or lesser extent (in the UK to a comparatively low extent) without in any way impairing their function as capital. Control takes the minimum form of 'prudential regulation' such as governments requiring banks to hold a proportion of their assets in non-interest-bearing cash to meet depositors' withdrawals. Such controls are not our main concern but conflicts do arise when banks shy away from high ratios - they have recently forced the Bank of England to abandon its initial suggestions for new prudential ratios. Our subject is the question of control over all aspects of the banks' and other institutions' disposition of assets: over the purposes for which they can buy and sell foreign exchange, over the types of loans they can make and over their commitment to financing government expenditure. Similarly, with regard to nationalisation, we do not deal with the creation of state-owned profit-maximising institutions. Instead, our concern is whether financial institutions should be nationalised as a condition for planned economic growth and social improvement regardless of the institutions' own profitability except when it furthers these aims.

Consider first, the question of controls. Since the Second World War, British governments have maintained various controls over the banks and some other financial institutions (such as hire purchase companies), but have consistently pursued a policy of attempting to dismantle controls. The Heath and Thatcher governments, in particular, have taken quite determined steps. In 1971 the Heath government brought in a policy, 'Competition and Credit Control', which attempted to simplify controls over the institutions in order to permit greater competition between them; in October 1979 the Thatcher government took a step as dramatic and important as its monetarist deflation when it abolished, for the first time for half a century, all controls over the export and import of money. We say 'since the Second World War' to highlight the fact that during the war the City was subject to comprehensive controls from which lessons can be learned for today. (16)

Controls were of two types: first, capital issues control and control over bank advances which were designed to restrict and direct the ability of firms and other enterprises to borrow money on the capital and money markets; and second, foreign exchange controls which were directed towards conserving foreign exchange and ensuring it was used for the war effort. The statutory capital issues control over the sale of new securities and related bond market operations was exercised by a Treasury Committee. Non-statutory control over bank advances was loosely practised by the Treasury through the (then still private) Bank of England so that borrowing from the banks could not be used to thwart any restriction of funds through capital issues control. These controls worked, but that does not mean they are appropriate in the Alternative Economic Strategy. First, they were implemented with the support of the City at a time when government controls were legitimated by patriotism - the Alternative Economic Strategy's background will be one of intense conflict over national aims. Second, the controls did not really succeed in directing the activities of enterprises by controlling their ability to borrow; firms were more effectively constrained by shortages of labour and materials and by physical controls. However, the capital issues control was very important in affecting the terms on which money could be raised and in controlling the capital market so that the government itself could raise money in the amounts and on the terms needed to finance its expenditure. Foreign exchange controls were imposed only gradually as the war progressed; they were resisted at first by the Treasury and the City for fear of the City losing its international role forever. Nevertheless, a complex system of controls over foreign exchange was instituted in the summer of 1940. It proved broadly effective and, although there were disagreements over the particulars, it was not the subject of strong conflict between the City and the State.

Controls over foreign exchange, capital issues and other forms of lending are an essential part of any strategy to build a planned economy. However, it is important to consider whether controls over the operation of the capitalist financial institutions are alone adequate for the task, or whether nationalisation is a prerequisite. We shall not discuss exchange controls here since they are the subject of another paper. Controls over capital issues and other forms of lending are directed towards influencing the quantity and terms of credit given to enterprises and the state. During the war the terms of credit proved to be the most important aspect. Since the war the flexibility of the financial system has proved to be such that controls alone are inadequate for directing and financing enterprises. The system has shown that as soon as controls are imposed upon one type of lending operation, new institutions and techniques develop to provide uncontrolled financing. This phenomenon was remarked on by the Radcliffe Committee at the end of the 1950s and has subsequently been manifested in the growth of unstable fringe banks (free of the controls that affected the commercial banks in the 1960s and early 1970s) which channelled funds into the property market. In addition, the flexibility in the development of international financial markets raises problems which we will return to. The banks themselves sought directives on their advances during the war and the system of exchange controls in the post-war years was operated by the banks willing to act as agents of the state. In a situation of conflict, however, the personnel and structural position of the private financial institutions cannot be relied on to ensure that controls are operated in accordance with planning priorities.

Nationalisation of the financial institutions could contribute to overcoming these problems, but there are various types of nationalisation. Nationalising the major banks, insurance companies and pension funds - a version of the strategy of controlling only the 'commanding heights' - may be a popular policy and relatively easy to implement, but it is not wholly adequate. A few major institutions have a dominant effect on interest (and exchange) rates on the wholesale money market thus affecting the state's ability to control the interest rates at which it borrows to finance its expenditure (assuming that exchange control prevents overseas institutions from dominating London's credit markets). However, if the takeover is limited to the major institutions then it is not possible to control the direction of credit granted to firms. The flexibility of the financial system will ensure that new institutions and techniques develop to fill unfulfilled needs. The only type of nationalisation that can overcome that problem is the establishment of a legal monopoly for the state in the provision of credit.

There are, nevertheless, severe limts to the control of industrial finance that can be obtained by either controlling or nationalising the finance system. The first is that industrial capital in Britain is not very dependent on external finance; firms have historically relied on internally controlled funds (retained profits and depreciation funds) to finance their growth.

The second limit is that the growth of multinational corporations concomitantly with the expansion and increased sophistication of international ('Euro') credit and capital markets over the past two decades means that some of the most significant decisions on investment and production are in the hands of firms whose external finance is derived from international sources. These limits highlight the fact that control of financing alone will not be adequate to ensure that firms' activities accord with the state's priorities; control and nationalisation of financial institutions is only viable if it is part of a policy to nationalise industrial firms themselves and thereby control their activities directly.

That perspective, however, presents the matter very much as an all-or-nothing question, a problem of how to build a planned economy once secure state power has been gained. The Alternative Economy Strategy has to be considered also as a strategy for immediate policies to improve the economy's growth (without which the position of the working class cannot be improved under capitalism) while increasing control over market forces. Under that heading two particular measures are presently on the agenda. The first is the creation of local enterprise boards, such as the West Midlands Enterprise Board and the Greater London Enterprise Board. These boards have the potential for using locally raised money and the pension funds controlled by local authorities to finance, gain strategic control and enforce planning agreements with local industry. (17) There is no simple mechanism for these boards to change the way in which the industries they finance operate: for one thing they will not have a monopoly of finance in the firms they fund, and for another the control of finance does not ensure control over production, investment and the firms' operations as a whole. Nevertheless, the boards are structures which can divert some pension fund money towards more socially controlled uses and thereby protect to some extent local industries and employment. The second measure is intervention to prevent the collapse of banks involved in international lending. The growth of international lending during the last decade (the recycling of the surpluses achieved by some oil exporting countries) has placed some banks in positions where their ratio of debt to capital is higher than many would consider prudent. Moreover, these international credits are concentrated on a few countries (such as Brazil and Poland) which, because of their high borrowing, can face difficulties in repayment. The danger of a bank's crash resulting from these circumstances and causing a general financial crash is a real one. If it were to occur, it would bring an intensified crisis with increased costs to the working class. There is, therefore, a case for demanding that a Labour government intervene to enforce high capital ratios and other prudential regulations upon London banks operating in the international markets. Such a policy would reduce the attraction of London as an international banking centre, it would also be part of a policy, backed by exchange controls and taxation, to dismantle the City of London's role as a centre for international banking. The ending of that role can only have a positive effect upon the freedom of a popular left-wing government to direct the economy.

NOTES

1. See, for example, Aaronovitch et al., 1981, Ch. 14, and Aaronovitch, 1981.
2. Committee to Review the Functioning of

Financial Institutions, 1981, Report (hereafter the Wilson Report).

3. A similar failure to recognise the specificity of financial capital is contained in Cutler et al., 1978, where the authors characterise financial institutions as merely a set of accounts.

4. The relation between finance capital's policies on the exchange rate and industrial and commercial capital's profits is discussed in its theoretical and empirical aspects in Ch. Five above.

5. Wilson Report, op.cit., Ch. 13.

6. See Bank of England, 1980A.

7. See Marris, 1964. For an alternative view of size of firm as a defence against takeover see Singh, 1971.

8. See the Wilson Report, op. cit., pp.252-3.

9. See Minns, 1980. For further evidence on the concentration of shareholdings see Minns, 1981.

10. Bank of England, 1980A, loc. cit., p.322.

11. See Financial Times, 13 April 1981.

12. Committee on the Working of the Monetary System, 1959: Report. The view to only a small extent appears to be supported by a survey being conducted under the Open University research project 'The Interrelationship between financial, industrial and commercial capital in the UK'.

13. See Bank of England, 1980B.

14. The changing nature of loan agreements is examined in Kurz, 1981.

15. See Lex, Financial Times, 25 June 1981.

16. A full examination of wartime financial controls is to be found in Sayers, 1956.

17. Minns, 1981, discusses the case for local enterprise boards.

REFERENCES

Aaronovitch, S. (1981) The Road from Thatcherism, Lawrence and Wishart, London.

------ Smith, R., Gardiner, J. and Moore, R. (1981) The Political Economy of British Capitalism, McGraw Hill, London.

Bank of England (1980A) 'Financing British Industry', Bank of England Quarterly Bulletin, vol. 20, no. 3, pp.319-23.

------ 1980B, 'Corporate Insolvency', Bank of England

Quarterly Bulletin, vol. 20, no. 4, pp.430-6.
Coakley, J., Harris, L. (1982) 'Industry, The City and the Foreign Exchanges: Theory and Evidence', British Review of Economic Issues.
Committee on the Working of the Monetary System (1959) Report, Cmnd 827, HMSO, London.
Committee to Review the Functioning of Financial Institutions, Report and Appendices, Cmnd 7939, HMSO, London.
Cutler, A., Hindess, B., Hirst, P., Hussain, A. (1978) Marx's Capital and Capitalism Today, Volume Two, Routledge and Kegan Paul, London.
Kurz, W. (1981) 'New Form in the Loan Agreement', Euromoney, February, pp.47-59.
Marris, R. (1963) The Economic Theory of Managerial Capitalism, Macmillan, London.
Minns, R. (1980) Pension Funds and British Capitalism, Heinemann, London.
------ (1981) 'Challenging the Bankers', New Statesman, 21 August, pp.6-10.
Prais, S. (1976) Evolution of Giant Firms in Britain: A Study of the Growth of Concentrations in Manufacturing Industry in Britain 1909-70, Cambridge University Press, London.
Sayers, R.S. (1956) Financial Policy 1939-45, HMSO, and Longmans Green, London.
Singh, A. (1971) Takeovers: Their Relevance to the Stock Market and the Theory of the Firm, Cambridge University Press, London.

Chapter Seven

THE MANAGEMENT OF SHAREHOLDINGS IN LARGE MANUFACTURING COMPANIES

Richard Minns

The research I report on here aimed to discover more about the extent to which investment management institutions such as merchant banks, clearing banks, insurance companies and other institutions manage shareholdings in large companies. The methodology includes the use of information on nominee shareholdings obtained by companies through the use of Section 27 of the 1976 Companies Act. The use of this legal provision allows the public to find out far more about shareholdings than normal share registers allow. It is also then possible to calculate who has the responsibility for making decisions about buying and selling shares on behalf of the share owners, and then to construct an initial categorisation of management control over shareholdings.

BACKGROUND

There have been five major surveys of shareholdings in the UK in the last 20 years; in 1963 and 1969, conducted by the University of Cambridge (1); in 1975 conducted by the Department of Industry (2); in 1978 contained in the Wilson Report on the Functioning of Financial Institutions (3); and in 1980 conducted by the Stock Exchange (4). Definitions and methodology have varied and the Wilson survey concentrated chiefly on the financial institutions; the 1975 and 1980 surveys went into additional detail for companies of different sizes, or market valuations; and the 1980 survey was based on information compiled by companies themselves. All the surveys have pointed to the rise in share ownership by financial institutions and the decline in individual holdings. The 1963 survey found that financial institutions owned 30.4 per cent of quoted ordinary shares, the 1969 survey showed that this had risen to 35.9 per cent, the 1975 survey 47.9 per cent, 1978 49.5 per cent, and 1980 51 per cent. Individual holdings declined from 54 per cent to around 36 per cent over the period. Pension funds showed the most dramatic increase in share ownership, from 6.4 per cent to 18 per cent of quoted shares according to the 1980 survey, or 20.4 per cent according to the 1978 survey. All the surveys concentrated on the beneficial ownership of shares. Pension funds and unit trusts, for example, are listed according to the shares they own. But many funds delegate the management of their share portfolios to merchant banks or other managers and many unit trusts are part of banking and insurance company management groups. It has been estimated that in 1978 two-thirds of all pension fund shareholdings were under the 'discretionary' management of banks, brokers and other 'external' managers. These estimates were published in <u>Pension Funds and British Capitalism</u>. (5) This discretionary management entitled them to buy and sell shares according to the investment policies of the banks, as agreed by pension fund trustees. Another survey has since estimated that banks manage over 50 per cent of pension fund assets. (6)

Table 7.1 reproduces figures from <u>Pension Funds and British Capitalism</u> which compared the ownership of shares from the 1975 Department of Industry survey with figures for the management of shares estimated for 1978. Around 20 per cent of individual shareholdings were estimated to be under the discretionary management of banks and brokers. (7) In addition, 67 per cent of pension fund shareholdings, and large parts of unit and investment trust shareholdings were reallocated according to whether they were part of insurance and banking groups. Finally, part of charities' holdings were also reallocated according to 'independent' investment groups. Stockbrokers were treated, like banks, as external managers for the most part, for although they argue that they only 'advise' funds, their advice is frequently crucial in investment decisions. (8)

The reallocation of shareholdings according to investment management rather than ownership showed that pension funds, while owning 16.8 per cent of quoted shares according to the 1975 survey, only directly managed 5.6 per cent. Banks only owned 0.7 per cent of shares but they

Table 7.1: The ownership and control of company shares (per cent)

	Ownership (1975)	Control (as of 1978)
Persons	37.5	29.9
Charities and other non-profit-making bodies	2.3	0.2
Stockbrokers (and jobbers)	0.4	6.3
Banks	0.7	17.6
Insurance companies	15.9	17.1
Pension funds	16.8	5.6
Unit trusts	4.1	
Investment trusts and other financial companies	10.0	11.1
Industrial and commercial companies	3.0	3.0
Public sector	3.6	3.6
Overseas sector	5.6	5.6
Total	100.0	100.0

Source: *Pension Funds and British Capitalism*, Heinemann, 1980.

managed 17.6 per cent. In fact banks emerged as the largest managers of shareholdings. They included clearing banks and their trust departments as well as merchant banks. The investment management was also concentrated in a few institutions with, for instance, about 30 external financial bodies managing half of all pension fund investment. Certain banks lead the field in investment management: Hill Samuel, Schroder Wragg and Morgan-Grenfell manage between £1.5 and £3 billion of pension funds and other discretionary funds.

It was also argued in *Pension Funds and British Capitalism* that the concentration of investment management had contributed towards a tendency to invest in large companies. This was partly because the relatively small number of major investing institutions dealt with enormous cash flows for investment. It was possible to invest substantial amounts of money in large companies without acquiring too large a proportion of a company and without significant effects on share price. The investment in large companies increased over the 1970s as funds and cash flows grew. Large companies (the 250 or so with over £40 million market valuation) represented around 79 per cent of the total valuation of all quoted companies in 1972 and also in 1977. However, the proportion of pension fund share investment going into large companies increased from 81 per cent in 1972 to 88 per cent in 1977.

Research on investment management and bank control of funds has advanced much further in the United States and West Germany than it has in the UK. In the United States, where the rise of pension funds has paralleled that of the UK, the Patman Report of 1967 found that 147 of the 500 largest manufacturing and mining companies had 5 per cent or more of their shares held by a bank trust department. The banks involved in this were the 49 leading trust banks, dominated by the two main asset managers, Morgan Guaranty and Citibank. These 49 banks between them controlled 54 per cent of the trust assets of all commercial banks in the US in 1967. As in the UK, the holdings favoured the large companies: bank pension and trust holdings were three times as great in the top 500 companies quoted on the New York Stock Exchange as in other companies quoted on the Exchange.

In 1971 the US Securities and Exchange Commission (SEC) found that 10 or fewer institutions, predominantly banks, held at least 10 per cent of 316 companies, 15 per cent of 203 and 20 per cent of 100 companies. Like Patman, the SEC decided that any institution holding 5 per cent or more of a company's equity was deemed to have effective control. The SEC went on to criticise the institutions for not being involved in companies' decisions except for takeovers where, it alleged, the institutions were attracted by the prospect of a relatively clear profit. (9)

More recently, Herman has reported on information obtained in 1979. Data generally is more readily available in the US than in the UK insofar as institutions had to report their holdings to the SEC if they exercise investment discretion over equities valued at $100 million or more. By the end of the 1970s there were 99 financial institutions that held shares worth over $1 billion, and these institutions held over 70 per cent of all institutional shareholdings. Of the 99 holders, 43 were banks, 31 were investment companies or advisors, 10 were insurance companies, 6 were government-sponsored trust funds and 6 were self-managed pension funds. The 43 banks held 50.5 per cent of the total for the 99 institutions. (10) Herman doubted whether the institutions had effective 'control' over companies as earlier reports had argued, because the bulk of ownership of the large companies lay outside this group of institutional investors. But, he continued, 'these institutions' overall large holdings in giant companies are substantial enough so that major shifts would surely have stock price and other implications. If institutions decided collectively how to vote corporate stock, or which ones to favour or disfavour as investments, even greater consequences would ensue.' (10) This theme was to have particular relevance to the UK in 1980-1 as I shall discuss below.

In West Germany, shareholdings appear to be more concentrated than in the UK or US, especially with large individual or family holdings still remaining. This must be partly the result of not having the funded pension system which characterises the UK and US. But German banks do still have a very important role which arises from their management of individuals' shareholdings. Share transactions are usually conducted through the banks and many small investors deposit their shares with banks. A bank has to inform investment clients of forthcoming company meetings and advise them of which way to vote. Usually the bank is left to vote according to its own recommendations.

The German Monopolkommission investigated the implication of this in 1975. Direct voting rights held by the banks amounted to under 5 per cent of all votes in the top 100 companies. But the banks actually controlled 36 per cent of the total votes when the proxies were included. It has been argued that because small investors in particular use the banks to hold their shares, the banks have most voting power in the companies with most shareholders, and these are often the largest companies. On average the banks control a majority of votes in the ten largest companies, and over 20 per cent of the votes in the next 90 largest. (11)

In the UK the significance of investment management discretion has been highlighted by the 40 'dawn raids' and 'sudden death' takeovers in 1980-1. The raids involved the transfer of large blocks of shares (up to 30 per cent until February 1981 and 15 per cent thereafter) from one company to another, often in a matter of minutes after a premium on the share price had been offered. The raids could be used as a basis for a full takeover bid, giving the bidder an initial stake in the company. Over a third of dawn raids were followed by a bid. The raids have been conducted on a range of companies, including larger companies such as Consolidated Gold Fields, British Sugar Corporation (twice),

Rank Hovis McDougall, Chloride and Thomas Ward, as well as BPC, Serck and Croda International.

A 'sudden death' takeover involves a bidder again offering a premium on the share price but this time the bidder aims to acquire a majority stake. The takeover of Amalgamated Power Engineering by Northern Engineering Industries occurred without an offer document issued by the bidder and without a defence document from Amalgamated Power.

It could reasonably be argued that these activities were facilitated by the concentration of fund management described above. A stockbroker would find it almost impossible to contact thousands of individual holders to offer to buy their shares at an attractive price. But with far fewer institutional holders, and with investment managers such as banks effectively coordinating the decisions of many pension funds and unit trusts, the whole process is much more straightforward. In the dawn raid on Eagle Star Insurance, stockbrokers Rowe and Pitman instructed 30 staff to make three phone calls each to a total of 90 institutions. As a result 14.9 per cent of the shares at a cost of £59.2 million was bought in minutes.

It appears that there is at least some superficial difference between the approach of the various categories of institutions. In the raid on Revertex Chemicals in April 1980, Prudential and Britannic Assurance Companies, each with over 5 per cent, refused to sell. In the raid on British Sugar in June 1981, the Prudential again refused to sell, and the same happened in the raid on Thomas Ward in November 1981 where the Prudential owned 8 per cent. However, the Prudential has sold in dawn raids, and so have other leading insurance companies, but they would still appear to be under-represented, along with self-managed pension funds, when compared to bank and broker-managed funds. (12) This may be because there is less pressure on insurance companies to sell in raids than there is on funds managed by merchant banks. This is perhaps because of the need to boost short-term performance, especially when merchant banks are competing for fund management business. (13)

Another aspect of the role of the banks was revealed in the bid by Trusthouse Forte for Savoy Hotels in 1981. The merchant bank S.G. Warburg was financial adviser to Trusthouse in the bid. It was reported that 15.4 per cent of the Savoy's A shares (with restricted voting rights) and 1.4 per cent of the B shares (with four times as many votes) were under the investment management of S.G. Warburg. Trusthouse acquired 52 per cent of the total Savoy equity and 32.5 per cent of the votes. The Savoy shares under Warburg's management were sold to its Trusthouse client.

Various attempts have been made to tighten dawn raid and takeover rules during 1980 and 1981. One amendment proposed to the Takeover Code by the Council for the Securities Industry would have treated a financial adviser, such as a bank or broker, as 'acting in concert' with its corporate client in a bid. All its shareholdings and dealings would then have been circumscribed by the rules applying to the bidder. The Takeover Panel however felt that it was excessive to assume that all dealing activities within a bank or broker's should be regarded as directed in common with the corporate department's advice to its clients. The panel agreed instead that the code would contain a warning that a bank's actions may be seen in this light in certain circumstances, thus raising the whole issue of conflicts of interest between the corporate department of banks and their investment management sections.

Thus, in both the work conducted in the US and West Germany, and in recent events in the UK, a number of questions have been raised about the management of shareholdings in different companies by the various financial institutions. Two crucial questions appear to be, how far do merchant banks control the shares of companies, and how does this control vary according to the different kinds of company. Since pension fund investment in particular has tended towards the large company, it was felt appropriate to examine initially the management of shares in large companies, concentrating on manufacturing companies.

The results of the survey are contained in the main table in the Appendix. The figures are underestimates for four reasons. First, the figures refer only to shareholdings of 100,000 and over. Second, there are still many nominee holdings that have not been identified. Third, individual holdings, 20 per cent of which are managed externally, are also under-represented because many companies using Section 27 do not enquire about small holdings. Even if they do, it is difficult to identify their investment managers. Fourth, some nominee holdings are difficult to disaggregate. For example, some externally managed pension funds use more than one type of manager, perhaps an insurance company and a bank, but the same nominee name is used for both managers. Where it is difficult to split up a holding according to the different managers, the shareholding has been discounted. The under-representation in general applies more to bank-managed holdings than to any other categories, especially that of insurance companies and self-managed pension funds.

One nominee holding is specifically exempt from complying with Section 27 of the 1976 Companies Act, and that holding belongs to Bank of England Nominees. This nominee company holds shares on behalf of the Queen and members of the Royal Family, as well as that of other heads of state and governments. The company has included the holdings of the Shah of Iran, for example, and it is also known to include holdings of the Kuwait Investment Office. In some companies Bank of England Nominees have a not insignificant holding. In 14 of the 50 companies in the survey, Bank of England Nominees holds over 2 per cent of the share capital (Rowntree, BPB, BET, Dalgety, Imperial Continental Gas, ICL, Plessey, Reckitt and Coleman, Consolidated Gold Fields, Rio-Tinto Zinc, BAT, Glaxo, Pilkington, Beecham).

Identifiable nominees and bank trust accounts fall into four categories:

(a) Multiple holders: Barings Nominees, Morgan Nominees, Schroder Nominees, for example, can cover dozens of beneficial owners in any one share register. These refer to the discretionary clients of Baring Brothers, Hill Samuel, Morgan-Grenfell and J. Schroder Wragg respectively.

(b) Smaller 'plain accounts': these are accounts with fewer beneficial owners, but one manager. Barclays Nominees (Aldemanbury) covers investment trusts managed by, Kleinwort Benson.

(c) Numbered, or designated accounts: these always refer to a particular beneficial owner and manager. Midland Bank Trust Co. 672760 a/c refers to the part of the BL Hourly Paid pension fund which is insured with, and managed by, Legal and General Assurance Co.

(d) Non-designated single accounts: these are non-numbered accounts which also always refer to a particular owner and manager. Junction Nominees refers to the part of the British Rail pension fund which is managed by S.G. Warburg.

Some further details of managers, allocations and categories are contained in the explanatory notes in the Appendix.

The main table in the Appendix shows the management categories for the 50 UK manufacturing companies. The most popular pattern is for insurance companies to manage the largest percentage of shares accounted for. Banks normally come second, followed by self-managed pension funds, self-managed investment and unit trust groups, or stockbrokers, and then other corporate and financial bodies. In nine of the companies, however, banks manage the largest institutional shareholding. Four of these are oil companies.

In 13 companies there is a major external interest in the form of another industrial company, a trust, the Kuwait Investment Office, or the Government and Bank of England. These interests are listed in the explanatory notes. The effect of such an outside interest is frequently to limit and distort the holdings of other categories, as in the case of BP, Lonrho, Charter Consolidated and Wimpey: these are four of the nine cases where banks manage more than insurance companies.

Table 7.2: Large holdings in the 50 companies by different institutions

	Insurance companies		Banks	Self-managed pension funds
Over 10%	43	companies	38	29
Over 15%	36		16	6
Over 20%	25		4	-

It is apparent from the main table that insurance companies, banks and self-managed pension funds manage large blocks of shares. Table 7.2 summarises some of the figures. For example, insurance companies managed over 10 per cent of the share capital in 43 companies, banks in 38 companies and pension funds 29. Insurance companies are the most easily identifiable category in the survey, but it is interesting to see that banks managed over 15 per cent of the capital in 16 of the top UK manufacturing companies, including Racal, Thorn-EMI, Plessey, ICL, Bowater, BOC, Bass, Pilkington, Burmah and BTR.

But equally important is the concentration of holdings amongst a few institutions. In the 50 share registers examined in the survey, the insurance company holdings are accounted for by no less than 84 insurance groups and independent insurance companies (including two foreign companies). But 17 leading UK composite and life assurance companies alone manage 75 per cent of the insurance

Table 7.3: Ownership and management of shares in large companies (average percentages, unweighted)

	Ownership (all quoted companies)	Ownership (large companies - over £150 m) (1)	Management (large companies - over £150 m) (2)
Insurance companies	19	18.7	19.0
Banks	-	-	13.0
Brokers	-	-	1.9
Pension funds	17	18.7	9.9
Unit trusts/investment trusts	15	12.0	3.4
Other institutions	14	14.7	2.1

average % = (1) Stock Exchange survey: average for 3 bands starting '£151 m. - £200 m.' and ending 'over £500 m'.
(2) Open University survey: average % of all 50 companies for each management category.

company holdings in 34 companies, and over 50 per cent in 47. (15) The banks' holdings are accounted for by 32 banks (including 10 foreign banks acting as investment managers), but 11 of the main UK merchant banks (the leading investment managers amongst the 17 accepting houses) (16) manage 75 per cent of the shares held by banks in 26 companies and over 50 per cent of the shares held by banks in 43 companies.

The final table, Table 7.3, compares the average percentages owned by institutions in large companies (market valuation here of over £150 million), taken from the 1980 Stock Exchange Survey, with the average percentages for investment management by the institutions in the 50 manufacturing companies (which roughly correspond to the £150 million and upwards market valuation). The Stock Exchange survey covered 64 companies with over £150 million compared to 50 companies in the present study. Of these 50 companies 30 were covered in the Stock Exchange survey. The table attempts to compare share ownership with share management in the large manufacturing companies.

Insurance companies stay about the same on this

measure of comparison, but pension funds drop from 18.7 per cent to just under 10 per cent when self-managed pension funds alone are considered. Although the Stock Exchange survey does not list banks separately as an ownership category, it is likely to be very small because UK banks do not usually own shares in their own account. However, the management role of banks appears as the most outstanding feature when comparing the ownership and management of the shares of large companies.

THE SURVEY

An initial study of the 50 largest manufacturing companies was carried out under a research grant from the Open University in 1981. The companies were taken from the Stock Exchange Factbook for September 1980 which lists the 100 largest UK Companies by Market Valuation. Financial companies were eliminated, along with companies that were predominantly involved in retailing, trading and property, while oil companies were included. Foreign-owned companies were left out (namely Standard Telephone and Cables), and also government-owned companies (BL). Allied Breweries, Imperial and Dowty were left out because the date of their share register which was available was pre-1980. Distillers, Redland and Thomas Tilling were also dropped either because of the availability of information or inadequate resources. This left 50 companies for the research.

Shareholders with 100,000 shares or over were selected from share registers. These shareholders usually represent at least 50 per cent and often 60 per cent of a company's share capital. The registers varied in date from January 1980 to July 1981 depending on the availability of the register at the Registrar of Companies, or at the company's own offices or at their registrar's offices. Most of the companies' registers were for 1981. As with the 1980 Stock Exchange survey of Shareholders, the aim was to obtain the most complete and up-to-date information which the companies had, or which was already publicly available.

The shareholders with 100,000 shares or more were identified as far as possible. Many holdings (often over 30 per cent) are held in the names of nominees or bank trust departments. Under Section 27 of the 1976 Companies Act, a quoted company can require any of its registered shareholders to state the capacity in which they hold any of the company's voting shares. If the shares are held on behalf of someone else, the company can require similar information from this holder too, until the ultimate beneficial shareholder is identified. If a company makes such an enquiry, the information must be entered in a register which is available to the public. Sixty of the top 100 companies were contacted to see if they had used Section 27. In fact 27 out of 60 had used this provision. The details are contained in the Appendix at the end.

Some companies have very extensive Section 27 registers, which are regularly updated, others have only used the provision on one occasion for one shareholding. One major difficulty arises with overseas shareholders. This is all the more important since the abolition of exchange controls. Under exchange controls overseas buyers had to secure Bank of England approval to buy more than 10 per cent of a UK company. The removal of the controls and the increase in dawn raids and takeovers has led to large holdings being obtained by overseas interests under a nominee name without the victim company being able to identify the buyers. This is because overseas holders are exempt from UK company legislation and do not have to respond to a Section 27 enquiry. A special investigation was even launched by the Department of Trade into the ownership of 30 per cent of the share capital of Dunlop by Middle East interests using nominee names, but without success. (14) The Department of Trade had no more success with a holding in Bond Street Fabrics registered under the name of National Westminster Guernsey Trust Company. Eventually the Secretary of State for Trade froze the transfer and voting rights in the shares.

Lastly, in July 1981, Sangers Group disenfranchised a block of shares held under London Wall Nominees because it had failed under Section 27 to identify the beneficial owners who were outside the UK. This followed an amendment to Sangers' articles in 1980 allowing disenfranchisement where the identity was concealed. In April 1981, Bowater Corporation also amended its articles to try to restrict the activities of foreign shareholders. Companies where there are large foreign interests, such as some oil and mining companies, will therefore have shareholders whose identification is more difficult.

Twenty-one of the 50 companies in the survey had used Section 27. Along with the six other companies that were approached and which had used the section, and five other companies (see Appendix) a directory of nominees was compiled for use in all the companies. Beneficial shareholders were identified as far as possible, and then their investment managers were located from pension fund yearbooks, investment and unit trust yearbooks, Crawfords Directory of City Connections, and from some shareholders themselves. Investment and unit trusts were reallocated to the banking and insurance groups to which they belonged.

NOTES

1. R. Stone, J. Ravell, J.P. Moyle, The Owners of Quoted Ordinary Shares - A Survey for 1963, Chapman and Hall, 1966: J.P. Moyle, The Pattern of Ordinary Share Ownership, 1957-1970, Cambridge University Press, 1971.
2. Central Statistical Office, The Ownership of Company Shares: A Survey for 1975, HMSO, 1979.
3. Committee to Review the Functioning of Financial Institutions, Appendices, HMSO, Cmnd. 7937, 1980, p.498.
4. The Stock Exchange, Shareholder Analysis, A Supplement to the Stock Exchange Fact Book, December 1980.
5. R. Minns, Pension Funds and British Capitalism: the ownership and control of shareholdings, Heinemann, 1980.
6. 'Banks and pension fund investment', Pensions, vol. 3, no. 7, July 1981.
7. These figures are confirmed by R.A. Vernon, M. Middleton and D.G. Harper, in Who Owns the Blue Chips? A Study of Shareholding in a Leading Company, Gower Press, 1973.
8. For details of all these calculations and assumptions see Pension Funds and British Capitalism.
9. Securities and Exchange Commission, Institutional Investor Study Report, Washington, 1971.
10. E.S. Herman, Corporate Control, Corporate Power, Cambridge University Press, 1981, p.146.
11. J. Cable and M.J. Dirrheimer, 'The Multidivisional Hypothesis', paper for the Workshop on the Economics of Internal Organization, Berlin, June-July, 1980.
12. 'The institutions at work', New Statesman, 24 October 1980.

13. 'The trigger-happy pension funds', Financial Times, 15 June 1981; also 'Neglecting the decencies', Financial Times, 3 August, 1981.

14. Department of Trade, Dunlop Holdings Ltd. Investigation under Section 172 of the Companies Act 1948, HMSO, 1981.

15. The 17 insurance companies are: Commercial Union, Royal, Prudential, Legal and General, GRE, General Accident, Sun Alliance, Pearl, Sun Life, Equity and Law, Norwich Union, Standard Life, Scottish Widows, Eagle Star, Cooperative, Provincial, Phoenix.

16. The eleven merchant banks are: Hill Samuel, Schroder Robert Fleming, Rothschild, Hambros, Morgan-Grenfell, Baring Bros., Kleinwort Benson, Charterhouse Japhet, Lazards, S.G. Warburg.

APPENDIX

Explanatory Notes to Main Table

Column 1: Insurance companies: Shares owned by life and composite insurance companies and their managed funds: plus shares of unit trusts which are part of insurance groups; shares of pension funds under discretionary management of insurance companies; insurance company pension funds.

Column 2: Banks: Shares of pension funds, charities and others under management of UK banks (clearing banks and merchant banks) and foreign banks; shares of unit trusts and investment trusts in banking groups (the Save and Prosper unit trust group is taken to be part of Robert Fleming since there were close links between them and a 26.5 per cent shareholding owned by Fleming until August 1981 when Fleming acquired a majority stake. However M&G - another of the largest unit trust groups - is treated separately despite Kleinwort Benson's 42 per cent stake): bank pension funds; Bank of England pension fund.

Column 3: Brokers: Shares owned by brokers directly: shares of pension funds and others managed by brokers; shares of unit trusts managed by brokers.

Column 4: Self-managed pension funds: Shares owned by pension funds where management is conducted directly by the pension fund itself: shares of investment trusts owned by self-managed pension funds.

Column 5: Self-managed unit trusts and investment trusts: Shares owned by investment and unit trusts which are not part of any other financial group: pension funds managed by unit trust groups; independent fund managers, eg. Geoffrey Morley and Partners, where not part of any other group and not managing unit or investment trusts.

Column 6: Other corporate and financial bodies: Church Commissioners; Church of England; Public Trustee; Official Custodian for Charities; Salvation Army; Building Society pension funds; Abu Dhabi Investment Authority; Kuwait Investment Office; Crown Agents; Bank of England Nominees; banks and insurance companies which are part of non-financial groups (eg. Singer and Friedlander, Cornhill Insurance); other non-financial companies.

Column 7: Other major external interests: Other corporate and financial bodies with over 5 per cent are listed separately because they can affect the amounts available to other shareholding interests:

1. BP 25.02 - HM Government. 19.61 - Bank of England.
2. Consolidated Gold Fields - De Beers Consolidated Mines and Anglo-American Corporation of S.A.
3. Unilever - Leverhulme Trust.
4. LASMO - Cawoods Holdings.
5. Associated British Foods - Wittington Investment (through George Weston Holdings).
6. Whitbread - Whitbread Investment Co.
7. Rank - Rank Foundation, Prize Funds and Group Charity.
8. Lonrho - Gulf Fisheries and Co. WLL along with two Sheikhs' declaration of trust in favour of Gulf Fisheries.
9. Charter - De Beers Consolidated Mines and Anglo-American Corporation of S.A. (through Minerals and Resources Corporation).
10. Burmah - Kuwait Investment Office.
11. Johnson Matthey - Charter Consolidated.

Main Table: The Management of Ordinary Shares in the 50 Largest UK Manufacturing Companies (1980-1)

		1 Insurance companies	2 Banks	3 Brokers	4 Self-managed pension funds
1.	BP	9.40	10.63	1.12	3.88
2.	Shell	17.52	11.91	2.38	7.84
3.	GEC	24.27	11.99	2.33	11.22
4.	ICI	17.82	12.14	2.51	11.15
5.	Rio Tinto Zinc	22.25	13.02	1.78	8.54
6.	Beecham	20.57	13.66	2.94	10.50
7.	Consolidated Gold Fields	12.98	8.05	1.49	3.61
8.	BAT Industries	19.96	13.12	2.15	11.11
9.	Unilever	17.95	7.87	1.63	8.82
10.	Racal Electronics	22.41	19.22	1.45	10.11

Main Table: continued

5 Self-managed investment & unit trusts & other managers	6 Other corporate & financial bodies	7 Other major external interest	8 Total shares accounted for	9 Date of share register
1.10	1.76	44.63	72.61	June 80
4.09	2.19	-	45.93	April 80
3.32	1.95	-	55.08	Sept.80
1.53	2.48	-	47.63	April 80
3.10	4.01	-	52.70	July 80
5.32	3.41	-	56.31	Feb. 81
2.85	3.46	28.81	61.25	Dec. 80
4.38	2.75	-	53.47	Sept. 80
1.66	2.64	18.45	59.02	March 81
5.77	2.05	-	61.01	Apr. 81

Main Table: continued

	1 Insurance companies	2 Banks	3 Brokers	4 Self-managed pension funds
11. Bass	25.81	16.12	2.46	12.08
12. Thorn-EMI	27.82	15.92	2.69	13.54
13. London & Scottish Marine Oil	17.14	12.01	0.88	7.10
14. BTR	19.60	20.49	1.34	11.90
15. Plessey	24.34	18.19	2.34	10.94
16. Ultramar	7.02	14.08	0.49	6.10
17. Hawker Siddeley	13.02	12.29	0.75	8.94
18. Glaxo	22.97	16.20	1.86	10.42
19. Associated Dairies	19.31	20.02	1.11	11.14
20. Associated British Foods	7.08	2.91	0.48	6.13

Main Table: continued

5 Self-managed investment & unit trusts & other managers	6 Other corporate & financial bodies	7 Other major external interest	8 Total shares accounted for	9 Date of share register
3.40	1.08	-	60.95	Feb. 81
2.35	1.04	-	63.36	March 81
9.23	3.75	9.13	59.26	May 81
8.53	0.93	-	62.79	Feb. 81
4.80	4.11	-	65.38	March 81
4.93	2.26	-	34.58	Dec. 80
0.93	0.61	-	36.54	July 80
2.93	3.02	-	57.40	June 80
4.14	0.98	-	56.70	March 81
0.55	0.36	71.0	88.51	July 80

Main Table: continued

	1 Insurance companies	2 Banks	3 Brokers	4 Self-managed pension funds
21. Whitbread	19.75	14.50	3.16	12.75
22. Pilkington	15.81	17.06	2.00	8.44
23. Sears	22.85	13.58	4.66	16.12
24. Imperial Continental Gas	11.18	12.65	3.69	10.22
25. Blue Circle	26.21	14.97	1.34	10.10
26. De La Rue	21.19	15.72	-	7.25
27. Rank	23.26	21.34	3.06	10.53
28. BOC International	30.13	15.32	2.67	14.98
29. Lonrho	2.72	4.70	0.33	1.19
30. Charter Consolidated	9.39	8.19	0.77	1.77

Main Table: continued

5 Self-managed investment & unit trusts & other managers	6 Other corporate & financial bodies	7 Other major external interest	8 Total shares accounted for	9 Date of share register
3.36	3.13	5.29	61.74	July 81
1.90	2.96	-	48.17	Sept. 80
4.64	1.71	-	63.50	Dec. 80
6.61	4.41	-	48.76	March 81
1.21	1.83	-	55.66	June 80
2.40	0.48	-	47.04	March 81
5.03	0.35	10.20	73.77	Apr. 81
3.01	1.46	-	67.57	Jan. 81
2.59	1.28	19.26	32.07	March 80
2.43	1.06	35.80	59.42	July 81

Main Table: continued

	1 Insurance companies	2 Banks	3 Brokers	4 Self-managed pension funds
31. GKN	23.58	11.11	2.20	15.08
32. Burmah Oil	11.46	10.97	0.19	4.77
33. Bowater Corporation	22.09	15.28	1.35	16.07
34. Johnson Matthey	22.12	9.41	2.05	6.60
35. United Biscuits	25.21	20.78	3.37	15.15
36. Cadbury Schweppes	24.51	14.72	2.75	11.16
37. BICC	25.29	14.51	4.12	10.40
38. BPB	33.06	8.42	3.25	13.80
39. Tricentrol	3.21	15.23	0.17	4.02
40. Unigate	14.30	7.94	3.46	9.27

Main Table: continued

5 Self-managed investment & unit trusts & other managers	6 Other corporate & financial bodies	7 Other major external interest	8 Total shares accounted for	9 Date of share register
2.49	1.96	-	56.42	Dec. 80
4.04	0.67	6.42	38.52	April 81
2.42	1.42	-	58.63	June 80
2.34	1.33	28.07	71.92	Feb. 81
4.72	1.91	-	71.14	June 81
2.15	2.39	-	57.72	Feb. 81
3.04	0.94	-	58.30	Jan. 81
2.75	5.45	-	66.73	July 81
3.05	1.89	-	27.57	Jan. 81
1.53	1.17	-	37.67	Sept. 80

Main Table: continued

	1 Insurance companies	2 Banks	3 Brokers	4 Self-managed pension funds
41. Wimpey	6.62	11.29	0.59	7.10
42. ICL	23.27	18.39	1.70	17.93
43. Reed International	27.10	12.77	1.23	12.35
44. Metal Box	25.32	9.60	1.87	14.38
45. Reckitt & Colman	23.93	7.88	2.56	11.03
46. Dalgety	12.38	10.14	1.87	5.81
47. British Electric Traction	17.36	8.44	3.00	7.52
48. Rowntree Mackintosh	26.78	15.76	2.53	16.24
49. Hanson Trust	11.02	6.34	0.30	5.61
50. Northern Foods	17.85	14.96	0.89	10.08

Main Table: continued

5 Self-managed investment & unit trusts & other managers	6 Other corporate & financial bodies	7 Other major external interest	8 Total shares accounted for	9 Date of share register
2.26	-	49.9	77.76	July 80
5.60	4.54	-	71.43	Feb. 81
4.85	1.02	-	59.32	Jan. 81
1.42	1.56	-	54.16	March 81
1.06	4.98	-	51.44	June 80
9.15	3.42	-	42.77	May 81
3.17	2.08	-	41.57	March 81
0.89	3.37	12.1	77.67	July 81
3.22	0.48	-	26.97	Jan. 80
2.01	0.25	-	46.04	March 80

12. Wimpey - Grove Charity Management.
13. Rowntree - Rowntree Trusts.

Supplementary Information

Section 27 Enquiries

GKN
Beecham
IC Gas
De La Rue
Boots
ICL
Rank
Consolidated Gold Fields
BTR
BAT
Imperial Group
Bowater
Lonrho
Unigate
Redland
Dowty
Tricentrol
Distillers
Allied Breweries
Associated Dairies
Racal
LASMO
Burmah
Charter Consolidated
Sears
Rowntree
Hanson Trust

I visited 20 out of these 27. The ones I left out only did a S.27 enquiry on one occasion and/or did it years ago. The seven are Boots, Unigate, Redland, Dowty, Distillers, Ass. Dairies, Sears. In addition the following companies have used Section 27, and their registers were also used in the research:

BPC
Petrocon

Marshall Cavendish
Dunlop
Anderson Strathclyde

Chapter Eight

BANK LENDING AND THE CONTROL OF INDUSTRY: AN EMPIRICAL STUDY

Jerry Coakley

> To use a military analogy the banks in their traditional role as providers of short-term finance might be regarded as the frontline infantry troops in the contact between financiers and industrialists, whilst the investment institutions are the heavy artillery.

This opinion articulated in 1982 by Sir Arthur Knight, former Financial Director and Chairman of Courtaulds is characteristic of the view that banks play second fiddle to the investment institutions (insurance companies and pension funds) in their role as suppliers of finance to industry. As a result one might expect the major investment institutions, if not the banks, to exercise some control over industry. Such a view, however, is at odds with most of the literature on the theory of the firm.

The purpose of this chapter is to investigate the hypothesis that banks can and do exert control over industry as a consequence of an emerging banks-industry nexus. Following a brief discussion of the theoretical and empirical background the results of a sample survey of large engineering companies are presented. In a final section the implications of the findings are related to the theory of the firm literature.

Background to the Survey

This section summarises the views on the role of financial institutions vis-a-vis industry implied by the neo-classical and managerial theories of the firm and some of their critics. It also reports on developments in the UK corporate finance market in the 1970s and on the related growth of finance departments within large corporations. These latter developments provide the justification for the nature of our survey.

In the pure neo-classical theory of the firm the capitalist entrepreneur owns the assets of the firm and thus is believed to exert complete control over the destiny of the firm subject to the technological constraints of production. The managerial theories of the firm take as their starting point the large joint stock corporation with its implicit separation between equity owners or rentiers and professional management. These theories conclude that management is only weakly constrained by the equity markets and that it pursues objectives such as growth maximisation which are at variance with the interests of the equity owners.

In brief then, both sets of theories deny that financial institutions exert any direct control over companies. And whilst the managerial theory does admit some influence for the stock market via the takeover mechanism it explicitly rules out any degree of control exercised by or through banks (Marris, 1964).

Given the documents on the institutional domination of the capital markets and of the existence of specific mechanisms for institutional intervention (Wilson Report and Appendices, 1980) it is perhaps not surprising that critiques of the orthodox theories have tended to focus on the control of equities. For example, Kotz (1978) has argued that in the United States banks now control firms through their control over the shareholdings of their trust departments and through credit relationships. In the United Kingdom, Minns (1980) has documented the control of substantial parts of total pension fund investment assets (including equities) by merchant banks. Moreover he demonstrates that control of pension funds' equities by merchant banks is substantially more concentated than their ownership by the pension funds might suggest.

Echoes of these empirical studies are found within recent developments in the theory of the firm literature. Here Stiglitz's (1985) exposition of the notion of bank control over firms is particularly interesting since it is derived from a modified neo-classical stance. Stiglitz argues that the control mechanisms of financial markets have failed. This has the dual implication that shareholders do not

Table 8.1: Companies Sources of Funds 1963-82

£ billion	Total funds	Internal funds Total	Internal funds % of Total funds	External funds	Bank total	Borrowing % of external fund
1963	3.4	2.4	70.6	1.0	0.5	50.0
1964	4.2	2.8	66.7	1.4	0.8	57.1
1965	3.7	2.7	73.0	1.0	0.5	50.0
1966	3.4	2.3	67.6	1.4	0.2	14.3
1967	3.6	2.6	72.2	1.0	0.3	30.0
1968	4.5	2.9	64.4	1.6	0.6	37.5
1969	3.1	3.4	66.7	1.7	0.7	41.2
1970	5.2	3.1	59.6	2.1	1.1	52.4
1971	6.0	4.1	68.3	1.9	0.7	36.8
1972	9.3	5.0	53.8	4.3	3.0	69.8
1973	12.8	6.2	48.4	6.6	4.8	72.7
1974	12.3	4.6	37.4	7.7	4.1	53.2
1975	10.0	5.6	56.0	4.4	0.5	11.4
1976	13.6	7.8	57.4	5.8	2.8	48.3
1977	17.5	12.0	68.6	5.5	2.7	49.1
1978	21.7	16.2	74.7	5.5	3.0	54.5
1979	25.9	17.5	67.6	8.4	4.8	57.1
1980	24.3	13.7	56.4	10.7	7.2	67.3
1981	27.3	15.5	56.8	11.8	7.1	60.2
1982	24.2	13.4	55.4	10.8	7.3	67.6

Source: Bank of England Quarterly Bulletin.

control large corporations nor does management maximise stock market value. However to the extent that any control over corporations is exerted Stiglitz maintains that it is exercised by the banks or lenders rather than by the equity owners. It will be seen that the findings of our survey point to a similar conclusion from a different angle.

Another but distinct aspect of the background to the survey was developments within the corporate finance market in the financing of industry. Here the picture of British companies being self-financing had to be modified since the relationship between the relative shares of internal and external funds had shifted somewhat. Between 1963 and 1969 internal funds accounted for an average of 68.7 per cent of total new funds but during the 1970-82 period their contribution had shrunk to 58.5 per cent (see Table 8.1). At first glance this does not appear to signal a dramatic shift in sources of funds. The important point however is that the ratio between new internal and external funds diminished from a mean of 2.2 in the 1963-9 period to a mean of only 1.4 in the 1970-82 period.

Within this general shift towards external funding other changes were occurring. First bank borrowing as a proportion of external funds had increased from 40 per cent in the 1963-9 period to 53.7 per cent in the 1970-80 period (see Table 8.1). This was not surprising given the temporary demise of the UK corporate bond market as a source of company finance since the early 1970s and its replacement by bank borrowing (loan finance). Second, the nature of borrowing was itself being transformed from predominantly the short-term overdraft variety to comprise a mix including a growing proportion of medium-term borrowing. The latter is defined as borrowing contractually available for periods of one year and more.

The enhanced role of banks as the major source of finance for industry was paralleled by a related development within large corporations. We refer to the emergence of centralised finance departments at head office level and within them to the establishment of the treasury division or function. These developments have been documented by a survey of some 113 companies undertaken by the Association of Corporate Treasurers, an organisation which has mushroomed to a membership of some 800 in the space of just four years. Just over 50 per cent of the respondent companies had treasury divisions, over half of which had been established only since 1975. The treasury divisions were found to have four core areas of responsibility, borrowing, banking, investment of surplus cash and currency management. The typical division was small consisting of five or less non-clerical staff and had discretion over cash management and short-term borrowing.

To understand these developments it may prove helpful to outline the potential elements of a centralised finance department within large British companies:

Finance Director

Financial Controller

Treasury Division   Accounting Division

Evidently a number of permutations of these elements is possible with only the largest companies exhibiting a developed division of labour. However within the evolving division of labour our interest lay in the development of the non-treasury division of those non-accounting functions of the finance department involving relationships with banks since we wished to test the hypothesis of an emerging banks-industry nexus. For convenience we shall refer to the non-accounting function of the finance department as the treasury function.

This then was the background against which it was decided to undertake a survey of the corporate treasures of engineering firms further to investigate the links between them and their creditor banks. To our knowledge no other systematic investigation of these links had been undertaken.

The Structure of the Sample

The sample comprised the largest non-electrical engineering companies included in the 1981 Times 1000 list of top British companies controlling for location in two contrasting regions - Greater London and the West Midlands (see Annexe 1). Its focus therefore was on mechanical engineering as opposed to the modern electronics oriented companies in the electrical engineering sector. Mechanical engineering here is broadly defined to include not only SIC (standard industrial classification) order VII but also SIC VI (metal manufacture) and SIC XII (metal goods not elsewhere specified). Although all the sample companies had substantial mechanical engineering interests the range of their activities spilled over the boundaries of the traditional engineering industry into industries like consumer durables and even beyond the pale of the manufacturing sector into the services sector. In its 1980 Annual Report, for example GKN the leviathan of British engineering and indeed of British manufacturing listed three general thrusts to its programme for strategic change and development. The first two concerned the manufacture of technologically oriented products of high added-value and a focus on world rather than on national markets. The third may shake some people's preconceptions about the objectives of a manufacturing conglomerate:

> to increase substantially the Group's involvement in the services sector both in wholesale and industrial distribution and in a variety of problem-solving services to industry, commerce, construction and the community at large (GKN, (1980), Annual Report, p.3).

The engineering industry was selected as the basis for the sample since it was commonly recognised as a traditional industry confronting relatively acute structural adjustment problems by the late 1970s. These adjustment problems were brought to a head by the deepening of the recession from the second half of 1979 onwards and by the general inability of many companies successfully to compete internationally without undertaking substantial restructuring and diversification. Such companies then faced the dilemma of having to incur restructuring costs precisely at the stage in the cycle when their cash flow or retained profits were weakest. These companies frequently found that bank borrowing was the one readily available source of external financing and that banks were prepared to advance the finance only subject to detailed and sometimes onerous financial conditions.

These detailed conditions generally attached to medium term rather than short-term bank borrowing and monitoring them meant that banks were forced to alter their erstwhile attitude of allowing overdraft finance to look after itself save for the ritual annual meeting with the finance director to confirm or arrange new overdraft limits for the next financial year. Moreover the increased proportion of instances of non-compliance with loan conditions had swollen the ranks of companies in banks' so-called 'intensive care units' and had nudged banks and the finance departments of such companies into a closer relationship in an effort to protect their joint interests.

The total number of engineering companies in the sample was 48. A total of 36 agreed to participation in the survey yielding a sampling proportion of 75 per cent. Interviews were conducted with the member of the finance department directly responsible for the treasury function. In the larger companies this was the corporate treasurer or the financial controller whilst in the medium-sized companies the finance director had responsibility for all finance department functions. The interviews took place in 1981 and 1982. The mean duration of interviews was one and a half hours and a high level of cooperation was achieved. The results of the interviews together with the companies' annual reports provide the source of the information in the following paragraphs.

The turnover of the sample companies as measured by sales revenue for the 1980 financial year yielded an average of £282 million. The range of turnover varied from the £1923 million of GKN on the one hand (number 20 in the 1981 Times 1000) to the £31 million of Deritend Stamping on the other (number 981 in the 1981 Times 1000). Not all of this turnover was generated within the United Kingdom. Some was contributed by the companies' overseas subsidiaries and associate companies since all but one of the sample companies had overseas representation. Four of the 48 sample companies consisted of the UK operations of parent companies based in the United States or Canada whilst the remainder were British. During the course of the study three of the sample companies were the subject of successful takeover bids whilst another, Stone-Platt Industries, was placed in receivership to become the largest international casualty of the 1980s recession.

NATURE OF THE TREASURY FUNCTION

The survey indicated that a total of 16 out of 36 survey companies had separate treasury divisions supervised by a group treasurer. The size of these divisions varied considerably from just one (the modal size) in the generally smaller companies to as many as 18 in the larger companies. In a further eight survey companies the financial controller combined both accounting and treasury functions as part of his responsibilities whilst in the remaining 12 survey companies the finance director subsumed the treasury function as part of his overall finance department responsibilities.

The majority (23) of survey companies operated without explicit internal treasury objectives. But just over one in three of the companies pursued an internal capital gearing objective and one in seven operated with an internal objective for interest cover. The capital gearing objective took two forms split fairly evenly as between survey companies. One was an upper limit on the company's capital gearing ratio. This limit ranged from a debt/equity ratio of 60 per cent to a ratio of 100 per cent. The other form which the capital gearing objective assumed was that of a long-term target. In this context companies pursued debt/equity targets ranging from $33\frac{1}{3}$ per cent to 50 per cent. The modal interest cover objective was 3:1 although it ranged from 2:1 to 4:1. In addition all the survey companies pursued some type of rate of return on assets objective but we do not define this as a treasury specific objective.

It will be seen in the following pages that all the principal treasury functions directly or indirectly entail relationships with banks. The survey revealed the principal treasury functions to be bank relationships, liquidity management and credit management. All of these involve banks (indirectly in the case of liquidity management) and are also related in other ways. For instance there is an obvious connection and trade-off between the amount of a company's liquid balances and the extent of its borrowings.

Bank Relationships

One of the characteristics of the sample companies was the increasing density of their bank relationships. Although UK companies in contrast with American companies cannot boast of a tradition of multibank relationships, the evidence from the survey suggests that this has begun to change even if a small proportion of companies, including some of the medium-sized ones, still rely largely or exclusively on the services of one or two of the clearing banks. Before presenting the evidence on bank relationships, it needs to be stressed that all the survey companies had to rely on one or more of the London clearing banks for cheque clearing and domestic money transmission services and so one clearing bank invariably featured as (one of) the lead or major banks of all companies.

This situation may change in the near future since the clearers' monopoly over cheque-clearing services has been challenged by an American bank, Citibank, and by Standard Chartered Bank. They have become members of Bankers Automated Clearing Services (BACS), the cheque-clearing company jointly owned by the London clearing banks. The implication for bank-industry relationships in the UK is that companies will no longer be tied exclusively to the London clearing banks for cheque clearing. Precisely because of their exclusion from cheque-clearing and domestic money transmission services foreign banks have been forced to compete for companies' other banking business.

As we point out elsewhere the tactic generally adopted by American banks has been to concentrate their marketing efforts on particular sectors of industry represented in the upper echelons of the Times 1000 top British companies and this focus is supported by the evidence presented below. For all survey companies the mean number of relationships with banks in the UK was seven (rounded to the nearest whole number) bearing out the hypothesis that British companies have become multi-banked. Nonetheless the mean conceals a considerable degree of variation since 20 per cent of survey companies had two or less bank relationships on one hand whilst some of the larger companies had as many as 30 relationships. An average of three out of seven UK bank relationships were with the clearing banks whilst virtually all the others involved overseas banks among which American banks clearly predominated.

The density of worldwide banking relationships was even more impressive averaging some 31 relationships. Here again the range was even greater extending from two to as many as 200. This is a reflection of the multinational nature of the largest engineering companies' activities.

Liquidity Management

Treasury responsibility for the management of liquid assets was not surprising given that the sample companies could boast of mean liquid assets of £88 million at the end of the 1980 financial year. Liquid assets are defined to comprise two components. On one hand they consist of cash or transactions balances employed by companies in the normal course of their business. On the other, they include liquid short-term investments or surplus cash balances which companies may accumulate from time to time. No equivalent of ICI's £1.3 billion cash mountain was found within the ranks of the sample companies though in general engineering companies with contracting interests did hold higher than average liquid assets reflecting in part prepayments for contracts in progress.

All of the survey companies operated a system of centralised cash balances which summarised companies' net cash position of the previous day with their bank(s) and the mean length of operation of such a system was some 10.5 years. Here the history was one of large companies centralising their cash balances in the late 1960s and of smaller companies following suit in the course of the 1970s. In a number of cases the impetus towards cash centralisation was provided by the tightening of financial management resulting from the company experiencing financial difficulties. Cash centralisation was seen to give rise to surplus balances over and above the (non-interest paying) compensating balances which companies may have agreed with their principal clearing bankers. These funds required investment and the survey indicated that treasurers generally employed money brokers to obtain the highest return on such balances.

Since the date of the survey the large American banks and some of the clearers have stepped up competition for the provision of corporate cash management services to companies. This provides further evidence of the growing importance of the liquidity management function for both banks and companies.

Credit Management

As the external borrowings of UK companies increased during the 1970s so the most important function of the treasury division became the management of such borrowing. As mentioned in the introduction the increased level of external borrowing was only one new aspect of company financing during the 1970s. Equally if not more important was the growing complexity of borrowings as compared with the 1960s when they virtually totally comprised overdrafts and bonds. By the late 1970s treasury divisions had to evaluate the relative merits of competing types of finance such as short-term versus medium-term borrowings, of sterling versus foreign currency facilities and of overdraft versus money market or acceptance credit short-term facilities.

The sample engineering companies had mean external borrowings of £38.7 million outstanding at the end of their 1980 financial years of which bonds accounted for an average of 22 per cent and bank borrowings for the remaining 78 per cent. The preponderance of bank borrowings is explained by the inactivity of the bond market during the latter half of the 1970s. For the survey companies the outstanding bonds assumed the form of loan stock (which essentially is an unsecured type of bond) or debentures. The latter are bonds which are secured on the assets of the company or its subsidiaries or are conditionally guaranteed as to interest and principal payments by the parent company.

The conditions attaching to loan finance generally were formalised as covenants in trust deeds held by the trusts to the bond issue (which invariably was an insurance company). Some of these covenants did restrict companies' borrowings but only borrowings on the bond market and so did not act as a material constraint on companies at the time of the survey. For this reason and because of the declining importance of bond finance we do not discuss bond finance further in this chapter. Rather we focus on bank borrowing.

CHANGING CHARACTER OF BANK LOANS

Of the average of £30.2 million bank loans outstanding at the close of the 1980 financial year an impressive 46.6 per cent consisted of medium-term loans (that is loans contractually available for periods of twelve months or more) with short-term borrowings making up the remaining 53.4 per cent. Accordingly, we may conclude that the picture of British engineering companies relying exclusively on short-term overdraft financing is now dated even if the average conceals some large divergences.

For example seven of the generally smaller companies relied exclusively on short-term financing whilst many of the larger companies held an above average proportion of their outstanding bank borrowings in medium-term loans. This offers some support for the hypothesis that banks (overseas and British) compete most vigorously for the loan business of the largest companies whilst the clearing banks still enjoy a virtual monopoly over the financing of smaller companies. As a corollary smaller companies are locked into relationships with the clearing banks. It emerged from the survey that the major reason for smaller companies not availing themselves of this category of finance was the cost and conditionality of medium-term borrowings which we now discuss.

The cost of borrowing is seen by neo-classical economists as the principal factor influencing companies' decisions on the level of their borrowing or their capital gearing. The survey revealed a major division between overdraft and committed money market facilities in terms of the cost of borrowing. On one hand the cost of overdraft finance was standard for all the survey companies being fixed at 1 per cent over base rate. The explanation for this uniformity of cost lies in the fact that overdraft finance is relatively risk-free being repayable on demand <u>in principle</u> even if in practice it is unusual for banks to accelerate a company's overdrafts except in cases of potential receivership. Money market facilities (excluding lines on short-term advances) by contrast are generally contractually available for fixed periods of three months or more and so incorporate a risk premium in their cost that generally varies with the size of the company.

For medium-term facilities the range of interest rate costs varied from 3/8 per cent over the London Inter Bank Offer Rate (LIBOR or the cost of deposits to banks) for the larger companies to as much as $1\frac{3}{4}$ per cent over LIBOR for the smaller companies. Clearly these levels of interest rates as compared with 1 per cent over base rate do represent a significant cost factor for smaller companies which acted as a deterrent against medium-term borrowing. However cost was not the only deterrent against medium-term borrowings for the survey indicated that the conditions inscribed in medium-term loan agreements represented an even greater disincentive against such borrowings.

Of all the characteristics of medium-term bank loans the question of conditionality has aroused greatest controversy particularly, but not only, when breach of such conditions has led to a bank placing a company in receivership. The controversy surrounding the receivership of one of the sample companies - Stone Platt Industries - is perhaps the best publicised but, here we emphasise that disagreement and conflict between banks and industry is not confined to receivership. The latter may be regarded as merely a manifestation of a more fundamental conflict of interest between banks and companies over the drafting and formulation of the details of loan agreements.

The survey of engineering companies indicated that the switch from short-term overdraft to medium-term financing was accompanied by a shift in the nature of loan agreements. To appreciate this we first outline the typical arrangements prevailing for overdraft finance until the late 1970s. Prior to the growth of medium-term financing after 1975 company bank borrowings consisted almost exclusively of overdraft finance. These overdrafts were not generally subject to the type of detailed loan agreements today associated with medium-term finance. Instead they were advanced subject to only one condition in that they generally were secured on the <u>securable</u> assets of all but the largest companies. We stress the concept of securable assets since not all of a company's assets could legally be captured within the security instruments available to the banks; in particular it is only since 1978 that a company's debtors (which generally comprise a large proportion of gross current assets) have been legally recognised as falling within the remit of security agreements.

Accordingly the conflict or bargaining process over loans between banks and companies prior to 1975 revolved around the nature and scope of the security offered as collateral for loans. Security instruments included fixed charges or mortgages over a company's fixed assets and floating charges over some elements of its current assets such as stocks and work-in-progress and liquid assets. After 1978 a company's overdrafts could be secured by both types of charges since the floating charge additionally offered the benefit of conferring on banks (or other creditors) the unique power of placing a company in receivership.

The survey indicated that two interrelated factors were responsible for the demise of security instruments attaching to banks' loans since at the end of 1980 only 9.8 per cent of survey companies' bank borrowing was secured. The first reason was the competition offered by American banks in that they were prepared to lend on an unsecured basis to large companies. Second the increasing share of medium-term loans prompted a growing elaboration of the conditionality terms of loan agreements which required banks to employ more systematic monitoring procedures.

Previously commercial banks' monitoring of the financial performance of companies remained minimal so long as the agreed upper limits on (secured) overdraft facilities were not exceeded. Under this approach to lending the banks relied on the value of liquidated assets as the ultimate source of repayment for loans.

It was for this reason that the American banks in their evidence to the Wilson Committee described the clearing banks' approach to the lending as the 'liquidation' or 'gone concern' approach. The accuracy of this description had been eroded by the time of the survey since the clearing banks had begun to alter their erstwhile hands-off approach to industry. By 1981 clearing banks were, like the American banks, advancing medium-term loans subject to detailed loan agreement conditions. Let us now examine the nature of medium-term loans obtained by the survey engineering companies.

Medium-term Loans

Perhaps the most striking factor about the growth of medium-term loans among the sample companies is that 1969 was the first year in which any engineering company raised a medium-term loan and that generally it was not the largest companies which were the leaders in raising medium-term loans. The explanation for the latter is provided by the fact that the largest companies could avail themselves of bond market finance until the early 1970s.

The survey indicated that the mean number of years since companies raised their first medium-term loan was 5.3 years. Some twelve of the sample companies raised their first medium-term loan from one of the clearing banks, seven from American banks, six from merchant and eleven from other sources. This provides another indication that the clearers have begun to alter their approach to lending to industry even if this change occurred only in the late 1970s. In three quarters of the cases where they supplied companies with their first medium-term loan they did so in 1978 or later.

Let us now examine what the survey revealed about the detailed conditions contained in medium-term loan agreements. All but two of the survey companies with medium-term loans had loan agreements which contained a capital gearing restriction. This basically had the effect of restricting their net outstanding borrowings. The most common form of this capital gearing condition was the ratio of net borrowings to net worth. The modal value of this condition was 1:1 which meant that if a company's net borrowings exceeded its net worth it would constitute an event of default and enable the bank to call in its loans. The mean value for the capital gearing ratio was somewhat higher at $1\frac{1}{4}$:1. In the case of twelve out of the company loan agreements containing a capital gearing ratio another form of gearing restriction was also included. This was the minimum net worth clause which stipulated a lower bound (in absolute terms) for a company's net worth. The mean value of this bound expressed as a percentage of companies' net worth at the end of the 1980 financial year was 83 per cent.

Only two companies had loan agreements which did not contain a capital gearing restriction. One large company had no gearing restrictions whatsoever but instead had a no material adverse change clause inserted in its loan agreements. This rather vague clause protects banks against major changes in a company's financial position and was included in a total of three survey company loan agreements. The no material adverse change clause was also included in the loan agreements of the other company which was not subject to a capital gearing restriction. This latter company managed to exclude all the usual ratio covenants from its loan agreements but upper limits on the borrowings of its UK subsidiaries were inscribed in its loan agreements.

Only a small proportion (17 per cent) of the company loan agreements contained an interest cover clause which specifies a limit on the relationship between pre-tax income and net interest payments. In general, companies were opposed to the inclusion of this ratio in agreements since its two components are only partially susceptible to company control. For example, companies are not able to exercise such influence over the level of LIBOR and many external factors such as the general level of aggregate demand impinge on the ability of companies to determine the level of their income. The mean level of the interest cover (or income gearing) ratio included in the sample was $2\frac{1}{4}$:1.

Apart from capital and income gearing restrictions the other most common type of ratio covenant disclosed by the survey was liquidity ratios. All except two company loan agreements contained some type of liquidity ratio. Among those agreements all except four included a current ratio clause specifying a relationship between current assets and liabilities whose mean lower value was 1.2:1. The other types of ratio clauses to be included were the working capital ratio with a mean value of 1.3:1, the quick ratio (liquid assets to current liabilities), a ratio of debtors to creditors and of stocks and work-in-progress to net current assets.

The remaining four major types of clauses were standard in all the company loan agreements. Two of these were designed to protect the banks' interests in the absence of any specific provision for security and these are the alienation of assets clause and the negative pledge clause. The former clause prohibits companies from disposing of substantial assets or subsidiaries without the express agreement of the banks where a range of 15-20 per cent of total net worth was deemed to be substantial.

The negative pledge clause prevents companies from granting security on any further borrowings with the object of protecting the interests of existing unsecured lenders. Exceptions to the negative pledge clause were standard; the two modal types being security on the assets of newly acquired subsidiaries and security on the assets of overseas subsidiaries. Although as mentioned the proportion of survey company borrowing covered by explicit security instruments is now very small a rather larger proportion of company borrowings is subject to parent company guarantees or cross-guarantees which may be viewed as a weaker form of security.

The perhaps most controversial clause included in all the survey company loan agreements was the cross-default clause. This provides that a default on any one of a company's loan agreements effectively triggers off a default on all of its loan agreements. A total of six companies managed to negotiate the exclusion of some or all of their overseas subsidiaries' borrowings from this clause. The object of this clause is to protect the interests of banks as a whole by preventing individual banks from adopting a policy of 'cut and run' when companies get into financial difficulties. The disadvantage to companies is that this clause forces them to negotiate with all their creditor banks as a whole rather than with individual banks should they run into financial difficulties.

The final clause common to all loan agreements was the affirmative covenant which specifies that companies supply banks with copies of their interim and annual reports within stipulated time limits of the end of their financial half-year and financial year respectively. Of these the audited annual report is the most relevant from the viewpoint of banks monitoring the ratio and other covenants of their loan agreements. The survey disclosed that this monitoring of published reports is invariably supplemented by a minimum of one visit by bankers to the company, generally just prior to the publication of the annual reports.

The monitoring of the covenants of medium-term loan agreements described above means that banks take a closer interest than hitherto in the financial performance of companies. It also means that a company's financial performance is to a greater or lesser degree influenced by the knowledge that it must conform to and fall within the limits imposed by loan agreement covenants. This is tangible evidence of the fact that banks do exert a measure of influence over the performance of companies. This influence is at least on a par with the takeover threat since the consequence for management is the same in both instances.

THEORY OF THE FIRM IMPLICATION

What do these findings imply about the relationship between banks and industry and more specifically about the influence of banks over industry? Does it remain valid within the theory of firm context to dismiss the influence of banks over industry as imperceptible? Here it will be helpful to distinguish between two opposing sets of influences.

On one hand the increased sophistication of the money markets in terms of both loans and deposits has provided a major impetus to the development of a treasury division within engineering companies. This in turn has heralded an increasing centralisation of purely financial activities within companies in areas such as cash and liquidity management and in the negotiation of the terms and conditions of loan agreements. The form of loan agreements has been especially important in this trend towards centralisation for it makes the head office of the company legally responsible for the financial performance of the group as a whole: hence the logic of centralising the treasury function within head office.

The logical next step in the development of the treasury function is that companies establish an in-house bank encompassing its treasury function. Although none of the engineering companies has done so a number of large multinational companies such as British Petroleum has set up a banking subsidiary. The implication of a developed treasury function or an in-house bank is to lessen the degree of influence of banks over companies.

The elaboration of medium-term loan agreements and the monitoring of their financial and other covenants by banks represents a second but opposing set of influences. In normal circumstances one may view the contents of such agreements as imposing a broad financial discipline on companies. As such they may be seen as exerting an indirect influence on the direction of strategic corporate decision-making which we believe is as significant as (though distinct from) that exercised by the Stock Exchange. However so long as a company remains profitable banks' involvement with it remains at this arms-length legal level. This is some distance from banks' traditional hands-off attitude to industry in Britain but equally it is also some distance from the banks-industry nexus in countries like West Germany and Japan.

However, the enhanced role of medium-term and other bank loans in the external financing of industry does provide for potentially closer relationships between banks and selected parts of industry. This is the case when companies run into financial difficulties and have to engage in a process of financial restructuring in conjunction with their major bankers and shareholders. In these circumstances (in which four of the survey companies found themselves) banks have become very closely involved with the management of companies. They generally have been allowed access to monthly management accounts, have taken substantial (quasi) equity stakes in companies and have even taken seats on the board of directors. However, such financial restructurings are limited in number and while they create an important precedent they cannot be taken as heralding a totally new set of relationships between banks and industry in the UK.

These two sets of influences work in opposite directions with regard to the degree of control banks might exert over industry. On one hand the development of a specialist treasury division at head office level has served to enhance the relatively autonomy of companies vis-a-vis banks. On the other the monitoring by banks of conditions attached to medium-term loan finance has imposed on external discipline on companies complementary to that exercised by the Stock Exchange.

In sum although the relationship between banks and industry has grown in complexity our results do not provide an indication for an emerging banks-industry nexus. The results also indicate that the influence of banks over industry cannot simply be dismissed as trivial. Rather the influence of banks has to be incorporated into any well-developed firm as the work of such diverse writers as Katz (1978) and Stiglitz (1985) demonstrates.

NOTE

The survey was carried out as part of a project funded by the Open University Research Committee. I am grateful to the Open University, and I thank Laurence Harris for comments.

ANNEXE 1: SAMPLE OF MECHANICAL ENGINEERING FIRMS

<u>Greater London</u>

Babcock
Davy Corporation
Hawker Siddley
Massey Ferguson
John Brown
Vickers
Chubb
M. Hall
Laird Group
600 Group
Staveley
Haden
Molins
RHP
Ingersoll Rand
Acrow
Butterfield Harvey
International Harvester
Expanded Metal
Smiths Industries
Mitchel Cotts
Delta Metal

<u>West Midlands</u>

GKN
Tube Investment
Associated Engineering
Glynwed
Birmid Qualcast
Duport
Hall Engineering
Serck
Ductile Steels
CMT
Folkes-Meto
APE
Barton
Redman Heenan
Wagon
Concentric
B. Priest
Mitchel Somers
McKechnie Brothers
F.H. Lloyd
Triplex
Deritend

Martonair
Otis
IMI
Blackwood Hodge

REFERENCES

Committee to Review the Functioning of Financial Institutions Report and Appendices, Cmnd. 7937, London, HMSO (the Wilson Report).

Katz, D.M. (1978) Bank Control of Large Corporations in the United States, Berkeley, University of California Press.

Marris, R. (1964) The Economic Theory of Managerial Capitalism, London, Macmillan.

Minns, R. (1980) Pension Funds and British Capitalism: The Ownership and Control of Large Shareholdings, London, Heinemann.

Stiglitz, J.E. (1985) Credit Markets and the Control of Capital, Journal of Money Credit and Banking, vol. 17, no. 2, pp.133-52.

Chapter Nine

AMERICAN BANKS' CREDIT TO UK INDUSTRY

Jerry Coakley

When in 1960 the Radcliffe Committee Report on the Working of the Monetary System was published it could only identify the presence of 26 foreign banks in the United Kingdom, six of which were American. The report distinguished these foreign banks from the 'British overseas banks'. The latter comprised those Commonwealth and international British banks (like Barclays DCO) whose operations focused on the Sterling Area, the trading bloc of countries centred on the United Kingdom and more specifically on the City of London. 1960 is also significant in that it was the year in which Chemical Bank of New York became the first American bank since 1938 to open a branch office proper in the City.

With hindsight one can see that Chemical's move heralded the beginning of what was subsequently to become a rush of American and other foreign banks into London. By the end of 1980 the number of foreign banks with a London branch office had leaped to 214, of which no less than 40 were American. In addition, a further 137 foreign banks had by then opened representative offices in London, whilst as many as 50 more could claim to be represented in London through a stake in consortium banks.

American banks were initially attracted to London to compete for the banking business of the 800 or so subsidiaries of American multinationals which, by 1961, had located in the United Kingdom (1) and thereafter by the burgeoning growth of the Euromarkets. Borrowing and lending Eurodollars in London enabled them to engage in lending with a freedom and at interest rates that at the time were denied them in New York dollar-based business.

By competing vigorously for these two types of banking business the American banks undermined the cosy monopoly of City banking business hitherto enjoyed by the London clearing and British overseas banks. Moreover, they gradually began to encroach on one of the traditional markets of the clearing banks, namely the corporate finance market. Within this market the nature of relationships between banks and corporations remains a largely unexplored topic. This chapter explores the relationships between large corporations in the UK and the largest American commercial banks. Conventionally, these largest banks are known as multinational banks (MNBs) and are distinguished from the smaller American regional banks.

Very little detailed information is available on American banks' corporate relationships in the United Kingdom. Kelly's (1977) study is of historical interest but its treatment of banking relationships is not systematic. The only directly relevant treatment of the subject was provided by the London trade association of American commercial banks (the American Banks Association of London or ABAL for short) in its evidence submitted to the Wilson Committee. (2) ABAL's analysis of the contrasting approaches of the American and clearing banks to credit analysis and banking relationships received short shrift from members of the committee. The committee implied that it had overstated the differences between the two sets of banks.

Given this paucity of information it appeared worthwhile to investigate further the approach to credit analysis adopted by American MNBs. The results of our investigation did point to contrasts between the American MNBs and the London clearing banks which were found to derive from the distinctive traditions of wholesale and retail banking (Coakley & Harris, 1983). They suggest that the system of banking prevalent in the United States conferred a comparative advantage on American MNBs in the field of wholesale banking which had expanded so enormously since the 1960s. This comparative advantage in wholesale banking gave American banks in London a headstart over the clearing banks whose traditional metier had been retail banking. It also helps to explain many of the peculiarities of the nature of American MNBs corporate relationships in the United Kingdom.

Survey and Sample Design

Unlike the case of securities which are publicly traded at known prices and under known conditions, bank loans are subject to private confidential contracts. Eliciting the details of these contracts is one of the major hurdles confronting any research on the nature of banks' operations in the credit markets and especially on corporate relationships. It is precisely for this reason that much banking research has concentrated on analysing the general trends indicated by published aggregate data. This chapter reports on one attempt to circumvent the confidentiality issue by means of a sample survey.

Against this background of confidentiality the survey technique deemed most appropriate to the circumstances was the interview survey technique. The merits of this technique were considered to be the ability to probe responses in more depth than a questionnaire survey would allow and the general belief that the interview technique offered the best possibilities of coming to terms with confidentiality issues.

The sample comprised the senior bank credit officers of US MNBs who were responsible for lending within the UK. The interviews were conducted in the first half of 1981 with officers employed at the vice-president level of management and above within their respective banks. The mean duration of the interviews was one and a half hours. A 100 per cent response rate to requests for interviews was achieved and a high level of cooperation was received. The credit officers had been appraised of the framework of the enquiry in an aide-memoire which had been dispatched prior to the actual interviews. The aide-memoire was employed to achieve a comprehensive coverage of relevant topics and to ensure comparability and consistency of response as between banks. Following each interview detailed notes were written up as a full record and were supplemented by published statistical material.

The sampling frame utilised was the list of 40 American commercial banks with full branch offices in London as published in the November 1980 issue of The Banker in its annual survey of 'Foreign Banks in London'. These are listed in descending order of size by total assets in Annexe 1. The overriding criteria in sample selection was the size of banks as measured by total assets controlling for east coast, mid-west and west coast head office location. The implication was that the sample comprised the largest 17 American commercial banks ranked by total assets and known as multinational banks (MNBs). Until 1983 the MNBs had enjoyed a privileged capital reserves status since their diversified asset portfolios were deemed to be less risky than those of other commercial banks. In mid-1983 the international debt impasse induced the American banking authorities to ask the multinational banks to comply with the general capital gearing requirement. (3)

A sample of 17 out of 40 American banks might suggest an overall sampling proportion of 42.5 per cent. But since our major concern was corporate banking relationships in the United Kingdom a more accurate index may be loans to such corporations which are not proportional to numbers of banks. Unfortunately disaggregated data on American banks' United Kingdom assets by individual bank is not available. Assuming that their United Kingdom assets are distributed pro rata to their global assets we find that our overall sample of banks was responsible for 86 per cent of the assets of the 40 American banks in London and that the top five banks alone accounted for 71 per cent.

But these figures are underestimates since the longer established London branches of the larger banks account for a disproportionately high fraction of their global assets as compared with the London branches of the smaller banks. On this basis we estimate that our overall sample was responsible for approximately 95 per cent of American bank lending to the United Kingdom private sector corporations. This was the reason why our survey focused on the MNBs.

The Corporate Finance Market

To appreciate the development of relationships between US MNBs and the UK corporate sector, it will be necessary to place these relationships within the context of the corporate finance market. The latter is taken to refer to the financing of those corporations and their subsidiary or associate companies which are located within the United Kingdom. In other words, it embraces both British and overseas companies. It will become apparent that the US MNBs have enjoyed a long tradition of participation in this market.

It is now almost a century since Chase Manhattan's predecessor (Jarvis Conklin Trust Company) became the first foreign bank to establish in the City in 1887. The mean

Table 9.1: American Banks' Lending in the United Kingdom

<table>
<tr><th rowspan="2">End year</th><th rowspan="2">Total UK assets (1)
(£ million)</th><th colspan="2">Advances to UK private sector (2)</th><th rowspan="2">(2) as % of (1)</th></tr>
<tr><th>Sterling</th><th>Foreign currency</th></tr>
<tr><td>1951</td><td>97.9</td><td colspan="2">16.0</td><td>16.3</td></tr>
<tr><td>1955</td><td>134.5</td><td colspan="2">29.5</td><td>21.9</td></tr>
<tr><td>1960</td><td>390.7</td><td colspan="2">78.0</td><td>20.0</td></tr>
<tr><td>1965</td><td>1435.9</td><td>240.2</td><td>73.9</td><td>21.9</td></tr>
<tr><td>1970</td><td>11,579.0</td><td>369.0</td><td>285.0</td><td>5.6</td></tr>
<tr><td>1975</td><td>37,185.0</td><td>1965.0</td><td>1725.0</td><td>9.9</td></tr>
<tr><td>1980</td><td>59,964.0</td><td>4440.0</td><td>2361.0</td><td>11.3</td></tr>
<tr><td>1981</td><td>78,345.0</td><td>4084.0</td><td>5394.0</td><td>12.1</td></tr>
<tr><td>1982</td><td>95,139.0</td><td>3946.0</td><td>7201.0</td><td>11.7</td></tr>
<tr><td>1983</td><td>102,945.0</td><td>4314.0</td><td>7474.0</td><td>11.5</td></tr>
<tr><td>1984</td><td>116,250.0</td><td>5849.0</td><td>9957.0</td><td>13.6</td></tr>
</table>

Source: Bank of England Quarterly Bulletin.

length of establishment in the City by the top five MNBs was no less than 70 years in 1981 whilst that for the total sample of 17 MNBs was some 33.5 years. For all but two of the 17 MNBs London was their largest overseas unit in terms of total lending. It was the largest funding centre for all of them, reflecting London's pivotal role in enabling banks to raise deposits in the Euromarkets. Table 9.1 gives an historical record of all American banks' lending to the UK private sector in the post-war period. It will be evident from this table that lending to the UK private sector is not the major activity of American MNBs in London; their principal activity like that of other foreign banking groups is Eurobanking business. Nonetheless of all the identifiable foreign banking groups in London the share of American banks' lending to the UK private sector outstrips all others in both absolute and relative terms, an indication of their deep involvement with this sector. Moreover American banks' lending denominated in sterling consistently exceeded that denominated in foreign currency between 1965 and 1980. Since 1980 III aggregate sterling lending actually declined for a period while currency on Eurolending has increased sharply.

The banking operations of American MNBs in the UK are predominantly wholesale: of the total sample of 17, only one bank (Citibank) was identified as engaged in limited retail operations. The focus on wholesale banking is borne out by the paucity of banking units the MNBs have established in the United Kingdom. Twelve of the 17 MNBs have a London location only, whilst of the remaining five, one can boast of four offices outside London, another of three offices and the remaining three banks of two offices each outside the capital. And of these 13 offices outside London four were located in Scotland (Edinburgh) and one each in Wales (Cardiff) and Northern Ireland (Belfast).

Two reasons can be adduced for American MNB's wholesale banking focus in the United Kingdom. The first - that the United States has long enjoyed a history of unit banking which basically prohibited retail branch banking between and occasionally within states (the two Chicago banks in our sample fall within the unit bank jurisdiction of the State of Illinois). This unit bank structure had encouraged the development of wholesale banking with its characteristic interbank market for inter-state banking transactions. Secondly, in the post-war period the restrictions on domestic expansion and on interest rates furnished an important impetus for the internationalisation of American banks through the development of the Euromarkets.

The Euromarkets have since become associated with the emergence of a distinctively new type of banking which I have elsewhere described as Eurobanking which is wholesale banking par excellence (Coakley, 1984). In this respect, American banks' long experience of wholesale banking has afforded them a comparative advantage over some banking groups like the British clearing banks which, since the mid-nineteenth century, have been developing and consolidating a branch banking structure.

The wholesale banking focus of American MNBs has a number of implications for their approach to the corporate finance market. First, it has enabled these MNBs to follow existing corporate customers and markets to the UK at a relatively low cost in terms of both labour and capital (typically one City office). This has meant that their initial and obvious target corporate clients were the UK subsidiaries and associate companies of American parent multinationals and, in the case of the larger MNBs, the UK subsidiaries of their worldwide multinational customers. All the MNBs in the total sample had just targeted this segment of the UK corporate market after establishing in London. That this provided a ready market for the MNBs since the 1960s is evidenced by the 800 American multinational corporations that had established themselves in the UK by 1961. That is to say that meeting some of the UK banking requirements of their existing multinational customers offered all the American MNBs in our sample a ready entree into the UK corporate market though clearly the lists of multinational customers of the smaller MNBs could not hope to compete with those of the top five MNBs.

We have emphasised above that American MNBs can only offer a limited range of banking services to their UK corporate clients and this is a second implication of their focus on wholesale banking. Because of their generally limited branch networks it would prove difficult in principle for the American MNBs to compete with the London clearing banks for cheque-clearing services. (4) Interestingly, the clearing system monopoly was the only aspect of the financial system which the Wilson Committee seriously considered as a candidate for nationalisation. Direct access to the clearing system is a very significant advantage which the clearers enjoy over all foreign MNBs (except two at present) for all UK corporations require ongoing clearing facilities. Given that American banks are forced to compete for other non-clearing corporate banking services the areas in which they can most vigorously compete are those of international and specialist banking. Here we need to distinguish the top five American MNBs which can offer corporations the service of lead international banks and a range of specialist banking and the other sample MNBs which can only supply more limited and/or specialised banking services.

So, in addition to servicing their existing multinational customers the American MNBs have only begun to market their services to the UK indigenous corporate sector relatively recently. Indeed, with the exception of two large MNBs which both entered this segment of the corporate market in 1965 the remaining sample MNBs encouraged by Competition and Credit Control in 1971 tapped this market at various stages during the 1970s. Three criteria were employed in targeting particular segments of this market. The overriding criterion employed by the MNBs in all cases was the size of corporations as measured by sales turnover in the Times 1000. For the top five MNBs competition was extremely keen for the lead international bank position to the top 250 companies (in the Times 1000) whilst all the sample banks competed for business among all or a segment of the top 500 companies whilst the opportunities for banking business below the top 500 divide were limited except for the case of three smaller MNBs.

A second criterion identified by the MNBs was the potential for international banking business generally defined in terms of exports or overseas sales comprising a minimum of 30 per cent of turnover. The international and size criteria are correlated since most of the top 250 companies are internationalised. The final criterion employed by the MNBs was industry specialisation. That is, the American MNBs unlike the British clearing banks did not direct their marketing efforts at all sectors of the UK corporate market but rather, on the basis of both the specialisms of their parent banks and their analysis of market potential in the UK, targeted specific sectors.

The modal sectors targeted in order of importance included commodities, energy (North Sea oil and gas), finance houses, insurance, real estate, shipping and chemicals. These specialisations are, with the exception of North Sea oil and gas and chemicals, closely bound up with the City of London's international trading and financial activities which is not so surprising given the MNBs' location there. In addition to these sector specialisations, the American MNBs also offer specialist financial services such as foreign exchange services, acceptance credit facilities, correspondent banking services and securities trading services like American depository receipts. Moreover, the American MNBs were able to offer UK-based corporations a range of new loan finance or credit facilities which their domestic competitors - the clearing banks - were not supplying at the time.

Loan Finance Facilities

Traditionally, the clearing banks had developed a focus on overdraft facilities as the major form of loan finance. Although technically such facilities could be recalled on demand, in practice the facilities frequently were rolled-over or extended thus constituting what is called hard-core overdraft facilities. This provided an informal if somewhat unsatisfactory means for extending the maturity of what were in essence short-term facilities. To compete with the overdraft American MNBs from the late 1960s began to offer a line for short-term advances which is the main short-term Eurocurrency facility. It is normally available for periods of three months upwards and is funded on the interbank market. Its advantage over overdrafts is the ability to fix an interest rate over the term of the facility. The line for short-term advances was the most important component of the MNBs' short-term loan facilities which in aggregate accounted for some 53.3 per cent of all their outstanding facilities at the end of 1980.

However, American MNBs' major contribution to extending the range of loan finance facilities has been the promotion of medium-term facilities by which we mean facilities contractually available for a term of one year or more. The main form these have assumed has been the revolving commitment and fixed term facilities. The former is simply an extension of the short-term line while the latter, as the name implies, is available for a fixed period of time. Both types of term facility are available subject to conditions for periods of up to seven years or more and are funded from the wholesale interbank markets. The American MNBs interviewed defined some 46.7 per cent of their outstanding facilities as medium term. This contrasts with our estimate of 20-25 per cent for the clearing banks' medium-term sterling facilities to the corporate sector. (5) In brief, the American MNBs' corporate loan facilities had a more than 2:1 chance of being medium term in nature as compared with the clearing banks' corporate advances. One may wonder whether this emphasis on medium term rather than short-term loan facilities implies a different approach to credit analysis by the American MNBs and this indeed turns out to be the case.

Approaches to Credit Analysis

In this section, our concern lies with the manner in which the American MNBs approach the question of the evaluation of corporate clients' creditworthiness and whether, as the American Bank Association in London claimed in its written evidence to the Wilson Committee, the American approach contrasts sharply with that of the clearing banks. Before we examine credit analysis it will be necessary to point to some organisational differences. One such difference in the approach to bank relationships is American MNBs' use of the account executive concept. That entails a single individual being responsible for a limited number of clients (or a single client in the case of the largest corporations). The account executive is generally the clients' initial point of contact for any of the bank's services including that of its subsidiaries. Another important point about account executives is the extent of their lending discretion. Although this varies as between American MNBs, for banks comparable in size to the clearers the discretionary limits of account executives exceeded those of the regional managers of the most decentralised clearing bank. The clearers are responding to this competition by centralising to a greater or lesser degree responsibility for the accounts of their largest corporate clients. That is, regional and head office rather than local managers are increasingly assuming responsibility for these accounts.

A further difference in the American MNBs' approach was the division of labour between account executives and credit officers in all the sample MNBs. This division of labour entailed the account executive being responsible for the marketing of banking services whilst the credit officer specialised in risk assessment. These two functions were seen as separate in the MNBs and they reflect the specialist credit analysis training which is standard practice of American banking education.

The American banks' approach to credit analysis has been characterised as the going concern approach. Its essential elements as revealed by the survey are a financial analysis of company accounts over a minimum period of three years accompanied by an evaluation of management capability, the employment of financial projections over the life of the loan facility (two smaller sample banks did not use projections), the detailed documentation of loan agreements and a systematic monitoring of clients throughout the term of the facilities. All the MNBs used spread sheets or a similar exercise to facilitate their financial analysis of company accounts in which the values of various financial ratios over the preceding three years were calculated. For example, balance sheet strength was assessed through the calculation of various capital gearing and liquidity ratios, some of which were later included in the loan agreements. One might add that balance sheets are also employed to some extent in the gone concern approach. In addition to the balance sheet, American MNBs analysed the sources and uses of funds statements to highlight trends in respect of plant closures, disposals and reorganisation costs. However, all the sample MNBs in their financial analysis placed most emphasis on the profit and loss account and, particularly on the concept of cash flow.

Central to American MNBs' going concern approach to credit analysis is an examination of cash flow as the source of repayment for loan finance. Definitions of cash flow vary but it was commonly taken to comprise retained profits, depreciation and deferred taxation. Examination of cash flow involved an analysis of various measures of company profitability and expenses. Among the latter dividends were seen as a major item. Since cash flow is taken as the source for the repayment of loan facilities an income gearing ratio or times interest earned was central to American MNBs' determination of debt capacity. Income gearing is defined as the ratio of retained profits to interest payments. A small number of banks also calculated the ratio of cash flow to total liabilities in this context. Where possible, American MNBs disaggregated their financial analysis by product, geographical area or subsidiary as part of their financial analysis.

All American MNBs saw the evaluation of management

capability as part of the going concern approach but were vague in describing how this was achieved in practice. All the interviewees conceded that assessment was a subjective art but proved useful as part of an overall assessment. Some banks relied on the company's actual financial performance as an indicator or management quality while some looked at how management had reacted in times of crisis.

As mentioned already, the financial analysis of past accounts was in the case of medium-term loan facilities complemented by projections over the life of the facilities by all but two of the smaller MNBs. In most cases companies would be expected to supply projections of their major financial variables but in cases where these were not forthcoming the larger MNBs were prepared to do such projections on behalf of the companies. One feature of all this which was striking was that the MNBs invariably used historical cost figures in their financial analysis. Moreover all except one MNB did not consider current cost or inflated adjusted accounts as being relevant to their analysis. As Walton (1981) has shown the use of historical and current cost data leads to significant differences in the calculation of gearing ratios. In particular historical cost figures underestimate capital gearing and overestimate income gearing as compared to their current cost counterparts. Finally, it was curious that only one MNB explicitly mentioned that an evaluation of the state of labour relations within corporations formed part of their credit analysis.

Conditionality of Loan Agreements

Over the past decade, the nature and extent of the conditionality of IMF loans to Third World countries has developed into a well-known contentious issue. By way of contrast the conditionality of loans to corporations had remained a closed book for all except corporate treasurers and bankers. However, in recent years, the frequency with which banks have invoked loan agreement clauses to place companies in receivership has begun to focus public attention on the exact nature of corporate loan agreement conditionality.

In the following pages, we set out the novel approach to corporate loan agreements pioneered by the American MNBs in the UK corporate finance market. We set out the types of terms and conditions commonly included in such loan agreements and which the clearing banks have begun to adopt since the late 1970s in their formal facility letters. The new agreements mark a distinct shift away from the passive banking relationship characteristic of traditional secured bank lending for they include the monitoring of companies' financial performance as an integral part of their overall approach.

The loan agreements attaching to medium-term loan finance facilities are formal contracts defining the parties to the facilities and their rights and obligations, the use(s), terms and conditions of the facilities and the remedy for breach of contract or the precise circumstances under which the facilities may be called in or accelerated. Much has been made of the legal complexity and length of American banks' loan agreements. However, for the most part they merely codify aspects of informal contracts even if in doubt in that it must nevertheless be pointed out that some of their clauses can potentially be highly contentious as we see below. From our survey it was possible to distinguish the following components of American MNBs' corporate loan agreements.

Conditions Precedent

This component is standard in all loan agreements and was employed by all the MNBs in our sample. Conditions precedent as the term suggests imply that the loan agreement remains inoperative until certain conditions have been complied with. Such conditions are concerned with the corporation's legal right to borrow in the first instance as set out for example in its memorandum and articles of association. In addition to these general conditions, a corporation has to comply with a further set of conditions before the drawdown of any particular loan facility. These invariably include the clause that the representations and warranties are correct and that no event of default is operative (see below for a definition of these terms). One can distinguish between conditions precedent and those that comprise the remaining conditions of loan agreements.

We focus here on the latter which are known as continuing conditions. This is because they apply throughout the life of the loan facility and constitute the conditions which are regularly monitored by the banks.

Financial Terms

Financial terms concerned with the details of the drawdown, repayment and interest rate(s) of the loan facility were standard in the loan agreements of all the sample MNBs. Normally a loan agreement will stipulate a fixed period during which the facilities may be drawn down and the commitment fee (if any) which is payable on the undrawn portion of the facilities. The American MNBs' wholesale banking approach and its focus on cash flow is linked to the regular repayment schedules of their loan agreements although occasionally grace periods are allowed in respect of the early repayments. Prepayment terms specify the conditions under which the oustanding portion of a loan facility may be paid off in advance for in their absence a borrower generally has no legal right to prepay.

The interest rate terms indicate the cost of the facility usually in terms of a margin over the London interbank offer rate (LIBOR) or other rate and the period over which the interest rate has been fixed. Finally some medium-term loan agreements incorporate multicurrency options with their associated interest rates under which part or all of the facility may be converted from one currency to another on specified rollover dates.

Representations and Warranties

These were included in all MNBs' standard loan agreements to define the factual basis of loan agreements. In legal terms representations are statements made prior to the actual loan agreement while warranties are included as terms of the loan agreement contract so that each has different legal remedies.

Representations and warranties serve two purposes: one gives assurances as to the legal validity of the corporation's obligations under the loan agreement and the other represents its financial and commercial position. It is becoming more common that warranties should apply at all rollover dates throughout the life of the loan agreement rather than just at the initial signing of the loan agreement. Such continuing warranties are known as evergreen warranties and thus constitute a continuing condition rather than a condition precedent to the loan agreement.

Negative Pledge and Pari Passu Clauses

These clauses were a standard part of all the American MNBs' unsecured loan agreements since they are designed to offer protection to both the unsecured or undersecured creditors. The function of the clauses is to establish equality between the same class of creditors and to place a somewhat indirect restriction on indebtedness. Both clauses have a long history in the corporate bond market but American banks can take the credit for disseminating their use in the UK loan finance market.

At its most basic the negative pledge prohibits a corporation from granting any future security interest on its assets or revenues while the pari passu clause requires that any indebtedness being incurred shall rank equally with the borrower's other indebtedness. Clearly the negative pledge appears to be more restrictive but in practice exceptions are built in. The modal types of exception identified by the MNBs were outstanding secured debenture bond issues and existing security on after-acquired property.

Unlike the normal types of security employed by banks the negative pledge has the disadvantage that remedies for breach are weak. However, if the pari passu clause is included as a warranty the remedy for breach (as with other warranties) entitles the bank to accelerate the loan as in the case of breach of contract with normal security clauses.

Financial Covenants

From an economic viewpoint, the most interesting if also the most controversial component of loan agreements is the range of financial covenants that may be included. Again such covenants are one of American MNBs' innovations even if financial covenants have enjoyed a long and relatively uncontentious history in the corporate bond markets. Financial covenants define financial performance norms for corporations which are monitored during the term of the facility agreement and are generally derived from industry or banking averages. A number of different types of financial or ratio covenants were distinguished in the survey:

(a) **Gearing restrictions.** All the MNBs interviewed saw one or more types of gearing restrictions as integral to the normal process of loan agreement negotiation. The type of capital gearing restriction employed by all the banks was a maximum capital gearing or leverage ratio defined as net borrowings divided by shareholders' funds or net worth. The purpose of the gearing ratio was to place a relative ceiling on net corporate borrowings. Twelve out of the 17 MNBs employed a minimum net worth restriction as a necessary part of the loan agreement negotiations to complement a conventional leverage ratio. Three MNBs used a limitation on capital expenditure and two MNBs specified a limitation on total debt as other supplements to the leverage ratio. On the other hand, five MNBs employed a cash flow/liabilities ratio as an alternative to the leverage ratio, the advantage of the former being that it captured off-balance sheet indebtedness such as leasing and other contingent liabilities.

A different measure of gearing is given by the interest cover or times interest earned covenant. This like the capital gearing covenant seeks to limit a corporation's indebtedness by relating a measure of its liabilities such as interest payments to its ability to generate earnings or cash flow for purposes of regular repayments. Because it remains sensitive to two parameters beyond the remit of individual corporations - interest rate levels and the general rate of corporate profitability - this covenant has generated a certain amount of opposition among corporate treasurers. Notwithstanding that eleven banks out of the total sample, including the nine largest banks, invariably considered an interest cover covenant (pre-tax earnings/interest payments) in formulating their corporate loan agreements.

(b) **Liquidity covenants.** This type of covenant was always considered by all MNBs in the total sample in drafting their corporate loan agreements. Its purpose is to warn banks of a deterioration in liquidity caused by losses or overtrading by their corporate borrowers. Liquidity covenants at their most basic relate current assets to current liabilities in various ways. The liquidity covenant employed by all banks was the current ratio generally expressed as a minimum ratio of current assets/current liabilities. In addition one-third of the banks considered a minimum working capital covenant where the latter is given by the difference between current assets and current liabilities. Finally, two banks used a quick ratio or acid test covenant (liquid assets divided by current liabilities).

(c) **Material adverse change.** Like interest cover/covenants the no material adverse change clause is regarded as contentious. When it is employed as an event of default (see below) it is viewed by some as conferring on banks a carte blanche over the fate of borrowing corporations. When not employed as an event of default banks used it as a last resort catch-all financial clause particularly in cases where corporations are loath to accept any of the previous financial covenants. Five of the total sample banks viewed this clause as an integral part of their loan agreement negotiations.

The definition of a material adverse change is something which will continue to exercise the imagination of the legal profession for some time for no satisfactory financial or legal formula has as yet been agreed. Of the responses received in the survey, the most plausible working definition adopted was 'changes of the order of magnitude of a 15-20 per cent movement in net worth.'

(d) **Other covenants.** These covered a range of aspects and were deemed to be appropriate for marginal credits. Eight banks in the total sample employed a covenant restricting disposal of assets and subsidiaries or other ownership changes; here the objective was to protect the banks' potential security. Seven sample banks employed a dividends restriction covenant which took two forms depending on the financial health of the borrower. In the worst cases dividends were completely prohibited while in less serious situations they were limited to a maximum proportion of total earnings. Again, this proved to be a contentious covenant.

Finally, it must be added that financial covenants required monitoring so that corporations were expected to supply regular financial information for this purpose. To this end the MNBs employed an affirmative covenant in their loan agreements stipulating that corporations supply them with copies of their annual reports and, where relevant, interim reports within specific time limits from the end of the relevant financial periods.

Events of Default

A critical component of all American MNBs' corporate loan agreements was the events of default clause which defines the precise circumstances and conditions under which a bank may accelerate its loan facilities; that is those circumstances where, in law, it can demand immediate repayment of its outstanding loans. Some transgressions have long constituted an event of default and were standard items in the events of default clauses. One is the failure to meet interest or principal repayments by the required date. A second obvious transgression of a loan agreement is receivership or liquidation.

More pertinent for our purpose is the link to financial covenants for breach of any of these was invariably judged to be an event of default by all the banks surveyed. Indeed much of the controversy surrounding financial covenants stems from the fact that they are defined to be events of default. Elsewhere Coakley and Harris (1983) have argued that such discretionary powers enjoyed by banks constitute a basis for the control of industry.

Cross Default

The final and perhaps the most notorious of all loan agreements clauses is the cross-default clause. This clause was standard in all the MNBs' loan agreements with the exception of a few conspicuous examples. (6) The cross-default clause is designed to protect the interests of all banks in the case of a multi-banked company running into financial difficulties and is based on the equivalent sharing of misery principle. Our survey revealed it can take three forms each one progressively more stringent.

At the simplest level this clause provides that acceleration of a debt or failure to meet payments by the due date under any one of a company's loan agreements automatically constitutes a default under all that company's other loan agreements. A second form of cross-default clause provides that default by a company on one of its loan agreements automatically triggers a default on its other agreements. A more stringent version of this clause is that a <u>potential</u> default under one agreement automatically constitutes a default on all the company's other agreements. (7) One exception to the general scope of the clause was identified and this was loan agreements covering borrowing by (some) overseas subsidiaries.

This then was the battery of financial clauses and covenants employed in corporate loan agreements by the American MNBs in London. Naturally the precise mix of covenants and their individual details depend on the interplay of a range of factors which underlie the bargaining process between banks and corporations and whose outcome was not really amenable to generalisations. Nonetheless a large number of the covenants discussed have become standard fare not only in American but also in clearing bank loan agreements as a process of convergence between the two approaches to loan agreements takes place through competition in the corporate finance market.

The Monitoring of Corporations

The detailed documentation of medium-term loan agreements and in particular the specification of financial ratio covenants logically leads to a consideration of how American MNBs monitor the continuing conditions of such agreements. It should be borne in mind that exclusion from direct access to the clearing system does deprive American and other foreign MNBs of one vital monitoring mechanism which is, of course, the corporation's bank current accounts. The ability to monitor corporations' up-to-date liquidity via the latter confers a considerable monitoring advantage on the clearing bankers over their foreign competitors. Thus it is that American MNBs have to adopt a more formal arms length approach to monitoring the basis of which is a standard American banking classification system which distinguishes credits as follows:

- 1 Unclassified credits where a formal annual review of facilities is standard procedure.
- 1-1A Watch list for deteriorating credits which are subject to increased informal monitoring.
- 1A Credits which require a quarterly classified loan report and a six monthly review of facilities.
- 2 Credits requiring a monthly classified loan report and a six monthly review of facilities.
- 3 Credits with non-accrual of interest payments.
- 4 Write-offs.

The amount of information required for monitoring varies according to the classification of the credit and is generally stipulated in the affirmative (information) covenants in loan agreements. Thus for unclassified term credits the normal requirement is that annual accounts be made available within six months of the end of the company's financial year and interim statements within 120 days of the relevant date. Other information required by some MNBs on a regular basis includes data on debtors, leases and other off-balance sheet items and any information which a company may from time to time provide to other competitor banks.

Watch list credits are deemed to require greater informal monitoring than unclassified credits. However, it is only in the case of classified credits, that formal monitoring requirements were increased. In addition the reasons for approving extended facilities to classified credits were more stringent. For example, a classification 2 company needed to be improving its credit situation before receiving additional facilities and such facilities were made available to a classification 3 company only in rescue operations. Also it was standard procedure that these facilities needed approval at a level of management authority one above the normal level.

Banks obviously were reluctant to elaborate on either the extent of their classified creditors or the number of insolvencies in which they were involved. Overall from the little evidence given on this topic the American banks have been involved in relatively few insolvencies in recent years and none appeared to have more than a handful of classified credits in its corporate portfolio including some of the publicised rescue operations. The main reason for the low number of problem credits is probably the American banks' focus on the larger UK corporations (most of which had until 1981 withstood the worst effects of the recession) which include a substantial number of non-manufacturing companies.

Other reasons may include the relative success of the wholesale banking approach as an effective early warning system and linked to that a tendency among a few smaller US MNBs to cut their losses when credits deteriorate. We emphasise the limited extent of this tendency since the majority of US banks were keen to establish long-term links with the US corporate sector.

Clearly one of the most controversial aspects of the MNBs' entry into the UK corporate finance market has been some of the financial covenants in their generally detailed loan agreements. Here a number of provisions such as the interest cover clause, the no material adverse change clause, the events of default clause, the cross-default clause have generated a certain amount of contention with finance directors and corporate treasurers. Nonetheless, it must be emphasised that some of these clauses and most of the other provisions have been standard in the corporate bond market or are also incorporated into the clearers' formal facility letters.

With their long history in the City the top MNBs are interested in building long-term relationships with corporations in the UK on the basis of acting as a lead international bank. Citibank's successful application to become an indirect member of the clearing system has marked a new stage of development in such relationships. The smaller MNBs evidently cannot hope to compete with either and the evidence from the survey suggested that some of these adopted the approach of cutting their losses when their clients got into financial difficulties. A more serious threat to all the MNB's relationships with corporations in the UK could be the repercussions of the recent debt problems elsewhere which could force banks into a general or sectoral balance sheet contraction directly impinging on their UK activities. The departure from London in mid-1985 of Wells Fargo Bank (the 12th largest US commercial MNB) is indicative of some of the problems currently faced by multinational banks.

Conclusion

Although the top American MNBs have enjoyed a long stay in the City of London, they and the other MNBs which began to arrive in the 1960s initially focused on American and other client multinationals as their target corporate market. Indeed it is only since the advent of Competition and Credit Control in 1971 that American MNBs have begun to make inroads into the upper echelons of the UK corporate market and here they have posed a challenge to the clearing banks both for sterling and foreign currency lending. Most of the distinctive features of their corporate relationships in the UK can be explained by their focus on wholesale banking.

Thus American MNBs' wholesale banking orientation has led them to concentrate their banking business particularly on the top 250 companies in the Times 1000 and on those other British companies with a strong overseas presence or export potential. In the context of such large and viable companies, the merits of the wholesale banking approach to credit analysis with its emphasis on unsecured medium-term loan facilities can be appreciated. We estimate that for example the proportion of outstanding MNB loan facilities which can be defined as medium term is close to 50 per cent or rather more than twice that for the clearing banks. Having said that, it must be borne in mind that the MNBs also engage in secured lending in the traditional areas of commodities, shipping, some oil finance and to companies in financial difficulties.

NOTES

I am grateful to Laurence Harris for his helpful comments on this chapter and to the Open University Research Committee for financial assistance.

1. Bank of England Quarterly Bulletin, September 1961, p.22.
2. Committee to Review the Functioning of Financial Institutions (1978) Evidence on the Financing of Industry and Trade: American Bank Association of London, pp.25-70, London, HMSO.
3. The Banker, July 1983, p.7.
4. In September 1983 it was revealed that Citibank had applied for membership of the clearing house system. One of the reasons for this application was the higher cost of transacting the volume of its sterling business through agency clearing banks as compared with directly transacting such business itself. In 1985 Citibank succeeded in becoming an indirect member of the clearing system.
5. The Committee of London Clearing Banks has estimated that 23 per cent of the clearing banks' lending to non-personal borrowers had a residual maturity of one year or more in August 1981. See the Financial Times, 26 October 1981.
6. For example, Burmah Oil Company succeeded in excluding cross-default clauses on an eight year $120 million facility from twelve banks in 1981.
7. For some of the controversy surrounding cross-default clauses see Youard (1981).

REFERENCES

Coakley, J. (1984) 'The Internationalisation of Bank Capital', Capital and Class, no. 23, reprinted in Part II of this volume.

Coakley, J. and Harris, L. (1983) The City of Capital: London's Role as a Financial Centre, Oxford, Basil Blackwell.

Kelly (1977) Bankers and Bonders, Cambridge, Mass., Ballinger.

Walton, P.A. (1980) 'Assessing Debt Capacity', The Treasurer, vol. 2, no. 5.

Youard, R.G.A. (1981) 'Why the Cross-Default Clause won't go away', Euromoney, July.

Annexe 1

American Banks with London Branches in 1980

	Bank	Assets less contra accounts ($ million at end 1979)
1	Bank of America	103,919
2	Citibank	102,742
3	Chase Manhattan Bank	61,975
4	Manufacturers Hanover Trust Co.	45,877
5	Morgan Guaranty Trust Co. of New York	43,486
6	Chemical Bank	37,826
7	Continental Illinois National Bank & Trust Co. of Chicago	34,697
8	Bankers Trust Co.	29,771
9	First National Bank of Chicago	29,201
10	First Interstate Bank of California (1)	28,821
11	Security Pacific National Bank	24,922
12	Wells Fargo Bank	20,052
13	Irving Trust Co.	16,475
14	Crocker National Bank (2)	15,643
15	Marine Midland Bank	15,162
16	First National Bank of Boston	13,262
17	Mellon Bank	12,725
18	First National Bank in Dallas	11,121
19	Republic Bank of Dallas	10,282

20	First City National Bank of Houston	9,275
21	Detroit Bank and Trust Co.	9,213
22	Texas Commerce Bank	9,061
23	First Pennsylvania Bank	8,880
24	Bank of New York	8,725
25	Seattle - First National Bank	8,316
26	Harris Trust & Savings Bank of Chicago	6,842
27	North Carolina National Bank	6,220
28	American Express International Banking Corporation	5,969
29	Northern Trust Co.	5,113
30	First Wisconsin National Bank of Milwaukee	5,062
31	Detroit Bank & Trust Co.	5,046
32	Rainier National Bank	4,372
33	Girard Bank	4,245
34	First National Bank in St. Louis	3,828
35	Bank of California	3,370
36	Fidelity Bank	2,798
37	Riggs National Bank of Washington DC	2,631
38	American National Bank & Trust Co. of Chicago	2,482
39	Allied Bank International	2,247
40	First National Bank of Maryland	2,088

Notes
(1) Formerly the United California Bank
(2) A subsidiary of Midland Bank

Source: The Banker, June and November 1980.

Chapter Ten

MODELLING THE FINANCE OF INVESTMENT

Martin Croasdale

Neo-classical theory, in its simplest form, suggests that profit-maximising firms are indifferent when they make their investment decision, to whether the finance for that investment comes from internal sources (principally profits) or external sources (principally borrowing). This is because it is assumed, amongst other things, that firms can borrow without limit at a fixed rate of interest and can always lend their internal funds at a rate of interest equal to the borrowing rate, the opportunity cost of such internal finance thus being the same as that of borrowed funds. The result has been extended to include the case of uncertainty (the risk of default by borrowers) in the famous theorem of Modigliani and Miller (Modigliani and Miller, 1958) and in the subsequent discussion (see King, 1977). Jorgenson's popular model of investment (Jorgenson and Siebert, 1968) is developed along these lines, as is the more recent example applied to UK data in Bean (1981).

Nevertheless, there has been a long tradition in modern economics of incorporating some form of a firm's internal finance (profits, retained earnings, cash flow) as an explanatory variable for its fixed investment expenditure. The theoretical justification (due to Duesenberry) which is most usually advanced is based on a standard Keynesian model of investment, with the particular feature that the marginal cost of funds rises with investment because of the risk involved in high levels of borrowing. Duesenberry measured the risk by a firm's 'gearing ratio', and his theory is outlined in Part 1 of this paper.

In Part 2 it is argued that the usual practical implementation of Duesenberry's theory is not correct because it does not take account of the influence on a firm's gearing of all its various sources and uses of funds. An omission which is particularly relevant to the UK in recent years is that of stockbuilding (including unplanned stockbuilding), which can have serious consequences for a firm's borrowing. As a practical solution to this problem, it is suggested that empirical models might include an appropriate borrowing variable rather than the usual internal finance variables.

Finally, in Part 3, the paper is summarised, and empirical research in this area is reviewed in the light of arguments here presented. It is seen that almost all implementations of Duesenberry's theory suffer from the criticism made in the present paper.

Investment and Internal Finance

Duesenberry (1958) introduced a theory of how the internal finance available to a firm might influence its investment stock, and this framework was subsequently adopted, or at least quoted, by Kuh and Meyer (1963), Meyer and Glauber (1964), Resek (1966), Evans (1967), and Meeks (1981), amongst others. Duesenberry worked within a standard Keynesian model where firms maximise profits each period by choosing that optimal capital stock at which the marginal efficiency of capital (mec) is just equal to the marginal cost of funds (mcf).

The situation can be illustrated graphically as in Figure 10.1 where the optimal capital stock is K*.

Figure 10.1

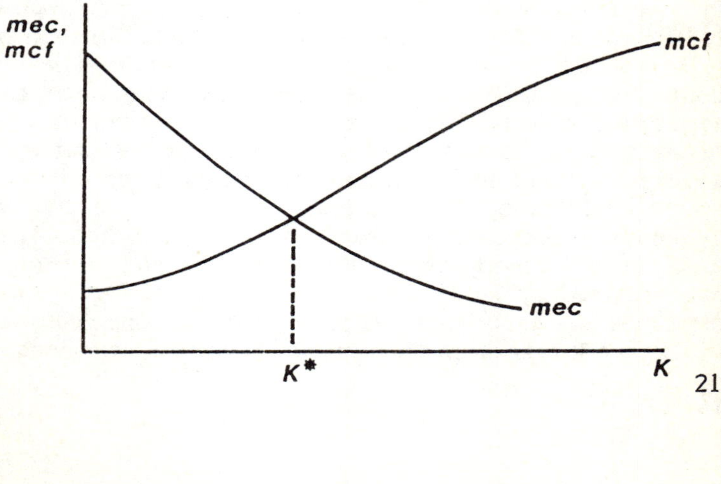

If the horizontal scale is taken to begin at K_o, the existing level of capital stock at the beginning of the period less the depreciation which is expected to occur, then the graph can equally well be drawn with investment I along the horizontal axis (Figure 10.2).

Figure 10.2

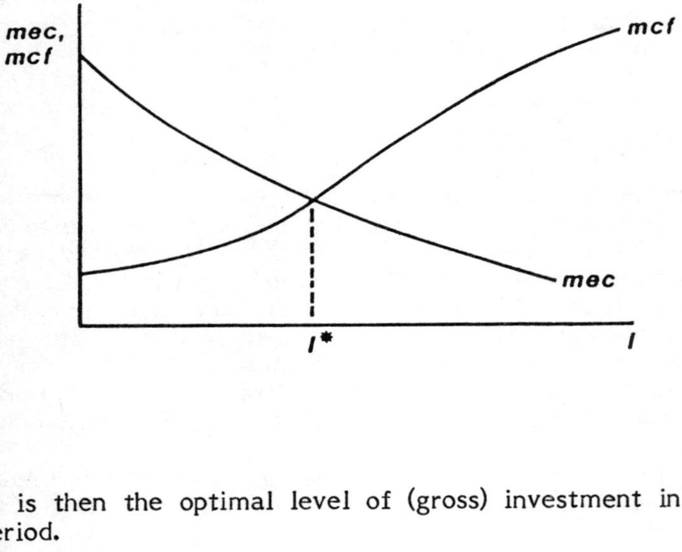

I* is then the optimal level of (gross) investment in the period.

The mec schedule slopes downwards because at low levels of investment it is only the most profitable investment projects which are undertaken, but less profitable ones are adopted as investment increases. Duesenberry assumed that the mcf schedule is flat at first as internal sources of funds are used. These consist of depreciation expenses (set aside to cover expected depreciation of the existing capital stock) and retained earnings (profits, less tax, interest and dividend payments), together often referred to as cash flow. Their cost is an opportunity cost - the return the company could have obtained by lending the money, or investing in other companies' shares, or repaying some of its existing debt.

Higher levels of investment will have to be financed by

borrowing more. Duesenberry assumed that firms and their creditors are concerned about the risk of borrowing (the risk of being unable to maintain payments of interest and principal, and hence becoming a 'necessitous' borrower, or even bankrupt). Borrowed funds will thus have an imputed cost above the level of interest rates, rising rapidly above what is considered to be a 'safe' level of borrowing. Duesenberry took this steeply rising part of the mcf curve to be a function of D/Π (a measure of 'gearing') where D is the level of outstanding debt consequent on the investment taken, and Π is profits in the period concerned. He then rewrote D as D_o - RE - A + I, where D_o is debt at the beginning of the period, RE and A are retained earnings and depreciation allowances in the period (both of which decrease D), and I is investment (which increases D). The mcf in this region is thus an increasing function of I.

The mcf will continue to rise with increasing investment, until the point is reached at which it becomes cheaper to raise finance by issuing new shares on the stock market (a source of finance which is considered by Duesenberry to be much more expensive than internal sources). At this point the schedule flattens out again, though still rising.

Given these two schedules, the optimum level of investment is fixed. Any factor which shifts either of the schedules may move their point of intersection, so that investment becomes a function of such factors. The mec curve will be shifted by, amongst other things, changes in expected demand and by 'animal spirits'. Duesenberry assumed that, for most firms, the intersection would occur on the upward-sloping part of the mcf schedule, so that investment will depend on the various factors which determine where the schedule starts to rise and how steeply it rises. These factors include the existing level of debt, the level considered to be safe, and cash flow in the period concerned (RE + A). Hence the justification for including cash flow in investment equations.

Although Duesenberry does not carry out the exercise, it is straightforward to develop the above argument algebraically, using linear approximations to the relationships. Suppose the mei in the period concerned is given by

$$\text{mei} = a - bI$$

and the mcf schedule is given by

$$\text{mcf} = c + d\left(\frac{D}{\Pi}\right)$$

$$= c + d\left(\frac{D_o - RE - A + I}{\Pi}\right)$$

Then the optimal level of investment I* will be where

$$\text{mei} = \text{mcf}$$

$$\text{i.e. } a - bI^* = c + d\left(\frac{D_o - RE - A + I^*}{\Pi}\right)$$

$$I^* = \frac{(a - c)}{b + \frac{d}{\Pi}} - \frac{d\,(D_o - RE - A)}{b\Pi + d}$$

Thus, other things being equal, an increase in cash flow (RE + A) will result in an increase in the desired level of investment. The level of existing debt (D_o) should be considered together with cash flow, which not all authors do, though this may be excusable if attention is being focused on changes in investment rather than on the level of investment (since the change in debt just involves the appropriate flows of retained earnings, depreciation allowances and investment expenditures).

The optimal level of investment will also be influenced by profits, since both terms on the right hand side of the equation above are positively related to Π (remembering that a-c is positive, and that the second term is preceded by a negative sign). This just reflects the fact that, for any given level of debt, an increase in Π will reduce the measure of gearing D/Π and thus shift the mcf schedule to the right. It might be thought that cash flow and profits are not at all independent of each other, but Duesenberry considered that the appropriate measure of profits would be an average of several preceding years, and this will fluctuate more slowly than current cash flow. Some authors do not include any measure of profits at all, apart from cash flow, and this might be justified if a common measure of gearing of the firm (D/W) is employed, where W is some measure of the net worth of the firm. As measured in company accounts, W tends to change very slowly and steadily, particularly in the aggregate.

The Sources and Uses of Funds

Given the simple algebraic development of Duesenberry's argument outlined above, it can be seen that the common practice of merely including a cash flow variable in an investment equation is open to many criticisms. But it is the purpose of this paper to concentrate on only one, viz. the failure to take account of other sources and uses of funds besides investment and those involved in the calculation of cash flow.

The most important sources and uses (as presented in the UK national accounts - differing in detail, but not in principle, from company accounts and US accounts) are:

sources:
- gross trading profits (including depreciation allowances)
- interest receipts
- investment grants
- new share issues
- new borrowing

uses:
- tax payments
- interest payments
- dividend payments
- fixed capital formation
- investment in stocks and work in progress
- acquisition of non-liquid 'financial' assets (principally direct and other investment abroad)
- acquisition of liquid financial assets

They are linked by the necessary identity that total sources equal total uses each period. It follows that new borrowing (one of the sources) must equal total uses less all other sources each period. But Duesenberry assumes that new borrowing is just equal to I - RE - A, where retained earnings only involves profits and tax, interest and dividend payments. This fails to take account of the consequences of, say, a high level of (perhaps unplanned) stockbuilding. This would mean that the level of debt consequent on any given level of investment would be higher, i.e. it would shift the mcf schedule to the left. Similarly, a high level of, say, investment grants from central government would relieve the pressure of borrowing and shift the mcf curve to the right.

An analogous algebraic expression to the equations

developed earlier would replace the cash flow term (RE + A) by cash flow plus all omitted sources of funds, less all omitted uses of funds. This would involve identifying all the relevant sources and uses from the accounts. But a simpler procedure, which also emphasizes more explicitly the central role of borrowing in determining the cost of funds, is the following:

$$\text{mei} = a - bI$$

$$\text{mcf} = c + d\left(\frac{D}{\Pi}\right)$$

$$= c + d\left(\frac{D_o + B}{\Pi}\right)$$

where B is new borrowing in the period concerned. The optimum level of investment* will be when

$$\text{mei} = \text{mcf}$$

$$a - bI^* = c + d\left(\frac{D_o + B}{\Pi}\right)$$

$$I^* = \frac{a - c}{b} - \frac{d\,(D_o + B)}{b\Pi}$$

As before, it can be seen that investment is positively related to profits and negatively related to the initial level of debt D_o. But now it is new borrowing B which appears (with a negative coefficient) rather than cash flow (with a positive coefficient). The inclusion of new borrowing in investment equations in place of cash flow correctly takes account of all sources and uses of funds (since borrowing will be low when, for example, either cash flow is high or stockbuilding is low) and is simple to implement (since a single figure for new borrowing is readily available in accounts). It should not be confused with 'credit-rationing' models where it is assumed that firms are constrained in the amount they can borrow, and borrowing appears with a positive coefficient. Duesenberry does not consider that firms are rationed - only that the cost of funds increases with gearing.

One slight problem with this formulation is that econometric estimates of the equation may suffer from simultaneous bias, since B on the right hand side is related to I through the accounting identity. But this could be overcome by the use of some appropriate instrumental variables method of estimation.

It might be thought that the sources and uses of funds omitted by Duesenberry are negligible in comparison with cash flow, but this is not so. The mean value of quarterly investment abroad, for example, by UK industrial and commercial companies over the period 1963-81 was £204 million, while the mean value of quarterly cash flow was £1439 million (data published by the Central Statistical Office). This comparison of means underestimates the much larger error which occurs in certain quarters or years, due to the fluctuation of the two variables. In the third quarter of 1979, for example, investment abroad was very nearly a third of cash flow.

The fluctuations in variables like stockbuilding are very much greater, even if their average values over long periods are small. Extreme examples are provided for the UK by the periods 1972-5 and 1979-80. Relevant data for industrial and commercial companies appear in Table 10.1

Table 10.1

	Cash flow (£ million)	New borrowing (£ million)	Stockbuilding (£ million)
1972	4686	750	-84
1973	5783	2599	1292
1974	4275	4360	1271
1975	5397	-844	-1680
1979	12,403	4687	2284
1980	9523	3342	-3486

Source: Central Statistical Office.

Note that new borrowing is all forms of borrowing (short-term and long-term) less acquisition of liquid assets. This is the appropriate measure of the risk (and hence imputed cost) of new borrowing, since increased borrowing matched by an equal increase in liquid assets involves no extra risk. Although Duesenberry does not deal with this point explicitly, it seems to be what he intends when he refers to 'repaying debt or holding liquid assets to balance it' (Duesenberry, 1958, p.94).

From Table 10.1 it can be seen that between 1972 and

1975 cash flow remained fairly steady, suggesting that this component of the factors affecting the mcf schedule did not vary. But new borrowing actually increased substantially over this period, and then plummeted in 1975, mostly due to the sudden swing from stockbuilding to de-stocking, a factor neglected by concentrating on cash flow only. In the period 1979-80 cash flow fell, suggesting that borrowing increased. In fact the level of new borrowing was reduced, this time due to the massive de-stocking of 1980. In both these cases, the use of cash flow as a measure of the cost of funds seriously distorts the true picture.

Conclusion

In summary, it has been argued that the inclusion of a cash flow variable in an investment equation is an inadequate specification of the effects of current income and expenditure on the mcf schedule, since it omits the effects of many important sources and uses of funds. For the UK the omission has been particularly serious in periods when stockbuilding behaviour has been erratic. A correct specification would adjust cash flow to take account of all the sources and uses, but it has been suggested that a simple solution is to replace cash flow by a borrowing variable.

It is of interest to examine how Duesenberry's theory was implemented by later researchers. Kuh and Meyer (1963) employ a 'cash throw-off' variable, defined as 'net profits plus depreciation less dividends'. They do not include Duesenberry's initial level of debt D_o, nor do profits appear separately. Meyer and Glauber (1964), as surveyed in Jorgensen (1971), include 'profits after taxes minus dividends plus depreciation expense' in their equations. Resek (1966), after testing several variants, finds the best variable is a similar measure of gearing to that used by Duesenberry, but with assets in the denominator rather than profits. His numerator is existing long-term non-bank debt less cash flow. This is one of the most faithful implementations of Duesenberry's theory, but still suffers from the main criticism made here in Part 3. Evans (1967), quoted in Jorgenson (1971), uses the same cash flow variable as Meyer and Glauber. The theoretical arguments in Eisner (1978) are vague, but include the suggestion that external sources of funds cost more than internal funds. He uses profits (without any deductions) in his investment equations.

Clark (1979), in testing various theories of investment against each other, includes an 'accelerator - cash flow' model (partly based on Duesenberry's theory) with a real cash flow term. Meeks (1981) includes the Duesenberry argument in his justification for having investment influenced by internal finance, and employs separate 'liquidity stock', depreciation provisions, and 'disposable retentions' variables, the latter being 'profit after depreciation, tax, dividends, interest and stock appreciation'. Lintner (1967) develops his theory separately from Duesenberry, but appealing to the same considerations of increasing risk with leverage, and the variable he employs is (LTD-RF)/SP where LTD is the stock of long-term debt, SP is the stock market value of firms' equity, and RF is cash flow. Coen (1971) accepts the argument that increased leverage may affect the cost of funds, but argues that this will affect the speed of adjustment to the optimal capital stock, rather than the optimal stock itself (p.150). He includes a cash flow variable in his investment equations.

Of the authors who base arguments on a Duesenberry-type theory, only Anderson (1964) correctly includes borrowing variables (both the stock of existing borrowing and the flow of new borrowing), in what is a very comprehensive model of the financial behaviour of companies. But although he criticises the work of other authors, including Duesenberry, he does not point out why the use of borrowing variables is superior to that of cash flow variables.

REFERENCES

Anderson, W.H.L. (1964) Corporate finance and fixed investment: an econometric study, Harvard University Press, Boston, Mass.

Bean, C.R. (1981) 'An econometric model of manufacturing investment in the UK', Economic Journal, vol. 91, pp.106-21.

Clark, P.J. (1979) 'Investment in the 1970s: theory, performance and prediction', Brookings Papers on Economic Activity, 1, 1979, pp.73-124.

Coen, R.M. (1971) 'The effect of cash flow on speed of adjustment' in G. Fromm (ed.) Tax Incentives and Capital Spending, North Holland, Amsterdam.

Duesenberry, J.S. (1958) Business cycles and economic

growth, McGraw-Hill, New York.

Eisner, R. (1978) Factors in business investment, NBER, New York.

Evans, M.K. (1967) 'A study of industry investment decisions' Review of Economics and Statistics, vol. 49, pp.151-64.

Jorgenson, D.W. (1971) 'Econometric studies of investment behaviour: a survey', Journal of Economic Literature, vol. 9, pp.1111-47.

------ and Siebert, C.D. (1968) 'Optimal capital accumulation and corporate investment behaviour', Journal of Political Economy, vol. 76, pp.1123-51.

King, M.A. (1977) Public policy and the corporation, Chapman and Hall, London.

Kuh, E. and Meyer, J.R. (1963) 'Investment, liquidity and monetary policy', in D.B. Suits et al. Impacts of Monetary Policy, Prentice Hall, Englewood Cliffs, N.J.

Lintner, J. (1967) 'Corporation finance risk and investment' in R. Ferber (ed.) Determinants of Investment Behaviour, NBER, New York.

Meeks, G. (1981) 'Cash flow and investment', in W.E. Martin (ed.) The Economics of the Profits Crisis, HMSO, London.

Meyer, J. and Glauber, R. (1964) Investment decisions, economic forecasting and public policy, Harvard University Press, Boston, Mass.

Modigliani, F. and Miller, M.H. (1958) 'The cost of capital, corporation finance, and the theory of investment', American Economic Review, vol. 48, pp.261-97.

Resek, R.W. (1966) 'Investment by manufacturing firms: a quarterly time series analysis of industry data', Review of Economics and Statistics, vol. 48, pp.322-33.

The financial support of the Leverhulme Trust is gratefully acknowledged.

Chapter Eleven

INTERNAL FUNDS AND INVESTMENT

Martin Croasdale and Laurence Harris

Recent economic circumstances have made UK companies at times particularly prone to a shortage of internal finance. Meeks (1981) demonstrates that trends in (historic cost) profits minus stock appreciation, taxation, interest payments and depreciation allowances significantly reduced the availability of internal finance for other purposes in the 1970s. And it has been claimed that the historically high nominal interest rates experienced between 1980 and 1982 particularly attenuated firms' retained earnings. If fixed capital formation depends on internal finance these trends will have had some role in accounting for the UK's low rate of investment, and if the availability of internal finance is negatively related to firms' interest payments, dear money policies will have constrained investment quite apart from any disincentive effect of the cost of capital.

The idea that investment is a function of firms' internal finance has gained some credibility from the fact that UK industrial and commercial firms finance an unusually high proportion of their uses of funds from internal sources instead of external borrowing or new issues (see e.g. Wilson, 1980), but the observation cannot support any causal inference. However, empirical studies on US and UK data do give the hypothesis some support, particularly in the US case. (1) For the UK, Meeks (1981) finds in a cross-section study that investment is related to the availability of internal finance, at least in the late 1960s and 1970s, and Anderson (1981a, 1981b) finds a significant long-run equilibrium relationship between investment and total finance. Anderson's study, however, is weakened by the dynamic instability of his estimated equation and by problems in the specification of the model (see Hibberd, 1981).

In Section 1 we set out the derivation of a model relating fixed investment to internal finance and relating the latter to interest payments; in Section 2 we summarise our empirical results; and in Section 3 we draw conclusions.

Investment, Internal Finance and Interest Payments

Although we are only seeking to model the effect of one source of funds (internal finance) on one use of funds (investment), this is part of a more general relationship between all sources and uses of funds. Thus:

1. Internal finance might be plentiful, but investment could still be constrained if other sources of finance were low, or if other uses of funds were high.
2. If investment is constrained by internal finance because of, say, high interest payments, we expect 'interest shifting' (analogous to tax shifting) to take place, as other uses of funds (for example, dividends) are cut back, or other sources of funds are increased (for example, profits may be increased by raising prices).

We have therefore to set out the investment equation in the framework of a simultaneous model of all sources and uses of funds of the firm. We have adopted a 'managerial' view of the firm, where ownership is separated from control, and internal finance is important because managers are reluctant to engage in high levels of borrowing, since this leads to loss of control to 'outsiders' and increasing risk of default as interest-bearing liabilities accumulate (see Kalacki, 1937 and Marris, 1967). We have taken the capital gearing ratio (defined as the ratio of all outstanding debt, net of liquid assets, to net worth) as the most appropriate measure of this risk. The evidence suggests (2) that, in the UK, more reliance is placed on this as an indicator than on income gearing, partly because the latter is so subject to fluctuations in interest rates which are out of control of firms.

Assume that each period the firm has the sources of funds B (new borrowing less retirements, all net of acquisition of liquid assets) plus other sources S_i (profits, new share issues, grants etc.). The firm's total borrowing will be associated with a certain level of interest payments INT, and it will also have other uses of funds U_j (tax payments, dividends, fixed investment, stockbuilding, acquisition of non-liquid financial assets etc.). If there were no constraint on the amount of internal finance, the flows of sources and uses each period would be functions of vectors of determinants X_i and Y_j, say:

$$S_i = f_i(X_i) \qquad (i = 1, \ldots, m)$$
$$U_j = h_j(Y_j) \qquad (j = i, \ldots, n) \qquad (1)$$

This would result in a certain level of new borrowing, B*, necessary in order to balance sources and uses, given by:

$$B^* = \sum_j h_j(Y_j) + INT - \sum_i f_i(X_i) \qquad (2)$$

B* is thus a residual, but it is not simply a passive residual: it is assumed that firms have some desired optimum level of new borrowing $\hat{B}$, and that they make some 'partial adjustment' of B* towards $\hat{B}$. (3) They achieve this (if B* is higher than $\hat{B}$) by cutting back to some extent on their uses of funds and seeking extra funds from other sources. Suppose that a certain proportion of the discrepancy between B* and $\hat{B}$ is cut from each use or added to each source, as firms seek to moderate the effects on their gearing:

$$S_i = f_i(X_i) + \alpha_i(B^* - \hat{B}) \qquad (i = 1, \ldots, m)$$
$$U_j = h_j(Y_j) - \beta_j(B^* - \hat{B}) \qquad (j = 1, \ldots, n) \qquad (3)$$
$$B = \sum_j U_j + INT - \sum_i S_i$$

B is actual borrowing and it is easily shown that

$$B = (1 - \theta)B^* + \theta\hat{B} \qquad (4)$$

where

$$\theta = \sum_i \alpha_i + \sum_j \beta_j$$

One of the uses of funds U_i will be fixed investment, and the effect of internal finance thus enters it through the 'unconstrained' borrowing requirement B*, which will be high if internal finance is low. The role of borrowing in this model should be clearly distinguished from that in 'credit-rationing' models, which embody a different view of the financial constraints on firms. In those models investment would be positively related to borrowing, but in this model it is negatively related. The advantage of formulating the internal finance constraint on investment in terms of the borrowing requirement is that it takes account of other sources and uses of funds. Models which have some variable such as retained earnings in the investment equation imply:

1 That the dividend decision is given absolute priority over the investment decision,
2 that the investment decision is taken independently of other uses of retained earnings, such as stockbuilding,
3 that other sources of funds are irrelevant.

B^* and $\hat{B}$ are latent (or unobservable) variables, but from equation 4:

$$B^* = \frac{1}{1-\theta}B - \frac{\theta}{1-\theta}\hat{B} \qquad (5)$$

Making this substitution and absorbing $\hat{B}$ into the constant terms of $f_i(X_i)$ and $h_j(Y_j)$, equations 3 become:

$$S_i = f_i(X_i) + \frac{\alpha_i}{1-\theta}B \qquad (i = 1, \ldots, m)$$

$$U_j = h_j(Y_j) - \frac{\beta_j}{1-\theta}B \qquad (j = 1, \ldots, n)$$

$$B = \sum_j U_j + INT - \sum_i S_i$$

Interest payments INT enter directly into the identity for borrowing B, but it is important to note that the effect on investment of a change in INT is not measured simply by the coefficient $\beta_j(1-\theta)$ on B in the investment equation. This is because the initial change in B would lead to all sources and uses being affected, and in their turn modifying B.

These 'shifting' or 'feedback' effects would lead to a net effect of a change in INT on investment less than that given by $\beta_j/(1-\theta)$. In fact, the net effect is given by β_j, the coefficient on $(B^* - \hat{B})$ in equation 3.

This simplified model has ignored the dynamics of the

equations. Our estimated equations incorporate lagged terms.

Estimation Results

The most general investment equation estimated was of the form

$$I_t = C + \sum_{k-1}^{9} a_k I_{t-k} + \sum_{k-0}^{9} b_k Q_{t-k} + \sum_{k-0}^{9} C_k B_{t-k}$$

$$+ d_2 S_2 + d_3 S_3 + d_4 S_4$$

where I is fixed investment, Q is output and B is borrowing (see appendix for data details). The quarterly dummies S_2 - S_4 were included because of the very strong seasonal patterns in the data, much of which must be due to reasons exogenous to the relation modelled. Initial estimates using ordinary least squares yielded a positive coefficient on the current borrowing variable. This would seem to be due to simultaneous equation bias (borrowing is positively related to investment by the sources and uses identity), since re-estimation by instrumental variables (using various other components of the identity as instruments) reduced the coefficient to zero and left the rest of the equation largely unchanged. The results obtained using the GIVE package, are reported in Table 11.1, with standard errors in parentheses.

The final restricted equation is given in equation 8, where L is the lag operator. In case of any remaining simultaneity bias due to the current output variable, this final equation was estimated by instrumental variables using lagged values of consumers' expenditure, government expenditure and exports of goods as instruments.

$$\begin{aligned}
&(1 - \underset{(0.04)}{0.34}L(1 + L^2 + L^6) + \underset{(0.10)}{0.58}L^8)\, I_t = \\
&\quad (\underset{(5.1)}{15.3} - \underset{(4.7)}{9.7}L\,(1 - L^4 + L^5) + \underset{(1.8)}{6.3}L^7(1 + L))\, Q_t \\
&\quad - (\underset{(0.011=}{0.048}L^2(1 + L^7) + \underset{(0.016)}{0.074}L^6)\, B_t \\
&\quad + \underset{(44)}{353}S_2 + \underset{(59)}{436}S_3 + \underset{(42)}{446}S_4 - \underset{(224)}{1107}
\end{aligned} \qquad (8)$$

Table 11.1: Unrestricted estimates of (7) (standard errors in parentheses)

k	0	1	2	3	4	5	6	7	8	9
I_{t-k}	-	0.44 (0.18)	0.06 (0.19)	0.34 (0.19)	-0.09 (0.21)	0.09 (0.21)	-0.14 (0.19)	0.42 (0.21)	-0.74 (0.24)	0.21 (0.23)
Q_{t-k}	21.7 (8.0)	-13.3 (12.1)	-4.1 (11.0)	-3.8 (11.9)	-3.2 (13.0)	16.0 (13.5)	-12.2 (13.0)	5.8 (13.1)	5.8 (13.3)	0.9 (8.3)
B_{t-k}	-0.001 (0.036)	-0.008 (0.024)	-0.044 (0.026)	0.025 (0.027)	0.001 (0.028)	0.007 (0.030)	-0.084 (0.025)	0.001 (0.028)	0.010 (0.030)	-0.054 (0.027)
S_k			500 (219)	554 (157)	565 (219)					
Const	-1007 (359)									

standard error = 70.8 (4.1 per cent of mean value)

The standard error of this equation is 58.1, the Durbin-Watson statistic is 1.90, and the Box-Pierce residual correlogram statistic with eight degrees of freedom is 3.91. A chi-squared test of predictive power over four quarters yields a statistic of 0.51 (four degrees of freedom).

The long-run equilibrium solution of the investment equation 8 is

$$I \; 0 \; 32.8Q - =.307B + 636S_2 + 786S_3 + 804S_4 - 1994 \quad (9)$$

As explained above, 0.307 is an estimate of $\beta_j/(1-\theta)$ in the investment equation of equations 6. It cannot be used directly to estimate the effect on investment of an increase in interest payments, because not all of this increase will be passed on into the borrowing requirement. The net effect would be given by β_j, but it will not be possible to derive a value for β_j until we have estimated all the equations of the system. All that we can say at present, since $\beta_j \leqq \theta$, is that $0 < \beta_j \leqq 0.235$.

Conclusions and Policy Implications

The regression results reported in equation 8 suggest that in long-run equilibrium gross fixed capital formation in UK industry and commerce is positively related to output and is negatively related to firms' actual borrowing. The structure of the underlying theoretical model implies from this that investment is positively associated with firms' internal financial resources: if an external shock reduces that source of funds it causes an increase in borrowing which induces a reduction in investment.

One such external shock that has been the subject of recent policy disputes is a rise in interest rates which, by raising total interest payments (INT), cuts firms' internal funds and forces them to borrow more. Since 1979 nominal interest rates have been historically high and our estimates enable us to assess their maximum possible effect on investment. They suggest that the effect has been less serious than claimed by industrial critics of monetarist policies; a much larger effect on investment is exerted by the fall in output.

Between 1978 and 1981 the category in industrial and commercial companies' appropriation account which approximately equals their annual interest payments doubled from £4,437 million to £9,193 million. However in our model of sources and uses of funds interest payments net of receipts is the relevant variable and that increased from £2,702 million to £5,715 million or, appropriately deflated for inflation, from about £1,890 million to about £2,730 million. According to our estimates the worst possible effect on the long-term equilibrium value of investment as a result of a rise in interest payments of that magnitude would occur if the increase were not shifted onto other uses of funds (for example dividends were not cut) or onto any sources other than borrowing. In that case $\beta_i = 0.235$ and the real value of annual investment would be reduced by only about £200 million or 2.3 per cent of 1978 fixed capital formation (at 1975 prices).

Nevertheless, our estimates suggest that there is a significant, if small, relation between investment and interest rates which occurs through a different channel from the impact that interest rate changes may have through the relative cost of funds. Given the relative lack of success in the UK of attempts to find interest rates significant in investment equations, we would suggest there is a case for further investigation of this internal finance effect in the context of a complete model of all the sources and uses of funds of industrial and commercial companies.

APPENDIX

All data is quarterly and unadjusted for the UK industrial and commercial sector, unless otherwise stated. I (gross domestic fixed capital formation) and B (bank borrowing plus other loans and mortgages, less acquisition of all liquid financial assets) were taken from the 1982 edition of Economic Trends Annual Supplement. They are measured in millions of pounds at 1975 prices, using the price index implied in the CSO Macroeconomic Data Bank series for real and nominal gross domestic fixed capital formation by all industries. The output series Q was constructed as a weighted average of the index of industrial production and the output-based measure of GDP for various component sectors (1975=100), using series from the CSO Data Bank. The estimation period is 1965 (ii) to 1979 (iv), and the prediction period is 1980 (i) to 1980 (iv).

NOTES

1. Kuh and Meyer (1963), Dhrymes and Kurz (1967), Lintner (1967), Coen (1971), Kuh (1971), Clark (1979).

2. This has been confirmed by the results of a recent survey by Jerry Coakley at the Open University, of banks and engineering companies.

3. $\hat{B}$ has been treated in this version of the model as constant, although it may well be the case that it varies through time, for example, as gearing itself varies. Attempts to include gearing in the estimated equations (using data made available by the Bank of England), in addition to the flow of borrowing variable, did not obtain significant results. This may have been because it was necessary to impose (possibly unjustified) constraints on the coefficients of the lagged gearing terms in order to avoid first difference terms which are high correlated with the flow of borrowing.

The authors gratefully acknowledge the financial support of the Leverhulme Trust for this research. This is an amended version of a paper delivered at the RES/AUTE Conference, Oxford, 1983.

REFERENCES

Anderson, G.J. (1981a) 'A new approach to the empirical investigation of investment expenditures,' Economic Journal, vol. 91, pp. 88-103.

------ (1981b) 'Investment and profits in the industrial and commercial sector', in The Economics of the Profits Crisis (ed. W.E. Martin), London, HMSO.

Clark, P.J. (1979) 'Investment in the 1970s: theory, performance and prediction', Brookings Papers on Economic Activity, 1, 1979, pp.73-124.

Coen, R.M. (1971) 'The effect of cash flow on speed of adjustment', in Tax Incentives and Capital Spending (ed. G. Fromm), Amsterdam, North Holland.

Dhrymes, P.J. and Kurz, M. (1967) 'Investment, Dividend and external finance behaviour of firms', in Determinants of Investment Behaviour (ed. R. Ferber), New York, NBER.

Hibberd, J. (1981) 'Comment' on Anderson (1981b), in The

Economics of the Profits Crisis (ed. W.E. Martin), London, HMSO.

Kalecki, M. (1937) 'The principle of increasing risk', Economica, vol. 4, pp.440-7.

Kuh, E. (1971) 'Capital stock growth: a micro-econometric approach', Amsterdam, North Holland.

------ and Meyer, J.R. (1963) 'Investment, liquidity and monetary policy' in D.B. Suits et al., Impacts of Monetary Policy, Englewood Cliffs, N.J., Prentice Hall.

Lintner, J. (1967) 'Corporation finance: risk and investment', in Determinants of Investment Behaviour (ed. R. Ferber), New York, NBER.

Marris, R. (1967) 'The economic theory of "managerial" capitalism', London, Macmillan.

Meeks, G. (1981) 'Cash flow and investment', in The Economics of the Profits Crisis (ed. W.E. Martin), London, HMSO.

Wilson, H. (1980) (Chairman, Committee to Review the Functioning of Financial Institutions) 'Report', London, HMSO.

Part IV

NEW TECHNOLOGY AND BANKING

INTRODUCTION TO PART IV

Laurence Harris

Changes in money and finance have long been intimately bound to changes in technology. A well-known, graphic example was the impact of the telegraph upon the development of world wide banking and money in the late nineteenth century's age of imperialism. Today in Britain the most famous example is the role of computer technology in the international capital market created in the 'Big Bang' of 1986 (albeit despite the fact that this fame rests partly on the technology's much publicised early breakdown). The new systems of information technology are also highly significant in revolutionising the retail services of banks, building societies and other financial institutions. The cash dispensers, automatic teller machines, and credit card systems based on new technology have rapidly transformed the money-using, credit and saving habits of the population and, hence, the deposits which provide a base for the wholesale credit and dealing operations of banks and other institutions.

These changes are rooted in technological innovation, and the technology perspective dominates most writings on the subject, particularly in the flood of popular articles and programmes which present an imminent prospect of a science-fiction, automated cashless society. In fact, the application of new technology is determined in a fundamental way by economic and related social factors rather than the abstract, pure and undoubted smartness of the technology itself. The example of one technology, Electronic Funds Transfer at the Point of Sale (EFTPOS) examined in the first chapter of Part IV, is a pertinent illustration of this. The widespread use of EFTPOS is central to 'the cashless society' dream but, while the technology is already well developed, Smith and Wield show that its relative absence from Britain's high streets in the mid-1980s was attributable to such economic problems as 'who is to pay for it?'

The conjunction of new information technology and economic factors pushing toward its adoption (although Smith and Wield's work suggests that some of the judgements regarding cost saving may be misplaced) have, nevertheless, transformed the financial system at all levels. The ramifications are widespread and diverse. At one end of the spectrum is the effect on the character of money and monetary policy. Two decades after the Radcliffe Report concluded that 'money' is an elusive category constantly merging into new types of deposits and financial instruments (which, to maintain some analytical boundaries, were called 'near-money') new technology has increased that elusiveness to the point where the monetarist government of Margaret Thatcher had to abanadon the central policy instrument, control of the money supply. The rapid development of new money and credit operations in the information technology age make it even less possible than it was in Radcliffe's day to define the money supply as one thing (in those days, cash and demand deposits at banks) and then control it. At the other end of the spectrum, the new technology has had a considerable impact on the working lives of bank employees and the employees of other financial institutions. Smith and Wield's two chapters are to a large extent concerned with this relation between new technology and labour in banks.

Both the chapters by Smith and Wield are significant contributions to the small number of pioneering studies which, on the basis of fieldwork, provide reliable information on the impact of new technology on employment in the financial sector. Banking on New Technology examines this from the point of view of the interaction between information technology and the clearing banks' considerations of cost and product competitiveness. Their approach contrasts with other studies which treat new technology as a given instead of recognising the choices banks make between different forms of innovation. Smith and Wield's second chapter, New Technology and Bank Work, is pathbreaking in financial economics because it uses concepts well established in 'labour-process' and 'management' theories to study banking in Britain. They show that the introduction of new technology in banks' clerical work is related to conflicting tendencies in the organisation of bank work. The traditional method of organising, training and controlling bank workers has been challenged by some move toward 'Taylorism' where the processing of data and paper is organised on the lines of a factory-type division of labour and repetitive tasks. New technology is seen as a major factor in banks' choice between the different methods although its impact is not in one direction only.

These two chapters reinforce a theme that runs through this book, the perspective which sees financial institutions as real institutions with specific forms of power, specialised functions within the economy and distinct forms of operating. This perspective contrasts with the pure neo-classical theories of financial institutions. The dominant neo-classical writings treat them as financial intermediaries each of which is, therefore, no more than a balance sheet of financial assets and liabilities and a manager making rational portfolio allocation decisions. Another set of neo-classical writings is concerned with banks as firms producing and selling services but (with recent exceptions) this treats financial services as if they were indistinguishable from soap-powder or other commodities and able to be analysed in a comparative static framework which ignores their internal organisation. Smith and Wield, in contrast to these approaches, recognise that banks are organisations engaged in a specific type of competitive environment, competition in financial markets, while having to confront the problems of managing large workforces that are partly common to other commercial enterprises, and while being involved in a dynamic way with changing technology and product innovation.

Chapter Twelve

BANKING ON THE NEW TECHNOLOGY: COOPERATION, COMPETITION AND THE CLEARERS

Stephen Smith and David Wield

In this and the following chapter the implications of recent and future technological changes and choices in the banking industry are examined. This chapter tries to avoid the orthodox approach of: (i) a simple listing of new equipment, (ii) an assessment of how rapidly they will diffuse into the banks; (iii) usually followed by an assessment of the effects on employment and skills. This is because the orthodox approach has not been successful in building up a picture of the complex relationships between technological changes, employment and work. Instead our approach attempts to integrate a classification of technological changes within a study both of banking operations and of the relationships of competition and cooperation within and between banking and other financial organisations. The chapter introduces many of the issues surrounding technological innovations in the clearing banks, focusing on their money transmission services. This approach allows an assessment to be made of the interaction between organisational strategies and the production, choice, and management of technologies, and therefore a more realistic forecast of the future.

TECHNOLOGICAL CHANGE AND EMPLOYMENT

Studies of technological changes and their effects on the production of services are still rare. For different ideological reasons manufacturing is somehow taken more seriously than services. However, some writers have argued that the 'service sector' will take up the employment 'lost' by the shake-out in manufacturing industry (Sergeant, 1979; Nedo, 1983). In particular banking and financial services has been pinpointed as one sector which will significantly increase its number of jobs in the British economy (Rajan, 1984). Others go still further to argue that there is a shift from manufacturing to a 'new service economy' (Gershuny, 1978). But there are far fewer detailed studies of changes in the service sector than studies of changes in manufacturing. (Exceptions are Gershuny and Miles, 1984, Crompton and Jones, 1984; Child et al., 1984.)

Further, it can be argued that the category 'service sector' is so much more amorphous than the category 'manufacturing', that more work and more care is required when studying the effects of a particular technical change. The study of the introduction of word processors is a good example of some of the difficulties associated with an undifferentiated approach to these studies (Downing, 1981; Webster, 1984).

Very fundamental questions like 'do word processors cause job loss?', and 'do word processors cause deskilling?', have been adddressed using a very small, even if high quality, series of case studies. Little generalisable research has as yet been attempted about the differential impact of different systems on the vast spectrum of organisations using clerical and secretarial labour. Differences certainly exist between large insurance and mail-order houses, and bank branches, offices in manufacturing enterprises and in health and educational institutions. In fact the work of Green et al. (1980) pointed to very small changes in the numbers of clerical and secretarial workers lost in manufacturing units at least in the short term (Green Coombs and Holroyd, 1980). There are likely to be differences between integrated networked systems and stand-alone systems, as Amin Rajan has shown for the insurance industry (Rajan, 1984). Thus there are large gaps in even the relatively well-researched areas of technical change involving the introduction of the word processor - on the surface a relatively simple, discrete piece of equipment.

The word processor example is a good illustration of the difficulties in attempting to address the question of whether there is a direct relationship between technological change and employment. Our belief is that there is no such direct causal relationship, but we stress that we do not want to shy away from the big questions by hiding in narrow, 'technicist', sectoral or subsectoral studies.

One study which sets out a less simplistic framework whilst studying the relationship between new technologies and employment is that of Rajan. He sets out a framework which 'not only looks at the job saving potential of new technology but also its interaction with other factors that influence employment' (Rajan, 1984, p.17). He argues that the full impact of new technology on employment is mediated by a series of filters which he calls the economic, social and organisational 'moderators'. This work is a real advance.

We would argue, however, that a weakness of this approach is that it still appears to assume, as have so many studies, that a technology is available and is thrust at employees through a series of hurdles. The implication is that there are no choices of technology. We would argue rather that there is an articulation of on the one hand management organisational strategies, and on the other the production, choice, and use of technologies.

Having taken this step, a new series of 'big' questions then arises, different to 'does technology change employment?' Examples are 'How do relationships within and between organisations affect the introduction of technological changes?'; 'What are the effects of technological changes on organisations, and the different groups of people within them?'; and 'Is the experience of technical change always the same for all groups?' These questions seem a little easier to grapple with since they allow us to look directly at organisations, at who makes decisions in them, at the assumptions made of new technology and how these are broken and remade in the light of experience. They allow important issues, for example, like the changing balance centralisation/decentralisation, to be investigated.

We are attempting to address these questions focusing on the large clearing banks and particularly on changes in their money transmission services. We shall concentrate on two aspects. Firstly, what are the pressures influencing the investment choices of the banks on new technologies? Here we shall concentrate on their recent history (next section) and the contemporary competitive pressures on them (third section). And secondly, what do the relationships between organisational strategies and the production use and management of technologies tell us about how organisations react to supposed 'market forces' (fourth section).

TECHNOLOGICAL CHANGE AND BANKING EMPLOYMENT

We have tentatively divided developments in the 'retailing' operations of clearing banks into three periods:

1. The late 1950s and 1960s - a period of extensive growth with the introduction of semi-automated branch accounting systems and the gradual creation of task sub divisions in 'stand-alone' branches,
2. the 1970s - a period of more rapid technological and organisational change and competition with other banks,
3. the 1980s - a continuation of more rapid change and competition from other financial outlets, with some radical rationalisation of branches and some intensification of work.

1. 1950s and 1960s

The major clearers were already large in the 1950s and continued to grow rapidly in employment during the 1960s. For example, employment grew by 60 per cent from 1960 to 1970. The 'big four' clearers each had well over 2,000 branch outlets yet the total number of branches was not very different in 1978 to what it was in 1938 (Quinton, 1979). They each had a series of centralised head office functions, had limited international links, and were much more significantly oriented than today towards retail banking and internal credit operations than to international credit and foreign exchange operations. Together the clearing banks and their associates in Britain held over 85 per cent of all commercial banking business in sterling in 1955 (Fforde, 1983).

Average branch size was (and remains) small. The mean size even in 1979 was only between 12 and 14 employees. The general manager of one clearer argued that this extensive network of mostly small size branches arose primarily as a result of: the relatively low wages and other overhead costs of starting branches between the wars; the difficulties of handling and balancing hand-written book-keeping systems as branches grew; the fact that the clearers grew by acquisition tending to leave branches intact; and the view that bigger branches would become impersonal

(Quinton, 1979).

The banks invested relatively early in computer systems. In the 1960s large investments were made on mainframe computers linked to branch back office terminals. They were used principally for computerisation and centralisation of consumer credit and debit account records, and some associated interest calculations. The rapid growth of cheque usage still involved batch processing and a rapidly increasing flood of paper between branches (see Table 12.1). Increasing cheque usage led in the 1960s to the inter-bank cheque clearing system, involving the use of Magnetic Ink Character Recognition (MICR) and to the creation in 1968 of the Bankers Automated Clearing Services (BACS), a computer to computer electronic fund transfer system using magnetic tapes. Most salary bank payments including standing orders and direct debits, and inter corporation transactions now go through BACS, making it amongst the largest automated clearing house systems in the world with almost 700 million transactions in 1983 (Table 12.2). But these changes in centralised operations in the late 1960s did not begin to make an impact on bank productivity until the 1970s.

Table 12.1: Growth in the volume of payments (millions)

1960	753
1965	1004
1970	1342
1975	1953
1980	2860
1984	3551

Source: Committee of London Clearing Banks, (CLCB).

Table 12.2: (i) Numbers of transactions (million) (clearing banks)

	1972	1976	1980	1984
BACS	175.1	296.7	485.2	797.4
Credit Cards (Visa/Access)	n/a	71.0	150.4	319.8
ATM/CDs (England)	-	11.9	49.2	236.7
Cheques cleared (England)	1127.3	1467.2	1947.3	2326.9

Source: Committee of London Clearing Banks (CLCB).

(ii) Percentage increase in transaction volumes

	Annual increase (%)	
BACS	13.5	(1972-1984)
Credit Cards	22.7	(1974-1984)*
ATMs/CDs	46.9	(1979-1984)*
Cheques cleared	6.2	(1972-1984)

* Data not available from 1972

Table 12.3 is an attempt to measure the productivity change in the clearing banks. It is fraught with problems (1) but serves to give an indication of the growth of paper processing per employee. It shows rather low productivity growth in the 1960s - probably hiding central headquarter efficiency gains behind combined headquarter and branch equipment.

Table 12.3: Productivity increases* (English clearing banks)**

Year	Annual compound growth rate (%)
1960-1965	0.8
1965-1970	1.7
1970-1975	4.5
1974-1980	5.1
1980-1984	4.6

* Productivity measured by (volume of payments transactions)/(no. of employees).

** These are Lloyds, Midland, National Westminster, Barclays, Williams & Glyn's, Coutts.

Source: Frazer (1982) updated with CLCB data.

2. The 1970s

It was in the 1970s that a broad range of technological innovations were applied on a large scale in the banks, leading to confusing claim and counter-claim about impact on jobs and work. Table 12.3 shows the productivity indicator rising rapidly in that period, and we would argue that technological changes were the most important factor accounting for this increase.

The kinds of changes included: improved data processing systems like on-line links between branch 'back-office' and mainframe computers; cheque magnetic ink encoding systems to improve cheque throughput; non-return of cheques to personal customers; a rapid increase in BACS turnover, limited cheque truncation; the growth of centrally administered credit card use; more arguably, the beginnings of Automatic Teller Machine (ATM) installation and use, the SWIFT international interbank electronic funds transfer (EFT) system and some counter automation (Revell, 1983; Read, 1983).

In terms of branch organisational changes, the banks began experimenting. One clearer experimented in one location in the mid-1970s followed by a second pilot with a two-tier branch structure - an area branch concentrating on the broadest range of services, and satellite branches responsible for a smaller range of personal banking services. It didn't pursue the experiment, considering it 'inefficient', with an over division of labour, and 'costly'. But another clearer began a similar scheme in the late 1970s (Jones, 1981) which became quite widespread, and has been followed by the two other big clearers in the early 1980s with mixed results (as described in the next chapter).

Much of this more radical branch experimentation was a result of business premises arising outside domestic banking. The clearing banks' dominance of sterling deposit liabilities had dropped dramatically from 85 per cent in 1955 to 45 per cent in 1975. Banks began to think of rationalising their branch structures as their international operations began to play a more significant role in their activities. Barclays, for example, reviewed their retail banking structure and came up with the forecast that the number of medium and small branches and sub-branches would significantly decrease whilst the number of larger branches in central London and the larger provincial cities would increase (Table 12.4).

But these rationalisations did not occur very rapidly in the 1970s (Table 12.5). There was a small decline in branches. There was also the beginnings of a shift in headquarters type operations out of London to other regions, although compared with the insurance industry this shift was comparatively slow. However most new computer centres were established out of London, and two clearers moved a

Table 12.4: Barclays branch rationalisation forecast

	1975	2000 (Forecast)
Very large and large branches (>40 employees)	90	150
Medium branches (11-40 employees)	900	500
Small and sub-branches (<10 employees)	2050	1500
Total	3040	2240

Source: Quinton, 1979.

Table 12.5: Numbers of branches (full and sub-branches)

	1972	1976	1980	1984
The 6 London clearers	11,838	11,659	11,289	10,993
The 3 Scottish clearers	-	1541	1554	1478
Total	.	13,200	12,843	12,471

Source: CLCB.

significant proportion of headquarter operations to the north of England.

3. The 1980s

It is more difficult to point to one single factor influencing banking developments in the last few years. Rather, technological changes are having an increasing effect on banking operations but at markedly different scales and time frames. It is partly for this reason that they have not led to net redundancies but there are nevertheless major qualitative employment changes underway (see next chapter). We believe that banks are continuing with substantial if modified forms of restructuring that will involve some rationalisations of branch establishment structure, the closing of 'big four' branches in depressed regions and (more often) the downgrading of branches to a narrower range of services requiring fewer staff designated and paid as 'management'. It also involves some intensification of work. This is partly the result of network reorganisation, in conjunction with the uneven workload throughout the 'banking day'. For example, there is increased use of part-time women workers to cover for peak work periods in banks (Table 12.6). Since 1980 there has been a 32 per cent increase in this group, compared with very small decreases in male and female full-time employment due to non recruitment. Yet if anything the decision of the clearing banks to provide new financial services most notably mortgage (and related) services, stock broking and jobbing and other investment banking services makes the banking day and banking week increasingly lumpy. In these circumstances the arguments in favour of part-time work may be balanced by counter arguments about the quality of branch clerical 'marketing' staff.

Table 12.6: Employment in the English clearing banks

	Men	Women full-time	Women part-time	Total counting PT as 1	Total counting PT as 4/7
1980	98,980	123,287	15,307	237,574	231,040
1984	98,300	120,800	20,200	239,300	230,640
Percentage change	-0.7	-2.0	+32.0	+0.7	-0.2

Increases in Clearing Banks Employment (England) (Annual compound growth rate %)

Year	All employees	Counting part-timers as 4/7
1950-1955	1.2	
1955-1960	4.1	
1960-1965	5.1	
1965-1970	4.2	
1970-1975	3.2	
1975-1980	2.7	2.7
1980-1984	0.2	-0.1

Source: CLCB.

Our crude productivity measure from Table 12.3 shows a continued rise in the 1980s at a rate of 4.6 per cent per annum.

The fact that banks are increasing productivity at significant rates has had implications for employment in specific areas of their operations. Table 12.6 gives data on employment in the clearing banks. It shows relatively large increases in the late 1950s and 1960s, a slowing in the 1970s and stagnation in the 1980s. In fact if part-time workers are counted as 4/7th (on the assumption they work 20 hours a week) instead of one as the banks do, then bank employment in the 1980s has slightly decreased in the English clearers.

We will focus on this period in more detail in the next sections.

THE COMPETITIVE PRESSURES

The focus in this section will be on the increased competition facing the large clearers in that changes in the nature of competition will influence the speed and nature of innovation.

Over recent years they have been facing competition from a steadily increasing number of institutions in the savings, consumer credit and retail financial services area, as well as in the corporate and sovereign lending and other wholesale markets.

Changes in the City of London including competition in corporate lending and foreign market areas has been well treated elsewhere (see Coakley and Harris, 1983). We have seen a sharp increase in competition between British and a growing number of foreign banks, focused on lending to leading UK companies with good profitability (Coakley and Harris, 1983, p.138).

We will summarise more carefully the competitive pressures on banks in the area of retail financial services. This is an area of central concern to the banks with a host of competing institutions, leading to much more serious attempts to cut costs, including labour costs. Figure 12.1 sketches the important competing institutions in the area, and the important overlapping services on offer. For example, we have divided the financial sector from the retail sector, with which it competes over consumer credit and credit card facilities. Then we have divided banks from building societies and other financial institutions like

Figure 12.1 Competition for personal savings, consumer credit, use of ATMS, mortgage loans.

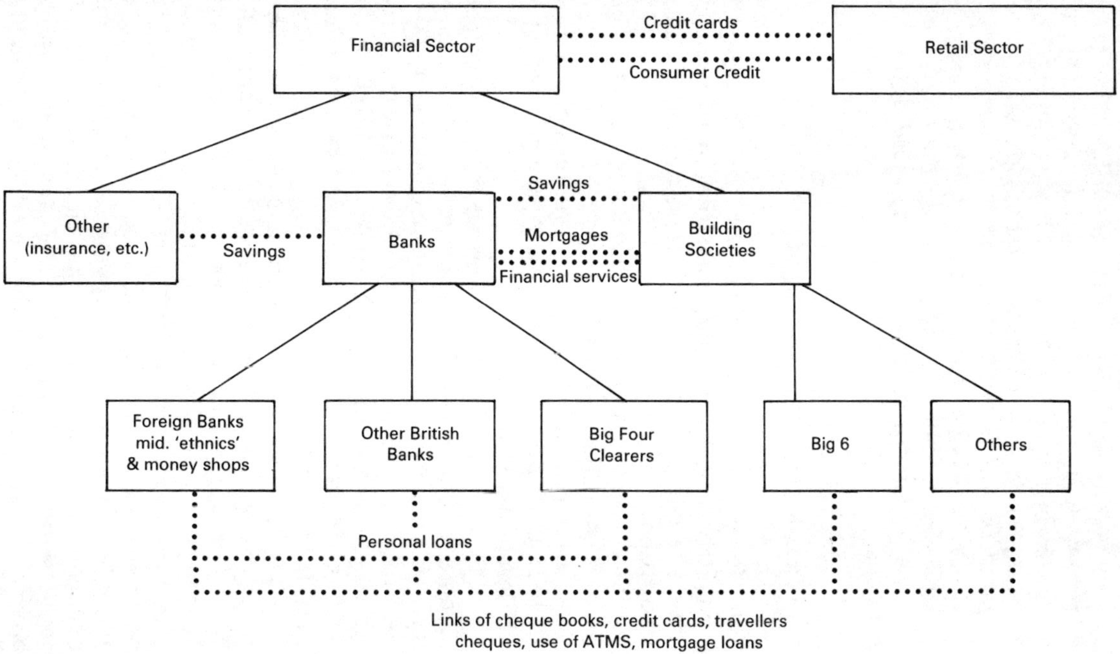

insurance companies.

We have divided the building societies into two groups: large and small. Those with large branch networks and assets are competing with the banks for savings business. At the same time individual building societies and small groups of building societies are cooperating with the smaller banks, with foreign banks and with the Girobank in order in turn to compete with the big four for example by obtaining ATM links, cheque clearing facilities and so on. The top 13 building societies have around 85 per cent of building society assets. These societies have the financial resources to invest in new computing and other information technology facilities, and several counter drive facilities are in place. Despite the prospect of many more product innovations the range of branch labour tasks remains very much simpler than in clearing bank branches.

We have also divided the banks into three groups, as follows:

1. The big 4 (Barclays, Lloyds, Midland, Nat. West). These have huge branch and ATM networks (see Table 12.5 and 12.7), and efficient cheque-clearing systems. They are attempting to remain dominant over the whole range of financial services with some product segmentation.

2. The smaller clearers, and British banks with retail outlets (Trustee Savings Bank, Co-operative Bank, Williams & Glyn's, the Scottish banks, Yorkshire Bank and the Standard Chartered (that applied to join the clearers in 1983). These banks have been able to increase their ability to compete with the big four through investment in new technologies, linked to a more flexible branch structure.

3. The foreign banks including Citibank with its expanding retail chain of about 50 outlets in late 1984 and the first foreign bank to apply to join the clearing system, the 'ethnic' banks like the Irish, Bangladeshi, Indian and Israeli banks, and money shops like Boston Trust and HFC Trust. These banks also offer a broad range of retail financial services with flexible opening hours, relatively higher interest rates on savings accounts than the other banks, and interest on current accounts.

From this short summary, we would suggest that there are a set of discrete instruments of competition, as follows:

(i) higher interest rates to savers,

(ii) lower margins between borrowing and lending rates (which requires lower costs or lower profits) particularly in the company sector,

Table 12.7: ATMs and cash dispensers installed by 1984 (English and Scottish clearers)

	Number
Barclays	787
Lloyds	1622
Midland	858
National Westminster	1544
Williams & Glyn's	185
Bank of Scotland	211
Clydesdale	225
Royal Bank of Scotland	317

Source: CLCB.

(iii) flexibility and ease of credit (say, for mortgages, retail credit and small personal loans),
(iv) more flexible money transmission services (like credit cards, ATMs, travellers cheques, cheque books), and
(v) breadth of branch network.

There have been changes in all these instruments of competition. The proportion of personal savings taken into the banks has fallen, whilst that of the building societies has risen. The building societies' new accounts with higher interest rates increased their share of new savings from 46 per cent to 57 per cent in 1980-82, whilst the banks' proportion plummeted from 45 per cent to 22 per cent. Thus the easy inflow of money from personal savers into high street branches all over the country slowed to a trickle. Banks have begun to respond by offering new types of account, like cheque accounts with higher interest rates and rolling credit/deposit accounts. The banks are aiming to increase their savings share by increasing interest rates and giving cheque accounts at the same time. This seems to be an example of the second instrument of competition, that of lowered margins. For their part, some building societies are offering cheque accounts, like Abbey National's account which offers a Co-operative Bank cheque book. Another example of the cooperative links between building societies and the smaller banks' 'retail' operations is Moneylink, which is a deal between Bristol and West Building Society and Standard Chartered. Customers with at least £500 at the Bristol and West earn 1 per cent less interest in return for free banking with Standard Chartered. Bristol's link with

Standard Chartered involves automatic transfer of non-interest bearing current account balances into the building society account. Of course, these developments depend on computer technologies, and automatic fund transfer systems.

Increased flexibility and ease of credit evolves from competition between banks and other financial and retail institutions. The banks expanded rapidly into the mortgage market in 1981 and 1982. The reasons suggested for this have been (i) that mortgage lending fits well into the banks' strategy to sell a broad range of financial services to personal savings customers, and (ii) that the building societies are easier competition in housing than the US banks in corporate banking (Crawley, 1982).

Competition between banks and the retailing sector is growing since both sectors are attempting to increase credit facilities in the personal sector. Credit card holders of Access and Visa totalled over 17 million in 1984 although average transactions remain quite low at under two per month. But also important in the light of technical possibilities for electronics fund transfer is the expansion of retailers' own cards. Some of these are run by an inhouse finance house. Debenhams, for example, through Debenhams Finance, has its own card. This puts these retailers firmly into the personal financial credit market into which the banks also wish to expand. Other retailers use specialised finance houses. D.H. Evans and Army and Navy use Midland Bank, Marks and Spencer use Citibank, Boots use National Westminster, and several others use Welbeck Finance. In late 1984 British Home Stores announced a link up with Boston Trust and Savings to offer savings, deposits, investment, mortgage, insurance and cheque cashing services as well as loans in selected BHS stores. Competition with retailing groups was one reason given for Nat West's decision to open on Saturday morning in some branches (Riley, 1984), a decision linked to selling personal services and non-staffed cash dispenser machine availability but no normal counter service.

The competition offered by the retailers is important in two areas. First is the experience in the United States where, greatly assisted by the restriction allowing banks to operate in only one state, Sears Roebuck has expanded dramatically in the credit market. Second, there is the technical possibility of electronic funds transfer systems (EFTS) linked to store point of sales systems (POS). The setting up of such systems on a national scale in Britain will require the banks to negotiate and work with credit companies and with the retailers who will insist on involvement in the EFTPOS arrangements, and who at least publicly protest that they have so far been excluded. This differs from automated clearing systems which the bank cartel controls but which with the publication of the Child report they have decided to open up (Lascelles, 1984). After the establishment of EFTPOS a branch network system will not necessarily be required for conducting retail operations involving money transmission. The banks then stand to lose their monopoly of money transmission systems. (2)

The fourth and fifth instruments of competition, money transmission services and branch networks, are traditional areas of dominance of the clearers. Money transmission remains a clearers' monopoly, certain until the Child report is implemented. The branch network has been under increasing pressure from the building societies. The banks have begun trimming their branch network and have downgraded hundreds of branches in attempts to cut costs, especially the costs of managers. At the same time extensions and alternatives to the branch network and the cheques are being developed and expanded. Examples are the Banks Automated Clearing Service (BACS), ATMs, EFTPOS, and the experiments with home banking. Certainly the banks see their branch network, without its traditional ability to bring in savings, as a major cost in the system, as they see the cheque system as a cost.

Until recently, the building societies gave the impression of having rather fewer proportional overheads than the banks - their network was smaller both in number of branches and in staff, and they have no cheque-clearing systems of their own. Yet they have little leeway, for in the period of competition over interest rates in late 1984, the building societies kept up the savers rate only at the expense of charging higher mortgage interest rates.

Whether the large clearers are now engaging more equally with the building societies or not (accounts vary), they are certainly considering a whole series of moves aimed at improving their competitiveness: both between themselves as a cooperating group (they are formally linked as members of the CLCB - the Committee for London Clearing Banks) and other financial institutions; and between themselves. We will summarise these moves in the next section.

We have detailed the competition element within personal financial services to show: (i) that many changes involve institutional and organisational innovations and not only technological innovations. The smaller clearers and the large building societies have organisational structures which make easier and cheaper the 'take-up' of new technologies, and they have sufficient size and business to invest in mainframe - mini computer - counter terminal systems, and (ii) that distinguishing between the instruments of competition is useful in beginning to characterise the use to which new technologies will be put. One such distinction is between technological innovation designed to cut branch overhead costs, or to improve delivery of a given service - so called process innovations, and innovation of a completely new financial product or service - a product innovation.

With such a distinction we may better be able to analyse the changes to date, and future changes within banks and other financial and retailing institutions, than by a simple listing of technical changes and how these will be mediated by social and economic forces.

Charles Read, former Director of the Inter Bank Research Organization, wrote that 'the most important effects of the new technology are not on the detailed systems designs but on major strategic issues such as who cooperates or competes with who, who should fund the technical developments, who has control and power in the new situations. In a word what are the politics of the technology?' (Read, 1983). Read here is referring to new technologies and to the politics and power of institutions to influence technical change. We would argue also that the politics of new technology internal to organisations (as for example in new branch design where systems design is political in a different 'work organisational' sense) is important (see next chapter).

NEW TECHNOLOGIES AND BANKING ORGANISATIONS

In this section we begin by characterising the technical changes taking place in banking. Then, using the examples of ATMs and EFTPOS we describe some of the contradictory tendencies occurring as choices are made on technology and organisation.

How to Characterise Technical Changes?

We argue that organisational and political aspects are of at least equal importance to any 'technical imperative' of the systems themselves and that any characterisation of the changes taking place in banks needs to take serious account of this. Clearly, technical change description cannot be a characterisation of the technical systems alone.

We have attempted several alternative types of characterisation (Tables 12.8a to 12.8d) to give an idea of the large and complicated range of technical changes taking place. Firstly, we tried characterising changes in terms of physical layout of bank branches (see Table 12.8a). This has the advantage of easily relating to organisation of work at branch level, but the disadvantage of not immediately illustrating the links between branches and head office functions.

Table 12.8: Alternative approaches to the classification of technical change in banking

Table 12.8a: Classifying from physical layout of bank branch

Lobby	- ATMs/Cash dispensers - Standing Order changes, customer aid systems.
Counter-Customer	- PIN number card link to cashier aid terminal.
Counter-Cashier	- Counter terminal system - Automatic cash dispensers - Use of plastic cheque guarantee cards.
Back Office	- Cheque processing, including truncation - Automation of accounts, through terminals to mainframes or distributed systems - Funds transfer electronically (EFT) - Computerisation of branch records - Word processing - Microfiche - Credit scoring for loans.

Outside the Branch
- ATMs
- Automated clearing through tape transfer (BACS)
- POS terminals linked to EFT switching network
- Home banking.

Table 12.8b: Classifying from types of electronic funds transfer (EFT) systems

- Automated Clearing House (BACS) for large batches of payments, substituting for paper flow
- ATMs/CDs, substituting for cheques
- Bank branch automation and cheque truncation substituting for paper flows, manual accounting systems, secretarial work and so on
- EFTPOS, substituting for cash, cheque, credit card
- Home banking, substituting for cash, cheque, credit card
- Corporate EFT, like the international Society for World wide Interbank Financial Telecommunications (SWIFT) and the City of London based same day Clearing House
- Automated Payments System (CHAPS) substituting for paper-based transmission.

Table 12.8c: Categorisation around concrete operations in the banks

- Automation of book-keeping and accounts
- Cheque handling
- Teller terminals at counter
- Removal of paper from information transmission using voice and data networks
- Self-service banking
- Automation of customer records
- Electronic corporate cash management.

Table 12.8b gives a characterisation based on changes in information transmission, particularly the use of electronic funds transfer (EFT) systems. It is an approach which relates more directly to the different types of equipment on offer.

Table 12.8c is a characterisation based on production operations mostly in the retail banking industry (Read, 1983). None of these characterisations is ideal. The types of

Table 8d: Summary of technical changes in banking, and its effects

Technical changes affecting bank operations	Automation of book-keeping and accounting	Administrative automation and reorganisation
Parts of banks affected	Branch 'back office'; computer centres management services	Branch 'back office' to central services and head office
Examples of changes, or problems	(i) In the 1960s branch terminals (like Burroughs TC 500) installed, linked to central mainframe computer (ii) In 1980s branch mini computers and micro-computers linked to main-frames, give increased flexibility and information at branch level, e.g. Nixdorf minis with VDU terminals and printers linked to IBM mainframes	(i) Automation of branch records, using mini computers, (ii) word processors or or upgraded typewriters for secretarial work (iii) Branch reorganisation with Area Offices for corporate business divided from personal customer services
Process/Product innovation		

Table 12.8d: continued

Improved cheque and voucher handling		Counter terminal systems
cheque clearing	credit clearing	('Teller aids')
Branch 'back office' and centralised cheque-clearing systems	Branch 'back office' and centralised clearing systems	Branch counter (front office) and lobby
(i) cheque encoding and 'reading' originally MICR (Magnetic Ink character recognition) increasingly OCR (Optical character recognition (ii) non-return of cheques to personal customers (iii) cheque truncation systems, possibly linked to computerised signature verification	(ii) credit encoding, usually MICR, beginning of OCR	(i) Cashier side cashier aid machines as in Building Societies and Bank of Scotland (ii) Cashier side machines for dispensing cash (iii) Customer side Pin number machines (avoiding use of cheques and guarantee cards at the counter)

Process

Table 12.8d: continued

Removal of paper processing from the branch		
Direct computer to computer transfer	Plastic card based system	
	Credit cards	Cheque guarantee cards
Substituting for cheques and vouchers in branch and elsewhere	Credit card subsidiaries Barclays, Access	Bank counter, cheque-clearing system, retailers
(i) Automated clearing house (BACS in Britain) substitutes magnetic tape systems for vouchers, for wage payment, etc. (ii) CHAPS for same day clearing in the city for payments of over £10,000	(i) Increased competition from retailers' own cards and entertainment cards (American Express, Diners Club) (ii) problems include security issues (limiting credit) and paper generation (iii) profitable, but ATM, EFTPOS and home banking are possible alternatives	(i) This system generates cheques at bank counters, requires the cheque-clearing system, and is considered expensive (ii) possible alternatives are ATMs, EFTPOS and home banking
	Process	

Table 12.8d: continued

magnetic stripe cards for ATMS, CDs ATMS, Cash dispensers	home banking	POS systems
substitutes for bank counter by situating machines in lobby, through the wall, or at 'remote' sites from branch	substitutes for cheques, etc. Avoids use of branch, uses customer terminal to LAN, mainframe	substitutes for branch network. Direct link retailer/LAN/mainframe or via BACS
(i) Simple single function machines like cash dispensers, account balance indicators (ii) ATMs with several functions as in most existing through-the-wall models (iii) sophisticated multi-function 'robot tellers'	(i) simplest systems allow account balance enquiry, standing order changes, bill paying (ii) Bank of Scotland, Nottingham Building Society allows travel service ordering, electronic mail service, broker service	(i) retailer terminal on-line to bank mainframe (ii) retailer terminal through LAN to mainframe (CLCB system) (iii) terminal linked to BACS

Product

operations in banking are difficult to characterise simply. Nor does there seem to be a simple characterisation of labour process used by the banks.

Finally, we attempt a comprehensive listing based on operations in banking as in Table 12.8c, but with a set of cross cutting columns detailing the parts of the banks affected, and examples of the detailed technical systems. Some of the changes took place in the 1960s, most have occurred in the last decade, and some are as yet experimental. The result is Table 12.8d, where the last columns give examples of equipment and systems, and the earlier columns the banking operations being changed. The list also divides process from product innovations. The advantage of this approach is that it shows the complexity of interaction between people, organisations and the determination of choices of technologies.

Table 12.8d does appear rather complex, and in fact serves to show that to talk of new technologies in banking is not to talk of narrow technical change, but of changes taking place at many levels. This approach does allow us to analyse contradictory tendencies. In this chapter we cannot be comprehensive but instead will consider a number of changes to illustrate the usefulness of this approach. We will look at ATMs and EFTPOS.

Introduction of Automatic Telling Machines (ATMs)

Automatic telling machines are machines operated by customers by putting a plastic card in a slot, and punching in a personal identification (PIN) number. This allows them to receive cash, and often credit balances. Customers can sometimes order statements and cheque books, and even move money from current to deposit accounts and vice versa. Cash dispenser (CD) machines just deliver cash.

ATMs have often been presented as an isolated technical change in their own right, but we would rather argue that they are a particular choice of technology for a twofold series of tasks. In Table 12.8d, for example, we have categorised ATMs in two ways: (i) as one element of self-service banking - as a means of delivering a service to customers without them meeting a cashier at the bank counter. This was originally characterised as a process innovation delivering a traditional service more productively. Sometimes however it has been seen as a product innovation delivering a new service to customers, as for example giving a 24-hour cash delivery service, and (ii) as a means of reducing paper in the system, clearly a process innovation.

We have chosen ATMs because superficially they appear to be an extremely simple innovation. However, the organisational issues associated with their introduction are still quite complex. We will summarise some of the most important here, as follows:

(i) issues of competitiveness, related to two of our earlier instruments of competition, namely more flexible money transmission systems, and the breadth of the branch network,

(ii) cost of delivery of the service,

(iii) choice of delivery of service between ATMs or improved cheque clearing,

(iv) relations between banks and equipment suppliers.

(i) Issues of competitiveness

If successful in gaining customer acceptance ATMs give the large banks a competitive advantage over smaller banks and building societies in this particular means of delivering a service. They give this advantage because each of the large clearers has a much larger potential ATM network than any of the building societies. Table 12.7 shows the extent of the bank's ATM network in 1984. Building on this advantage Nat West and Midland have linked their National Cash Register ATM machines and Barclays and Lloyds theirs, so that customers of either bank can use them. These machines, in their vast majority, are sited at bank branches, either inside the lobby or through-the-wall. But a few have been set up at retail and workplace sites on an experimental basis, thus beginning a trend to unstaffed bank service points.

The building societies and banks with a smaller number of branch outlets, realising that if they wish to compete in this they would need to co-operate between themselves, have made attempts to link with other institutions to set up an integrated system. One such consortium, called Fund Transfer Sharing, links Citibank Savings, American Express, Yorkshire Building Society and Western Trust, in a proposal to set up 230 ATMs, and link them with those operated by National Girobank, Abbey National, and the Co-operative Bank to form a network of 800 machines (Banking World,

1984).

(ii) The cost of delivering the service

Another important question is to what extent ATMs are being introduced to save employees and thus labour costs, to save other costs like paper processing and transmission costs, or to give an extra service to the customer. We shall approach this issue in two ways: firstly by summarising the history of ATM introduction, and then by looking at the cost questions.

Apart from the very simple electro-mechanical £10 cash dispensers, there have been three main phases in, or approaches to, ATM introduction. Lloyds Bank were the first to introduce this generation of ATM machines in the mid-1970s. At the beginning their approach seemed geared more towards lowering labour costs than increasing service, since they introduced their machines inside the bank lobbies, but not for 24-hour service. They were linked on-line to mainframe computers from branches where the lines were not active during the night. They introduced them with a notional half a cashier saving in each bank branch - notional in that ATMs were introduced into expanding branches.

Lloyds argued that the number of employees in these branches would increase less fast. ATMs would help given the rapidly increasing level of branch custom in branches that could not easily be physically expanded. The end result was that Lloyds had machines in the lobby only operating during the hours of business, or sometimes a little more.

However, when the other banks introduced ATMs later in the 1970s, they went for a 24-hour through-the-wall service. This involved quite expensive structural alterations. It also involved giving a 24-hour customer service, some banks say for little extra revenue and rather low cost savings on alternative paper transactions.

In fact more recently Nat West particularly have moved towards both through-the-wall ATMs and in-lobby cash dispensers, and separate machines for checking balances and paying in, thus mixing product and process rationales in mechanising facilities to free other staff for other tasks. Lloyds have in the meantime also come to view ATMs as product as well as process innovations. They have thus increased the hours of many of their ATMs in lobbies and redesigned some branches so that some in-lobby machines remain open until very late at night. So the history of ATM introduction over the last few years shows a move at the beginning balanced towards saving employees, then moving to increase the level of 24-hour cash service to customers for little extra revenue, and finally moving to a hybrid form of 24-hour and lobby ATM, and other self-service machines, in some cases inserting advertising into the ATMs.

The issue of ATM cost is also sometimes forgotten. ATM costs are significant and are a cost on branch services in the sense that they are an integral part of the retail banking service. It is not clear what the 'return' is on ATM machine costs. The cost of a through-the-wall ATM is about £30,000. It has been argued that to save the labour of one cashier an ATM requires a throughput of about 1500 cash transactions a week. That is about one transaction every six minutes over the 24-hour day. At that level of saving the payback period is calculated as between five to seven years. The average weekly number of cash transactions in the big four varied in 1984 from 850 for Lloyds to 1200 for National Westminster. The most used cash withdrawal from ATMs was the minimum (£5). Though it's recently increased to £20. Customers have taken to withdrawing smaller amounts more often. About 5000 of these through-the-wall ATMs were in place at the end of 1984 at a cost of about £150 million. It is clear that some banks feel under pressure to introduce ATMs in non-cost-effective sites because of the competition from other banks. Certainly the number of new through-the-wall ATMs being introduced has now dropped dramatically as the focus has turned to in-lobby cash dispenser and other machines.

(iii) **Choice of delivery of service between ATM or improved cheque clearing**

Another way of looking at costs is by looking at the way the banks estimate the cost of a transaction. In mid-1984 we were given the following estimate of relative costs of cheque clearing and ATM use. The cost of clearing a cheque was about 24p for a simple cheque-clearing operation between accounts in the branch, and went up to 65p for a cheque being cleared between two different banks. A transaction through an ATM was estimated as costing between 25p and 50p. But ATM use is increasing the volume of unpaid for transactions, and particularly the number of small value transactions, as we saw above. These estimates of relative cost once again illustrate that there are conflicting approaches to delivering services using different technologies with rather complex interactions. On the one hand the banks have successfully automated the cheque handling system, which is reputed to be the best in the world. But at the same time they have tried and continue to try to substitute for it by developing forms of self-service banking through automatic teller machines, cash dispenser systems, EFTPOS, home banking and so on.

(iv) The relationship between banks and equipment suppliers

This issue is particularly interesting in that the British clearers as users and the equipment manufacturers as suppliers have different views of the direction that technological innovation should take. Around the issue of ATMs the suppliers have tended to emphasise interactiveness and complexity of machinery and service functions, whilst the banks have emphasised simplicity, speed, ease of use and dividing services to customers into discrete machines.

The banks have argued that the ATM systems should not contain large numbers of alternative services. They argue for example that queues build up in the banks and that ATMs must substitute above all for cashing cheques in branches. They have therefore encouraged suppliers to supply cheap and very simple cash dispenser systems operating from customer cards. Banks pressured suppliers to design and produce and are now installing simple in-lobby cash dispensers costing around £9,000 to introduce rather than the £30,000 required for a through-the-wall ATM. The suppliers on the other hand, have attempted to get the banks to use more complicated systems involving more complex interactive systems such as those which are in place in the United States where customer behaviour and expectations differ. Despite these differences one consultancy is designing a workshop for suppliers which aims to assist them to communicate the virtues of more interactive systems to the major clearing banks.

The Introduction of Electronic Funds Transfer at the Point of Sale (EFTPOS)

Some EFTPOS systems are already in operation, but not on a generalised, integrated basis. There are several schemes in the United States and France. In Belgium EFTPOS is generally available at garages. In Scotland, Clydesdale Bank has a scheme operating at filling stations. The Anglia Building Society has begun a scheme in the Northampton area. Last but not least, the Committee of London Clearing Banks (CLCB) has a long-standing committee to develop a shared nationally unified EFTPOS scheme. This is planned to begin in 1988 and would be the first ever such network.

EFTPOS systems are innovations that can function in several ways, usually involving a customer's card to activate a terminal at a shop checkout: (i) the on-line type can make immediate transfer of funds from a customer's account to a retailer; (ii) there is an 'off-line' system which can store information to be sent through the BACS system for daily electronic funds transfer; (iii) this would require a security check to make sure the customer has enough money, but which could be an authorisation telephone; and (iv) in France, the 'smart card' has a memory chip which contains a particular quantity of 'money' from which each purchase is deducted.

Although there are some technical difficulties with the most sophisticated systems, it is not these which are holding back the growth of EFTPOS. It is organisational and institutional constraints which are holding it back, particularly the questions of who will cooperate with whom? on what terms? and who will pay the cost of setting up a national system? We will briefly introduce three issues, namely those of (i) cooperation between banks; (ii) cooperation between banks and retailers, and (iii) other issues of cost.

(i) Cooperation between banks

Cooperation between banks is needed to avoid duplication of terminal systems in retailing outlets. Difficulties in other countries have been caused by individual bank or finance houses going it alone. This has resulted in a plethora of exclusive systems, resulting in low volume use per terminal. Heffenan (1984) suggests that the only clearly successful

EFTPOS system is in Limoges, France, where one bank has a significant proportion of personal bank accounts and there is only one large hypermarket. The US has scores of local systems.

The CLCB's initiative is an attempt to avoid such problems by integrating the clearers, and debit and credit card companies. By early 1984, the planning group had had discussions with 13 such card companies (Clark, 1984). The CLCB team hoped that their initiative will avoid individual banks going it alone. It also hopes to stop Visa or American Express setting up competing systems.

But there are still unresolved problems. For example, when in 1984 the CLCB working team moved to select a joint British Telecom/IBM system for part of the network equipment, some banks appeared to be against such large companies (with no British computer equipment suppliers) monopolising a possible future standard. This has been resolved for the moment, with BT and IBM expecting to be given the first orders, and an agreement that standards will allow other companies to tender in future. Keeping this agreement constrains the design of the system.

However, it seems that the clearers will not be able to keep a monopoly control over the system, as they did over BACs and the cheque-clearing systems. The anti-monopoly Office of Fair Trading, and the National Consumer Council are watching too closely for that. Thus, one important question is whether the banks should underwrite a large proportion of the costs of a system which is an alternative to the clearing services they monopolise, with the danger of losing custom to other financial institutions and retailer-organised loan operations.

(ii) Cooperation between banks and retailers

One issue, arising partially from the costs of setting up the EFTPOS system, is that of relations between the banks and retailers. Some retailers have argued vociferously that there is nothing in EFTPOS for them, and they will not pay any of the capital cost of setting it up. This was estimated at around £400 million in 1984, £150 million for the banks (and possibly credit card companies), £150 million for the network suppliers and £100 million for the retailers. The retailers' portion is principally for terminals. They would therefore need to save costs or gain extra business to make the system pay. The banks will need to levy lower charges, in comparison to credit cards or cheque-clearing charges, for the retailers to accept EFTPOS.

A related issue is that of integrating the retailers' own credit card systems. These cards need to be integrated into the system to gain retailer acceptance and to gain transaction volume.

(iii) **Other issues of cost**

The volume of transactions will be an important determinant of the EFTPOS's success. The banks will need a tangible benefit, namely cutting down cheque use, and generally stemming the use of paper. The banks estimate that unit cost of electronic operations will be one-third to a half less than the costs of conventional clearing after seven years (Heffernan, 1984, p.22) although no data exist to verify this. Neither is there information to check whether this includes the cost of building up extra computer capacity to cope with the extra processing requirements of EFTPOS.

British Telecom will require revenue for the use of the network and will almost certainly require a minimum number of transactions so as to guarantee a profit.

The EFTPOS system aims to pick up about half of the retailers' share of cheques, i.e. half of 24 per cent. Banks hope that EFTPOS will thus account for 600 million transactions by 1996. But they also estimate that credit card use will still be higher (700 million), with cheque still the most popular payment form (1.6 billion).

Revell (1983, p.46) believes that the initial sales volume would not be reached even if the system completely replaces bank credit card use and half the cheque system.

Getting customer acceptance is another imponderable since they stand to lose both the three-day grace from cheque payment and the up to six weeks credit given by a credit card, a system which provides profits for the banks.

Finally, the banks must be aware of the large capital costs of installing an infrastructural technology as yet without clear national or international standards. This involves the danger of being 'locked-in' to a relatively obsolete system if say equipment linked to a more sophisticated system like the French 'smart card' became the international standard.

To summarise, we find once more that the issues

surrounding EFTPOS are complex, revolving around whether the banks can control and get overall agreement for a nationally integrated system, or whether competing financial institutions will operate separate localised systems if the banks delay their 1986 start. As retailers develop their own credit card systems, any nationally integrated system will become less easy to install.

CONCLUSION

'Revolution in banking' is the slogan of suppliers of information technology equipment to the banks. One conclusion from this chapter is that although the technology appears to be revolutionary, the reality is somewhat less so.

For example, the introduction of ATMs was originally seen by suppliers as a simple substitution of 'human' by 'automatic' tellers. But this equivalence has not been hard and fast. Firstly, productivity is difficult to measure; secondly ATMs have been used in a different way to that anticipated, e.g. generating more smaller cash withdrawals; thirdly, the banks are not agreed how sophisticated their systems should be; fourthly, competition between banks means that ATMs have been put in sites of low usage; and so on. Similarly, EFTPOS is one means of eliminating paper. However, its capital cost is very large, negotiations are unfinished as to who will pay for it, and it is clear that it will make only a small dent in the number of cheques cleared. It also looks unattractive as a product.

All the signs are that these and other technical changes are steady rather than 'revolutionary'. What we do see, however, is that the large gamut of technical changes is significantly affecting the organisations of banks, and other financial institutions. The relationships between technical change and organisation are two way. Changing conditions of competition and cooperation are affecting technological innovations and technology choice in a complex way. For example, the introduction of through-the-wall ATMs with 24-hour service forced Lloyds to change its in-lobby ATM policy. And the cost of through-the-wall systems has affected the decision of other clearers to introduce simpler, cheaper in-lobby cash dispenser machines. The moves against monopoly practices of the clearers, though hotly denied by them, have changed the environment in which EFTPOS can be introduced compared to say that of the banks' control of the cheque-clearing and BACs systems.

The availability of new technologies is affecting conditions of competition and cooperation. For example, customer acceptance of ATMs has forced clearers to increase their number, and moved the building societies and non-clearing banks to introduce them. This is a costly operation, and requires a large number of outlets. It is being planned as a cooperative venture between groups of competing institutions. This chapter includes other examples reinforcing the conclusion that the introduction of new technology is central in the competition between financial and retailing institutions.

Moving to the effects on internal bank organisation, if tendencies continue, we are witnessing the end of big employment growth in banking. But there will not be, for a number of years at least, any real decline in banking employment. We are nevertheless witnessing very significant changes in work organisation and career structure. This chapter describes the planned rationalisation of the branch network. It also shows employment stagnation among the clearers, balanced by a rapid increase in women's part-time employment. The following chapter focuses on these changes and their relationship to technical change, showing the implications for the quality of working life. There have been some surprises.

NOTES

1. Accurate productivity measures in many service sectors are extremely difficult to find. For example, the Central Statistical Office uses a simple measure of the number of people employed, to measure the output of some service sectors like education, resulting in a complete inability to measure labour productivity (CSO, The measurement of changes in production, 1976). It measures banking output, principally from financial data like total bank deposits and quantity of bank advances made.

Serious research work on bank productivity have used financial information alone - like assets per employee, and revenue per employee. These indicators cannot measure added value since they depend on bank assets and interest rates (see Frazer, 1982). We agree with Frazer that labour productivity measures must use some indicator of labour output. Although many banks have complex organisation and method productivity measuring systems, these are very complex indeed and are neither publicly available, nor available with long time series. But one key measure is the processing of payments. In the large clearers it is said that a large proportion of staff time is spent in these activities. Furthermore it seems reasonable to suppose that more staff time is being spent in the last few years on new activities not relating to money transmission (international, mortgages, marketing of services) so understating productivity. So actual productivity measures are perhaps higher than those calculated by dividing the number of payments processed by number of employees. However, in the absence of other productivity measures we have updated Frazer's table using CLCB statistics.

2. Please refer to footnote 3, Ch. 13.

This work is part of a research project 'The impact of new technologies on Greater London', funded by the Open University.

REFERENCES

Banking World (1984) '1984 Survey of ATM installations', November, pp.48-9.

Central Statistical Office (1976) The measurement of changes in production.

Clark, R.T. (1984) 'Electronic Funds Transfer', Telecommunications Policy, pp.29-43.

Coakley, G. and Harris, L. (1983) City of Capital, Blackwell.

Child, J., Loveridge, R., Harvey, J. and Spencer, A. 'Microelectronics and the quality of employment in service' in Marstrand, P. (ed.) New technology and the future of work and skills, Frances Pinter, 1984.

Crawley, F. (1982) 'Competition in retail banking', Long Term Planning 15, no. 3, p.72.

Crompton, R. and Jones, G. (1984) White Collar proletariat, Macmillan.

Downing, H. (1981) Developments in secretarial labour: resistance office automation and the transformation of patriarchal relations of control, PhD, Birmingham.

Fforde, J.S. (1983) 'Competition innovation and regulation in British banking' Bank of England Quarterly Bulletin, September, pp.363-76.

Frazer, P. (1982) 'How not to measure bank productivity', The Banker, pp.103-5.

Heffernan, S.A. (1984) New technology and competition in British banking, City University Business School Working Paper No. 63.

Gershuny, J. (1978) After Industrial Society, Macmillan.

------ and Miles, I. (1984) The New Service Economy, Francis Pinter.

Green, K., Coombs, R. and Holroyd, K. (1980) The effects of microelectronic technologies on employment prospects, Gower Press, Aldershot.

Jones, D. (1981) 'Midland pioneers area grouping', Bankers Magazine.

Lascellers, David (1984) 'Clearers promise to open up the field', Financial Times, 12 December.

Marshall, J.N. and Bachtler, J.F. (1984) 'Spatial perspectives on technological changes in the banking sector of the United Kingdom', Environment and Planning A16, pp.437-50.

NEDC (1983) 'Changing employment patterns: where will the new jobs be?' memorandum by the Chancellor of the Exchequer, November.

Quinton, J. (1979) Rationalisation of the branch networks: the Barclays experience, 8th EFMA Congress, June 1979.

Rajan, A. (1984) New technology and employment in insurance, banking and building societies: recent experience and future impacts, Gower.

Riley, B. (1984) 'Automation is the key to six day opening at Nat West', Financial Times, 14 September.

Sergeant, J.R. (1979) 'UK performance in services' in Blackaby, F., De Industrialization, Heinemann, pp.102-16.

Read, C.N. (1983) 'Information Technology in Banking', Long Range Planning, vol. 16, pp.21-30.

Revell, J.R.S. (1983) Banking and Electronic Funds Transfer, OECD, Paris.

Webster, J. (1984) Word processing and the secretarial labour process, B.S.A. Conference Paper, Bradford.

Chapter Thirteen

NEW TECHNOLOGY AND BANK WORK: BANKING ON IT AS AN 'ORGANISATIONAL TECHNOLOGY'

Stephen Smith and David Wield

The financial institutions of the City of London have been unsettled by a series of overseas and domestic changes as post-war regulatory conventions have been broken down. The changing capital flows through the City thus reveal the making and remaking of the world economy and changes in the balance of international influence between London, New York and Tokyo.

However, City institutions may be thought of in a quite different way. They also represent the apex of a complex division of labour tasks: millions of physical operations performed by thousands of people throughout the UK. It is this 'technical division of labour' which we will concentrate on, and more particularly the organisation of work in the branch networks of the London clearing banks.

As we shall see the division of labour in banking is inherently difficult to manage. This is essentially because the efficiencies to be gained from the centralisation and specialisation of labour-tasks may conflict with the 'service' nature of much of the banks' business. This conflict is expressed in the recent history of new technology and work reorganisation at the branch level.

The general ambiance of the City is one of major change, or even of a 'Revolution in the City', and, as we will show, the banks have looked for ways to 'revolutionise' the organisation and productivity of work in branches. Certainly the technology suppliers have borrowed this imagery in selling their products. New technology has been presented as the basis of a 'revolution in the financial services industries in the 1990s'.

In the recent past, some banks have pursued

information technology as an 'organisational technology' which might overturn the classical patterns of bank branch work organisation. This departure from established assumptions has not always been well received by bank workers. Men and women, managers and non-managers, senior and junior staffs have each been affected in different and sometimes negative ways by the new thinking.

It is even suggested that management strategies may have led to some 'proletarianisation' of a workforce usually renowned for its conservatism.

We have argued in the previous chapter that new technology has certainly contributed to moderate and steady increases in the efficiency of bank workers over a long period. But we will explain that recent radical management strategy towards technical change has not markedly increased productivity but has instead generated some new problems in place of those they were intended to solve. This has led at least two banks towards a new and more conservative approach to new technology.

ORTHODOX BRANCH WORK ORGANISATION

The classical model of bank work involved customers and staff in face to face trust relations. Banking was thus far from an exclusively impersonal set of accounting calculations and ledger entries. It was, and to a declining extent still is, based on intensive and often long-standing personal relations. In the Protestant Ethic and the Spirit of Capitalism Max Weber hints that banks may indeed be among the very last businesses to adopt a thoroughly modern rational-bureaucratic form of organisation (Weber, 1930). This paper will present some reasons why this is likely to be the case.

Under the classical pattern of bank work organisation, the recruitment, pay, training and career assumptions which applied to bank staff were above all directed at maintaining a financially secure, dutiful, deferential and therefore trustworthy workforce. In addition, a presumption in favour of wide ranging apprenticeships in banking created operational advantages at the clerical and at the higher, 'appointed' grades of work and was designed to result in rounded, 'generalist' and therefore flexible bankers for ultimate promotion to corporate management.

Later on we will show that there is considerable

evidence that the banks have sought to dismantle this structure of bank work and to replace it with a more intensive or 'Tayloristic' division of labour. In doing so they seem certain to undermine their traditional personnel objectives. Indeed they have already done so.

The traditional bank branch created a particular form of control over work and bank workers. The established ideal in banking was that every branch manager was theoretically capable of performing most if not every branch operation, on the basis of his training and practical experience. A branch manager might be a lending manager, personnel manager, training manager and operations manager. In theory, promotion was open to anyone who could demonstrate the necessary 'aptitude' and 'dedication' (Bunyan and Youdale, 1981). The apprenticeship was long and comprehensive. It began with employment as a 'junior' at 15 or 16 years of age and might in theory at least end in a general managership at corporate HQ. These assumptions are represented in the statement that some recruits joined believing they carried the proverbial 'chief general manager's baton in their knapsacks'. The career paths of senior managers show that this representation of career planning stands up to examination and that managers received their management education within the system.

The dominant principle for promotion was that one would be nominated for career steps to jobs one could not yet do (the opposite of Taylorian specialisation, which regards this as wasteful). The newly promoted would learn the job by the example of somebody who had already mastered it, and who would eventually be moved on in turn to a task which he was not yet competent to perform. Over time this knowledge would be entrusted to the next generation of employees. The ethos of the banking apprenticeship was paternal-autocratic (Rix et al., 1979). Employees were held in trust and received a career in return for deference to the bank's code of ethics. Indeed the research has shown that banks remain prepared to help employees through periods of illness or where there are difficult domestic considerations, by altering their workload to suit. On the other hand, the banks may expect staffs to implement changes with little advance warning on the assumption that 'the bank knows best'. In principle, nonconformity was devalued. Wide experience and knowledge as a 'general practitioner' in banking might qualify a manager for senior management after a career spanning some 35 or 40 years. Clearly, this picture is somewhat over-drawn but it is a reasonable indication of how 'old school' bankers were promoted; authority and confidence to manage came with age, experience, generalist skills and a particular outlook. (1) The prerequisite 'passport to success' was, and to an extent still is, the examinations leading to recognition by the Institute of Bankers. We consider possible changes to this system later.

The generalist principle was evident at the clerical level where people have been trained to do a comparatively wide range of tasks. This brought immediate operational advantages, and the principle has not been completely eliminated.

Because the banking day involves considerable qualitative and quantitative variations in inputs and outputs, staff flexibility is advantageous if a branch is to operate efficiently. For example, an enquiry clerk might be expected to be able to cashier, under some circumstances to 'input' account changes on a terminal, to encode cheques, to move around the branch doing a small number of different operations at different times of the day and to be prepared to cover for colleagues in emergencies. This is how the 'traditional' branch meets its peak loads. There is a certain camaraderie and collective pressure amongst clerks to work well and not to create difficulties for others to deal with later, and in a crisis employees will help each other out. There is reciprocity. The smaller the branch the greater the interdependence of people and tasks. A clear majority of clerks interviewed expressed a preference for working in smaller traditional branches over larger branches where they had experience of both.

Within the traditional branch, day to day managerial control rests with the branch accountant, while ultimate control rests with the manager. The accountant's title is misleading, for in fact he or she is closer to the roles of production, personnel and training superintendent rolled together. The accountant has a considerable say in the allocation of work, in the deployment of staff and in arranging for training. A successful accountant must carry a great deal of knowledge about the branch staff. This is part factual and part intangible. We estimate that an accountant in a large branch probably carries several hundred, perhaps thousands of such mental rules in addition to formal procedural rules. After 'generalist' training accountants may operate these rules quite fluently and carry far more implicit knowledge than they may consciously realise.

The actual balance of power and working relationship between the branch manager and accountant varies between branches according to personalities, despite the presumption in favour of conformism inherent in the organisational structure. This means that branches may vary according to the 'atmosphere' set by this working relationship. Comparable branches thus vary considerably on financial and operational performance. The performance of the same branch might change radically with a change of manager and accountant and their skills are fundamental to effective performance. A good lending manager may raise branch profitability as much as 500 per cent or better.

The term apprenticeship is used quite deliberately in order to suggest parallels between banking and crafts normally associated with manufacturing industry. 'Old school' managers have often referred to this system as 'coming up the hard way'. They identify themselves as 'Bankers' - their own term - rather than as 'Professional Managers'. The emphasis was on gaining new skills through experience.

But as technology was introduced, new design and organisational values were incorporated into bank work. These threaten to overturn the orthodoxy at the first stage: clerical work.

TAYLORISATION

The traditional structure is only one of a number of ways through which managers seek effective control over work. An alternative is to break jobs down into smaller, technically interdependent parts. This lowers the discretion, necessary skills and autonomy of individual workers and is believed to be more efficient than craft forms (Taylor, 1967; Braverman, 1974).

Here we argue that although this 'Taylorist' management strategy is now evident in banking, it remains incomplete. This is because it has thrown up new and unexpected problems of its own. Indeed, it is by no means clear that the productivity gains which were envisaged from a more intensive division of labour are materialising.

Partly on the basis of the design values of largely US technology suppliers, corporate managements in banking have overseen considerable changes in bank work and organisation. An extreme and widely quoted statement of supplier values was presented by Franco de Benedetti, managing director of Olivetti, at a Financial Times conference in March 1979. He anticipates that new technology will lead to a new form of work control, which would amount to an industrial revolution for white collar workers.

> The Taylorism of the first factories ... enabled the labour force to be controlled and was the necessary prerequisite to the subsequent mechanisation and automation of the production processes. In this way, Taylorised industries were able to win competition over the putting out system ... information technology is basically a technology of co-ordination and control of the labour force, the white collar workers, which Taylorian organisation does not cover ...
>
> However, EDP (Electronic Data Processing) seems to be one of the most important tools with which company management institutes policies directly concerning the work process conditioned by complex economic and social factors. In this sense EDP is in fact an organisational technology, and like the organisation of labour, has a dual function as a productive force and a control tool for capital (cited in Downing, 1981).

Similarly, Docherty (1978) observed that within the branch increased automation converted tellers who were in effect mini-bankers into 'automatons'.

Advantages have also been sought from further managerial specialisation. In keeping with most clearing banks, one recently announced:

> For some time, we have been moving away from the concept of a generalist banker and have now decided that we must provide a greater degree of specialisation to serve our personal and corporate customers (Press Release).

Such a process is not new but appears to have accelerated during the 1970s.

As we explained in the last chapter, the primary application of new technology in banking has so far been the automation of the branch accounting system. Branch ledgers have been progressively replaced by mainframe files: mens' italic book entries by womens' key board entries. Indeed, business growth and information control could not have been handled without new technology. While the accounting principles have remained the same, the social organisation of the accounting process has changed in important ways, particularly with the feminisation of the workforce. The direction of change points towards Taylorism, although as we shall see later, the banks are far from convinced that this is the best approach. Furthermore while banks clearly seek productivity gains, the use of technology as a form of control is far from most managers' minds (see Taylor, 1984, 280-1).

There has been progressive specialisation and several tiers of entry have replaced common entrance at 15 or 16. The career structure has become horizontally and vertically segmented; men and women tend to do different jobs, often physically segregated within a branch. What were once stages in a long career have tended to become more or less permanently staffed by one segment of the labour force, and what were a series of more or less coherent clerical processes have been progressively broken down into detailed stages.

A number of banks have taken this division of labour to its logical conclusion and piloted American-style Hub and Satellite banking, where specialist tasks are geographically and hierarchically defined. At the hub branch a full range of services are provided and this is where a management team of specialist lenders, administrative and training managers may be found. The processing of remittances may be undertaken in this building, or in a separate data processing office. Payments handling is usually done by women on a semi-automated basis, sometimes working part-time or in shifts. This layout has, at least until recently been articulated by US suppliers of new technology as the best fix to rising costs (for example at the recent Financial Times banking and new technology conferences, and in interviews).

Standing order clerks and many 'appointed' grades are also grouped centrally in this local network, as is typing/word processing. The hub and DP offices are linked to satellite or service branches, which offer a narrower range of services directed at the personal customer and which therefore house only a fraction of the range of bank jobs. Many satellite branches have no managers and the banks have achieved this partly by non-replacement of a post-war age cohort of generalist or 'general practitioner' branch managers. Instead, central managers nominally cover a number of satellite branches each. In most clearing banks the lines between the branches largely represent van-runs for voucher and other collections and deliveries, relief staff cover and journeys by the management team who oversee the network. A separate corporate branch may be established for purely business custom and may have no counter service (Figure 13.1).

Figure 13.1

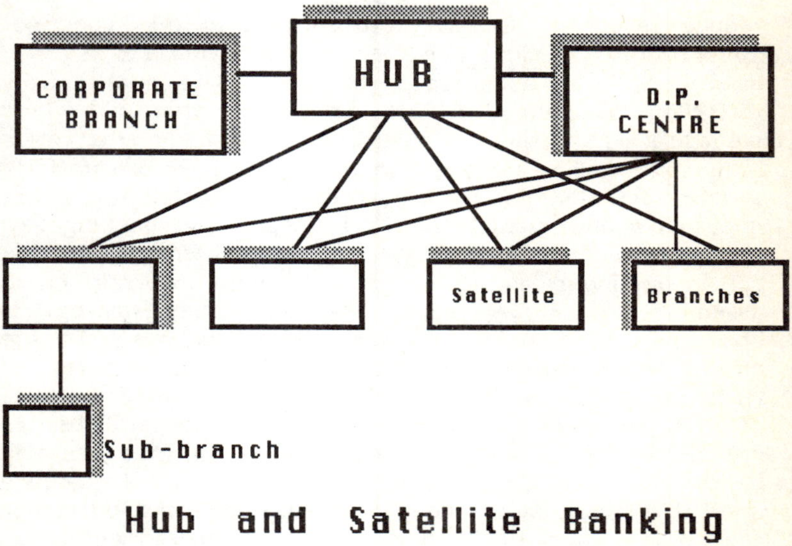

This form of reorganisation has been successful on the lending-side provided that the network is not too geographically dispersed, nor its corporate customers too conservative. It is not ideally suited to rural areas. Specialised lending managers are almost unanimously pleased with reorganisation because it enables them to concentrate on marketing the bank's services. This is seen as rewarding work. The younger lending specialists clearly welcomed not having to perform the wider administrative functions which a generalist branch manager would deal with. In some networks administrative managers have no lending responsibilities at all while in others they do have limited lending duties.

However, reorganisation in this form has brought a series of new problems. The management, administrative and coordination input is increased with specialisation despite reductions in branch managers. Banks which have piloted hub and satellite banking have found that there are few if any clerical staff savings - clerical staffing seems to rise by degrees and appointed or intermediate staffing also seems to increase (by as much as 32 per cent in one bank (EFILWC, 1984, 95). These changes can be a little more than proportionate to the increase in business which banks have been enjoying. In other words specialisation may slightly reduce labour productivity. It quite definitely does not 'revolutionise' clerical work performance. Hub and satellite banking has also accentuated the need for a qualitatively different management style of supervision which old school managers may find difficult. But probably the most immediate reason for the disappointment over productivity is that specialisation tends to reduce staff flexibility. The qualitative and quantitative variations in the 'banking day' are inconsistent with Taylorism which works best on continuous inputs and outputs, for example, as occurs on an assembly-line. A Tayloristic new technology strategy is bound to create some important new difficulties given the nature of the business which clearing banks undertake, the range of products to be serviced and the face-to-face nature of much service delivery. Many new messenger jobs are created in the network and considerable van mileages may be run up. These are a quantifiable symptom of the new control difficulties of hub and satellite systems, but other real, if less quantifiable, disadvantages from reorganisation may be as decisive.

QUALITATIVE CHANGE IN BANK WORK ORGANISATION

Specialisation highlights differences between groups of employees in a new way. Young 'specialist' graduate managers and older GP managers are conscious of profound differences of outlook which separate them. The graduates have intimated that they may feel uncomfortable in a branch environment and that older bank workers find it difficult to 'place' them in the status hierarchy. One old school manager complained of new school managers that 'you can't just inject people with thirty years' experience.' Old schoolers are inclined to argue that they can understand balance sheets in a rapid, intuitive way, and can better understand the branch staff milieu. This they claim only comes with experience. On the other hand, new schoolers suspect that such GP 'intuition' represents benign prejudice rather than strict business sense. The new managers seem more inclined to treat branches as industrial systems rather than as a particular or special form or organisation. GPs regard this as a regrettable offence against a revered way of working life. These views surface infrequently in the banking press but they form an undercurrent of debate among bank branch personnel.

There is also a hiatus between women who predominantly work as cashiers, standing order clerks, personal bankers (upgraded enquiry clerks) and 'mech' (machine)room operators, and men on the accelerated career programme. Men appear to be put through these grades more quickly, particularly through the mech rooms, probably as a gesture towards the old notion of a banking apprenticeship. We have thus found men allocated for no more than several months as part of their 'man management training' to mech rooms run by women. There is an obvious association between the historical automation of clerical work in banking and the recruitment of women.

The overall proportion of women to men has steadily risen (Table 13.1), though not so rapidly in London (Table 13.2).Table 13.2 also shows that female part-time working in London declined between 1974 and 1981.

Table 13.1: Percentage of men and women working in the banks, national

Year	% women	% men
1959	40.5	59.5
1965	47.6	52.4
1970	53.0	47.0
1975	(54.5)	(45.5)
1979	(55.5)	(44.5)
1984	(57.1)	(42.9)

Notes: Figures in brackets count part-timers as a half. This data only available from 1975.

Source: Palmer (1983).

Table 13.2: Employment composition in banks, Greater London

Year	Total women	Total men	Total part-time women	% women	% of women working part-time	% part-time women out of total bank employment
1974	57,992	62,044	10,975	48.3	18.9	9.14
1981	66,024	69,233	7,921	48.8	12.0	5.90

Source: Department of Employment.

The proportion of women to men appears to be higher in the satellite branches than in hub branches, while in the mass processing centres, women are in the majority by far.

Staff morale in DP is quite variable. However there were numerous complaints that women staff who joined as bank workers find themselves limited to repetitious 'factory work' as dedicated machine operators. Several complained that 'This isn't Banking, it's Factory Work'. The changing morale of staff and the weakening of certain incentives to work hard - collective pressure to finish and go home, reciprocity, the satisfaction of seeing a task through to completion, the promise of a career in return for conscientious work - may have contributed to some 'proletarianisation' of staff in these areas. (See also Crompton and Jones, 1984.) Two groups of Taylorised clerks in the research complained of boredom from the sameness of their work. The groups of interviewees were in a surprisingly volatile mood.

In some branches, men and women seem to have clearly accepted the division of labour between them. Both men and women thus responded to questions on this issue by pointing to the different social expectations held by men and women. And it was certainly true that a majority of younger women interviewed emphasised that bank employment was not the central feature of their lives and that marriage and childcare were valued more highly than 'getting ahead'. Some found male competitiveness and ambition to be distasteful, or 'OK for them but not for me', while certain women were ready to assume that 'career women' in the bank had otherwise failed in their domestic lives. However, in other branches there was an undercurrent of tension, especially among women of around 30 years old and above whose values had shifted with their experience both in banking and in the home. Here earlier objectives - marriage, childcare - had proved unsatisfactory; for example those who had divorced or were childless. They felt that they could have achieved more in banking. In the most closely studied branch networks, trades union membership was slightly higher among older compared with younger women.

MANAGEMENT AND WORKFORCE STYLES: NEGOTIATING CONSENT FOR NEW SYSTEMS

All clearing banks have progressed some way towards

factory-like work at most levels or stages in the production of standardised services. This has dictated the need on the banks' part to develop factory management styles and has necessarily altered workforce images of the situation. This is particularly evident in the banks' central clearing where work conditions resemble batch processing in manufacture. It has enabled banks to cope with a long history of cheque growth and new centralised services. As one moves closer to the branches, however, the logic for this pattern of organisation looks progressively weaker.

The essence of the difficulty is that branches are called upon to conduct two rather different types of work which cannot easily be separated for practical purposes: meeting customers (with different needs) and processing large quantities of information. Given the lags and leads in the banking day referred to above there is a good case for fitting these two spheres into the one branch workforce, in order to gain maximum utilisation of people, machines, skills and time.

Clearly, hub and satellite banking is a radical attempt to divorce the two types of work with partial automation. As we have suggested, this strategy has failed to prove itself conclusively. But only in the crudest sense is the productivity of bank work set by the machines themselves. It must also be realised that neither are even the formal organisational structures directly linked to performance. The same organisation with the same machines may produce one set of outcomes in one place which will not be reproduced elsewhere and this is admittedly true of traditional 'free standing' branches, of networked branches and of factory-like processing units. Within a bank there will be famous and infamous examples of each kind.

An intensive division of labour can be made to work under certain conditions. The key here is whether or not both men and women, managers and non-managers broadly accept or reject a view of their work drawn more or less in 'factory' terms. There is no guarantee of this happening. In one case staff had accepted these terms and the unit in question was considered a success. A manager explained his approach:

> Anyway right at the beginning I sat down at the machines and said 'Right girls I've got no idea. Show me what I've got to do' ... Getting stuck in. The spirit was 'This is our job. This is what they want. This is what

> we'll do.'
>
> What they'd said was 'revolutionise ... So we made our own way forward, developing in isolation. The rules were very vague really you know. Anyway we looked at them and asked what needed doing.
>
> What we got was strong staff loyalty. There was a lot of overtime and the girls could have walked out, right? They could have walked out the door but didn't. Sometimes you'd see a boyfriend in the foyer two hours after he was due to meet his girlfriend here.
>
> It wasn't at all bad going was it?

By getting 'stuck in' this relatively young manager had set aside the social distance between mens' and womens' jobs and between the manager and non-manager that we found elsewhere. He stressed solidarity, and was proud of his 'girls'. The clerks came to accept their work as a 'job' to be done alongside the manager. Staff knew what 'they (the Bank) wanted' and they 'did it'. Interviews with the staff confirmed this view.

The inherent staff inflexibility of specialisation had presented problems he admitted. Staff cover for holidays and sickness was difficult to organise. One set of dedicated machine operators were unfamiliar with the work of another and were therefore in no position to help out. When crises occurred these were difficult to manage. He continued:

> Well o.k. we did have problems. I could easily talk about problems it's true. The overtime bill soared. But we did fantastic stuff really ... That must be a plus ... The staff couldn't be faulted ...
>
> But they had far narrower experience. That was a problem ... because the (staff) on one floor couldn't do the job (of those) on the next floor, even if we were short somewhere because of sickness or holidays ...
>
> (the place) worked like a time-bomb. We were always working to a time-constraint (but) we always beat the deadlines in the end ...

Traditional forms of work organisation, for example in a bank branch, did have their advantages, he said, explaining that staff and task flexibility was inherent in these circumstances:

> Now if you take a small branch then a clerk is going to

> have to do the lot. Standing Orders, Open and Closed Accounts, Inputting. Seeing to the customer. Everything ... (But) some of our girls had never seen a customer. They didn't know the beginning parts of jobs.

Though reasonably successful, due to the overriding importance of premises costs it had been closed down. It was 'efficient but not cost-effective.' We must point out that had the machinery and the organisational forms been as effective as originally claimed by the advocates of a 'revolution' in bank work, the premises costs factor might not have proved as decisive as indeed it became.

One other comparable unit, had proved very successful largely because it had taken in work from outside to fill in during 'slack' parts of the day. But in many, the inflexibilities already referred to had caused some frustration among managers and staff alike.

For example, due to peaks and troughs, the overall throughput might be moderately good, while at certain times, machinery (and staff) were under employed and at other times machines were forced well beyond design capacity, occasionally resulting in temporary failures. Fluctuations in the demands on staff could only be smoothed by a limited amount of other work. Some machine operators with conventional branch work experience expressed doubts over the systems design.

Most operators were women, a number of whom suspected that older, male managers were uncomfortable in this environment because they were not familiar with the machines, nor with the difficulties and psychological stresses of machine operation. This meant that it might be difficult to establish the rapport which we described above. Certain managers were equally disturbed by these developments. For some indeed older managers, it offended their sense of 'what banking should be all about'. They expressed a preference for the free-standing branch milieu. In short, their training as 'Bankers' did not prepare them for 'Factory Management'.

TRAINING

With the intensification of the division of labour and the tendency to place many more women at machines than men, a double problem had emerged around the question of bank education and training.

The belief that women had 'nimble fingers' and were therefore better suited to machine work came up with striking regularity. Because keyboard skills take time to acquire, and because women spend longer at machines, this belief became self-reinforcing. The stereotype is coming under strain because a growing percentage of women are seeking Institute recognition and staying at work longer. Further, when few promotions are on offer, staff perceive an added incentive to take their examinations. It is unfortunate that a more egalitarian view of women by banks has coincided with employment stagnation.

The IOB qualification means that women have increasingly won what theoretically might have functioned as a 'passport to success' under the old orthodoxy. As one manager explained:

> Men don't have as much dexterity as women. They just don't have it. They're all fingers and thumbs. On the other hand come to think of it we did have one keyboard operator once and he was really good.
>
> The thing was too that women didn't do their (IOB) exams and they often didn't stay for long before leaving the bank. But now values are changing. And they are staying on. In fact there is a majority of women among my senior clerks now and they are passing their exams.

At a time of employment stagnation, promotion opportunities are necessarily limited. But increasingly formal career ceilings have been placed across the paths of employees comparable to the civil service.

There have been two responses to these developments. Firstly, the banks have sought to limit day release provision for IOB courses. To date this has not significantly reduced the record number of candidates registered as students (self-tuition and evening classes remain options).

Secondly, specialisation appears at least partly to be having an impact on the structure of the Institute's syllabus and examinations. Probably because the IOB's role as a 'passport' contradicts the growing horizontal and vertical segmentation of the labour force, the Institute is placed in a difficult position.

A compromise is being sought which might channel students either to an upgraded form of banking qualification or to a new diploma in financial sector services work, possibly beyond banking as such.

This development could have further effects on the gender and career structure of banking employment and might conceivably underscore the separation of womens' and mens' work in the industry as well as in related financial service industries.

Much remains to be decided, not least whether the existing membership of the Institute of Bankers will be prepared to vote through such changes. Old schoolers might be expected to resist them.

These few examples show that technical and organisational change raises questions far beyond the machines and that new technology of itself does not bring clear and self-evident advantages. The Olivetti claim that information technology is a Tayloristic "organizational technology" ... which lends itself to the co-ordination and control of the labour force' seems to have proved premature in the case of banking. Should specialisation result in workforce dissatisfaction particularly at the clerical level, then IT may instead be in the process of generating entirely new control problems for the banks. We have some evidence that this had indeed happened and that the loss of career prospects and work satisfaction has caused clerks to becomes less 'duty-bound' by their employment. Bankers have certainly referred to 'motivation' problems among non-career staff (for example at the 1982 Cambridge Seminar on The Banks and Technology in the 1980s).

However, as we will now explain, information technology does not have to take a Tayloristic path. There is a more conservative alternative.

TOWARDS A MORE CONSERVATIVE VIEW OF NEW TECHNOLOGY IN BANKING

Recently, observers have detected a sense of disappointment and surprise among senior bankers over new technology. A recent report (Touche Ross, 1985) has placed the blame for this on the banks themselves and in particular on the 'old culture' of the banks. At least one software supplier has made similar comments (Arthur, 1985).

While it is true that bankers are having real doubts about some systems they have bought, we feel that it is misleading to blame systems failures on the 'old culture' as such. It is fairer to say that Tayloristic forms of design embodied in some systems show a lack of fit with branch banking and that problems then result from organisational change around the kit. IT as an 'organisational technology' has proved inappropriate, and if bankers are to blame, then it is for accepting suppliers' productivity claims and design-values. To do this, they had to unlearn some old lessons on the organisation of work which they surely assimilated while serving their 'generalist' apprenticeships in the branches during the 1950s.

We will list some of the limits of new technology as both product and process innovations. But we will close by explaining how the current shift of thinking provides an opportunity for a paradoxically more conservative, yet more imaginative, organisation of bank work and technology. There are signs that this is happening.

It is now realised that the interaction of inputs and outputs at branch level is extremely complex, and not capable of at-a-stroke technology fixes. According to one clearer, even the most important process innovations envisaged in the next five to ten years 'may not produce as much as one whole staff or equivalent time saving per branch!' Far from 'wiping out' clerical staff, one further 'revolutionary' innovation will save an estimated five person-hours per branch per month.

Technical and organisational changes have brought other surprises. Two major clearing banks have found that the most operationally efficient branch is the 'traditional' 15-person branch and that reorganisation 'hasn't produced any staff savings really'.

One experience with a prominent innovation has underlined the inadequacy of Taylorian assumptions about efficiency, the 'Automated Teller Machine'. To the American suppliers who coined the term, the terminal was primarily a process innovation, literally an automated teller. Obtaining cash by customer self service at a machine was thought equivalent to between one-third and one human cashier, a calculation initially accepted by the UK clearing banks.

The problem was that this was a very rough approximation greatly affected by considerations apart from the nominal 'efficiency' of the machines. With hindsight the notion of the human equivalence of an ATM is misleading particularly in a European context where, despite the advance of specialisation, 'cashiering' has not been sufficiently split up to allow for one-for-one machine replacements of human operations. The two are not comparable. Cashiers perform many operations which machines cannot conveniently reproduce yet which must still be performed for most customers. The assessment of ATMs as a process innovation is complicated because customers use ATMs in a quite unanticipated way. We showed in the last chapter the typical cash withdrawal at an ATM was surprisingly small. This pattern simply has no equivalence with customer behaviour at the cashier position which involve fewer visits for larger amounts and other queries besides. (Counter transactions continue to rise despite ATM usage.) Here IT has made a difference but not necessarily the one that was anticipated. Certainly useful but again not 'revolutionary'.

However, the suppliers did not rest their efficiency arguments there. They have attempted to persuade European banks that the ATM should form a more sophisticated 'self service banking terminal'. Sited in the wall, the lobby or at a remote site, customers might transfer funds across their accounts, initiate payments, set up standing orders, all without the intervention of bank staff (or in supplier terminology without a 'warm body'). (2)

The clearers are hesitant and although many innovations are operational, including 'home banking' terminals, uptake appears to be restricted to a narrow segment of the customer profile. Another 'substantial' innovation saved more in postal charges than it did in staff costs.

DISCUSSION AND CONCLUSIONS

Our research has led to two conclusions. Firstly, the productivity gains which were sought through a more intensive division of labour in the branch network have not materialised. In this form information technology has not lived up to the claims made for it. Secondly, a better understanding of bank work organisations is causing the banks to think again about new technology, and to evolve a new, yet paradoxically more conservative view of technical change.

In the light of both these findings, many forecasts of the employment effects of new technology in banking are beginning to look unrealistic.

Attempts to increase productivity by specialising

clerical work have been compromised by the loss of operational flexibility which this has created. In some areas this loss of flexibility has been compounded by a reduction in staff morale, though in others the changeover to a new regime at work was accomplished more successfully. Yet there has been no 'revolution' in labour productivity. Moreover the more carefully one looks at the branch networks of the major clearers the less easy is it to see where technically-induced job-loss might occur. This leads us on to a different view of what the role of information technology might be (below).

Our conclusions that the overall figures for banking employment may stagnate but not decline over the next eight to ten years broadly fits with Rajan (1984) but not with most other studies known to us which posit more or less 'substantial' to 'massive' labour reductions. For example, Shaw (1980), Game et al. (1981), BIFU (1980) and Hewlett (1985).

The reasons for these different estimates are almost certainly methodological. Rajan's study was distinguished by reporting senior management estimates of job-loss in a number of service industries. However, the mechanism of the relationship or what he terms the 'mediating factors' between technology and employment change is not properly explored.

The higher job loss forecasts found in other studies are clearly linked with a method which estimates the theoretical capabilities of innovations on a machine-by-machine basis. (Suppliers may be forgiven for thinking of change in this way.) It seems to us extremely unlikely that this method of forecasting will prove accurate. The approach probably guarantees that overestimates will be produced. This method merely establishes the absolutely worst case conceivable.

The other major weakness of the piecemeal method is that it seriously understimates the nature, complexity and particularity of technical change as it affects the quality of employment. It is most unwise to isolate 'the new technology' from changes in career, work, organisational structure and management. These issues are additional to the question of how customers will react to new systems. (3, 4)

However, new technology need not primarily be thought of in terms of labour productivity and the fragmentation of tasks as it most often is.

In order to develop an alternative to the strategy of work specialisation it is necessary to make a shift in emphasis around some basic assumptions. Instead of assuming that the banking day can be remade in order to fit the (theoretical) advantage of a more intensive division of labour, one may begin with the traditional branch as it stands and what it is supposed to do.

Although the banks have reduced the 'service' content of many of the services they provide, the raison d'etre of a bank branch is customer contact. Yet historically new technology has not really been directed at enhancing this function, but has instead been concentrated on the branch accounting system: and on the back office. The information produced for accounting purposes is relatively opaque and a number of older managers and many back office clerks have complained that they have lost contact with the customer in the meantime.

However, recent proposed developments would establish a transparent 'information' system operating separately to the opaque 'data' generated by the automated accounting system. Personnel would be able to ask the system sensible questions on the nature and spread of customer accounts in order say to get to know about their account holders and devise marketing strategies. 'It's back to the old days!' said one supplier. Jobs could then be constructed around 'service' and information. There are no technical reasons why for example personal bankers (enhanced enquiry clerks who are usually women) should not be given access to any such system and be allowed to develop 'banking' skills further, thus demonstrating old style 'commitment', 'aptitude' and 'dedication'. This might even lead to new 'appointed' job status for successful personal bankers, involving not simply selling but also marketing financial services. They would become 'bankers' in the old sense.

This policy of using new technology to upgrade the marketing skills of bank workers would be compatible with a number of recent developments in branch work organisation. Several steps have been taken which promise to recover the traditional control skills of the clerks (clerical work having been broken up over a period of several decades).

For example the trend is now against separate local processing centres which represented the ultimate in task fragmentation. New open-plan branch layouts are a physical recognition that cashier and 'mech' operations are best shared by several employees. Here there are few specifically back office clerks as such, and efficiency gains have resulted. This widening of clerical duties has recovered much of the camaraderie and spirit of mutual helpfulness (and mutual coercion) among clerks. For clerks at least, the notion of knowing each other's jobs and seeing work through a reasonable number of steps is becoming re-established. We have seen just how well this can work in a branch that was very short staffed through sickness and leave yet which was coping well with the intensive peak loads of the week. Staff found satisfaction in meeting the challenge, though men admitted some reluctance at using the terminals.

Even within the hub and satellite pattern which formally centralises the management function, clerks may find themselves enjoying more rather than less autonomy.

Some satellite branches from which the manager has been removed, are left in charge of grade four clerks - often women. It is quite clear that their work involves management responsibility. The problem is that these skills are not actually recognised or rewarded as management skills - especially as these clerks spend much time cashiering and machining alongside more junior clerks (wherein lies the secret of their authority and success). Although the organisation chart may indicate a certain centralisation of control this may paradoxically leave clerical workers in a more autonomous position than before the removal of the manager.

In recognition of this change there was considerable debate in one bank as to what the senior clerk in managerless branches ought to be called. Part of the difficulty in finding a form of words involved deciding whether or not the job involved 'management'. In effect the definition of management compared with operational skills was being negotiated.

Indeed we have been struck by the degree to which technology, work organisation and the roles of men and women in banking are subject to tacit negotiation. This contradicts the conventional wisdom on technical change in a number of ways. For example, there is a mythology that technical change carries a coherent logic which organisations simply must pursue and which then have an 'impact' on the workforce. Certainly technology in banking has been followed as if it did possess a correct logic, notably a logic of efficiency through an increased division of labour. But if technology had this simplistic quality then it would surely not have presented the banks with the difficult issues which have arisen. As we have explained neither is a more conservative approach to bank work organisation and new technology guaranteed of success. But given the context it seems less of a risk than the radical strategy of specialisation.

A 'traditional' approach may succeed where a 'factory' approach has not and *vice versa*. Much depends on the managers and the non-managers concerned, on the balance of new and old schools, and on the perceptions of men and women. To this may be added the character of the local labour-market, the degree of unionisation, regional labour and household traditions and the nature of the local demand for bank services.

The future involves choices both for management and the trades unions.

Within management there is a struggle of ideas between those who believe in the advantages of task specialisation and those who do not. This debate is far from being settled.

The trades unions in the industry also appear to be cross-cut by competing caucuses, though on the surface the issues seem clear cut. Trades unions are understandably concerned primarily with job security and pay in relation to new technology and seek to link them in 'new technology agreements' (BIFU, 1980). The union approach is to negotiate a 'share in the benefits' of new technology in terms of a shorter working week, earlier retirement and improved pay. Unions also seek consultation in advance of the implementation of new technology in order that negotiations can be made meaningful. In the absence of such agreements, trades unions are inclined to fear job-loss.

Here we would make two points:

Firstly, it would appear that the unions' fears over job-loss are exaggerated. As the employers have discovered, what a machine implies in theory is not at all the same as what a machine may mean when placed within the structure of an organisation.

Secondly, the mix of traditional and rationalised branches present the trades unions with different sets of members working in very different circumstances. Because new technology does not therefore affect workers in anything like the same way there are some difficulties in identifying a common set of worker interests. There are differences of interest and perception between men and women, between those who have joined the union because they have become 'proletarianised' and those who have joined because they do not wish to become proletarianised, and who seek to retain staff status; between 'job' people and 'career' people and between managers and non-managers.

Each of these issues ultimately expresses itself in terms of technical change and the way staff are allocated to tasks. These decisions have important consequences for the well-being, security and work satisfaction of staff. However, despite the different circumstances of bank workers in the branch network, the majority clearly valued customer contact, flexible task sharing, group camaraderie, trust and skill.

This means that there is a happy coincidence between staff values, efficiency and the conservative approach to new technology and clerical work organisation in branches. Our proposal that both unions and employers should embrace some old school, or Banker, values might even seem bizarre. Yet we conclude that trades unions, employers and suppliers should cooperate to develop model technology design values which articulate what is at heart a conservative concept of banking.

Many permutations exist, and an ideal technical and organisational form will never be found. It is an elusive chimera. Our broad conclusion remains that a stronger case can be made for the traditional form than for the factory form of branch organisation. Indeed, as Weber seems to argue, it may prove irrational to 'rationalise' bank work. As one experienced clerk explained:

> You see we somehow knew that reorganization wasn't going to work. You could see it right from the start, and I think a lot of managers feel the same way about it!

Tailpiece

> We trained hard ... but every time we were beginning to form up into teams, we would be reorganized. I was to learn later in life that we tend to meet any new situation by reorganizing ... and a wonderful method it can be for creating the illusion of progress while producing inefficiency and demoralisation (Petronius, AD 66).

NOTES

1. For a discussion of managerial 'schools' see Wilkinson and Smith (1983). Smith and Wilkinson (1984), Gouldner (1954a, 1954b) or Spybey (1984).

2. A most reliable source in banking has reported that the simple, limited function ATM is not necessarily proven. Because ATMs have been placed at many sites where usage is low it can cost more to dispense cash through ATMs than via a 'warm body' human cashier.

3. It is more likely new technology will continue to be used to partially automate various tasks. Cheque truncation which involves stopping cheques and sending information about their value electronically (so avoiding the paper-based clearings) falls into this category. (At present truncation is very expensive). So too electronic funds transfer at the point of sale (EFTPOS). This involves persuading customers not to use their cheque books or credit cards in shops but to pay by electronic means directly from their bank accounts into the retailer account. Again, far from eliminating the clearing of cheques which is possible in theory, the most the banks can expect from the 'EFTPOS Revolution' is that a proportion of customers will move from cheques at the point of sale to EFTPOS. But as only a minority of cheques are written in stores the potential employment impact of EFTPOS must be considered small in the foreseeable future.

4. For further useful discussions on new technology and banking see Taylor (1983), Read (1983), Child et al. (1984) and Marshall and Bachtler (1984). For further union research see BIFU (1983a, 1983b) and for an introduction to industrial relations in banking see Lowe (1979).

REFERENCES

Arthur, C. (1985) 'Bankers begin to doubt technology' in Computer Weekly, 961, 2 May.

Braverman, H. (1974) Labour and Monopoly Capital, the degradation of work in the twentieth century, New York, The Monthly Review Press.

BIFU (Banking Insurance and Finance Union) (1980) Microtechnology a Programme for Action.

------ (1983a) Microelectronics Briefing No. 1, BIFU Research, January.

------ (1983b) Microelectronics Briefing No. 2, BIFU Research, April.
Bunyan, D. and Youdale, R. (1981) Report of a case study on the impact of New Technology on women and Trade Union Organisation in Banking, Bristol, Bristol Resource Centre.
Child, J. (1984) 'New Technology and the service class', paper to the Annual Conference of the British Sociological Association, Bradford, April.
Child, J., Loveridge, R., Harvey, J. and Spencer, A. (1984) 'Microelectronics and the quality of employment in services', in Marstrand, P. (ed.) New Technology and the future of work and skills, Frances Pinter.
Crompton, R. and Jones, G. (1984) White Collar Proletariat? London and Basingstoke, Macmillan.
Docherty, P. (1978) Automation of the Service Industries, IFAC Round Table.
Downing, H. (1981) Developments in Secretarial Labour: resistance, office automation and the transformation of patriarchal relations of control, Ph.D. Dissertation, University of Birmingham.
EFILWC (European Foundation for the Improvement of Living and Working Conditions) (1984) Technological Developments in Banking and Insurance: The Impact on Customers and Employees, United Kingdom, Dublin.
Game, A. and Pringle, R. (1984) Gender at Work, Pluto Press.
Goulder, A.W. (1954a) Wildcat Strike, Yellow Springs, Ohio, Antioch Press.
------ (1954b) Patterns of Industrial Bureaucracy, New York, Free Press of Glencoe.
Hewlett, N. (1985) 'New Technology and Banking Employment in the EEC' in Futures 17, 1, February.
Lowe, J. (1979) 'Staff Representation in Banking', Industrial Relations Journal, 3, 195, March.
Marshall, J.N. and Bachtler, J.F. (1984) 'Spatial perspectives on technological changes in the banking sector of the United Kingdom', in Environment and Planning, 16.
Palmer, L.S. (1983) Technical Change and Employment in Banking, Brighton, Sussex University Dissertation.
Rajan, A. (1984) New Technology and Employment in the UK Financial Services Sector; past impact and future prospects, Institute for Manpower Studies.
Read, C.N. (1983) 'Information Technology in Banking' in Long Range Planning, 16 August.

Rix, A., Keates, L. and Rees, T. (1979) Employee Attitudes to Representation in Barclays Bank, University College of Wales, Cardiff.

Shaw, E.R. and Coulbeck, N.S. (1983) UK Retail Banking Prospects in the Competitive 1980s, Loughborough: Staniland Hall Associates.

Smith, S.L. and Wilkinson, B. (1984) 'From Old School Hunches to Departmental Lunches' in Sociological Review, 32, 1 February.

Spybey, T. (1984) 'Traditional and Professional Frames of Meaning for Managers', in Sociology, 18, 4, November.

Taylor, A. (1983) New Technology in Banking, Insurance and Finance, Research Report 59, London Borough of Hammersmith and Fulham.

------ Coppin, P. and Wealthy, P. (1984) The Impact of New Technology on Local Employment, Gower.

Taylor, F.W. (1967 (1911)) The Principles of Scientific Management, New York, W.W. Norton.

Touche Ross, (1985) The Impact of Technology on Banking, London, Touche Ross and Co.

Weber, M. (1976 (1930)) The Protestant Ethic and the Spirit of Capitalism, Trans. Parsons, T., Giddens, A. (ed.) London, Allen and Unwin.

Wilkinson, B. and Smith, S.L. (1983) 'Management Strategies for technical change', in Science and Public Policy, 10, 2, April.

Part V

THE LOCAL STATE, PENSION FUNDS, AND INDUSTRY

INTRODUCTION TO PART V

Laurence Harris

The concern felt in Britain over the City's role and, in particular, over the adequacy of its industrial finance - the issue considered in the chapters of Part III - has led to a wide range of proposals. The most far-reaching have been for the nationalisation of the City in order to restructure its industrial finance in line with a regeneration of industry under state leadership and to control the power it exerts through foreign exchange operations and international finance. The argument is that regulation and controls over the financial system are necessary and, to reduce the inconsistency between them and financial capital's drive for profits, liquidity and mobility on a worldwide basis, state ownership is necessary.

None of the main political parties has that on their agenda. The policy has been promoted by sections of the Labour Party and has, at times, made headway within it, but under the leadership of Neil Kinnock and Roy Hattersley the Labour Party has concentrated on more modest proposals. Their policy in 1987 is for tax penalties to encourage financial institutions to reduce partially their overseas investment and for additional institutional sources of finance for UK industry.

Any such policies for the City as a whole depend upon government at the national level and, given the policies the Conservative government has pursued, they depend upon a change of government. A significant feature of British politics in the 1980s, however, has been the strategies of socialists in local authorities or other institutions who attempt to use the levers of power they legitimately control to institute socialist changes even under a Conservative government. A combination of three factors: the growth of pension funds' significance on the stock exchange; Labour control of local authorities; and pension fund trustees who represent Labour local authorities as employers or who represent employees, gave rise to a new socialist strategy for finance. It was argued that local authorities should set up enterprise boards to invest in local industry and that part of their funds should come from pension funds such as the local authorities' own. The following two chapters discuss divergent assessments of this strategy by two economists who were involved in implementing it.

Robin Murray had responsibility for the Greater London Council's economic policy when it was controlled by Labour under Ken Livingstone. As such, he was closely connected with the establishment of the Greater London Enterprise Board. In Pension Funds and Local Authority Investments Murray argues that there are severe limits to the role pension funds can have in a socialist strategy based on the local state alone. If pension funds (and insurance companies and similar institutions) have provided inadequate finance for industry over the years it is not a matter of their own volition, or capriciousness on the part of their managements. Instead, their concern for purely financial gains and for profits from property and other 'unproductive' investment derives from the nature of financial capital itself and its role in the capitalist economy. Changes at the level of pension fund management decisions will, therefore, be constrained by the funds' underlying role unless there are special circumstances. Murray emphasises that if the direction and character of finance is changed a prerequisite has to be to interrupt its existing links and isolate it to some extent from market forces and the domination of the profit motive. Using the example of the Greater London Council's own pension fund he discusses the limits and possibilities of such strategies which 'are testing the social control of finance in practice'.

Richard Minns was one of the earliest and foremost proponents of using pension funds to alter the direction of finance, and he has been involved in the practice of 'the social control of finance' in the West Midlands, the Greater London Council and the Greater London Enterprise Board. In Pension Funds: An Alternative View he takes issue with Robin Murray's general argument. To a large extent the disagreement between these two writers is over the relative weight attached to, on one hand, the economic laws determining the role and character of finance in general and, on the other hand, the specific character and role of the particular institutions that make up the British financial system. Minns emphasises the specifity and unique historical development of the City and argues from this both that the City has considerable responsibility for Britain's industrial weakness and that there is much greater scope for local investment strategies related to pension fund finance than Robin Murray believed possible.

One conclusion that may be drawn is that 'the general laws of financial capital' and 'the specificity of the City' are not sharply polarised alternative perspectives but are, instead, complementary. At the theoretical level of the specific character and history of Britain's financial system has to be analysed in the light of the general principles, while at the practical level both Minns and Murray have argued for national control of the City to effect more fundamental changes than local strategies alone can achieve.

Chapter Fourteen

PENSION FUNDS AND LOCAL AUTHORITY INVESTMENTS

Robin Murray

This paper deals with what existing local authorities can do particularly those authorities currently under socialist control to use pension funds for the purpose of long-term investment. (1) National law must therefore be taken as given, though as with so many fields of local authority initiative at the moment, precisely how we should interpret the law is a major variable. But part of the importance of these local initiatives is that they are testing the social control of finance in practice, and they are testing it as one part of a much wider investment strategy.

The Significance of Finance

To begin with we should be clear about the significance of finance in a progressive economic strategy. It is one moment in the overall circuit of capital, a circuit that also embraces (i) the purchase of inputs for the production process; (ii) the production process itself; (iii) the sale of the output. In as much as a progressive strategy envisages that some form of capital circuit will continue and not be substituted by, say, a planned use value form of economy which does not use money as capital, then the question of the significance of intervention at the money capital point of the circuit becomes important.

There are three lines of argument we can distinguish in the current debate. First, there are those who argue that the financial institutions in Britain are a major cause of British economic decline, and their regulation and/or control would be crucial for any arrest in that decline. The financial institutions are attacked for:

(a) failing to provide long-term investment funds in the UK;
(b) investing abroad;
(c) investing in unproductive assets, or on speculative landed property.

The Wilson Committee (2) considered these points, particularly that relating to long-term finance, and different sub-groups offered various answers: a medium-term re-discounting facility to counter the drying up of long-term industrial bonds; a more active involvement of the long-term financial institutions in industry; and the TUC proposal of a National Investment Bank, to be jointly funded by the state and the long-term investing institutions. Many have followed this general approach both before and after Wilson, emphasising the lack of venture capital for new business, and the more general absence of funds for fixed assets and the long-term.

The major response to this - and not merely from the financial institutions defending themselves - has been that it is not the institutions which are to blame but the lack of projects in which they can securely invest. There has been a steady decline in the profitability of productive industry both in the UK and elsewhere, and it is to the root causes of this that we should address ourselves. There is in fact a surplus of investment funds, but a dearth of profitable outlets. As Marx and Keynes would say, at a moment of crisis money capital is withdrawn from the circuit of productive capital. The crisis is reflected in the monetary sphere, but the money sphere does not cause the crisis.

In broad terms I would support this latter line of argument. Capitalist money cannot alter its intrinsic character, which, like capital in general is to drive always for maximum self-expansion. It invests abroad because there is greater profitability overseas. The fault lies with the removal of exchange controls not the managers of the funds. It invests in property, but the fault lies in an organisation of landed property which permits secular real increases in urban rent, and therefore offers a secure hedge against inflation. It eschews new, small, untried ventures because of the risk relative to investment in large concentrations of capital. In this by and large money capital is right, for it is not just a question of attitudes towards risk, it is that in general large corporations are economically stronger than small firms, and the real risk is correspondingly less.

It may be that some parts of the British financial establishment are risk averters; that some of them take unnecessarily short views, and are in brief bad managers from the point of view of capital profitability. But the financial institutions attract more criticism because they are managing capital well (from capital's point of view) than because they are managing it badly.

Our experience at the GLC (Greater London Council) suggests we can go further. We have found a number of financial institutions taking a longer-term view than the government would have wished. Major clearing banks (Barclays and the Midland) have been rapidly expanding their industrial first-aid departments. The aim is to avoid a devaluation of their capital by restructuring firms which on the criterion of profitability should be dispatched to the receiver. Major receivers, too, have been involved in many of the restructuring operations - both before they are called in (when they act as advisers to the bank in their capacity as accountants) and as active receivers trying to restructure their assets as a going concern. The Bank of England, likewise, has been active in forestalling bankruptcy by coordinating intervention. All these financial institutions have a self-interest in avoiding capital devaluation, and preserving a productive industry capable of reproducing profits in the long run. From what we have observed in a number of cases, the financial system can be seen as operating an alternative industrial policy to the government, more active in its intervention, and less short-term in its financial criteria.

I say 'short-term' to relate this recent experience to the debate. But in many ways the emphasis on the period of capital funding mis-specifies the issue. The question is whether particular projects are ever likely to be profitable, or put in another and more positive way, whether the criterion of profitability is any longer appropriate for the allocation of resources.

Take first the case of a firm on the verge of bankruptcy. The GLC has been approached by some 30 such firms in the last nine months. The issue in each case is not the absence of long-term funds, but whether (a) there is any hope of the enterprise ever earning a normal rate of profit; and (b) there is a long-term non-market case for supporting the enterprise. As far as (a) is concerned, there are instances of firms which have expanded too fast, and been caught short by the collapse of demand after 1979. Here there is a case for long-term capital investment. But often these are found in sectors already heavy with overcapacity, when even newly equipped firms may have no long-term security. More common were firms which clearly needed restructuring if they were ever to achieve market profitability: old plants, with old machinery, in some cases producing commodities which were becoming rapidly obsolete technically (such as push-button B telephone boxes) or facing a long-term declining market (for instance in the up market furniture trade). The question in these cases is how the restructuring is to take place (if at all), who is to carry it through, how long will it take, with whom would it make sense to merge. These are the issues - restructuring the use value side of production - rather than the availability or not of long-term finance.

In the Wilson Committee discussion, there were two groups of dissenters to the majority opinion that no new long-term investment agency was required. One group was composed of TUC representatives and Harold Wilson himself, who argued for a new investment agency, capable of investing £2 billion a year in productive industry, and funded from the institutions and North Sea tax revenues. The other group contained significantly Sir Kenneth Cork, who, as the country's most eminent receiver, could be described as capital's official restructurer. This group argued that a new institution was needed which 'would depend partly on its own resources and partly on the number and size of investment programmes it could discover or create. Its own resources consist almost entirely of skilled staff and finance. Of these two, we believe the more important constraint is the staff'. In as much as the issue for the British economy is one of restructuring, the Cork group argued that what was needed was a public body of restructurers who should build up their financial resources in line with their staff capacity. They point out that fund managers do not have skills which are 'appropriate to appraising new projects'. They criticise the TUC line on the grounds that it concentrates on exchange value (finance) and not on use value ('men and machines'). It is the right projects which need to be developed, and only then does finance need to be made available. (3)

What is interesting in this proposal is that it emphasises that a 'shortage of demand for finance is a major part of the problem' rather than the shortage of supply of long-term funding, but at the same time argues for state intervention in the development of new projects. 'In our view present arrangements need to be buttressed by a new facility (probably organised in a decentralised way) through which new projects and new firms are actively sought and promoted.' (4) It shifts the criticism of financial institutions from their short time horizons to their incapacity to actively develop new projects. The financial institutions might say that restructuring is not their job (though they are increasingly being drawn into it - witness for example Lazards' plan for restructuring the foundry industry by widespread closures with cross compensation). They might argue that it is industrial not banking capital which should restructure production. What the Cork group were suggesting was that, blame aside, if neither were doing it, then the state should intervene.

My argument here is that the main issue is active restructuring rather than long-term finance. The discussion has focused on the inadequacy of institutions to provide appropriate finance, whereas it should first consider the inadequacy of institutions to restructure whole sectors of the national economy. Long-term finance without detailed plans for restructuring will be of limited value as far as projects which will be profitable in the long-term are concerned.

The second issue which tends to get underplayed is whether there are projects which may never make a profit, but which are still important in the long-term. The question here is not short-term as against long-term availability, but whether on market criteria there will be any funds at all. In public investment circles there is a tendency to refer to such projects as 'social'. In the guidelines to the National Enterprise Board or the Scottish Development Agency, they are given only passing reference. These public agencies in order to show themselves rigorous in approach adopt relatively stringent criteria based on expected market profitability, which they apply to new projects. The Cork group argue that their proposed state investment bank should appraise projects which are financed at below market rates against strict criteria, linked principally in to manning and productivity levels agreed with the unions. (5) The new facility should not be used for 'propping up firms for social or political reasons'.

In all these instances the projects are envisaged as

being 'viable' in the long-term. Those that are not are regarded as in some way soft. But this is to accept that market valuations are accurate reflections of social valuation, which is clearly not the case. Some projects may be important for stimulating others, or because they use otherwise wasted resources, or because they might have to be protected against international competition in the long-term because they produce socially useful products with methods of work which do not degrade labour in the same way as international competitors. If we link this back to the earlier discussion, restructuring may take place in a number of ways with very different implications for labour. Some ways involving adequate wages and working conditions will be at a disadvantage in the market vis-a-vis enterprises that have been restructured by and for capital. It is therefore important to have a funding institution which can support and protect projects which have been restructured for labour.

A third type of project we should consider is that where the market is no longer an adequate mechanism for determining the type and pace of technical change. In a number of industries technical change is taking place so fast that any new plant built will be rapidly obsolete. This often discourages investment in research and development. Given the uncertainties, firms wait for others to make the initial moves. Only the largest can carry the costs in these circumstances, and these, too are having to scrap virtually new plant (ICI for example), or to judge constantly the trade off between investing and waiting, or developing a type of technology with a long commercial life, rather than a type with longer-term technical possibilities. The technology of cables is one example, or of electronic switching systems, or types of videodisc.

In the case of technological development, as in the previous point about desirable projects which are unlikely ever to reach market profitability, it is not the financial system but the market system as a whole which is inadequate. Improving the flow of long-term funds aiming for market profitability does not address these problems, and it is these that are further aspects of the process of industrial restructuring.

I have not wished to suggest that adequate long-term finance is not important for any programme of active restructuring. But it should be seen as part of a package, and not as the principle variable. Furthermore, in as much as it is used as part of a package, its character as capital must be recognised. Its aim is always the maximum expansion of its value, and this remains true whether the banks are run by old Etonians or by socialists in government.

A second line of argument about financial institutions is that they are not like any other private enterprise (as the Wilson Committee implied) but that they form an economic 'estate'. Most recently, this argument has been developed by members of the Open University Financial Studies Group (Coakley and Harris (6)). Finance capital - as we may call this estate - has acted economically and politically as a macro force whose results have been to keep up interest rates and the exchange rate in order to maintain the strength of sterling. This has put British industry in a weak position economically, which it has not been able to remedy politically. For these reasons, the destruction of this political power is needed, via the nationalisation of the financial institutions, following which interest and exchange rates will be adjusted downwards.

This tension between industrial and finance capital is an important one, but the social control of finance capital and a lowering of the cost of capital and the value of the pound is again too restricted a financial view of the necessary conditions for industrial revival. If the issue is as I have posed it, namely one of restructuring, the question is to what extent low interest and exchange rates will encourage restructuring. It can be argued that such falls by providing a degree of protection, would encourage restructuring (certainly Mrs Thatcher thought that the opposite moves of raising interest and exchange rates would lead to restructuring according to her preferred path). It is part of a more active policy of restructuring for labour that these adjustments in circulation are important.

A third line of argument is that the financial institutions are now the commanding heights of the economy, and that their nationalisation will give a socialist government control over finance and industry. A recent and closely reasoned case of this sort has been made by Richard Minns (7) of the West Midlands County Council, but it has a longer tradition in socialist thinking, having much in common with Hilferding's programme for the control of money. In a curious way it is an inversion of the macro monetarists. Friedman, Harry Johnson and their Chicago colleagues, always saw the control of money as offering a path to influence every pore of a country's economic life without direct intervention by the state. The state could adjust the supply of money, and autonomous citizens would respond according to their felicific calculus. The problem for the monetarists has always been that the state does not have monopoly control of the supply of money in a modern credit economy. For Hilferding, as for Richard Minns, the nationalisation of the banks would give the state that control which it could use for progressive purposes.

The question for Richard Minns, as for Rudolf Hilferding, is whether in an economy of private industrial capitalists, the socialist government control of the issue of money alters the character of money as capital. If a nationalised bank issued long-term credit to a firm which could not repay, what would happen to the financial system? Would the state bank devalue the capital and bankrupt the firm? If it did not receive interest, how would it finance new investment? Would it create money, and if so within what limits? What would happen to the rate of exchange of this nationalised currency? I would suggest that as long as money performs the role that it has always done in capitalism, as a medium of exchange, and means of payment, a store of value, a unit of account, and above all as the money form of capital, then the socialist control of money cannot alter its character. For the nature of money is determined by its part in the process of economic reproduction. If this process remains capitalist (with private ownership of the means of production, and circulation via a market) then money will be called upon to play a particular role, regardless of who formally controls it.

My argument has been that many of the criticisms of British financial institutions in this country should be seen first as criticisms of money as capital ruled by the law of value rather than criticisms of the financial institutions as such. Overseas investment, investment in property, selling out in dawn raids, the paucity of venture capital, all might be expected from money capital which seeks maximum self-expansion. The institutions are bearers of these forces, and we may see them as doing their job too well as they shun long-term investment, manufacturing industry and the British economy.

Having said this, however, two further points arise. First, the law of value as imposed through the market is problematic for capital. The size of investments and their gestation periods are expanding and this increases the uncertainty of any long-term profitability. Industrial capital needs long-term finance, but money capital as such - whose essence is self-expansion - is no longer an adequate source. Similarly the market's traditional mechanisms of crisis and restructuring are increasingly self-wounding. As the direct interdependence of production grows, so does the severity of a crisis of restructuring since new planned systems of production have to be introduced on an ever wider scale. It is not just a question of the bankruptcy of a small firm and the transfer of its assets to a larger more productive one. It is rather one of massive devaluations, affecting simultaneously great aggregations of capital and whole national economies. Financial institutions are inadequate because money capital guided by the lodestar of market profitability is inadequate, not because the institutions as institutions are at fault.

This leads to the second point, which is the extent to which finance can be insulated from the daily discipline of market profitability (the law of value). Can institutions be set up which perform the functions of financial institutions - as providers of long-term finance, as active restructurers - but obey other economic laws? This is the main issue of this paper. I have not wanted to play down the importance of institutional change, or the question of ownership. But both must be seen in terms of alternative economic forces. If we nationalise the banks we do not abolish the law of value. It reimposes itself through the international money and commodity markets, and through the role of money in the internal capitalist economy. But we can insulate at least part of the national economy from the immediate laws of the market. This is particularly important with respect to the restructuring of production, for it is on this that long-term competitivity (or put another way, long-term insulation from the international law of value) depends. It is then in terms of an alternative economics of production, rather than a modified economics of circulation (the provision of long-term capital, the modification of the exchanges and interest rates) that the change of ownership and control of financial institutions should be judged.

The National and Local Significance of Pension Funds

Pension funds have to come to play a major part in UK finance. Their size has grown from £3 billion in the late 1950s to £64 billion in 1982. Of this £8.66 billion (14 per cent) is in local authority funds, and £18.66 billion (29 per cent) in other public sector funds. As finance they have a number of distinct features:

(i) The final purpose of pensions is use values rather than exchange values. The retired pensioner wishes to consume goods, rather than re-invest. The pension in money form should thus be seen as primarily a medium of circulation and the employer's liability ultimately a liability to provide use values.

(ii) They are not intrinsically self-expanding. Whereas banking capital has its only meaning as self-expanding value (moving from M-M'), pensions have a different logic. They take the form of wage payments paid after the worker has ceased to work. In private pension schemes the employer's liability builds up during a labourer's active working life. This is why pensions are often seen as a deferred wage. But in fact they amount to no more than a liability, and the history of pensions is a history of the nominal size of this liability, its guarantee, and its funding. Pension funds are one way in which this liability can be met. But they are only one way. Current liabilities can be funded by current contributions or from the employer's current general income (pay-as-you-go). This is effectively what happens in state insurance. In these cases pensions are not paid out of accrued money capital but out of income. This point is clearest when pensions are non-contributory - as they could be and have been in certain periods. Contributions make it appear that pensions are paid out of capital - the invested worker's wages - but in macro terms (and intrinsically) there is no necessity for them to be so.

(iii) Since pensions are closely tied to wages and work, they are subject to decentralised agreement by employers and workers, and therefore are subject to collective bargaining. The question of the control - and within limits the use - of pension funds does not depend on state action, but can be contested by organised labour (the Lucas shop stewards combine is an early example). Local authority pensions funds have further characteristics:

(iv) They are index-linked (thus guaranteeing inflation-proof pensions) and thus involve a liability of a constant real value, approximating to a constant purchasing power or bundle of use values. There is thus no commercial risk for a local authority contributor.

(v) Shortfalls are funded by the local council, effectively from taxes. Rate funds are not capital. They have no requirement to expand. Rather they are a transfer from private income to (in this case) former state employees. As a matter of practice the guarantees are paid into the pension fund following five-year actural revaluations, so that they become capital prior to their pay out as pensions.

(vi) Since contributions by both employer and employee are funded from taxes, and since the guarantees are likewise paid from the rate fund, we can see local authority pensions as a relation between rate payers and former council employees, and local authority pension funds as a relation between the timing of rate payments to settle a future liability.

(vii) With private company schemes, workers clearly have an interest in an independent fund as a guarantee of their future pensions because of the danger of the company disappearing or not being able to pay when the pension is due. This is much less the case with a local authority. The local authorities' power to tax provides a much firmer guarantee and makes funding less necessary.

When considering the use of local authority pension funds, therefore, we should not be misled as to their nature. They are merely a device for setting aside rate and government grants to meet an eventual liability, constant in use value terms. There is no necessity for them to be used as capital. If they do not earn the maximum rate of return, then current rates may make up the difference. Indeed they could in principle be entirely funded by current rates, or by current rates plus current contributions (in the GLC fund total outgoings in 1980-1 were £30.2 million, while current contributions - excluding investment income - were £52.5 million).

The point here is that there are strong pressures for local authority pension funds to treat those funds as capital. The Local Government Superannuation Regulations 1974 require surplus funds to be invested in accordance with a modified version of the Trustees Investment Act 1961. This lays down guidelines for investment. For example, it requires that the fund be administered with the advice of qualified financial consultants, that the fund be diversified, and that no more than 10 per cent of investment be in unquoted companies.

However, the emphasis of the Act is on prudence rather than maximisation. Under the heading of diversification, divergence from immediate profit maximisation may be justified. Most significant, up to 25 per cent of the Fund can be used for purposes for which Local Councils have statutory borrowing powers. The Council acts not as trustees but as if they were trustees. It can immediately be seen that there is considerable leeway in how these funds are used.

In 1982 the GLC Pension Fund has assets amounting to £556 million with 39,000 contributors and 22,000 beneficiaries. Its administration is formally in the hands of the Finance and General Purposes Committee, but it is effectively managed by officials in the Finance Department with a team of City advisers. It has been run on conventional lines, treating the fund as capital. The recent report on investments says 'The Fund must be maximised within an acceptable and minimum pattern of risk. Both prudence and legal requirements dictate a wide diversification of investments'. This is reflected in Table 14.1 below:

Table 14.1: GLC Funds 1978-82

	GLC		1981-2	
	1978	1982	Other local authorities	Private sector funds
Fixed interest	35	23	27	24
UK equities	38	41	40	27
Overseas equities	-	7	17	28
Property	19	23	10	15
Other ('short-term' and cash)	8	6	6	6

Source: CIPFA (Chartered Institute of Public Finance and Accountancy).

This indicates a lower proportion of overseas equities than the norm, and a higher proportion of property. Within property, however, there was a low proportion of investment in Central London. As with overseas investment, these divergences were undertaken for policy reasons. In the past few years the policy has been to restore the 'normal proportions' - that is to say further insulate the fund from policy considerations. Thus last year 50 per cent of investments went overseas, and significant property investments have been made in London.

The GLC Labour Manifesto of 1981 contained two commitments vis-a-vis the Pension Fund:

(a) to give the members of the Fund - the GLC employees - a full say in its administration and investment. A panel of 27 has now been set up consisting of nine members and 18 union representatives, with the unions representing pensioners and those contributors not in a union;
(b) to persuade the Fund 'to invest a substantial and increasing proportion of the cash flow of the fund to GLEB' (Greater London Enterprise Board). In 1981-2 the surplus for investment of the Fund was £65 million. This is the stage at which we are now.

There are two directions for advance. The first is the more modest, in that it recognises the Fund as capital and works within those broad limits. Already, the GLC Fund - as the result of initiatives by Finance officers - have invested in a CIPFA consortium for the finance of small industrial premises. This is a sector of the market which until recently was avoided by private property companies, in part because of the costs of management. The GLC fund justified its investment on grounds of diversification, in that they have no investment in that branch of the property market.

But there is a wide scope for the Fund to play in the projects which GLEB (and the Council) are currently putting together, even given conventional interpretation of the nature of the Fund. The most immediate area is property. In all five major rescue attempts we have been involved in to date, the financing of the factories has been a central lever. The GLC has powers under the 1963 Local Authority Land Act to invest in land and buildings, but may contribute only 90 per cent of the value that should be secured on a mortgage. Nor may GLEB use the GLC's money for this purpose other than as an agent. The mortgage still has to be held by the GLC, and GLEB's independence is thereby limited. The aim of the Act, and the modifications in the 1982 Miscellaneous Provisions Act, was to involve private sector finance. For this purpose GLC Pension Fund money can be used as private finance, either to fund all property operations, or to complement GLC funding.

Secondly, all these investments have had two parts: the first is commercial. For example, property has to be valued at market prices (though property valuation is hardly science or art - but rather a question of convenient formula). Interest on loans has to be charged at market rates. The second part of GLC agreements has been sub-commercial. We have provided revenue funds to make up the difference between expected performance and the normal rate of return. We thus are able to subsidise interest rates (as the West Midlands do), or rents, or provide contributions to other running costs. It has proved quite possible to involve private sector funds in the commercial parts of the package: Barclays have invested in two of the schemes, the Midland Bank in a third. There is no reason why the GLC should not invest likewise, even in equity, given that foreign securities (unquoted on the London market, but quoted overseas) are no longer included in the 10 per cent limit on unquoted company investment. The usefulness of the Pension Fund, as with all internal sources of financing, is that it can be synchronised more easily with the rest of the package.

Thirdly, the Fund is legally permitted to spend up to 25 per cent of its value on capital investment for which the Council has statutory borrowing powers. Given the restrictions currently being imposed on capital spending in the GLC (£10 million in 1983/4), this would enable a significant increase in capital available for industrial investment undertaken directly by the GLC.

Fourthly, the Fund could invest more generally in GLEB projects without specific guarantees (e.g. through a charge on project assets) but with the guarantee of a given rate of return by GLEB. This might take the form of fixed interest loans (the GLEB equivalent of gilts) or of loans with a base rate guaranteed but no limit on maximum returns. There is, of course, an issue about guarantees. Why should the GLC via GLEB shoulder the risk at the expense of private capital? The point in general holds water, but is clearly not applicable in the case of the GLC's own Pension Fund. Given an expected actuarial liability, the GLC will have to make up any shortfall directly from the rates. A guarantee given by GLEB merely obviates the need for guarantee payments by the GLC on that part of the Fund capital. If the Fund's investment earns more than the expected rate of return, this - ceteris paribus - reduces the deficit to be made up from the rates on the Fund as a whole. Hence in the case of Pension Fund money, guarantees can be given in the knowledge that this is effectively a self-guarantee. For this reason, the Council should be able to borrow more cheaply from the Pension Fund than on the open market - particularly if the guarantee rate is taken as the rate on gilts.

An alternative form of guarantee would be of capital losses on a particular investment rather than on an overall rate of return.

The significance of local authority pension funds in the above cases is:

(a) it allows local authority instruments such as the GLEB, or the Council itself, to get round certain government restrictions on capital spending and property investment;
(b) because of the guarantees which it makes sense for the Council and GLEB to offer to pension fund investments, it should be possible to obtain funds at lower interest rates and for longer-term periods than ordinary commercial loans. (It should be remembered that GLEB and the Council would be offering the fund something it would not normally get in the open market - even were it to lend to other local authorities and public bodies - and that is hard guarantees);
(c) given that it would effectively be a source of internal finance, it could be more easily managed as part of an overall package.

There remains the question of the best means of investment. One proposal we are considering is a financial subsidiary of GLEB to manage pension fund investment. This fund would have an overall guaranteed rate of return, and individual investments would be left for it to manage. This has the advantage of avoiding the formal procedures of Council assessment, and placing control of the funds directly in the hands of GLEB financial officers. West Midlands have pioneered this approach, and are involved in developing different types of funds of this sort, one for the inner city, another for a particular sector.

The above I see as the minimum use that can be made of pension funds. The proposals acknowledge the requirements of the pension fund as capital, but use this capital for wider purposes. One of the dangers of public investment bodies such as GLEB seeking external funds is that they gear their investment criteria to those of the financial market (see for example the Scottish Development Authority) or make a compromise which still ties broad policy to the law of value. This I regard as unnecessary. It is quite possible to separate any investment into its commercial and sub-commercial components. Pension funds may be incorporated in the first.

The question remains: how much further can pension funds be taken? Can they be of wider use than a secure, internally managed commercial source of finance? To begin with, direct control by an investment panel composed of unions and councillors can direct the funds in the commercial market to link in with the Council's wider economic and political policies. For instance the Council operates an early warning system to indicate which plants in London are threatened with redundancy or closure. Major firms identified can then be talked to and offered some carrots if necessary. There are also some sticks: GLC's purchasing powers are one such (for instance Plessey has recently announced a closure in Romford and we have found it is bidding for a large computer project for the London Fire Brigade); our planning powers are another (which we investigated in relation to the closure of Hoover's in West London). The Pension Fund's investments are a third. Table 14.2 shows the largest 20 holdings of the Pension Fund in British equities.

Large manufacturing companies are significantly under represented, but many have substantial operations in London, and two have recently been involved with the Council in discussions about closures.

There are many other policies for which pension funds could be used as a lever. The GLC is currently starting a contracts compliance unit which seeks to use its purchasing power to induce employers to put into practice the principles of Equal Opportunity legislation. Pension fund investment could be used similarly. The GLC has used its purchasing power in RTZ and Shell to object to policies followed in the Third World, particularly in South Africa. The American unions are using pension fund power over these and wider forms.

What is needed in this respect is coordination between authorities. The GLC fund at the moment restricts its investments in any one firm. For instance the £9 million invested in BP is only 4 per cent of the £229 million invested in UK equities, and less than 2 per cent of the fund as a whole. It also represents only a small proportion of BP shares. However, together the major local authority and public sector shares would control a substantial proportion

Table 14.2: Twenty Largest Equity Holdings at 31 March 1982

Position	Company	Market value (£000)
1	British Petroleum Co plc	8990
2	Shell Transport and Trading Co. Ltd.	8213
3	BAT Industries, plc	6270
4	General Electric Co. plc	5245
5	Marks & Spencer, plc	3813
6	Barclays Bank, plc	3790
7	Beecham Group Ltd.	3259
8	Prudential Group, Ltd.	3237
9	Imperial Chemical Industries, plc	3228
10	Lloyds Bank Ltd.	3198
11	BTR, plc	3006
12	Boots Co. Ltd.	2994
13	Grand Metropolitan, plc	2943
14	BPB Industries, plc	2800
15	Royal Insurance, plc	2700
16	Northern Foods, plc	2667
17	National Westminster Bank, plc	2653
18	Rio Tinto-Zinc Corp., plc	2653
19	Hanson Trust, plc	2592
20	Unilever, plc	2571

of the major companies shares. Richard Minns estimates 20 per cent of all UK equities are held by pension funds, but in individual cases this will be significantly higher. (7) The West Midlands have taken the lead in trying to coordinate local authorities' pension funds in this regard, and to build parallel systems to those in the United States where the trade unions have developed a computer system on company information and pension fund holdings.

The wider issue, however, is whether it is possible to break the close link between pension funds and commercial rates of return. Given the inadequacy of profit as a guide to major long-term investments, what is necessary is a fund which can be used for restructuring without the constant discipline of the money market hanging over it. There are strong arguments why pension funds should be used for this purpose: they derive from the rates whose purpose is more generally to provide services and infrastructure for Londoners. The long-term economic health of London is in the interests of those who work in London, both as citizens, and (with some mediation by the rate support grant) because the future rate income will in part depend on the general level of economic activity. Most important of all, if the restructuring of production in London is to take place in a way different to the process as organised by capital, if it is to be a restructuring in the interests of labour both as workers and consumers, then the GLC employees as workers have a clear interest in providing a source of finance for this end.

This brings me to the final emphasis of this paper. The main issue in the UK (and in London) at the moment is restructuring. Capital through monetarism is carrying through their version of restructuring at the expense of labour, with enormous waste, and with fearful consequences so far as the state of the world economy is concerned. The task of socialists is to resist this version, and instead to work through alternative versions which we have called restructuring for labour. This involves workers, and socialist-controlled authorities, developing projects which can hold their own in the long run, but which produce outputs which are directly related to working people's needs, in ways which build on the skills of labour rather than deskilling them. The main problem in this process is the construction of the projects. In this sense, the Cork group in the Wilson report is right, though they envisage the process of restructuring taking place in another way. Finance is one part of this package, but only a part. It cannot lead it. In our first year of operation we have found money to be the least of our problems: at times it has even been a negative factor. However, the particular character of pension funds as not inherently capital, means that they can usefully be used (even with procedures which regard them as capital), and in the longer term may be the source for supporting a much wider programme of restructuring than any individual local authority or group of workers can currently mount.

NOTES

1. This is the text of a paper delivered on 21 January 1983 at the Future of Finance Conference organised by the Open University Financial Studies Group.

2. Committee to Review the Functioning of Financial Institutions (1980) Report, Chairman the Right Honourable Sir Harold Wilson, HMSO Cmnd 7937.

3. Ibid, p.271.

4. Ibid, p.271.

5. Ibid, pp.265 and 272.

6. J. Coakley and L. Harris (1982) 'Evaluating the role of the financial system' in D. Currie and M. Sawyer (eds), Socialist Economic Review, 1982.

7. Richard Minns (1982) Take Over the City, Pluto.

Chapter Fifteen

PENSION FUNDS: AN ALTERNATIVE VIEW

Richard Minns

It is indicative of how far we have moved on in our thinking over the last few years, that we can now discuss boring old local government in the same breath as the restructuring of British industry and the role of financial capital. In this sense Robin Murray's article raises, for me at least, a vitally important issue at the present time, namely, 'what existing local authorities can do ... to use pension funds for the purpose of long-term investment.' As he rightly states, 'part of the importance of these local initiatives is that they are testing the social control of finance in practice, and they are testing it as one part of a much wider investment strategy.' His article proceeds to question a number of points which critics of the City have raised. What emerges from the argument is that there seems to be some confusion amongst those involved in these issues not only about the political purpose of local initiatives, especially so far as pension funds are concerned, but also about what direction we should take in economic terms at the local level. This follows on from a difference of view about the City and its importance in Britain.

Firstly, I want to briefly summarise Robin Murray's line of thinking, and then to tackle the major points. In a nutshell, what he argues is that it is mistaken to attack the City for not providing long-term funds for investment in British industry. Finance is not the crucial problem - rather the issue is one of restructuring British industry, after which the necessary finance for profitable investment is a secondary issue. The City is only an expression of money capital which seeks maximum self-expansion through profitable investment. This, in turn, has implications for local initiatives. Pension funds can be used in various ways which build on their capitalist nature while the local authority can provide additional finance of its own to broaden the purpose of intervention and investment and to 'restructure for labour'.

This is a very crude oversimplification, but it goes to the heart of the issue - what is the role of the City and its financial institutions and what position should local authorities adopt? Let me now deal with some of the main points in more detail.

Does Finance Matter?

Robin Murray begins by attacking the view that the financial institutions are a major cause of UK economic decline. The fact that they fail to provide long-term investment funds, he argues, that they increasingly invest overseas, and that they invest in unproductive assets, arises because there is a lack of profitable projects in the productive sphere in the UK, a view taken by the City itself as Robin Murray points out. Capitalist money has an 'intrinsic character, which, like capital in general is to drive always for maximum self-expansion'.

> It invests in property, overseas assets, and the shares of large corporations rather than smaller untried ventures because it is simply more profitable to do so. Further, at a moment of crisis money capital is withdrawn from the circuit of productive capital. The crisis is reflected in the monetary sphere, but the monetary sphere does not cause the crisis.

There is therefore, in Robin Murray's view, probably something temporary about the current problem. Once the crisis is over, money capital will flow back into the circuit of productive capital. There are signs of something occurring already, according to this argument. In the GLC's experience, major clearing banks such as Barclays and Midland, have been taking a longer-term view in order to forestall company collapse. Along with the Bank of England, 'all these financial institutions have a self-interest in ... preserving a productive industry capable of reproducing profits in the long run'. In fact, the financial system is apparently 'operating an alternative industrial policy to the government, more active in its intervention and less short-term in its financial criteria.'

The issue anyway, according to Robin Murray, is not whether there is an absence of long-term funds, the problem is industrial restructuring and planning. The criticism of financial institutions is not their short-term horizons but their incapacity to actively develop new projects - 'long-term finance without detailed plans for restructuring will be of limited value as far as projects which will be profitable in the long term are concerned.'

I feel that there are a number of fundamental points here; disagreement on them affects any subsequent argument. Basically I do not feel that we can take theoretical concepts of money capital and circuits, and just read off from these what is occurring in Britain. In fact, Robin Murray also has trouble with this because he uses various concepts interchangeably to deal with the problem of theoretical and empirical analysis; see his use of 'finance', 'financial institutions', 'money capital', 'banking capital', 'issue of money', and even 'finance capital'. In some cases theory swamps the empirical, as in his reference to money capital being withdrawn from the circuit of productive capital in a moment of crisis. As I understand the historical evidence, the remote, or withdrawn relationship of financial capital (the institutions broadly summed up in the concept 'the City') to productive capital (manufacturing and certain service industries) has a long history (1) which is more substantial than that reflected in what I take Robin Murray to be referring to as the present crisis of the last ten years or so.

In other cases, the empirical swamps the theoretical. The fact that the GLC has found a number of financial institutions taking a longer-term view and presumably willing to finance GLC projects does not convince me that their position has changed. Barclays and the Midland may well have their industrial first-aid developments; but how long was the institutions' new found long-term view in the cases of Stone-Platt and Airfix where financial reconstruction was followed by the same institutions pulling out after a year? Even in the huge reconstruction of Massey Ferguson, the institutions had more to lose by collapsing the company as their first option, than by writing off some debt and converting some other to equity or risk capital. This in no way can be construed as 'preserving a productive industry capable of reproducing profits in the long run.' It is equally the same short-term view being demonstrated. Banks seek maximum security on the assets of a company before any loan is forthcoming. In the case of financial trouble in a company, their reaction is 'how do we get out?' By calling in a receiver they can sell assets and retrieve their loan. In some cases, the collapse of markets may make the assets worth less than the books show, and in these cases, the banks can get out with what they can, or they may be pressurised to stay in if there is too much to lose. Even the Industrial and Commercial Finance Corporation (ICFC), the largest development capital organisation in the UK, tends to operate rather like a conventional bank, and ICFC was set up by the banks in 1946 to provide more risk finance to industry.

The City is essentially an international centre of finance. It does not exist, historically, to finance British industry. Even a bank, like the Midland Bank, more involved than most with lending to British industry, has been diversifying substantially into overseas banking. It describes itself as 'an international banking group' and its recent substantial acquisition of the Crocker National Corporation in California (as well as others such as the majority stake in Handelsfinanz in Switzerland) is seen as part of its 'long term plan' (sic) for the international expansion of the Midland Bank.

The financing of overseas ventures and foreign governments is the City's traditional role. However, I do not accept that this efficient, successful (in capitalist terms) group of financial institutions, is actually so successful even in its own terms. It makes mistakes, like the recent problems with sovereign debt in countries like Mexico and Poland. Other mistakes like the over commitment to property in the 1970s were baled out by the state. Its activities centre on world wide financial operations (2) rather than allying itself constructively for the long-term with any particular productive capital (however defined). This I feel is equally risky, in capitalist terms, because it involves a succession of short-term views of the location of the production of surplus value (to use the jargon). But then, even in theoretical terms, capitalism is based on contradictions and this does not preclude financial capital.

How successful have pension funds been - again in capitalist terms - in this system? Very few pension funds are in fact financial institutions. Most are just balance sheets which are effectively run by another institution -

merchant bank, stock broker, insurance company and others. At least 50 per cent of all pension fund assets are managed by merchant banks alone. These institutions obtain fees for management, as well as other more concealed benefits. (3) Stockbrokers, of course, receive dealing fees. Pension funds have nevertheless failed to produce real rates of return. Stockbrokers Phillips and Drew have shown that the average private pension fund achieved an annual rate of return of 9.1 per cent over 18 years to 1981, compared with average increase in earnings of 11.9 per cent. (4) Since pensions are linked to salaries, and most actuaries assume real returns of at least 2 per cent, this represents a significant real loss for pensioners.

But it has provided the City with some short-term income, and while this has been going on, the City has been moving more into international fund management. Robin Murray's question is the right one - why should the institutions invest in British industry when all these other avenues are open to them. The answer, however, is wrong. It is not necessarily the case that a series of short-term profitable outlets creates the conditions for greater returns in the long-term than commitment to one productive base does. The City has not invested in British industry, not because it is necessarily unprofitable in the long term, but to put it crudely, because current income is available elsewhere. The issue is the assessment of risk and security, which is different in Britain compared to countries like Germany and Japan. This is because of the different approach and international role of financial capital in Britain, however counter-productive this may be to the financial institution and to pension funds in the longer-term. This issue is the availability of long-term finance, no matter how much restructuring is undertaken. According to the Banking Information Service, (5) the official defenders of the banking faith, the banks of overseas countries are not less profitable than British banks (as a result of taking a radically different approach, we might add): the political danger of Robin Murray's line of argument is that we will spend more time controlling the industry and restructuring, and less time on how to control the financial institutions.

Of course restructuring is necessary. No one, I think has ever referred to the issue of controlling finance without considering the need to link it closely with the planning of production, in one form or another. British industry is too far gone after decades of lack of investment and long-term risk finance to think that finance is the be all and end all. What is at issue is the degree of emphasis given to different parts of the equation. For example, although restructuring is not defined in detail in the article, it might well of course include financial restructuring. This can arise where a company has invested in new plant and machinery, but in order to do so it has borrowed heavily. A classic case in the Midlands has been the ferrous and non-ferrous foundry aid schemes during the 1970s. These provided grants for a part of the cost of capital investment. Companies had to borrow the major part of the expenditure to make up the difference between the costs and grants. By the end of the 1970s this created a crippling interest rate burden. The ludicrous capitalist situation was emerging where companies which had not invested and borrowed could just about struggle on in the recession while those, not necessary in the same sector, that were more efficient and had restructured would go bust. These companies needed injections of equity capital either for the original capital investment or for subsequent working capital. Basically, in this and other companies, the most appropriate type of finance for capital investment, for working capital and even for mergers, acquisitions and demergers, is not available - even when the company is successfully restructured and has significant growth potential.

Whoever initiates the restructuring, industry or the state, finance too needs to be controlled because it will not offer itself. Financial capital in the UK operates differently to financial capital in, say, Japan, and has traditionally done so. The lending by the Japanese banks was controlled and directed by the government into priority industries. (6) It was not a matter of restructuring Japanese industry and then waiting for the banks to play their part. The problem of finance for industry in Britain is not just a reflection of a crisis in industry as a result of industrial decline over the last ten, 20 or even 30 years.

The political role of the City complements this. The City has successfully pressed for economic measures which benefit its international position rather than that of industry in Britain. This may partly explain why industry is increasingly locating overseas. Be that as it may, Robin Murray criticises this argument that the financial institutions are an economic estate. Far be it from me to defend Coakley and Harris who are cited as the latest proponents of this analysis, but it appears to me that Robin

Murray has begun to throw the baby out with the bath water. He argues that control of this estate in order to lower interest and exchange rates is not enough for industrial revival and I suppose that it is true. But Coakley and Harris state the following: 'Control and nationalisation of the financial institutions is only viable if it is part of a policy to nationalise industrial firms themselves and thereby control their activities directly.' In addition, as an analysis of the political power of the City which works alongside the City's approach to investment and risk assessment, the work of Coakley and Harris and others, is an essential part of the equation. Robin Murray tends to reduce everything to restructuring.

Next, he draws our attention to the argument advanced by others 'that the financial institutions are now the commanding heights of the economy, and that their nationalisation will give a socialist government control over finance and industry'. Arguments of this sort he attributes to me, and to Rudolf Hilferding. What is said by Robin Murray is, 'If we nationalise the banks we do not abolish the law of value.' In other words, nothing would change. 'Criticism of British financial institutions should be criticisms of money as capital ruled by the law of value rather than criticisms of the financial institutions as such.'

In my view this is an oversimplification which can emerge from reading off empirical events from the categories of the law of value. I believe that the institutions are different from the concept of money as capital. These theoretical categories direct our thinking, but they are very general. Within the concept, different manifestations of money capital, in this case British financial institutions, operate in a range of ways and guises in order to seek successfully or not, the maximum self-expansion. Just because a law of value exists, this does not mean all institutions in different nation states will operate in the same way empirically. British financial institutions seek self-expansion in an international role full of short-term assessments of speculation and surplus value extraction. Japanese financial institutions seek self-expansion in a national role linked to long-term risk taking and development in Japanese industry. In this context I do not agree at all that necessarily 'overseas investment, investment in property, selling out in dawn raids, the paucity of venture capital, all might be expected from money capital which seeks maximum self-expansion.'

The proposals I want to put forward still basically add up to capitalism - with that I agree. But intervention can at the same time be based on the advancement of socialist principles, such as greater accountability of capital (industrial and financial) to the workforce and to the community, and greater planning of investment and production in Britain which is less wasteful of human and environmental resources. Finance needs to be controlled in order to do this.

However, Robin Murray has an alternative. This is his suggestion that 'we can insulate at least part of the national economy from the immediate laws of the market. 'This' he continues, 'is particularly important with respect to the restructuring of production, for it is on this that long-term competitivity depends.' Robin Murray is considering projects which 'restructure for labour' as opposed to capital. These may involve better wages and working conditions which may put a company at a disadvantage in the market against others which have been restructured by and for capital. However, these projects must 'hold their own in the long run'. How this requirement squares with 'restructuring for labour' is not explained. But let us examine in more detail the basis for creating an 'alternative economics of production.' This brings us on specifically to consider pension funds and local government initiatives.

The Case for Mobilising Local Authority Pension Funds

Robin Murray argues that pension funds have distinct features as finance. 'They are not intrinsically self-expanding, because they aim to produce use-values for pensioners, rather than reinvestment.' Pensions could indeed be paid out of current revenue (rates or taxation), rather than out of a fund. But does this mean that pension funds are not capital? Presumably most people who insure themselves or their property are concerned with income, use values, for themselves or dependents, rather than reinvestment. In addition, insurance could be run completely by the state out of current revenue (and for various purposes, such as health and unemployment, to a large extent it is). But does this mean that insurance companies are not capital? Is the majority of money at the disposal of building societies or banks saving for a rainy day and for daily running expenses (income, use values), or does it accumulate for reinvestment? Maybe, it is a bit of both. But the line of argument confuses the concept with its purpose. Whatever its purpose, it functions as capital. Even if we scrap pension funds tomorrow for some alternative system, the accumulated assets are capital.

Furthermore, local authority pension funds may well be guaranteed by local authorities through the rates: therefore technically it does not matter to future pensioners if there is a deficit. But they are still capital because of their place in the structure of British finance and the City. Even if we could agree that they were not, politically they will be treated as such. Let us try to use a pension fund in a project which protects jobs with no prospect of long-term survival and then let us guess which way a court's decision will go. Hence the importance of the political battle with the City because its views about finance, prudence, security, benefits, duties, permeate other structures of society, in particular the courts and central and local administrations, as many of us are finding.

It is worth noting that there is no legal requirement in <u>any</u> pension fund, public or private, to invest for the maximum return. The duty is to invest prudently and not to deliberately lose money. As Robin Murray says, there is much flexibility in how the funds can be used. Take, for example, no less august a body than the National Association of Pension Funds (every investment manager's minder). Even <u>it</u> has taken the broad view on this subject; in response to a consultation document drawn up by the Lord Chancellor's Law Reform Committee it stated:

> The primary obligation of the trustees of a pension fund is provision of the intended benefits and these, in many cases, are linked to salary shortly before retirement or some similar concept. The liabilities often do not materialise for some two generations and the incidence of new money available for investment from contributions of the employer and employees is such that investments rarely require to be realised to meet benefit obligations. Thus the trustees of a pension fund are under pressure to invest with a view to appreciation, whether of capital or income, and may therefore feel the existing concepts of investment are not appropriate. In consequence pension fund trustees have regard for long term considerations including the possible purchase of non-income producing assets or

> income producing assets, on assumptions as to future market and economic conditions which, in the context of family trusts, would be regarded as speculative. It follows that the term 'investment' may, in relation to pension schemes, but not necessarily in relation to family trusts, include the purchase of assets which will yield a profit only upon sale and the purchase of assets justified only on the broad view that such purchase being good for the national economy is also good for trade in general and for pension schemes in particular. (8)

It is uncertain how broadly this can be interpreted, but I doubt whether it could be used to justify a policy of restructuring for labour with all the connotations that it entails.

Pension funds are also, of course, related to wages and work. Their control can therefore be contested by organised labour, as Robin Murray points out. I would just like to add that this is more problematic than it would seem. Many trade unionists are concerned about the loss of jobs in the UK, especially when they see pension funds being invested overseas. But when they become pension fund trustees they need to be supplied with a lot of detailed arguments in order to tackle the City's view. This is where Robin Murray's line of thinking will let them down. They need to know how they can divert some of the finance into industry. The only line that in my view will work is to argue that investment in industry, through local enterprise boards or whatever, will produce returns to the fund, and there will be no call on the rates in the case of a local authority fund. Trustees need to show the comparatively poor rates of return elsewhere; they can point to enterprise boards as organisations which can put together investment deals which the funds themselves are not equipped to do. As far as restructuring for labour is concerned, we can get away with arguing for an increase in the accountability of firms to their workforce and the community on the grounds that this is responsible investment and in the long-term interest of the firm. If we want to advance anywhere near controlling the financial institutions for productive investment, then that is the political reality. But perhaps this is premature: Robin Murray cites some examples and proposals from the GLC.

First, it is suggested that the GLC pension fund could be used to finance the property side of rescue deals in which the GLC gets involved. Property investment is of course nothing new to pension funds. Second, private finance is used in the commercial part of GLC projects generally, with revenue finance used to subsidise interest rates and rents to make up the difference between expected performance and the normal rate of return. It is proposed that the GLC fund could be used in the same way as private finance, even providing equity. The West Midlands Council is said to be subsidising interest rates out of revenue already. This is in fact as part of an arrangement with ICFC whereby an interest rate subsidy on loans made to companies in the Midlands by ICFC is given in exchange for a planning agreement specifying employment targets and various industrial relations conditions. As a personal view, I do not accept the logic politically for subsidising interest rates in this way, especially with an organisation like ICFC where we effectively contribute to clearing bank profits out of ratepayers' money. But then many of these economic policies are the result of pressures and compromises.

Thirdly, the fund is allowed to spend 25 per cent of its value on capital investment for which the Council itself has statutory borrowing powers. However, where fund money is used by the Council, the statutory borrowing power is to be deemed to have been exercised as though a loan of the same amount had been raised: in other words, it is not a way round government restrictions on capital spending.

Fourthly, the fund could invest in Greater London Enterprise Board (GLEB) projects with a guarantee given by GLEB itself. Because this is said to be a self-guarantee, it is argued that the Council should be able to borrow more cheaply from the pension fund than on the open market - 'particularly if the guarantee rate is taken as the rate on gilts'. It is unlikely to be so, because gilts are marketable, while GLEB guarantees are not (or at least not yet). So a premium will have to be paid for this.

The philosophy behind these proposals is to avoid gearing investment criteria to those of the financial market. GLEB would be able to separate investment into commercial and 'subcommercial' components, and put pension funds into the former. It may be possible to do this, but of course it does not challenge anything that financial institutions do - and this is consistent with the analysis in the first part of Robin Murray's article. Pension funds will be given property investments, security or a guarantee - otherwise the funds will want to know what happens when the present GLC administration ends. If the investments are made in the interest of restructuring for labour, the funds will want this security and guarantees. They will want to know that they will come out of it fully protected. But I would suggest that the challenge is to make pension funds do what they would otherwise not do. This is to provide long-term risk finance with no guarantees and minimal security. The challenge is in getting them to do this. But this of course is based on an alternative view about the need to control the financial institutions in the interests of people in this country, on the grounds that they are not serving the economy, other workers and future pensioners well even in their own terms.

In the West Midlands the Council has established the West Midlands Enterprise Board to invest sums of around £100,000 to £750,000 in equity and loan finance for medium-sized firms in the West Midlands. The Council has allocated £4.3 million from the rate fund to the Board, and by March 1983, £3 million had been invested or allocated in ten companies. The Council then set out to establish a specialised fund of up to £6 million; £3 million of this to be provided by the Board itself (via rate fund finance from the Council) and the balance of the fund provided by pension funds, including local authority pension funds. It will be a 'closed end' fund which means that there will be an identifiable portfolio of investments. The fund will be invested over an 18-month period in around 12 companies and will be drawn down from the participating institutions as and when investments are identified. The investments will belong to the participating institutions, but selected and managed by the Enterprise Board. The institutions have the right to exercise a number of safeguards which are felt to be necessary at this early stage. The investments of risk finance will be made with a view to capital growth, without necessarily any income in the short-term. Rate fund finance will be treated the same as pension fund finance and not as a subsidy to industrial or financial capital except insofar as it will take a larger share of any investment than any single pension fund.

The West Midlands Council has also drawn up a strategy for working towards restructuring proposals in the foundry industry which is one of the largest sectors in the area. In this the Enterprise Board can be actively involved because it has five investments in different parts of the foundry industry.

In addition it is proposed that local authority pension

funds should also consider investment proposals from each others' enterprise boards. This would create a network of cross-investments and allocations between local authorities which strengthen each individual initiative. It also helps in the general argument about pension fund investment in any local initiative because a network of enterprise boards and other local investment vehicles enables pension funds to diversify their local investments across different areas and sectors of the economy.

This and other issues, such as cooperation over shareholdings in companies that Robin Murray refers to, have been the subject of discussion and further work at special conferences for local authority pension funds. The first was at West Midlands in November 1982, the second at Merseyside in April 1983, and the third is to be held in London later in 1983. The conferences have challenged the record of pension funds and the role of the City and they are pressing for positive action by local authorities on the issue of the investment of their pension funds.

The danger of not taking on the funds head on, is that local authorities can get channelled into countless demonstration projects which are no challenge to the power structure at all. I imagine some observers will view this as sacreligious, but I feel that a few cooperatives each employing a handful of people, mainly in the service and retailing sectors, are harmless. We are fooling ourselves if we imagine that they are the root of some new economic structure, or that they and some other projects are islands of socialism, or socialism in one company. They give some people limited control over a part of their lives, and there is nothing wrong about that. But altering an economic structure, perhaps with large co-ops employing hundreds of people which can hold their own in the long run is a major exercise which needs big money, often in the form of risk finance.

Robin Murray gives the game away at the end of his article by summarising his view that restructuring is the main issue. 'Finance is only a part of this package. It cannot lead it. In our first year of operation' he writes, 'we have found money to be the least of our problems: at times it has been a negative factor'. The GLC must be the only local authority in the country able to say this. In Greater London the product of a 2p rate under Section 137 of the 1972 Local Government Act (what local authorities currently are using to spend money on economic initiatives) is nearly £40 million. In contrast, in the West Midlands it is just over £9 million, with about £8 million available for economic development (not just investment in companies). In other areas it is £3 million or £4 million. In a London Borough it can be less than £1 million. Let us contrast these figures with the local authority pension fund resources available. Ten per cent of the fund (what can be invested in unquoted securities) in the West Midlands is over £50 million, in Greater Manchester £55 million, in Derbyshire £12 million, in Islington £4 million. These vast pension fund resources are available. In some areas it is not a matter of the pension fund being prised open for some property investment as part of a bigger resource deal backed by Section 137 finance. Instead, pension fund money is virtually the only readily available source of local funds, if the local authorities are to have any effect. Hence the need to get their arguments worked out for an alternative investment strategy which confronts the City on its own terms. We can have all the restructuring proposals we care to devise, for foundries in the Midlands, for the fishing industry in Lancashire and the North East, for clothing, textiles and steel in Yorkshire, without knowing that we have control of finance, perhaps we should not get started.

NOTES

1. Yao-Su Hu (1975) National Attitudes and the Financing of Industry, PEP Broadsheet, No. 559.
2. William Clark (1979) Inside the City, Allen and Unwin.
3. Richard Minns (1980) Pension Funds and British Capitalism, Heinemann.
4. Phillips and Drew, Equity Market Indicators, October 1982.
5. 'The City: A Socialist Approach': A Response to the Report of the Labour Party Financial Institutions Study Group, Banking Information Service, 1982.
6. 'The financing of Japanese industry', Bank of England Quarterly Bulletin, December 1981.
7. Jerry Coakley and Laurence Harris (1982) 'Evaluating the role of the financial system', Socialist Economic Review, D. Currie and M. Sawyer (eds) Merlin.
8. National Association of Pension Funds; Response to Consultation Document drawn up by Lord Chancellor's

Law Reform Committee; reproduced in part in Pensions World, February 1983.

Part VI

STATE REGULATION OF FINANCE: THREE CASE STUDIES

INTRODUCTION TO PART VI

Laurence Harris

Michael Meacher's opening chapter and the debate presented in Part V address the urgent political issue of changing the financial system in Britain, and they are concerned specifically with the problems of the UK economy. At issue is the finance of industrial regeneration in Britain and international financial connections which are not debilitating or destabilising for the UK economy as they appear to have been in the past. These issues have, at different levels, been widely debated in the context of Britain's soul-searching exploration of its malaise. But although the debate is self-centred other countries' experience has been brought in regularly as a relevant factor.

Frequently, West Germany's financial system of close ownership and managerial links between firms and banks (with trade union involvement) has been cited as a factor in its industrial strength. Others point to the state regulation of the Japanese financial system with consequent low interest rates and credit rationing as having made a significant contribution to that country's growth and would argue for a similar degree of regulation (accompanied by state involvement in the direction of finance) in Britain. Sonja Ruehl's research (consisting of a major survey of banks in Japan) has been conducted at a significant time for evaluating that Japanese system, as Japan was beginning in the mid-1980s to modify and dismantle some of the cornerstones of its system of financial regulation. The new 'liberalisation' of finance in Japan appears to be the greatest example of the wave of financial liberalisation that has been sweeping the world since the 1960s, but has become a flood in the 1980s partly as a result of pressures on other countries from the United States and from institutions led by the International Monetary Fund. As Sonja Ruehl's chapter, Interest Rate Policy and Credit Rationing in Japan: The Evidence, makes clear, however, there is considerable doubt over whether such a clear-cut dichotomy between regulation and liberalisation exists. She examines the arguments of those who argue that the development of new financial markets in the 1970s, the existence of arbitrage, and the practice of banks made Japanese finance close to a free-market system although formally it was regulated. Assessing the evidence and theoretical reasoning, the chapter concludes that although regulation did not necessarily have the direct effects sometimes attributed to it, it did influence the direction, quantity and terms of credit. If we were to draw implications for Britain, Japan does not offer grounds for concluding that any state regulation is certain to be circumvented and made inoperative by the interest flexibility of financial markets.

The question Sonja Ruehl addresses is whether regulation was really regulation. In Chapter 17, Financial Reform and Economic Growth: A New Interpretation of South Korea's Experience, I ask whether deregulation was really deregulation. In the mid-1960s South Korea was one of the first Third World countries (after Taiwan) to abandon its policy of enforcing a low ceiling on all interest rates. The resulting high interest rates on bank deposits and some categories of bank credit, which were accompanied by the country's rapid industrialisation and growth led to South Korea being held up as an example of the benefits of financial liberalisation. However, this chapter shows that, in fact, state control of the financial system remained very high and state direction of credit was a major feature of South Korea's industrialisation. Far from that experience validating the arguments in favour of a free-market financial system, the financial reforms in South Korea appear to have increased the state's ability to direct accumulation through the control of finance and also to have been the pre-condition for a great inflow of American, European and Japanese finance to fuel the boom. Of course, profitable industrialisation in a rising Third World country like South Korea does not hold direct lessons for industrial regeneration in an advanced capitalist society like Britain's, but this chapter does provide a warning against taking the claims often made for the virtues of an unregulated financial system at face value.

The country that in recent years has been most frequently held up as the example of socialist financial policy is France which, in the early days of Mitterand's presidency, extended the nationalised banking sector and intervened in the foreign exchange and credit markets. This certainly produced no magic solution delivering France from the international economic crisis of the 1980s although this financial policy was one of the elements which, by acting as a buffer between France and the international financial markets, did contribute to a relatively high level of economic activity while austerity was at its height in Britain at the start of the 1980s. Nevertheless, these financial policies ran into severe problems and much of the strategy was abandoned. Naturally, advocates of free-market systems based on private enterprise draw the lesson that the nationalisation of banking is to be avoided while ignoring the fact that a high proportion of French banks were state owned throughout the post-war economic boom. By contrast, Alan Lipietz argues in the concluding chapter that the problem with Mitterand's strategy was not that the banks were nationalised but that they were not nationalised enough. In The Limits of Bank Nationalisation in France, Lipietz argues that although ownership was taken fully into state hands, the banks were effectively allowed to operate in almost the same manner as under the previous system.

One conclusion that can be drawn from the French experience is that if banks are to be part of a socialist economic strategy their role and modes of operation have to be radically re-evaluated and altered. State ownership itself is not necessarily socialist and does not automatically change anything; its importance is that it is a necessary pre-requisite for achieving significant changes in the way finance operates. That conclusion from the final chapter returns us to the issues raised by Michael Meacher in the first chapter. He notes that nationalisation of the Bank of England in 1946 was not accompanied by measures to achieve real changes in its operation and he poses the more general and highly pertinent question: 'if people argue for nationalisation, exactly what are the alternative criteria by which the financial system should then operate?' The question is urgent if we are to draw the lessons of British, French and other countries' experience. It is to be hoped that the anathemas provoked by mention of nationalisation do not deter analysis of what it really means.

Chapter Sixteen

INTEREST RATE POLICY AND CREDIT RATIONING IN JAPAN: THE EVIDENCE

Sonja Ruehl

While Japan has become increasingly firmly established as one of the leading advanced capitalist nations, a noticeable shift has occurred in academic commentary on Japanese economic 'success'. Many Japanese authors have become impatient with explanations that take other economies as a paradigm - usually, that of the United States - and that view Japanese growth and industrialisation as an intriguing deviation from that paradigm, a unique and exotic 'case' with its own interesting but non-generalisable features; a kind of Asiatic anomaly.

Instead, a recent trend has been to emphasise the transferability of features of Japanese economic organisation and the possibility of taking the Japanese economy itself as a paradigm or model. Instead, this trend has been marked enough to be picked out for comment in itself. (1) (2)

Possibly, some of the motivation behind this trend from the Japanese side comes from a resistance specifically to the idea that one of the pervasive features peculiar to Japan is a degree of government-private sector involvement unique to a capitalist economy. (3) Certainly, many of the current re-evaluations of Japanese economic success equate their rejections of Japanese 'uniqueness' with acceptance of 'the more universalistic terms of the market principle'. Thus the question 'What special factors explain Japan's economic success?' is being redefined as the question 'Why does the market principle work especially well in Japan?' (4) This fact, that a more 'general' interpretation is taken to be synonymous with an explanation in terms of market forces, means that more is at stake here than the explanation of recent Japanese economic history alone. If Japan is to be taken as a model for emulation - as it inevitably will be - then is it to be emulated as a model of market forces at work - or on the contrary, as as persuasive instance of the success, at least of government regulation and direction, if not planning?

This question is a pertinent one to pose, too, about recent work on the financial system specifically. A trend in recent writings, reinterpreting the post-war financial system both as less prone to government involvement, and as more competitive, than previously thought has emerged clearly enough to attract notice. (5) In one sense this is unsurprising, since the financial system has long been argued to hold a central place in explanations of Japanese high growth and rapid industrialisation. What does make it a surprising trend is the very pervasiveness with which the 'conventional' view has been held hitherto. A view stressing par excellence certain 'unique' features of the Japanese financial system and a view also giving credence to an important role for government in financial allocation, has been very widely accepted within Japan as well as outside it.

This 'conventional' view is well-enough known for its main features to be easily summarised. The financial system has been construed as highly regulated by the government, whose financial policies have been seen as systematically designed to support industrial policy priorities. Regulations on interest rates are held to have generally kept them below market-clearing rates so that controls have been possible on the quantity and distribution of credit. The financial system is thus seen to have played a key role in an investment-led growth strategy. In the conventional view, this high degree of government control characterises the decades from 1953-73, including the period of very high growth rates - and not simply the period of immediate post-war reconstruction.

Features of the financial system argued to underpin such government involvement, and quoted as unique to Japan include a predominance of financing by debt rather than equity; a very high degree of dependence of the corporate sector on bank borrowing; a chronic indebtedness of the banking sector as a whole to the Bank of Japan, known as 'overloan'; a high degree of specialisation of financial institutions; and a chronic imbalance of liquidity so that the money market persistently channelled funds from the smaller regional to the large, and 'overlent' city banks.

(6)

Most authors would probably still accept that this characterisation held true of the financial system until at least the early 1970s; though changes in the financial environment since then require a new interpretation of the system emerging over the last decade. In short, most would accept a radical change in the nature of the financial system since the early 1970s. But changes in the financial system (and in its legal framework) have also engendered some re-evaluation of the system prevalent during the high growth years. One aspect of such re-evaluation is a shifting in the period seen as one of active government control back in time, to the reconstruction era prior to high growth. This has been argued on the basis of a more precise examination of the extent of government involvement previously assumed. As a result, several aspects of the conventional view have recently been challenged. (7) (8) The conventional view has been, as it were, 'unpacked' so that different elements have been singled out and scrutinised separately.

Some of the apparently 'unique' and distinctive features of the financial system have been queried, among them the predominance of indirect (debt) finance and the high degree of government regulation, as well as its effectiveness. (7) Also, the links between features of the financial system and systematic and deliberate policy geared to growth and industrialisation have been scrutinised: the objectives of financial regulation other than growth; the pattern of allocation of government-controlled funds; the adequacy of mechanisms for alleged government control over private sector fund allocation; the causal connection between a low-interest-rate policy and growth. (8) (5)

In this paper I shall concentrate on just one of these areas of re-examination and re-evaluation. Looking at the workings of interest rate regulation and at the question of whether the Japanese banking system could be characterised as a credit-rationing system of fund allocation during the high growth period. This is important in itself - affecting a general assessment of the plausibility of credit allocation systems for promoting industrialisation and growth. Also, the interpretation of the financial system in the high growth period in Japan affects understanding of the subsequent process of financial reform there.

DISEQUILIBRIUM AND ARBITRAGE

The existence of interest rate regulations on deposits and loans has long created a presumption that the banking system in Japan has been a disequilibrium system, characterised by credit rationing, at least in the high growth period. Indeed, the Bank of Japan's own econometric model, published in 1972, embodies this presumption. (9) In this section, I want to look first of all at arguments for thinking disequilibrium did exist in bank lending and then in later sections at the mechanism by which the 'artificial low interest rate policy' was argued to result in credit rationing in the bank loan market. Lastly, I shall look at whether it is reasonable to concentrate arguments about credit rationing on interest rate regulation in the bank loan market alone, given developments in the money market in the late 1960s.

Several Japanese authors have applied econometric disequilibrium analysis to the bank loan market, but with conflicting results. (10) The most recent research, however, does lend support to the disequilibrium hypothesis for the high growth period. Yoshio Tsutsui (11) found the market in disequilibrium, by comparing actual loan rates with hypothetical equilibrium rates. His findings are that there was excess demand in 41 out of the 68 quarters examined during the period 1960 to 1977. Tsutsui examines not only nominal lending rates, but also a measure of 'effective' interest rates, to take into account the common practice in Japan of using compensating deposits as well as explicit interest rate setting. (It seems unlikely that effective interest rates were much affected by differentials in bank charges, commissions and fees given the cartelised nature of the banking system. But another factor enabling effective rates to diverge from nominal rates has been the provision of cheap loans through governmental institutions such as the Japan Development Bank and the Export-Import Bank. Because of their 'pump-priming' role in accompanying private-sector loans, these low-cost funds were able in effect to play the role of compensating balances for the private banks concerned.)

Ito and Ueda (12) in their earlier paper (1981) also find evidence of disequilibrium in their analysis because price adjustment in the Japanese loan market is too slow to establish equilibrium. Their later paper (1982) refines their analysis, as they try to distinguish adjustment in lending rates due to the pressure of excess demand, from adjustments directly related to financial regulations. Taking into account the influence of the Official Discount Rate of the Bank of Japan on the nominal lending rate - a direct effect of regulation which Ito and Ueda see as due to 'institutional rigidity' - the lending rate is still judged too inflexible to equilibrate demand and supply.

Thus, even if econometric evidence does point to the bank loan market being in disequilibrium, this may not be argued to result directly from government regulation. However, regulation often is argued as its basis, since the government's 'artificial low interest rate policy' is seen as having been a coordinated effort to maintain a system in which excess demand is endemic.

There is little doubt about the effectiveness of one arm of this policy, namely regulation over deposit rates, in the high growth period and beyond it. Rates have been overtly regulated under the Temporary Interest Rate Adjustment Law of 1947. Though not particularly low by international comparison throughout the period, (13) deposit rates have been set below rates prevailing in the call market, the short-term interbank money market, in which rates are thought to have generally equilibrated supply and demand, though with some Ministry of Finance influence. Non-price competition has also been controlled by strict regulation of bank branching by the Ministry of Finance.

However, the effectiveness of the other arm of the 'artificial low interest rate policy', regulation over bank lending rates, has generated more controversy. Maximum rates on the short-term loans (under one year) in which the city and regional banks specialise have likewise been regulated under the Temporary Interest Rate Adjustment Law; in addition, from 1958 until 1975, a further voluntary ceiling within the statutory ceiling was laid down by the Federation of Bankers' Associations, under Ministry of Finance influence. A basis for short-term lending rates has been constituted by Japan's prime rate system, under which rates on loans to prime borrowers have been linked to the Official Discount Rate; the rate at which the Bank of Japan rediscounts bills of the highest creditworthiness.

The macro economic framework within which these regulations were seen to result in credit rationing is taken to be one in which the only short-term money market was the call market, an interbank market closed to other participants. With 'overlent' city banks relying on loans from the Bank of Japan, in order to extend their own lending, any tightening of credit by the central bank would result in increased demand for call loans by them, until rising call rates choked off city banks' own supply of loans (at regulated rates) to non-financial firms' causing excess demand. On the other hand, non-financial firms' loan demand was taken to respond only to the level of regulated interest rates - since there was and is no access for them to the call market - and so, with regulated lending rates set relatively low compared to call rates, a situation of excess demand could arise and city banks have had to resort to non-price rationing of their credit.

One aspect of this picture that has been called into question recently is the assumption that bank loan rates themselves are determined outside the influence of any open money market rates. The reason this has been called in question (14) is the development of secondary bonds markets and in conditional repurchase bonds - the 'gensaki' market. Since the development of these markets is indeed a feature of financial innovation in Japan, this is an argument that deserves attention.

The argument Kuroda puts forward (14) is that an influence from these open market rates upon bank loan rate determination, through arbitrage, can be assumed; and econometric evidence is presented supporting the suggestion. I shall not, here, look in detail at these econometric results; but rather, examine the initial assumption, that the 'gensaki' and secondary bond markets were open markets, such that arbitrage relations would be assumed between them and bank loans, from a period as early as the late 1960s.

What Kuroda claims for these markets is not that they were open to all participants, but rather that interest rates on 'gensaki', secondary bonds and loans was 'mainly determined by market arbitration' (15) (my emphasis).

Kuroda does not describe the process of arbitrage, but Figure 16.1 illustrates in a simplified way one mechanism by which it could have taken place. Securities companies, short of liquidity, appear as fund-raisers in the 'gensaki' market, selling bonds to non-financial firms, with resale agreements giving an implicit, and unregulated, interest rate. Non-financial firms appear in the 'gensaki' market as fund suppliers, but also appear in the bank lending market as fund-raisers since excess fund supply is expected by them to be temporary. However, the rate they are willing to pay for bank loans could depend on the rate they can get in the gensaki market, when they have excess funds.

Figure 16.1

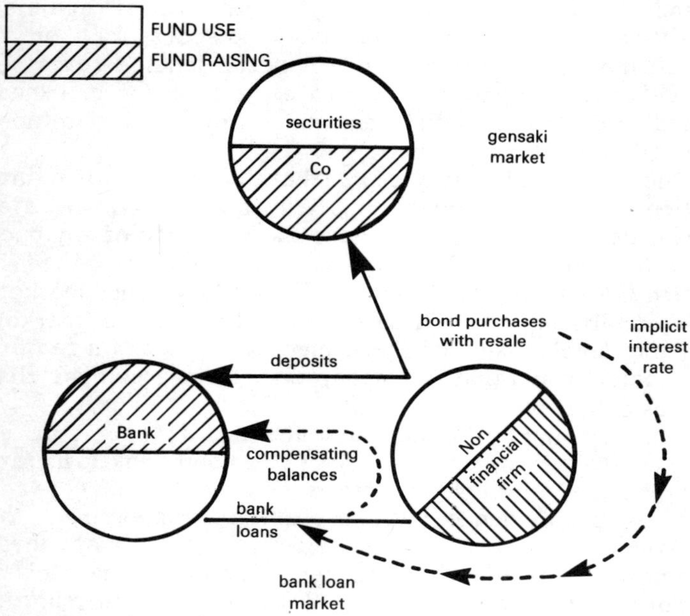

Development of Open Markets

In the early 1960s, a short-term trade arose in the sale of bonds with conditional repurchase agreements. In effect, these were short-term money transactions, using bonds as collateral. On the fund-raising side, the trade arose as a response by securities companies to the liquidity problems they faced in financing their securities inventories as dealers. On the fund-investing side, this 'gensaki' trade was used mainly by non-financial firms to place temporary fund surpluses, often of a seasonal nature. The trade in conditional repurchase agreements was at first a bilateral trade between securities companies and large non-financial firms, rather than a true 'market' open to a wide variety of participants (16); it had a seasonal nature; and it was small in scale until developments in the late 1960s and early 1970s boosted its expansion.

Through the early 1960s, the liquidity position of the securities companies worsened, precipitating financial crisis for many of them around 1965. The securities market had failed to develop to the extent anticipated; having initially taken up most of the new issues, securities companies were left with a mass of unsaleable equities. Further, the nature of government regulation over the bond market produced pressures on the financing of bond inventories. Rates in the primary market were held at a low level compared with those in the secondary market; hence demand for new issues was subject to rationing, which was carried out by the Bond Issue Council. Though made up of representatives of major banks and securities companies, the Council operated under the aegis of the Bank of Japan, and the Ministry of Finance. One of the aims of regulation of new issues under the Council is argued to have been to favour issues of public bonds such as government guaranteed bonds and local government bonds. (17) In these circumstances, new bond issues were allocated through 'underwriting' syndicates, whose members effectively subscribed to them on a compulsory quota basis. Securities companies alone were permitted to sell bonds on to the general public; and in the case of industrial bonds, underwriting and subscription was handled by a syndicate composed exclusively of securities companies. However, the syndicate through which new issues of government-guaranteed local authority and public corporation bonds were absorbed included securities companies as a minority, with most of the quota taken up by financial institutions. When the government began to issue long-term national debt, in 1966, the underwriting syndicate was composed of financial institutions, plus securities companies who alone were allowed to offer their share of bonds (about 10 per cent of each year's issue) to the general public. (18)

The composition of these underwriting syndicates points to the causes of expansion of the gensaki market in the late 1960s and early 1970s, when participation in the market widened; and helps explain why this expansion did not take place before. The role of national debt was one significant factor. With yields on national debt issues below other types of bond yields, prices were particularly likely to fall after issue, making national debt especially unsaleable to the public. Financial institutions therefore subscribed to nine-tenths of national debt issues, with banks taking up as much as half; these bonds were to be held in the institutions' own accounts and not liquidated for at least one year.

The first, indirect, effect of national bond issues from 1966 onwards was that the call money rate was stabilised by intervention from the Bank of Japan, in accordance with the yield on national debt, in order to assist the absorption of the new low yielding government bonds. (19) Making the interbank call rate less responsive to supply and demand for funds is argued to have stimulated the growth of gensaki transactions by banks in the late 1960s.

The second effect of national debt issue on the development of wider participation in gensaki trading did not occur until 1975, when the volume of national debt issue sharply increased. Since banks were absorbing a large quota of low yielding bonds which they were not permitted to sell immediately, these bonds had normally been purchased by the Bank of Japan after one year as part of the Bank's buying operations. After 1975, the Bank ceased to take up all the financial institutions' holdings in this way and so their holdings of low yielding government bonds began to increase. Government bonds have accordingly formed a growing portion of gensaki trading.

Changes in the Bank of Japan's buying operations had also affected participation in gensaki trading somewhat earlier, when in the late 1960s bank debentures were made ineligible for Bank of Japan bond operations. (19) In the situation prevailing in the late 1960s, incentives for commercial banks to hold securities were not great, in that yields were low and securities hard to liquidate; thus, the eligibility of securities either as instruments of Bank of Japan buying operations or else as collateral for Bank of Japan loans provided the chief incentive for bond holdings. Changes in the rules of eligibility were important to the liquidity position of the city banks in particular. Bank debentures at that time usually formed the largest category of securities held by commercial banks (a quarter of all securities holdings in 1970) and so the change in their eligibility for Bank of Japan buying operations prompted banks to begin selling debentures holdings on short-term repurchase agreements.

Thus by the late 1960s participation in the gensaki trade had begun to widen to include banks; but on the fund investing side, it was not until the early 1970s that non-financial firms turned in larger numbers to the gensaki market for protection against the inflation, following the oil-shock; protection which regulated low-interest bank deposits could not provide. It was not until the mid to late 1970s that it became apparent that many large non-financial firms would continue to have excess funds, not simply of a temporary or a seasonal nature, which they would want to place at market interest rates. Resulting pressure on bank deposits at regulated rates from the new gensaki instruments of the securities companies built up in the 1970s, but it was not until 1979 that banks were empowered to retaliate by offering Certification of Deposit which, in large denominations only, did carry market rates.

Therefore, although there were already some pressures for expansion of gensaki trading by the late 1960s, the major expansion into a gensaki market proper with wide participation did not occur until the 1970s; that is, not until after the high growth period had ended. The Securities Dealers' Association did not begin to produce a comprehensive survey of gensaki transactions until 1973. Though administrative guidance to securities companies meant there was government intervention in gensaki trading from 1974, (20) the market was not officially recognised by the Ministry of Finance until 1976. (21) That is not to say the authorities were ignorant of the development of gensaki trading well before that date; some opinion within the Bank of Japan had even predicted it in advance as an outcome of Bank of Japan policies. But it was not until 1976 that trading rules were laid down and the market thereby organised. The existence of a well-organised market with wide participation is necessary before arbitrage relations could be assumed as a major determinant of rates in any market.

In fact, even after recognition and regulation of the gensaki market, there are reasons to doubt the pervasiveness of arbitrage. Although permissible participation was wide (22) individuals have never been allowed to participate. City banks, though permitted to enter the market as fund-raisers, at first had a ceiling on gensaki fund raising of 5 billion yen per bank, which was relaxed in 1978 but not abolished until 1981. City banks were not allowed to invest funds in the market until 1981. Moreover, when the Ministry of Finance did begin to recognise the gensaki market formally in 1976, it simultaneously restricted access by raising the minimum trading denomination from 30 million yen to 100 million yen.

Altogether, it seems implausible to suggest that the

gensaki market was sufficiently organised by the late 1960s for arbitrage between it and the secondary bond markets to be as well developed as Kuroda's argument would require. The gensaki market has continued to be somewhat segregated even from other short-term money markets, still maintaining to some extent its seasonal character (23). In the early 1970s certainly gensaki rates moved to an extent out of step with market rates on corporate bonds and bank debentures as well as nominal bank lending rates (Chart 16.1), again indicating that arbitrage was at most only partial in its operation by that time. The removal of restrictions on bank participation in the gensaki market may have had a significant effect on increasing arbitrage between money markets, since the banks by definition operate in the inter-bank call market too; but removal of restrictions was not completed until 1981.

Chart 16.1

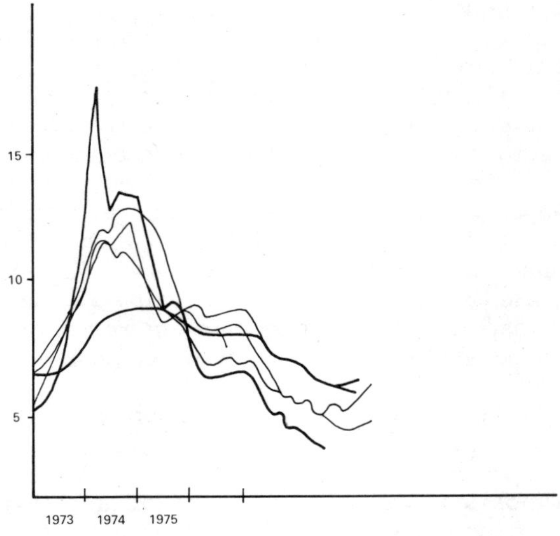

- nominal lending rate (all banks)
- rate on 3-month gensaki
- call rate
- market rate on 2½-year bank debentures
- corporate bond market rate

Source: Wakita, Yasuhiro (1983) in Kinyu Kenyu, vol. 2, no. 1 March 1983. Wagakusi no Kashidasi Shijo to Keiyaku toribiki.

Added to the undeveloped state of the secondary bond markets before national debt began to be issued on a large scale, the nature of gensaki trading before the end of the high growth period makes it unlikely that a chain of arbitrage relations between gensaki, bank debentures, secondary bonds markets and bank loans could have existed such that average bank loan rates were significantly affected by such arbitrage, as the last link in the chain, during the period of high growth.

Even so, to conclude that rate setting in the bank loan market was not significantly affected by arbitrage with open market rates does not show that the regulations on bank lending were in fact binding, nor that credit rationing was the result, in the period of high growth. But it does mean that it is reasonable to concentrate next on the bank loan market itself in examining those questions, to which I now turn.

REGULATION OF BANK LENDING

While regulations over the market for bank loans (here, the short-term market in which city and local banks are specialised were certainly explicit, there is considerable controversy over whether they actually have constrained bank behaviour. In the case of bank lending, regulations imposed statutory ceilings on rates for different loan categories while, from 1958 to 1975, the bankers' federation imposed voluntary ceilings within those limits, and changed them in line with changes in the Official Discount Rate (the Bank of Japan's 'Bank Rate'). From 1959, the bankers' federation also determined a floor to loan rates in the shape of the price rate, which was also determined by Official Discount Rate changes, being set 0.25 per cent above the Official Discount Rate. (24) Thus both regulated ceiling and floor fluctuated in line with the Official Discount Rate.

Were actual bank lending rates determined within this floor/ceiling framework? One piece of evidence suggesting that they were comes from examination of average (short-term) bank loan rates. Even those who are critical of an explanation simply based on the effectiveness of regulations over bank lending (25) do concede that there is a high correlation between actual average loan rates and the Official Discount Rate. Takeda in addition points out that the extent of fluctuations in loan rates and the Official

Discount Rate have corresponded (with an increase in the extent of fluctuations of both, after 1973). Though this link could be evidence in favour of the effectiveness of regulations, alternative explanations have however been suggested which rely on some notion of equilibrium loan rate determination. (26)

Another type of evidence adduced in favour of the effectiveness of regulations over lending comes from looking at the distribution of lending rates, rather than at average levels. It has been asserted (27) that the shape of the distribution of short-term lending rates mirrors the regulatory framework, with two peaks at the floor and ceiling attesting to their binding nature. Doubt has been cast on whether this two peaked structure still applied in the period after 1965 (28); but a more fundamental problem concerns the use of nominal lending rates as evidence at all. It has been argued that nominal rates cannot provide evidence of the binding nature of loan rate regulations, since it is precisely through a divergence of effective from nominal rates that regulations have been avoided. It is therefore necessary to look at the question of effective rates, and the 'compensating balances' which have enabled them to diverge from nominal rates.

An immediate difficulty arises when looking at effective rather than nominal rates, in that reliable data are lacking on the former. 'Compensating balances', that is, sums which borrowers are obliged to leave on deposit (usually a time deposit) with the bank making the loan, were made illegal in 1959. Although the continued existence of these compensating balances was widely known, being illegal they could not be made a formal condition of a loan agreement, but could only be the subject of an informal 'gentlemen's agreement', which banks would be reluctant to acknowledge publicly. It is therefore difficult to know whether the amount of compensating balances (in percentage terms) has been stable, so that the premium of the effective over the regulated rate was also stable, giving an effective rate which was also, in essence, regulated.

Despite this difficulty, some survey data is available from 1964 onwards on levels of compensating balances, collected by the Ministry of Finance and the Fair Trade Commission by questionnaires to borrowers and/or lenders. From Table 16.1, it can be seen that estimates of the actual level of compensating balances in any one year are very different as between surveys (part of the difference may

Table 16.1: Annual average ratio of compensating balances: loans (%)

Year	City banks (a)	City banks (b)	City banks (c)	Local banks (a)	Local banks (b)	Local banks (c)
1964	11.1	29.9	n.a	21.6	25.4	n.a.
1965	8.9	20.0	33.4	16.4	21.3	32.8
1966	8.2	12.4	22.7	13.6	12.0	21.1
1967	6.5	10.4	22.9	9.9	9.2	19.1
1968	5.8	10.2	25.6	9.0	8.0	19.1
1969	5.1	9.4	23.3	8.4	7.4	18.7
1970	4.1	8.2	22.2	7.5	7.8	20.2
1971	3.5	7.1	22.1	6.4	6.9	19.5
1972	3.1	6.7	21.4	5.4	4.8	18.2
1973	2.4	4.1	19.1	4.5	5.2	18.2
1974	2.0	3.4	18.5	3.9	2.6	14.6
1975	1.8	3.3	19.8	3.1	2.3	13.3
1976	1.5	2.5	18.1	2.7	2.1	13.5
1977	1.8	2.1	14.6	2.8	1.6	10.6
1978	1.8	2.1	14.2	2.6	1.4	9.3
1979	1.5	1.6	12.8	2.2	1.1	9.1
1980	1.5	1.7	11.8	1.9	1.3	9.0

Sources:
(a) Ministry of Finance, questionnaire to private banks.
(b) Fair Trade Commission, questionnaire to medium and small businesses; compensating balances narrowly defined.
(c) As (b); compensating balances broadly defined to include deposits a borrower cannot draw at will.

<u>See</u> Akiyoshi Horiuchi, op.cit., (13) for more comprehensive estimates.

arise from the inclusion of large firms in the Ministry of Finance lenders' survey, but not the Fair Trade Commission borrowers' questionnaire. But it is clear that the level of compensating balances was at a much higher level before the end of the high growth period, indeed exhibiting for the most part a steady decline from 1964 onwards; though the decline is by no means so clear until after the end of high growth, if compensating balances are interpreted broadly. It is difficult to disentangle debtors' deposits that are voluntarily held for transactions purposes, from those compensating balances whose withdrawal is de facto restricted. Despite these problems, effective loan rate series have been constructed (29) which do show effective lending rates to have been both higher and more prone to fluctuation than nominal rates, particularly before 1973 when nominal rates were very stable. But this does not in itself show that effective rates were actually equilibrium rates; as discussed in Section One, some econometric studies have cast doubt on this.

A doubt also arises as to whether a system of nominal rates plus compensatory balances functions in precisely the same way as a system of explicit rate-setting. This is a crucial issue: is this quasi-price mechanism exactly like a price mechanism when it comes to allocating credit? Many commentators would argue that it is; that it is just a way of avoiding regulations and the need to allocate credit by non-pricing means. But there are two distinct reasons for doubting that this is entirely true. Firstly, compensating balances exist in loan markets whose rates are not regulated (such as the United States) and their role is clearly not limited to adjusting nominal rates. Secondly, the use of compensating balances rather than explicit rates could have the effect of excluding some would-be borrowers, and the question then arises as to whether this is 'credit rationing' or not. In this connection, the provision of low-cost funds by government institutions, through the government's investment and loan plan (zaiseitoyushi) is a relevant consideration. Such loans, with a policy-implementing role also intended to guide the direction of private sector loan allocation, were not evenly made available to all industries or businesses. If they are seen as in effect substituting for compensating balances, these low-cost loans then operated to exclude some borrowers from receiving credit, as well as influencing the overall effective lending rate.

In the case of Japan, it is clear that nominal rates are even now still set up by banks with an appropriate level of deposits in mind and that the resulting effective rate is routinely calculated. But as well as adjusting the effective rate, from the point of view of the bank, borrowers' deposits may also provide information on the firm's financial situation and enhance the bank's ability to monitor the loan. Additionally, in Japan, where the bank's expansion chances (in branching, for example) would frequently depend on its ranking in terms of liabilities, banks have had a clear incentive to 'create' deposits by lending, as well as to collect them. From the point of view of the borrower, the compensating balance system might have advantages in terms of general perceptions of its credit standing; nominal lending rates more easily become public knowledge and so, if a higher rate than usual or than rivals were levied, the borrower's reputation would to some extent be protected if that were done through a compensating balance rather than an explicitly set rate.

But could the system also have had the effect of excluding some would-be borrowers, especially in tight money periods? This does seem possible, since a greater degree of trust would be necessary between borrower and bank if 'repayment' partly depended on maintaining deposit levels agreed only informally; and the bank might come under pressure to allow withdrawal of the borrower's deposits in case of difficulty. This would increase the desirability of lending to customers already known, customers of greater profitability showing higher growth rates. In the case of Japanese business groups, also, requests to keep 'compensatory balances' with a firm's main bank might not be made of larger companies central to the group. This again would imply differential access to credit.

Thus, even the compensating balance system fostered by the attempt to evade loan rate regulations may itself introduce an element of credit rationing; although it is one neither unique to Japan nor due solely to regulation.

This reinforcement of the preference for allocating credit to known corporate clients, and clients with deposit accounts at the bank, was further strengthened in Japan by the practice of rolling over short-term loans on a semi automatic basis. As long as there had been no deterioration in the financial situation of the company, short-term loans - well over half of which were loans on promissory notes, often of three months' duration, throughout the period in question were habitually renewed, although the lending rate might be renegotiated. In effect, these loans did have something of a long-term nature, although giving the bank more flexibility and the borrower correspondingly less stability than a long-term loan proper. Judging what proportion of short-term lending was actually long term in this sense is difficult, but one such estimate is given in Table 16.2. In that prime borrowers could be more certain that their short-term debt would be rolled over fairly automatically, this practice would have given the advantage in credit allocation to prime customers, when credit was tight. Thus exponents of the 'conventional view' that credit rationing due to government regulation did exist, have often argued that the decrease in the proportion of lending to medium and small business in tight money periods can be taken as a proxy for credit rationing.

Table 16.2

	Proportion of long-term loans in total loans. excluding rollover credit		Proportion of long-term loans in total loans including rollover credit		Proportion of rollover credit in total loans	
	1965	1968	1965	1968	1965	1968
City banks	12.2	12.9	23.4	24.4	11.2	11.5
Local banks	20.2	19.7	36.7	38.2	17.7	18.5

Source: Adapted from Table 3, Juro Teranishi (1982) 'A Model of the relationship between regulated and unregulated financial markets: credit rationing in the Japanese context', Hitotsubashi Journal of Economics vol 22, no. 2, February 1982.

(Table based on 'Kinyu Seido Chosaki Shinyo - Bekkan 1970')

Other aspects of bank lending practices do lend credence to the view that some categories of borrowers have habitually been de facto excluded from access to the short-term loans in which city and local banks specialise. Except for bill discounting, some kind of collateral security has almost invariably been required on loans and has formed an important criterion in loan evaluation, certainly over the period in question. Table 16.3 indicates the importance of different types of lending over the period. Views on acceptable collateral have, apart from deposits, often privileged real estate, although personal or corporate guarantees have sometimes been accepted where real estate was lacking. This emphasis on collateral and on real estate in particular would, at least until the 1970s, have operated to some extent to exclude would-be borrowers in service industries and start-up ventures where such collateral was lacking; not to mention the even more striking exclusion of the consumer sector.

Table 16.3: Composition of loans, advances and discounts

	1953	1958	1963	1968	1969	1970
Bills discounted (% of total loans)	38.2	32.6	35.2	34.7	36.9	37.3
Loans on notes (% of total loans)	54.6	64.2	62.5	58.9	63.0	62.7
% of total loans	92.8	96.8	97.7	93.6	99.9	100.0

Note: Loans on deeds and overdrafts, the other two types of lending undertaken by ordinary banks, have been almost negligible in amount.
Source: Economic Statistics Annual, Bank of Japan.

Credit rationing in some sense does then seem to have existed in the short-term bank loan market, at least in the sense that some categories of borrowers did not de facto have access to that market. (30) This is partly but not entirely due to overt regulation of short-term bank loan rates. To some extent, regulation could be and was avoided by using 'compensating balances' and so one cannot argue that interest rate regulations was entirely binding. But this very avoidance introduced a certain element of non-price rationing in itself, reinforced by other lending practices. The result was, at least until the end of the high growth period, that some categories of would-be customers were excluded from the market, a segmentation also constructed by the various laws governing the legitimate business areas of those other government and private sector banks and financial institutions operating outside the short-term loan market dominated by the 'ordinary' city and local banks.

For an understanding of credit rationing in Japan, then, one has to look beyond the short-term bank loan market itself, and consider its interrelations with other markets and the system as a whole which they constitute. Some arguments have thus been produced explaining how credit rationing could have existed in ordinary bank lending despite the partial but extensive ineffectiveness of overt regulations over it. One argument proposes that the binding nature of regulation in the long-term lending market, and consequent rationing of credit, permeated through to produce credit rationing in the short-term loan market too despite its being in effect non-regulated in itself. (31) A second argument suggests that allocation of cheap loans through the government's investment and loan programme affected even the short-term effective interest rate on private sector lending. Another proposal is that, in the Japanese system as a whole, the 'artificially low interest rate policy' has been affected by a combination of policy measures including strict regulation in some markets but not all. Royama suggests that it is in markets where customer segmentation is difficult - and so bilateral bank-client ties are weak - that interest rate control has been strictly enforced, e.g. deposits markets with numerous small depositors. The fact that interest rate control has not been strictly enforced in the bank loan market should be understood in terms of this market being one where bilateral relations predominate, a state of affairs reinforced by custom as well as law, bilateral relations naturally predominating in any bank loan market. As a whole, Royama maintains the effectiveness of the 'low interest rate policy' in the period before 1973. However, his is an argument which does not rely on interest rate regulation in short-term bank lending alone, but rather encompasses the fact that regulation was actually less than strict in this market, in an explanation which still upholds the existence of credit rationing in finance markets as a whole.

CONCLUSION

In the case of Japan, in the decades of 1953 to 1973, what is needed is to reconcile the perception that credit rationing was actually pervasive in bank lending, with the perception that overt interest rate regulation in that market was much less than completely effective. In assessing the 'artificially low interest rate policy', it is not just overt rate regulation in one market that needs to be examined, but rather the whole nexus of practices, policies and laws segmenting and regulating the activities of financial institutions overall. In the case of Japan, the necessity for credit rationing is over. But in the current movement toward liberalisation, it would be misleading to suggest that the policy never did exist.

NOTES

1. E.g. Haruo Shimada, 'Japanese Industrial Relations - A New General Model? A Survey of the English-Language Literature', in Taishiro Shirai (ed.), Contemporary Industrial Relations in Japan, University of Wisconsin Press, 1983.

2. E.g. Ronald Dore, 'The "Learn from Japan" Boom', in Speaking of Japan, November 1984, vol. 5, no. 47.

3. See, e.g. T.F. Cargill 'A U.S. Perspective on Japanese Financial Liberalization', In Monetary and Economic Studies, vol. 3, no. 1, May 1985, Bank of Japan, Cargill points out a recent resistance to the 'Japan, Incorporated' view of a financial system geared to government policies.

4. For instance, Isamu Miyazaki - himself a former Vice-Minister of Economic Planning - expresses this shift quite explicitly. See Miyazaki, 'The Real Reason for Japan's Success in Economic Growth', in Japanese Economic Studies, Spring 1982, vol. X, no. 3, pp.87-8.

5. See Cargill, op. cit.

6. See Yoshio Suzuki, Money and Banking in Contemporary Japan, Yale University Press 1980, for a comprehensive exposition of these characteristics.

7. E.g. Bakakibara and Feldman, 'The Japanese Financial System in Comparative Perspective', in Journal of Comparative Economics, vol. 78, no. 78, no. 1, March 1983.

8. E.g. Akiyoshi Horiuchi, Economic Growth and Financial Allocation in Postwar Japan, August 1984, University of Tokyo Discussion Paper 84-F-3.

9. See Iwao Kuoda, 'Mechanism of Bank-loan Rates Determination in Japan: Re-examination of the Traditional Theory and a New View', in Discussion Paper Series No. 3, The Bank of Japan Special Economic Studies Department, October 1980.

10. See Shoichi Royama, 'The Japanese Financial System: Past, Present and Future', in Japanese Economic Studies, Winter 1983/4, for a resume of research.

11. See Yoshio Tsutsui, 'Is the Japanese Bank Loan Market in Equilibrium? An Empirical Study', in Economic Studies Quarterly, vol. 23, no. 1, April 1982 (summary in English).

12. See Takatoshi Ito and Kazuo Ueda, 'Tests of the Equilibrium Hypothesis in Disequilibrium Econometrics: An International Comparison of Credit Rationing', in

International Economic Review, vol. 22, no. 3, October 1981 and 'Tests of Equilibrium Hypothesis in the Japanese Business Loan Market', in Economic Studies Quarterly, vol. 23, no. 1, April 1982 (summary in English).

13. See Akiyoshi Horiuchi, 'The "Low Interest Rate Policy" and Economic Growth in Postwar Japan', in The Developing Economies, December 1984, no. 4, vol. 22.

14. See Iwao Kuoda, op. cit.

15. See Kuoda, op. cit., p.50.

16. See Shoichi Royama, op. cit.

17. Kaichi Shimura, 1978, Gendai Nihon Koshasai Ron (An Essay on the Japanese Bond Markets), University of Tokyo Press.

18. Takeshi Goto, 'Bond Market - Current Situation and Legal Aspects', in Lectures on Japanese Securities Regulation, Japan Securities Research Institute, 1980 (p.31).

19. See Shoichi Royama, op. cit.; and Masataka Nakajima, 1977, Nihon no Kokusai Kanri Seisaku (Debt Management Policy in Japan), Toyo Keizai Shimposha.

20. Stephen Bronte, Japanese Finance: Markets and Institutions, Euromoney Publications, 1982.

21. Ministry of Finance circular, Okura-sho No. 287, March 1976.

22. Including not only securities companies, non-financial firms and financial institutions but also public organisations such as mutual pension funds and public corporations, plus the government Trust Fund Bureau, Postal Life Insurance and Postal Annuity Special Fund; non-residents have been allowed to participate in the market since 1979.

23. Because non-financial firms assist financial institutions with 'window dressing' by increasing their deposits at the end of reporting periods and because securities companies use gensaki transactions to adjust their inventories of government bonds at the ends of their accounting periods, gensaki rates tend to rise in March and September. See Sena Eken, 'Integration of Domestic and Financial Markets: The Japanese Experience' in IMF Staff Papers, vol. 31, no. 3, September 1984.

24. Though the prime rate did not strictly apply to loans made on bills secured by deposit, whose rates were based on deposit rates and thus could be below prime rate.

25. Kuroda puts forward an explanation in which there is an 'equilibrium of expectation', the ODR exerting an influence on loan rates merely through conveying

information about future money market rates. Takeda's explanation relies on the fact that regulated deposit rates have also moved in tandem with the DDR. It is deposit rates which he sees as affecting loan rate determination (via an objective function for banks which includes business scale expansion as well as short-term profits) rather than loan rate regulation itself. Thus his explanation relies on the effectiveness of some regulation (on deposits rates) but rules out credit rationing.

28. See Kuoda, op. cit., who does however conceded that the two peaked distribution was characteristic before that date.

29. See Yasuhiro Wakita, 'Wagakuni no kashidashi - shijo to Keiyaky - torihihi' (Loan markets and contracts in Japan) in Kinyu Kenkyu, vol. 2, no. 1, March 1983 and Takeda (op. cit.). Takeda points out that his series still exhibits strong correlations with the ODR and deposit rates.

30. Whether one does indeed label this 'credit rationing' is a matter of debate. The 'modern' school of credit rationing theory would argue that borrowers willing to pay the (interest rate) price on a loan, but who do not meet other loan conditions such as collateral requirements, are not really 'rationed out' of the market by these non-price conditions - rather, they have shown themselves unwilling to 'pay the price' of the loan in a wider sense, including all its non-price conditions too. See e.g. Ernst Baltensperger, 'Credit Rationing', in Journal of Money, Credit and Banking, vol. 10, no. 2, May 1978.

31. See Teranishi, 1982, op. cit.

32. See Royama, 1983/4, op. cit.

Chapter Seventeen

FINANCIAL REFORM AND ECONOMIC GROWTH: A NEW INTERPRETATION OF SOUTH KOREA'S EXPERIENCE

Laurence Harris

In September 1965, the government of South Korea carried out a major reform of that country's financial system. (1) Its most prominent feature was a large rise in the interest rates banks paid to depositors; the interest rates on time deposits were doubled (to reach 30 per cent per year on new 18-month time deposits or nearly 35 per cent compounded monthly) and bank lending rates, although subsidised, were also raised (from 16 per cent to 26 per cent per year). Although the rise in deposit interest rates was central, the 1965 actions should not be interpreted as a Keynesian stabilisation policy where high rates are designed to deflate aggregate demand and achieve balance of payments equilibrium by deflation-induced declines in imports and the attraction of foreign capital. Its purpose was to stimulate the growth and re-structuring of the financial system itself, and through this effect, to contribute to growth in output, capital formation and other real variables. The policy was implemented following the completion of a report of the US Operations Mission to Korea; written by Gurley, Patrick and Shaw by late July 1965. The report led the National Assembly to raise interest rate ceilings in August and to include interest rates in a wider package of reforms in September. The reform of the financial system by the end of September had been a condition for US aid, and the South Korean authorities had been interested in Taiwan's experience of high interest rates for some time before that. (2)

In the two decades which have elapsed, South Korea's 1965 reform has been regarded as a test case by economists writing on finance and development. It provided important empirical data for E.S. Shaw (one of its main architects) in the further development of his theory that a 'deepened' and market-oriented financial sector stimulates growth; and R. McKinnon's seminal work on a related theory was stimulated by the 'remarkable financial transformation that occurred in 1965-66 in Korea'. (3)

The remarkable development of the South Korean economy since these reforms, producing a real growth rate of approximately 10 per cent per year on average, has led to a view that the theories of Shaw and McKinnon are vindicated by it and that states in the Third World should eschew intervention or direction in financial markets, liberalising them to respond autonomously to market forces. To draw such a conclusion from the broad sweep of South Korean experience would, of course, be to use an assumption of post hoc ergo propter hoc in respect of very broad trends. But if high growth did result from the interest rate reforms there must have been specific channels, or transmission mechanisms through which the reforms made their effects felt. This paper attempts an evaluation of whether the transmission mechanisms predicted by McKinnon and Shaw did operate. The exercise is addressed to two questions: first, did the financial reforms contribute to the subsequent economic growth; and, second, if they did, did they do so for the reasons postulated in the McKinnon-Shaw thesis?

The conclusion I draw (Section 6) is that the evidence is consistent with the view that the reforms contributed to growth but that, contrary to the McKinnon-Shaw thesis, it did so because it increased the role of the state rather than by rolling it back to liberate private, market forces. The conclusion is unusual not only because other commentators interpret the reforms as being market oriented (albeit imperfectly so) but also because South Korea's popular image is as a success story of free enterprise.

In Section 1, I outline the transmission mechanism suggested by the McKinnon-Shaw model and in subsequent sections consider the extent to which they correspond to Korea's experience. In Section 2, I discuss the behaviour of domestic and foreign savings; in Section 3, I examine the allocation process of the financial intermediaries in distributing credit from savers and other lenders to investors; in Section 4, I discuss the impact of this financial intermediation on investment; in Sections 5 and 6, I evaluate the role of the reforms and the view that their significance lay in their being a foundation for state direction of the 'economic miracle'.

1. The McKinnon-Shaw Transmission Mechanism

The broad argument of the McKinnon-Shaw thesis is that a financial reform or liberalisation allows the banking system greater autonomy which will lead to higher interest rates on deposits and loans, and these changes in the financial sector interact with private firms and households making them change their saving and investment behaviour in directions that are beneficial for growth. Particularly in McKinnon's work the concept of private agents as all entrepreneurs or potential entrepreneurs is the foundation for the analysis of those changes in firms' and households' behaviour. The basic units in his model are essentially families, all of which are potentially 'firm-households'. These comprise the 'many entrepreneurs who provide labour, make technical decisions, consume, save and invest'. (4) Although McKinnon argues against distinguishing different groups as savers and investors, the transmission mechanism of the general model has three components: savers, investors and financial intermediaries (especially banks) linking them. Within the model, financial reforms generating high interest rates have effects transmitted through these three components and their links:

> Saving: It causes growth in domestic saving which replaces foreign loans as a source of finance for investment.
>
> Intermediation: This domestic saving is channelled through an integrated banking system rather than segmented 'unofficial' money markets. This operates as an efficient capital market in which the allocation of credit, rather than being discriminatory and rationed by quantity, is determined by the relationship of the real rate of interest to the marginal product of physical capital.
>
> Investment: The growth in domestic saving and the (high) level of real interest rates lead to an expansion of investment and an improvement in the efficiency of investment, or the marginal product of capital. This occurs through the responses of private agents throughout the economy (the 'firm-household') rather than a monopolistic or state sector. The outcome is an

increase in the rate of growth of per capita output.

In South Korea the 1965 reforms did not operate on this three-part transmission mechanism in the manner described. In particular it did not involve a discrete switch of the financial system toward a non-discriminatory allocation of unrationed quantities of credit. And the responses of saving and investment were not unambiguously of the type foreseen in the model. In discussing this I shall concentrate on the effects generated between 1965 and 1971 (although some will have appeared only after a lag) for those were the years when the real rate of interest on time deposits was significantly and consistently positive, which, on usual assumptions, signified that the financial market was closer to its equilibrium than would have been the case with negative real rates. Whereas this rate was -20.1 per cent in 1964, the increase in nominal rates in 1965 raised it to 20.1 per cent and it remained at double-digit levels through 1971 (when it was 13.2 per cent) declining sharply thereafter. (5) That period of high real interest rates also saw remarkable economic growth as non-agricultural production grew at an annual average rate of 15 per cent and real GNP also grew at a historically high rate. (6)

2. Domestic and Foreign Savings

An outstanding feature of the Korean economy in the late 1960s was the sharp rise in the private sector's saving which occurred at the same time as the financial reforms instituted high interest rates. As a proportion of GNP domestic savings in real terms more than doubled from 7.5 per cent in 1964 to 17.5 per cent in 1969. (7) This represented a substantial shift in the behaviour of the private sector; households and firms raised their aggregate saving rate from 4.3 per cent in 1964 to 10.9 per cent in 1966 and whereas between 1960 and 1964 its mean had been 5.4 per cent, its mean was 11.6 per cent in 1966-70 (8).

As predicted by the McKinnon-Shaw model, the rise in saving was accompanied by an increase in the real value of money balances for savings held in the form of bank deposits increased. The ratio of the money supply (M_2 which includes time deposits) to GNP increased from 9 per cent in 1964 to 15 per cent in 1966, reaching 33 per cent by 1969 and remaining at about that level through 1971 (9). There is no doubt that this decrease in the velocity of money was a response to the 1965 reforms which raised the real rate of interest on deposits. However, it should not be assumed that real interest rates are the only determinants of the demand for money. The desired ratio of money to GNP partly depends on the structure of production and exchange itself (10). If we take the level of GNP itself as a proxy to indicate that structure we would expect South Korea to have a similar ratio of money to GNP as other countries at similar levels of development. In fact, on one estimate, South Korea's money:GNP ratio before 1965 was less than half the level that would be expected on this argument, and the effect of the reforms was to bring it up to that level (11). In one sense, then, the reforms could be seen as an adjustment toward a structural norm.

The fact that real holdings of bank deposits increased as a result of the high interest rates and that private savings increased simultaneously suggests that the rise in deposit interest rates induced increased saving which was accumulated in bank deposits. That conclusion would conform with econometric studies of Asian less developed countries which find savings are interest elastic, although such findings have been contested. (12) But in this case it would be wrong to assume that all the increase in bank deposits represents new savings, as is assumed in McKinnon's model, for part of the rise in deposits may have come from a reduction in holdings of other financial assets.

The existence of a large and well developed 'unofficial' or 'curb' market for credit means that households and firms are able to acquire financial assets by investing in it (for example, lending to a money lender) as well as holding bank deposits. As a result, time deposits at banks are likely to be substitutes for deposits in the 'unofficial' market and the growth of time deposits will depend on both banks' rates (positively) and rates in the unofficial money market (negatively). A model estimated by van Wijnbergen finds that this assumption is able to explain changes in time deposits (13). In fact, he interprets the estimates as consistent with the view that the increase in time deposits at banks from 1965 was wholly a switch from assets in the unofficial money market rather than a rise in savings. To the extent that this did occur, it makes the central role the McKinnon-Shaw model gives to bank deposits as a channel for increased savings less plausible as an explanation of how the financial reform influenced South Korea's growth.

Whatever the role of the banking system in raising firms' and households' savings, saving did rise after 1965. In McKinnon's model such an increase should finance increased investment and replace foreign loans as a source of such finance. In the case of South Korea, however, the adoption of high interest rates was followed by a substantial increase in inflows of foreign capital. Until 1963, South Korea had no foreign debt. In 1964 and 1965, it received US$40 million and US$30 million of foreign loans respectively. After the reforms this approximately tripled to US$110 million in 1966 and rose to US$540 million by 1971 (and in subsequent years became much greater). (14)

The contribution of foreign capital to the finance of corporations' investment became large after the 1965 reforms. The ratio of foreign loans received by public and private corporations to their investment in fixed assets and inventories was only 5.7 per cent in 1964. But in 1966 it rose to 37 per cent and stayed at high levels (38 per cent in 1970 and 28 per cent in 1971) (15). Some estimates indicate that in the 1960s this inflow of foreign capital was concentrated on loans to import substituting industries and to 'tertiary' or 'social overhead capital' such as electric power and transport. One example was the large government borrowing agreement of US$150 million in 1968 to finance a tripling of the country's electricity generating capacity (16).

The greatly increased inflow of foreign capital after 1965 resulted from several factors including the high interest rate policy. The high interest rates engineered by the reform stimulated the demand for and supply of foreign capital, for it was a relatively cheap source of finance for Korean borrowers, while foreign lenders were able to obtain a higher return than previously. The other changes that encouraged the inflow were the 1965 normalisation of diplomatic relations with Japan, the settlement with that country of outstanding property claims inherited from the period of Japanese colonialism, and the establishment of a foreign loan guarantee scheme which removed the risk of defaults or losses through exchange rate changes. Thus, the high interest rates obtainable by foreign lenders did not include a risk premium.

The high inflow of foreign capital after 1965 indicates that the growth in investment in physical assets cannot be accounted for only by the increased availability of domestic saving resulting from the reforms. The inflow of foreign funds itself was partly caused by the high interest policy.

In addition to private domestic saving and foreign capital the state itself made a major contribution to South Korea's saving after 1965. The government sector had been substantially in deficit (dis-saving) throughout the 1950s and until a fiscal reform in 1962. A further fiscal reform in 1965 led to a substantial surplus which accounted for 20 per cent of national savings (gross and excluding foreign saving) in 1965. This rose to over 30 per cent in 1967 and to 42 per cent of national saving in 1971. (17) This important contribution to South Korea's saving in the second half of the 1960s cannot be credited to the 1965 financial reforms.

In sum, the McKinnon-Shaw view of the effects of financial reforms on savings only partially corresponds to South Korea's experience. The reform was followed by a substantial rise in private saving but there is reason to doubt whether this accounted wholly for the rise in bank deposits as the model predicts. That increase was not the only significant source of finance for new investment. The financial reform itself stimulated large inflows of foreign funds and, quite apart from the financial reforms, the government's own surplus made a major contribution to national saving. These elements of non-correspondence indicate that the reforms were not exactly of the type subsequently prescribed by, say, McKinnon; for example, South Korea took steps to encourage foreign credit whereas McKinnon recommends steps to discourage it.

3. Interest Rates and Allocation of Credit

In addition to their role in stimulating domestic saving, high interest rates are recommended in the McKinnon-Shaw model as a means of credit allocation which is superior to discretionary quantity rationing. If interest rates are raised to market-clearing levels, willing borrowers are never constrained by a shortage of funds; their only consideration is to match the marginal returns on the use of funds (their investment) with the high interest rate or the related marginal cost of funds. The purpose of reforms such as South Korea's is seen as an increase in the role of interest rates as an allocative mechanism. However, in South Korea itself the reform did not achieve this, partly because it was not a sufficiently thorough going reform and partly because of the role of the unofficial market.

Credit from banks to exporters was provided at low

interest rates and was in perfectly elastic supply at those rates: firms could automatically obtain short-term credit on production of a letter of credit or other proof of an export order. The interest rates the Deposit Money Banks were directed to charge was lowered from 8 per cent to only 6.5 per cent per annum in 1965 and, again, to 6 per cent in 1967, which, since the wholesale price index was rising at approximately 10 per cent in those years, meant that real interest rates were substantially negative. (18) Although a high proportion of such bank loans to exporters were formally short term (90 day or 120 day), the practice of automatically rolling over short-term loans so that they were effectively medium term was widespread and, according to Cole and Park, more common in Korea than elsewhere (19). A sample survey conducted by the Bank of Korea in 1968 showed that the actual term of general loans on bills was on average about three and a half years (20). Thus, medium-term bank credit, able to finance capital accumulation was automatically available at subsidised interest rates throughout the years after the 1965 reform. The size of the subsidy can be calculated in several ways, all of which indicate that it was substantial: the 6.5 per cent on banks' export loans may be compared with the rates, in 1966 for example, on general one year loans by banks (25 per cent), on loans in the 'unofficial' financial markets (59 per cent) or with the rate of return to fixed assets in the manufacturing sector (40 per cent) (12).

The growth of subsidised credit for exports led the authorities to attempt to ration the supply of credit for other purposes. Following 1965 they imposed restrictive ceilings on other types of bank credit. Other measures to restrict the rate of growth of total bank credit (and, hence, non-export credit since export credit was automatic) included the imposition of 50 per cent reserve requirements on increases in demand deposits from October 1966 to March 1967.

Thus, a central assumption of the McKinnon-Shaw model did not apply in South Korea: the 1965 reforms did not lead to a market for bank credit where funds were allocated by their price rather than quantity rationing and directives. An indication of the fact that demand for bank loans continued to exceed the supply was that it 'continued to be common practice to pay a 'finders fee' to someone who is believed to be able to get a favourable decision on your behalf.' (22)

The advantages McKinnon and Shaw saw in the creation of an efficient market for bank credit arose from their assumption that, in its absence, all other sources of credit are inefficient. It is assumed that in the Third World, non-bank sources of credit are fragmented, local, and discriminatory so that many projects in particular areas or sectors are unable to obtain finance even though the expected yield of new projects at best matches the cost of credit. Thus, at one extreme it is assumed that rural money lending is highly localised and unable to transmit funds from savers throughout the economy to high yielding projects; and, at the other extreme, state provision of finance in grants or loans is not made on market criteria related to rates of return but is allocated to favoured groups. In these circumstances the liberalisation and growth of the banking system is seen as the creation of the only efficient credit market.

In South Korea it is doubtful whether the growth of the banking system after 1965 did have that effect. Apart from the fact that bank credit itself was allocated on a favourable basis to the export sector and rationed for many other types of borrowers, the existence of a large and developed 'unofficial' financial market before and after 1965 suggests that the development of bank credit may not have been creating a new, efficient, credit market where none existed before. To assess whether this was the case some judgement has to be made on the character of the 'unofficial' market. The 'unofficial' financial market in the late 1960s included rudimentary money-lending, and rotating credit clubs (kye). Both of these have the characteristics associated with fragmented and, hence, inefficient markets: rudimentary money lenders use their own funds for lending to local borrowers and to relatives, while the rotating credit clubs are essentially local associations for pooling savings and employing them within the group. Such arrangements are common in the Third World, but South Korea also includes a large 'curb market' in its 'unofficial' financial markets. This (like the informal commercial bill discounters) was a large, well-organised system of credit brokers and dealers. Participants arranged credit between ultimate borrowers and ultimate lenders (that is, direct loans rather than borrowing and lending-on themselves) and also acted as financial intermediaries, borrowing and lending themselves.

These brokers' and dealers' operations suggest that the curb market was cohesive, with good information flows, rather than fragmented. They 'set the terms of and the interest rates on informal loans. They exchanged information about borrowers and ultimate lenders, sometimes made loans to each other and had market-sharing arrangements' (23). The loans in the curb market were principally, but not exclusively, to large corporations, but the sources of their funds were heterogeneous and included banks and funds invested by large rotating credit clubs. Therefore, the curb market provided the function of integrating other credit markets to some extent and reducing their fragmentation.

More direct indications of the degree to which the curb market itself is efficient with market-clearing interest rates and whether it decreased the fragmentation of the financial system as a whole may be derived from interest rate differentials. The existence of differentials in the interest rates changed to borrowers is interpreted by McKinnon (and by Wai in his seminal work on unofficial financial markets) (24) to introduce segmentation and the absence of market clearing. By that criterion the existence of differential rates within South Korea's curb market and between it and bank loans suggests that it was not an efficient market. However, as van Wijnbergen points out, in a market where borrowers have different characteristics differential rates which reflect this (by including differential risk premia for example) indicate that interest rates are acting as an efficient market-clearing mechanism. (25)

There are grounds for thinking, therefore that the growth of bank credit as a result of the 1965 reforms did not create an efficient mechanism for allocating credit where none had existed before. The banks' growth, moreover, did not lead to a shrinking of the curb market. This may have been partly due to the fact that loans from banks and the 'unofficial' market were, in part, complements because their effective maturity terms were different, (26) but it was also to a large extent due to the curb market's continuing role in integrating the financial system as a whole. Of particular significance here was the fact that cheap bank export credit was channelled to other sectors through the curb markets by exporters who borrowed more than their requirements from the banks and on-lent.

4. High Interest Rates and Investment

As we have seen, the 1965 financial reforms were partial compared to the policies prescribed by the McKinnon-Shaw model, and they did not unambiguously have the effects on saving and the character of financial markets that they would have had in that model. But they did involve a rise in real interest rates on bank deposits and loans. If the predictions of the McKinnon-Shaw model for the effects of financial reforms on real growth are valid, such interest changes will have had an impact on real investment. McKinnon predicts a dual impact. On one hand high interest rates will increase the volume of investment by increasing saving in the economy and thereby removing the excess demand for capital; on the other hand, it will increase the efficiency of capital by ensuring that investment projects are only undertaken if their yield is high. It is not easy to judge directly the extent to which these effects occurred in response to the 1965 increase in interest rates but several studies bear on the issue indirectly.

The McKinnon-Shaw model would lead us to expect that the investment rates or measures of the capital stock are positively related to the availability of credit and an inverse function of the real cost of credit. The investment function estimated by van Wijnbergen for the period 1966 through 1979, does conform to these expectations (27). However, the estimate was not carried out as a test of this against alternative hypotheses and the variance of investment is explained just as well by a simple accelerator in another econometric study (28). van Wijnbergen uses the change in the real value of debt to the banks as an indicator of credit availability and the real curb market lending rate as a measure of the cost of capital. This is based on the assumption that there is a rigid dichotomy between the curb market (which is in equilibrium) and the banking system (with rationing) as sources of finance which, as argued above, is doubtful. The assumption is, however, a means of overcoming the difficulty of interpreting the effect of a rise in real interest rates within a rationed or partly rationed market, for while a rise in rates on credit to firms would be expected to reduce investment (as in this equation) the accompanying rise in rate on savers' assets, which it would be proxying, would be expected to increase investment by increasing the availability of credit.

Bearing this in mind, the McKinnon-Shaw model should

lead us to expect a positive relation between the real interest rate on bank deposits and both saving and investment. Its relation to saving has already been discussed. In relation to investment, an interesting phenomenon is that, as Hong shows, substantial capital deepening occurred only after 1967. Excluding the ownership of dwellings, fixed capital per worker rose by 8 per cent per year from 1965 to 1967, but by an average of 13 per cent per year from 1968 through 1971 (29). This substantial increase coincided with a decline in the real interest rate on bank deposits. The real rate on time deposits rose to a peak of 23.6 per cent in 1967 and thereafter declined to 17.4 per cent in 1968 and 13.2 per cent in 1971 (30). If the speed of adjustment of the capital stock per worker is fast, this suggests that increases in that ratio have been associated with declining returns to savers; and evidence of machinery's young vintage and of short lags in the investment equations of simulation models suggest that even with a growing labour force the speed of adjustment is fast. (31) However, this phenomenon cannot be taken to give a strong indication of the effect of interest rates on investment through the availability of credit, for the effect of the interest rate may be capturing the cost of finance instead. Following that approach, Hong identifies the post 1967 rise in capital per worker with a rise in the ratio of wages to the cost of credit.

One approach to evaluating the impact of interest rates and credit-rationing on investment would be to note that interest rates were subsidised for the export sector and raised for other sectors from 1965. In a simple McKinnon-Shaw model, that should lead to relatively low investment and capital stock in the export sector because it would be constrained by a shortage of supply of credit. From that point of view, Hong's finding that the capital-intensity of South Korea's exports rose (between 1960 and 1973) relative to that of import substitutes suggests that such a mechanism did not operate (32). However, such a test is not possible since government directives ensured that the relative availability of credit was the opposite of that assumed in the model; that is, low lending rates to exporters were accompanied by a high (perfectly elastic) supply of credit while non-exporters faced both high rates and credit rationing.

Thus, the evidence on whether the 1965 increases in real interest rates had the impact on the level of investment and capital stock that McKinnon-Shaw predict is ambiguous. As soon as we attempt to go behind the gross fact that investment rate and capital:labour ratios did rise in subsequent years and inquire whether this occurred for the reasons postulated or because of some other factor, we find the existing evidence inconclusive.

The McKinnon-Shaw thesis on reforms' effects on investment, however, concerns not only quantity but quality. It is postulated that rising real rates of interest encourage a capital stock with a higher marginal productivity than would otherwise be the case. Again, the indirect evidence is ambiguous. Data on the average return to fixed assets in the manufacturing sector suggest that it did rise to 60 per cent in 1966 (from 33, 32 and 34 respectively in 1963 to 1965) but it declined strongly thereafter, reaching 23 per cent in 1971 (33). If we ignore the fact that average returns differ from marginal returns, these estimates would suggest that high interest rates did not have the effect predicted. But that interpretation would have to be qualified by the fact that the rate of return rose immediately after the 1965 rise in real rates and its fall coincided with the decline in real interest rates from 1967 that we have noted previously.

5. High Interest Rates and Economic Growth: Alternative View

The 1965 financial reforms in South Korea were followed by exceptional real growth. It is widely recognised that the Korean 'economic miracle' even in the 1960s cannot be attributed only to the financial reforms, but there is a strong presumption in the literature that the high interest rates they initiated were a major element in the package of reforms that generated it (including fiscal reforms, changes in foreign trade policy, exchange rate, and other reforms) (34). Subsequent reductions in interest rates and the partial character of the reform itself have been criticised on the grounds that they jeopardise these positive effects (35). The previous sections have attempted to evaluate whether the high interest rate policy did have these positive effects by examining the main mechanisms through which, according to the theory underlying the positive claims, their effect should have been transmitted. South Korea's experience between 1965 and 1971 casts doubt on the effectiveness of some of those mechanisms and is ambiguous on others. In this section I discuss an alternative view of the role for the financial reforms. The McKinnon-Shaw thesis is that complete financial liberalisation reduces the distortions imposed by state intervention and frees market forces which stimulate efficient capital accumulation by agents across the economy; the South Korean reforms, although partial, are seen as having worked by going some distance in that direction. The alternative view is that the financial reforms were part of a package of measures which increased the role of the state in the economy; if they were responsible for an increased rate of growth the experience suggests that appropriate forms of strong state intervention in finance may have a positive impact.

The McKinnon-Shaw and other models of how financial changes are transmitted to real economy have three components, savers, investors and financial institutions and markets which intermediate between them; the variables such as interest rates and quantities of finance which connect the financial markets to savers on the one hand and investors on the other are the means by which the effects of financial reforms are transmitted. In South Korea the state has had a major presence in each of these components as well as regulating the interest rates and quantities of finance that connect them; moreover, its role in each sector increased substantially in the 1960s. The 1965 reforms can be seen as a means to consolidate that role.

The role of the state as a saver has already been noted; the effect of fiscal reforms in 1962 and 1965 was to turn a substantial budget deficit into a substantial surplus which accounted for 42 per cent of the flow of savings (excluding foreign capital inflows) by 1971. This switch from deficit to a surplus in the mid-1960s represented a substantial increase in government savings, at least as important as the increase in private savings.

The state's role in carrying out fixed investment was also substantial because of the significance of public enterprise in national production and the public enterprise sector was also growing in the 1960s. By the early 1970s, South Korea had a large public enterprise sector whose contribution to non-agricultural production was comparable to the share of similar enterprises in India and probably higher than those of Britain or Italy. In 1960 the majority (about three quarters) of public enterprises had been inherited from the Japanese colonial occupation and the measures taken when it ended. From 1960 a large number of new public enterprises were created so that the total number rose from 36 in 1960 to 119 in 1971, and the greatest expansion was carried out after 1965 (from 59 enterprises in 1965 to 119 in 1971). The number of enterprises is an unsatisfactory indicator of the sector's size, but its growth is also evident from its contribution to Gross Domestic Product. In real terms the share of public enterprises in GDP increased from 6.6 per cent in 1963 to 10 per cent in 1972. The data for 1963 to 1972 shows 'a real average annual sectoral growth rate of 14.5 per cent over a period when the economy as a whole grew at 9.5 per cent and the non-agricultural economy at 12.2 per cent' (36). According to Jones, these public enterprises had a much greater incremental capital/output ratio than the economy as a whole (6.12 as against 2.25) so that its growth was accompanied by a disproportionately high rate of investment (37). He estimates that public enterprises, while producing 10 per cent of Gross Domestic Product, accounted for some 30 per cent of gross investment. In addition to public enterprises, the government's own fixed investment rose from 3.2 per cent of GNP in 1965 to 7.9 per cent in 1969 and 6.2 per cent in 1971.

The third component in the chain of transmission where the state had a major role was in the ownership and control of the financial institutions themselves (38). The commercial banks were nationalised in October 1961 and in May 1962 the Bank of Korea was placed fully in the hands of the Ministry of Finance. The other element in the construction of the state-controlled financial system that existed throughout the boom of the late 1960s was the creation of special state banks in 1961. The National Agricultural Cooperative Federation (NACF) was constructed to supply agricultural credit (reducing the role of 'unofficial' financial markets) within an integrated operation of supplying inputs to farmers and acting as grain purchasing and marketing agent. The Medium Industry Bank was established to provide loans to medium and small enterprise and the financial resources of the Korea Development Bank were enlarged. Each of these special banks and the newly nationalised commercial banks rapidly expanded their lending.

Thus, in Korea during the years we are concerned with, the state was a major economic agent in each part of the process that links finance with the real economy: as saver, financial intermediary and investor. Its control of the quantity of financial flows and their terms (interest rates) meant that, in addition, it controlled the way each part was linked. Thus, for example, it determined the direction of funds toward exports. Similarly, the state controlled the allocation of foreign capital which, in principle, could have short-circuited the system and directly financed investment; the state-owned special and commercial banks had a role in approving the guarantees given to foreign investors and state approval was required for such guarantees. In this context, the interest rate reform of 1965 can be seen as an instrument to increase the state's control of the financial process and it did so in two ways. First, it increased the flow of savings controlled by the state. The sharp rise in interest rates on bank deposits led to a remarkable increase in real holdings of those deposits. As we have seen, there is controversy over whether this represented wholly an increase in saving or a switch of existing savings into banks from the 'unofficial' financial market, but whichever phenomenon occurred the result was an extremely large increase in the volume of savings under the control of the state-owned commercial banks and the state itself. Secondly, the reform's increase in general bank interest rates increased the power the state had to determine the direction of credit by differential interest rates; it was a considerable increase in the subsidy represented by low interest rates to selected sectors. The differential between general interest rates and the rates charged to exporters and farmers could not have been attained without the rise in general rates (unless the politically implausible policy of charging negative nominal rates to such borrowers had been adopted).

Here I am concerned with the role of the state in relation to the financial system and the reforms' effects on it. A full evaluation of the state's role in South Korea's economic growth would require us to put those operations in the context of its activities in other areas. The South Korean state placed great emphasis on its five-year plans for the economy and intervened in several areas to implement them. And the political repression that accompanied this had strong implications for the working of the labour market. To analyse how, or through which mechanisms, the state's saving, investment and financial intermediation affected growth in its financial reform has to be examined as one element in those wider interventions.

6. Conclusion

South Korea's 1965 financial reform, marked by a significant rise in bank interest rates, was only a partial reform when compared with the liberalisation policies recommended on the basis of the McKinnon-Shaw model. Although interest rates were raised, financial markets were subject to considerable state control and intervention. Economic growth did follow, but the evidence does not strongly support the view that this occurred through the changes in saving, investment and intermediation that McKinnon-Shaw envisages would result from a full liberalisation.

Moreover, the type of widespread entrepreneurial accumulation and expansion that McKinnon envisages as the basis of such growth in the context of financial liberalisation appears not to have occurred. Jones and Sakong find that the 'entrepreneurial elite is emphatically not drawn from the population as a whole' but from a narrow selection of family occupational backgrounds - large to medium landlords, merchants, factory owners, civil servants and professionals. Since these occupations were confined to at most 16 per cent of the parental cohort, it is clear that the industrial elite has been derived from the pre-industrial elite' (39). They also infer from the data they have that business growth was accompanied by increased concentration; the growth of chaebols (large private conglomerates) has been faster than that of smaller enterprises.

While widespread enterpreneurial initiative may not have been stimulated by the financial reforms, economic growth was associated with the growth of the state as a saver, investor, and in financial intermediation. This suggests a new interpretation of the role of the 1965 reforms. Instead of being an example of financial liberalisation which increased the role of market forces and generated growth through free enterprise, they were an instrument for increasing the power of the state. It is widely agreed that South Korea's economic growth of the second half of the 1960s is partly attributable to the reforms. On the new interpretation, the lesson to be drawn would be that the growth resulted from an increased role for the state; on the old interpretation it would be that it resulted from (partial) liberalisation of market forces - a decreased role for the state - and would have generated greater growth if it had been more complete.

NOTES

The research for this chapter is part of the research programme of the Open University's Financial Studies Group and Development Policy and Practice Group. Financial assistance from the Open University research committees is gratefully acknowledged, as is the provision of facilities by the University of California, Irvine. I am grateful to Maxwell J. Fry and Mahmoud Meskoub for helpful discussion of issues considered here, and to Soo H. Kim whose work for the Open University introduced me to some of the paradoxes of South Korea's 'economic miracle'. Mohsin Khan and Stanley Fischer also made valuable comments for which I am grateful.

1. Brown (1973), Ch. 7; and Cole and Park (1983), Ch. 7.
2. Cole and Park (1983), p.201; and Chandavarkar (1980), p.516.
3. Shaw (1973); McKinnon (1973), p.2. Although there are significant differences between their models, their policy implications are similar. In this paper I shall, therefore, follow the common practice of identifying the theory as the McKinnon-Shaw thesis.
4. McKinnon (1973), p.10.
5. Cole and Park (1983), Table 45, p.230.
6. Cole and Park (1982), p.227.
7. Cole and Park (1983), p.266.
8. Kim and Roemer (1979), pp.55-6. These ratios are calculated with respect to a measure of 'private GNP'.
9. Cole and Park (1983), Table 45, p.230.
10. Gurley and Shaw (1960).
11. Cole and Park (1983), pp.19-20.
12. Fry (1978), Giovanni (1983).
13. van Wijnbergen (1982), p.157.
14. Hong (1976), Table 1.2, p.4.
15. Cole and Park (1983), Table 7, p.31.
16. Brown (1973), pp.213-18.
17. Kim and Roemer (1979), pp.51-5.
18. Cole and Park (1983), p.18.
19. Cole and Park (1983), p.324.
20. Cole and Park (1983), p.142.
21. The calculation of the exact value of these interest subsidies differs according to different assumptions regarding the norm with which the rates are compared.

Cole and Park (1983), pp.191 and 327, review some estimates.

22. Brown (1973), pp.206-7. In principle, however, the existence of a finders' fee need not indicate a generalised excess demand. It could arise from the existence of imperfect information about the characteristics of borrowers and lenders.

23. Cole and Park (1983), p.118.

24. McKinnon (1973), Wai (1957).

25. van Wijnbergen (1983).

26. Cole and Park (1983), Ch. 5.

27. van Wijnbergen (1982), p.141.

28. Norton and Rhee (1981).

29. Hong (1976).

30. Cole and Park (1983), Table 45, p.230.

31. Hong (1976) reports on machinery's young vintage; Wijnbergen (1982) and Norton and Rhee (1981) do not estimate long lags. Mason, Kim, Perkins, Kim, Cole (1980), p.279, report short lead times between conceptualisation and operation of investment projects.

32. Hong (1976). The interpretation of this finding, however, does not imply that capital/labour substitution did not occur within import competing industries. Within such industries substitution did occur, but because of the changing weight of particular industries in that sector, the average capital intensity was less affected.

33. Cole and Park (1983), Table 30, p.131.

34. A classic statement of this argument is Brown (1973), Ch. 7.

35. McKinnon (1976).

36. These estimates and the quotation are from Jones (1975), pp.73-5.

37. Jones (1975), p.86.

38. The value-added in their operation and their physical investment are included in the preceding discussion of public enterprises' own capital formation. Here I am concerned with their control over flows of funds.

39. Jones and Sakong (1980), p.301.

REFERENCES

Brown, G.T. (1973) Korean Pricing Policies and Economic Development in the 1960s, Baltimore, John Hopkins University Press.

Chandavarkar, A.G. (1980) 'Some Aspects of Interest Rate Policies in Less Developed Economies: The Experience of Selected Asian Countries' in W.L. Coats and D.R. Khatkhate (eds), Money and Monetary Policy in Less Developed Countries, London, Pergamon Press.

Cole, D.C. and Park, Y.C. (1983) Financial Development in Korea, 1945-1978, Cambridge, Mass., Council on East Asian Studies, Harvard University.

Fry, M.J. (1978) 'Money and Capital or Financial Deepening in Economic Development?', Journal of Money, Credit and Banking, 10, 4, November.

------ (1980) 'Saving, investment, growth and the cost of financial repression', World Development, vol. 8, pp.317-27.

Giovanni, A. (1983) 'The Interest Elasticity of Savings in Developing Countries: The Existing Evidence', World Development, 11, 7, pp.601-7.

Gurley, J.G. and Shaw, E.S. (1960) Money in a Theory of Finance, Washington, Brookings Institution.

Hong, W. (1976) Factor Supply and Factor Intensity of Trade in Korea, Seoul, Korea Development Institute.

Jones, L.P. (1975) Public Enterprise and Economic Development: The Korean Case, Seoul, Korea Development Institute.

------ and Sakong, I. (1980) Government, Business and Entrepreneurship in Economic Development: The Korean Case, Cambridge, Mass., Council on East Asian Studies, Harvard University.

Kim, K.S. and Roemer, M. (1979) Growth and Structural Transformation, Cambridge, Mass., Council on East Asian Studies, Harvard University.

Mason, E.S. et. al., (1980) The Economic and Social Modernization of the Republic of Korea, Cambridge, Mass., Council on East Asian Studies, Harvard University.

McKinnon R.I. (1973) Money and Capital in Economic Development, Washington, Brookings Institution.

------ (ed.) (1976) Money and Finance in Economic Growth and Development, New York, Dekker.

Norton, R.D. and Rhee, S.Y. (1981) 'A Macroeconometric Model of Inflation and Growth in South Korea', in W.R. Cline and S. Weintraub (eds), Economic Stabilization in Developing Countries, Washington, Brookings Institution.

Shaw, E.S. (1973) Financial Deepening in Economic

Development, New York, Oxford University Press.
van Wijnbergen, S. (1982) 'Stagflation Effects of Monetary Stabilization Policies', Journal of Development Economics, 10, pp.133-69.
Wai, U.T. (1957) 'Interest Rates Outside the Organised Money Markets of Under-developed Countries', International Monetary Fund Staff Papers, 6, 1, November.

Chapter Eighteen

THE LIMITS OF BANK NATIONALISATION IN FRANCE

Alan Lipietz

When I was asked to write about 'what the nationalisation of banks had brought to the socialist government', I said, 'Well, nearly nothing', but the response was 'Well, tell it'. So, although I've given that short answer, I will now say, more fully, what did happen and what could have happened.

The recent nationalisation of banks actually took place only eight months before writing this paper so we have not had long experience of what exactly can be done on the basis of this act. The decision to nationalise was taken nearly at the beginning of the presidency of Mitterand, so there was absolutely no doubt that it should be done and it was only because of filibustering by the opposition and by a series of legal battles that nationalisation of banks was delayed.

Just after Mitterand said 'We <u>are</u> going to nationalise <u>all</u> banks', a lady went to her bank, the Credit Lyonnais, and said 'I want to take back all my jewellery from this bank, because I know it will be nationalised.' The clerk said 'I am sorry, Madam, but we have been nationalised for forty years.' That was the case, in fact, for 50 per cent of the banks in France and nobody had noticed it. And I am afraid that, although today the rest of the banks have been nationalised practically nobody will notice.

To explain what happened and what could have happened I must first explain the role of the banks, paticularly the connection between banks and industry. The problem of the connection between banks and industry is the most important one in France, for there is not a great problem between banks and the state. The state is able and has been able to obtain the finance it wants from the banks without difficulty; when the left has been in government following 1936 (the Popular Front), 1945, and now funds have been made available to the state.

What is Banking?

Suppose you are a capitalist. You have money M, and with this money you buy productive capital P, which consists of machines (what is called 'fixed constant capital K_f) and labour force (which is called 'variable capital' V). But you buy also 'constant circulating capital' Kc (that is raw material etc.). Actually, circulating capital is at the centre of this discussion. You produce 'commodities' C, and you prove that you can sell them against money M. And then you divide the proceeds into the money you give the shareholders, and the money you put back into production.

For simplicity I said this money was the property of 'you', the entrepreneur or of the shareholders. But there is another part of the money which makes this turnover, which is the loaned capital. To the money M which is the property of the shareholders you can add another quantity of money, which is loaned from the banks, mainly. This money will circulate in exactly the same way as the owned money so that, in use, it cannot be visibly identified separately, but mainly this borrowed money serves to pay for 'circulating capital', K_c + V. When this money (I will call it 'borrowed money', BM) has made the circuit, it will have grown to BM'; part of it, the 'principal', is repaid to the bank, but the growth of this money (BM' - BM) due to the work of the labour force, is divided between 'profit of enterprise' and 'interest', which is paid to the bank.

So, if you own a firm, to your own money (what we call in French 'risked capital' or 'equity' in English) you can add a little more money, or sometimes it is a great deal more money, that the firm can use, financing a productive process with it. But out of additional profit that you can get by putting into movement this borrowed capital, you must give part to the bank.

What is the great difference between the borrowed money BM and your own money M? The difference is that the increment between M and M' depends mainly on the success in producing well, that is exploiting well the labour force, and selling a good product, at a sufficiently high price. It's a risk. You are not sure when you produce something that you can sell it. So the profit, which is the excess of the quantity of money M' on the quantity M, depends on your ability as an entrepreneur.

But in the case of the borrowed money, you will have to pay it back, and you will have to pay the interest which is in the contract from the beginning. Even if you fail in the enterprise, you must give back your borrowed money with the rate of interest which the bankers told you. For instance, now the rate of interest is around 12 per cent in France, so if in the process you make a profit of around 15 per cent, of course on your own money you will keep this 15 per cent, but on the part of the money which was borrowed from the banks you will have to pay back 12 per cent ('interest'), so the part that is left to you is only 3 per cent ('profit of enterprise').

Suppose, in fact, the global rate of profit on the two parts of money you put in action is only 10 per cent, you must still pay 12 per cent to the bank on what you borrowed, and you must pay with your part of the profit. That has been the great problem in France, during the crisis, as we shall see later.

Where does this money the banks lend, BM, come from? Well, in one sense it comes from nowhere, for banks create money. The bank says 'I lend you money' (the bank says that to firms, to households and to the state). Since (nearly) all the money which is lent is re-deposited in banks, (nearly) all the quantity of money they lend is at once a deposit in banks. Maybe not in the same bank, that is the problem for the bank which lent, but for the global system of banks, all that is lent is deposited into banks with the result that the quantity of money depends on the will of the bank to make loans.

Can the banks lend as much money as they want? Not exactly. Because each singular bank must be sure that, if somebody comes and says 'I have made a deposit in your bank, can you give it back to me?' it will be able to do it. So there must be a proportion of cash that the bank keeps, over the money that the bank lends. In addition the central bank (the Bank of France) says 'I want you to keep a fixed amount of money and not lend it again' (that is called 'obligatory reserves'). Also in France there is a system of directives under which the Bank of France is able to say to a bank 'Don't make more loans than such and such'. So for all those reasons, the banks cannot create as much money as they want.

Some banks lend more money than can be financed from deposits and they borrow money from other banks to finance this. There is a 'market for money' that the banks can use which is supplied and regulated by the Bank of France. The central bank effectively argues 'Well, you made a loan to this enterprise, this enterprise now has the money of the loan you made, and you have not got this money. Well we will lend you the money, but with interest'. So in that case it is the Bank of France behind the loan money coming from the bank and in that situation the Bank of France is able to choose the basis of the rate of interest. Because of this structure, the Bank of France is able to dictate the rate of interest. This is an important point, as you will see later.

Now, this Bank of France dictates only the rate of interest between banks, the rates at which they can have money when they need overnight money, for instance, to give to the enterprise. But that is not exactly the rate of interest between the bank and the firm. The rate of interest between the bank and the firm will be generally greater, of course, than the rate of interest between banks. What will determine the particular rate of interest between the bank and the firm; its premium over bank rates? It will be mainly the kind of risk the bank incurs in making a loan to this firm. Suppose that the firms' valorisation cycle is a complete failure, that those commodities C are not <u>all</u> sold, for instance, or only sold at 15 per cent of their value, then it will be absolutely impossible for the firm to pay back the bank, and there will be a failure of the firm. Everybody who can ask for repayment of debts by the firm will ask. According to the law banks loans are not given a high priority for repayment in these circumstances. In France the first ones are the workers. That is, when there is a breakdown of the firm the workers' claim for the wages the firm owes them receives first priority. Second the Social Security, of course. Third, taxes and only after that, the banks. Thus there is a great probability, if there is a failure of the enterprise, that the money will never come back into the pockets of the bank. The interest premium they charge corresponds to this risk.

Now I think we have enough general background now to situate the tragedy of these poor banks. Now I must explain in more detail the system of banking in France before nationalisation and the factors that led to the nationalisation.

The French Banking System

I have said that all the banks, or the banking system, make loans, and that all the money of these loans is re-deposited with the banks. It is not exactly true. We have a distinction in France between 'banks', strictly speaking, and 'non-banking financial institutions'. The banks are exactly what I told you, that is, when they make a loan to you, as a household, or to a firm, they say, 'Well you can use your loan, say £1,000; we have a place for you in our ledgers, you have cheques and with those cheques you can pay'. So it is really a money you can use. But non-banking financial institutions are not like that. They can make you a loan but the form of the loan is that they will open an account for you in a real bank. Of the total amount of loans 65 per cent come from banks and the rest (35 per cent) come from these institutions. Although they are not fully banks these financial institutions are an integral part of the French banking system and I will describe them first. They are mainly built around a peculiarly French institution, the 'Caisses d'Epargne'.

The Caisses d'Epargne is a savings institution where people put their money and earn interest on it but since no cheques can be drawn on your deposit you cannot use it as cash money. This money of the 'Caisses d'Epargnes' goes into a fantastic institution which is 'Caisse de Depots et Consignations' (CDC) which is even older than the Republic of France. This institution, the CDC, lends its money mainly to builders, municipalities, and so on, and a part of it to enterprises, through the 'Credit National'. The banks, in order to make loans, need to borrow from this system of non-bank institutions and this gives their operations a special significance.

Now let us consider the banks themselves which account for 65 per cent of all lending. We have several kinds of banks. First, what we call the 'banks of deposit', which make up 50 per cent of the banks' lending. We have the 'business banks', which make up 5 per cent. We have a little thing which is called the 'etablissments financiers', which are strongly connected to business banks and make up 10 per cent. Of great significance are the 'special status banks', mainly mutual credit institutions operating as full banks such as the Credit Agricole. These in total. The Credit Agricole alone is one of the world's largest banks. Its assets belong to all the peasants of France, or nearly all of them.

The great banks of deposit in France are three main banks 'Societe Generale', 'B.N.P.' and 'Credit Lyonnais', and these three banks are also in the top seven world banks. So these are great enterprises but you will notice that these three banks were already nationalised before Mitterand's measures. About half of the deposit banks' business was accounted for by these banks which were nationalised 40 years ago.

So what remained for Mitterand's government to achieve through nationalisation? First, from 50 per cent of the deposit banks, the nationalisation brought the publicly owned share to 80 per cent. The rest are mainly French offices in foreign banks. Second, the two main business banks, Paribas and Suez, were nationalised. Although these business banks accounted for only 5 per cent of total bank lending, Paribus and Suez are the two main structures of capital and finance in France. Suez is called 'Bank of Suez and Indo-China' indicating its origins as an old colonial bank which made a lot of money with the nationalisation of the Suez Canal and used that money to expand its business. That bank's history suggests that nationalisation is generally a very, very good thing for private capital, because you get plenty of money out of something that you didn't know exactly what to do with, and you can put it back into the more profitable activities available in the modern world. Paribas was the 'Bank of Paris and the Low Countries' and it is also a very old bank. Why were these remaining French deposit banks and these business banks nationalised? It was thought to be necessary to overcome certain problems.

It was widely believed that one great problem was that the banks who had the deposits were generally not the banks who made the loans. As I have mentioned, a lot of people make deposits in the Caisses d'Epargnes, but the Caisse d'Epargne does not make loans. The money of the Caisse d'Epargne goes to the CDC, which makes loans to the Credit National, and the Credit National makes loans to the banks and so on. Although the savings institutions are separate, the banks of deposit account for a high proportion of the circulating money because in nearly every street there is an agency of these banks and your money or the money of all the households of the street are in this bank. The mutual banks are more 'balanced' in one sense because they are multivalent banks for particular sectors. The money of the peasantry goes to Credit Agricole, and these banks make loans to agriculture. But, in fact, there is an excess of rural deposits over loans to agriculture for the Credit Agricole, and so it is now making loans to towns for instance, and also international loans.

Thus, there is always a problem of getting the money from deposit institutions like the Caisses d'Epargnes towards the banks that make loans. This problem is very crucial because at each moment a bank, which makes loans, must get money, and, as I have indicated, this money market is regulated by the 'spot market' between the Bank of France and the banks.

The rate of interest banks charge to firms depends on this high degree of intervention by the Bank of France. As you can imagine, the first problem for the Bank of France is not to fix the rate of interest, with a view to the cost of credit faced by firms; its primary task is to defend the value of the franc or, in other words, to make 'hot' money (the foreign money floating from one place to another) come to France. Thus, the problem of the Bank of France is to set a rate of interest high enough for instance for the OPEC 'countries' surplus at the beginning of the 1980s to come to France. If the rate of interest in the United States, for instance, or in London is very high, the rate of interest decided by the Bank of France, must be very high to attract into France a part of this hot money. Of course, if each particular French bank making loans to enterprises had its own money and had no connection with international credit markets this would not be a problem: that bank would make a loan to a firm at a rate of interest not connected with the international rate of interest. But since, as explained above, the division of functions between institutions means that most of the banks that make loans must go through the money market to get money, the rate of interest is fixed, in fact, in the United States. It is determined by the choices of the American Government whose policies largely determine the rate of interest on the dollar assets, and thus the rate of interest of the Bank of France, and the rate of interest between banks and the firms. That is the first great problem.

To see the second great problem, let's go back to Figure A. In the money committed to firms you have two kinds of money: the internal finance which is part of the firm's equity capital (M), and loan capital (BM). The problem is that it could happen that the owner of the equity capital is itself a bank. If the owner is a bank, that means that the money belonging to the bank will have a share of the profit of the risked profit, which will sometimes be lost, and so on. If there are weak profits, then there will be weak dividends coming to equities, thus to the bank.

In that situation, the bank takes the risks and the responsibilities of an entrepreneur. The bank suffers the crisis. It has to share the effects of good and bad markets, good and bad techniques of production, and good and bad marketing and so on, even though the people managing the bank are not the same as the people managing the firm. The risks of the firm are risks of the bank if the bank is the owner, or as far as the bank is owner of shares of the firm. But if the bank is only a lender, then the bank will ask at the end of its interest rate, for instance 12 per cent, or if it is a small firm it will ask more than 17 per cent, and since there is a risk they will ask guarantees. They will lend to a firm in proportion to the assets of a firm. 'What will happen if you break down? I must get back my money, so I will lend you money, only if you have good assets, buildings and machines and so on'.

The banks will not make loans according to the utility of the productive process even in the capitalist sense, but only according to the security given by the assets of a firm, and any way they will require a fixed interest commitment on what they lend.

The great characteristic of bankers, French bankers in particular, is that they nearly always engage their capital in this second and secure form. The only ones which put up money as the owner, as risked or equity capital, are the 'business banks', and these banks make 5 per cent of the credit loans by the banks. So for this 5 per cent, the reward of the money from the bank is risky because, as a dividend, it is variable; for all the other banks it is fixed interest. For each firm it is very dangerous to owe money to the banks, because if the firm does not do well, if the firm does not successfully exploit, or correctly control the work of the labour force, if they have not got a strong policy in buying the machines and a strong policy in selling their commodities, if the enterprise doesn't do that, it will have anyway to pay this 12 per cent or 17 per cent to the banks.

This problem becomes acute when, as in recent years, there is a general economic crisis. The share of profits in national income was 30 per cent before the crisis (say 1974) and it fell to 25 per cent during what I call the 'Keynesian period of the crisis' that is when the main industrial countries tried a social-democratic way of managing the crisis. And after the hegemony of monetarism came, in the midst of a breakdown of the world economy the profit of firms became still worse, and in France it went down to a 23 per cent share. When Mitterand came to power this share recovered to 25 per cent, because the volume of business increased, raising both profits and wages; but with the second 'recessive' phase of the Mitterand policy, profits are going to break down again.

That profit share represents the 'result of exploitation' for French capitalism as a whole. But there has to be a division of the profits between the enterprises and the banks, that is, the industrial-commercial part of capitalism and the financial part of capitalism. If you look at what was left to the firms after they had paid their interest (what we call 'gross savings of the enterprises') it was only 15 per cent of national income before the crisis. And after the first part of the crisis: 12 per cent. It appears as if from this time the workers in the capitalist system were less exploited by their own firm than by the banks. And now, with the monetarist policy, with high rates of interest, what is left to the firms is only 8 per cent.

Moreover these statistics are calculated on the basis of gross value added or gross national product. It is not exactly the value added by workers; it is the value added by workers in the year before subtracting the depreciation allowance. The latter represents (in principle) the labour which was expended years before, which was integrated into the machines the firm uses; through the value of the machine depreciating it goes into the value of the commodities and then to the cash flow. So, out of this 8 per cent you must still take the depreciation allowance, in order for the firms to pay back the same machine. I am not speaking of investing, creating more plants and so on, but only to pay again for the same machine you must pay about 8 per cent of this whole gross value added. So in fact, since 1980, the firms are working for no profit. No net profits. All the profits which are made are going to banks. These were the circumstances in which bank nationalisation has occurred in France and in which the nationalised banks have operated.

What to do with the Nationalised Banks?

What were the main ideas of Mitterand's nationalisation, nationalisation of the rest of the banks; the 30 per cent of deposit banks and the two great business banks? There were two ideas.

First, this nationalisation of banks was connected with the nationalisation of the main industrial firms (five or six were nationalised depending on how you count them). Since the business banks, and partly the deposit banks, had equities in these great industrial firms, in order to restructure industry it was very useful, it was absolutely necessary in fact, to have nationalisation both of the banks and the firms. If you nationalise only the firms but not the banks which are their partial owners, it is very difficult to make what we call the 'meccano' (putting the elements of one firm with those of another to make a new firm and so on). This industrial policy is very active under Mitterand and the government, owning all the banks and the main industry is nearly, although not completely, able to restructure all the industrial system.

Now, the main problem was to make the banks act, not as lenders but as investors, risking their capital, creating money and re-investing the interest as risk capital. That was the great aim of the nationalisation of banks. If you want to do something in the industrial sector you must get firms free of the banks. In a way, you must mix the two parts of the profit: the share which goes back to the bank, and the profit of the state-owned industry. That was the idea.

You may notice that this idea is not particularly socialist; in itself there is nothing at all socialist about it, it is a purely capitalist reform. It only involves making a new deal between two parts of capitalism, between the financial part and the industrial part. But it could be a socialist reform if within the industrial sector, socialist things are done. For instance, a firm which would try to make people work less hard in it, would make less profit, so its part of the profit would be still less and yet this firm would have to pay the same to the banks. So with that structure it is impossible for a firm to experiment with new social job-relations. Another example: if the firm has an ecological interest and wants to protect nature, it will use more fixed capital to make the same thing, so the firm will have to borrow from banks and pay the banks for it. But private banks only lend, not according to the social use of what the firm is doing, but according to the rate of interest the bank can get from these firms.

A third example: a municipality or a region may wish to help new forms of enterprise, cooperatives and so on, or unemployed people could decide to create their own job and offer some service to the neighbourhood. They need a little money to invest in such initiatives and they will ask for loans. The banks will say 'Where are your assets?' Of course they have not got any yet. 'But we are going to work' and the banks will say 'No, you have no assets you cannot have a loan' and the municipality, which was ready to help them, would say 'Well we can give you a little money but if no bank lends you more money you cannot start so we stop', and so on and so on.

So the nationalisation of banks is not a socialist measure in itself. It's only a modernist measure, for industry, but if there are socialist strategies in the political sphere it is necessary to nationalise banks in order to give a socialist content to industrial policy.

Well, actually very few things changed. Why? First of all, the Prime Minister said 'we have nationalised banks, now we have to nationalise the bankers'. What happened? They gave people new functions within a gigantic techno-structure, but this banking bureaucracy was competely monetarist, right-wing orientated and so on. In order to make the international bankers have more confidence in what the French were doing, they very often chose a new president for the nationalised firms, Giscaridan high civil servants, with very orthodox ideas. That was what they did for every bank, for instance Paribas. Even most of the socialists, I mean the members of the Socialist Party, who were already working in banks (some at high levels) were socialists for everything outside but within their job were bankers like the others. So, for this new direction the first thing to do was to get the confidence of this techno-structure, to get the confidence of their technocratic structure they had to prove their credentials, and to do this they acted exactly as strictly orthodox bankers should do. That is, lend money at higher rates, lend money only on the good securities, that is good firms having good assets and so on. And not lending for social experiments and so on.

The second point, there were still the other banks. They nationalised French banks but there is competition from foreign banks. The government wanted to have hot money placed first in France and second in the nationalised banks. But in fact international hot money is not obliged to come to France, and if it comes to France it can go to the Morgan Bank or other foreign banks in Paris.

Third point, there was absolutely no change in the

structure of the system. That's an important point. I have described the incredible structure where the banks having the money as a deposit are not the bank making the loans. The Mitterand government's idea was to make a great national investment bank. It would be able to raise loans from all the deposit banks, and itself make loans to the firms. This did not happen. Why? It was part of the programme of the two parties in Mitterand's government, the Socialist Party and the Communist Party, but it was not one of the ideas of M. Delors. Jacques Delors was the liberal wing of the government, he was the strong man of the government, the almighty Minister of Finance, and he said 'It is impossible to create a national investment bank because if you do that there will be great speculation against the franc and so on and so on'. And everybody said 'Well, O.K.'

You know, Jacques Delors presented himself as a Christian with a kind of 'duty': 'I am here for the credibility, external credibility of the French experience. So I must always prove that we are not doing anything unusual'. But in order to convince the Financial Times and so on that in France absolutely nothing unusual is happening, he is always telling other ministers not to do anything unusual. And so, to this day, there is no national investment bank (and there are a lot of other things that have not been done).

But had anything changed? First there are changes of the great enterprises, the giant firms were nationalised. Since they are the property of the state, these firms are very secure, because the French state is something which is old, important, and even with socialists in power is something very safe. Far more safe than the Polish state, the Argentine state, Brazilian state, and so on. So anybody may rely on something which belongs to the French state, and France's credit rating is still triple A in the international banking system. Thus it was very easy for the government to give orders to the banks, nationalised banks, to make loans to the firms which were now the property of the state.

In the seven years of the right, the last seven years of the right (Gistard D'Estaign) one and half billion francs, (there are eleven francs in one pound), $1\frac{1}{2}$ billion francs were given by private capitalists to the future nationalised firms as owners capital, risk capital. Six and a half were drawn back from these firms to private capitalists as dividends. So you see there were in fact 5 billion francs going from the pockets of the firms to the property of private households. In two years under Mitterand, 15 billion francs went from the state or from the nationalised banks, as owned capital or very long-term capital, to these firms. That is ten times as much as the bourgeoisie in the seven previous years. I must add that this 15 billion francs served mainly to pay for the losses of these firms during the very bad years, 1980-1. So anyway, I think that if there had not been the nationalisation of the banks and of the firms, in order to stop the crash of these great firms, there would have been money from the state and from the banks to these firms.

That is what they did, mainly. And there are other attempts at progressive measures. What they are doing now (which is so easy to do even for Delor) is first to make a kind of deconnection between international rate of interest and the rate of interest between banks and the firms. They make this deconnection by giving money from the state, from the government out of taxes, or by using several devices to achieve a mix of money coming from the deposit banks and the business banks. Another policy is to guarantee the risks of small firms. That is the state says: 'You, bankers, are afraid to give money to little firms or to social experiments. Well, OK, you make the loan and if it is a complete failure and you cannot get back your loan, we, the state, will pay'. That's a very good design, which is regionalised and there will be a new kind of structure to do that.

But of course, the long-term solution to the problem would be a national investment bank. To be relatively simple, the banks of deposit would be obliged to make some loans to this national investment bank. And the latter would inject risk capital into firms. So there would be some intermediation and reduction of the deposit banks' risks. This is very important, because since they borrow on the international market it must not appear that their lending operations are risky. They will make very safe loans to this national bank of investment, because there will be a strong guarantee from the state, so it would be possible to deconnect the international rate of interest and the risk in the bank. And this national bank would invest really its own money into enterprises, lending at low interest and long term and buying new shares, or helping new kinds of enterprise to exist, making socialist experiments, and so on.

But that, once again, is only a socialist dream. Even

though France has a socialist government, it is a project which has been completely blocked by the leaders of French finance, and especially by the Minister of Finance himself. That is the situation in January 1983.

INDEX